Jack Cavanaugh

DIMENSIONS OF FAITH

Edited by
WILLIAM KIMMEL
and
GEOFFREY CLIVE
With a Foreword by
JAMES LUTHER ADAMS

DIMENSIONS OF FAITH

Contemporary
Prophetic
Protestant
Theology

Karl Barth
Nicholas Berdyaev
Rudolph Bultmann
Oscar Cullmann
Feodor Dostoievsky
Soren Kierkegaard
Richard Kroner
Reinhold Niebuhr
Richard Niebuhr
Rudolph Otto
Paul Tillich

TWAYNE PUBLISHERS, NEW YORK

Library of Congress Catalog Card Number: 60-8551

MANUFACTURED IN THE UNITED STATES OF AMERICA

To

PROFESSOR RICHARD KRONER

in gratitude for the permanent
influence of his lectures at
Union Theological Seminary
1948-1950

PREFACE

In 1936 I attended in Switzerland an international conference of students and faculties of Protestant theology, a conference in which the Swiss theologian Karl Barth was a participant. At the very first session of the conference Dr. Barth filled every expectation of controversy. The first paper, presented by a theologian from the University of Geneva, dealt with the concept of religious experience, and it employed the language of psychology as well as of Christian theology. Before the speaker was well under way, however, Dr. Barth suddenly arose in the audience, interrupted the speaker, and addressed the chairman. "I shall not wait any longer. I want to ask the speaker a question now," he said, thereby of course throwing the meeting into an uproar of consent and dissent. The chairman replied that it is customary for questions to be withheld until a paper is finished, but that he would leave the decision to the speaker. With questionable judgment the theologian reading the paper agreed to accept the question immediately. Barth thereupon made frontal attack. "Is the speaker reading to us a paper on Christian theology or on the psychology of religious experience? If the paper is on the psychology of religion, why should we here listen to it? This is a conference of Christian theologians; only the Word of God, not talk about psychology and religious experience, is appropriate here." Immediately the assembly plunged into heated argument, a debate on the place, or lack of place, of secular science and of even apologetics in a Christian discourse. The heat of the controversy pervaded the remaining sessions of the conference. Indeed, the Barthian students within the week, I was told, delivered a formal petition to the Dean of the Theological Faculty at Geneva, pleading for the dismissal from the University of the beleaguered author of the paper and for the appointment in his stead of a *Christian* theologian. The Dean did not comply; he could not accept the presuppositions of the avowedly Barthian framers of the petition.

The reader may not feel disposed to accept those presuppositions either. Yet, one must recognize that Barth's interruption of the meeting is typical of what has been going on in Protestant theological circles in our time. From various quarters and in varying ways Protestant theology has been trying "to interrupt the meeting" in both the church and the world.

Already a century earlier Søren Kierkegaard in his *Attack upon 'Christendom'* anticipated the present confrontations and tensions by raising a radical protest against the so-called Christian society of his time and its churches. In face of the established church and the society of his day he rejected their claim to be Christian.

> "When all are Christians," he said, "Christianity *eo ipso* does not exist. The race of men have found a way to make Christianity comfortable. Gradually the human race came to itself and, shrewd as it is, it saw that to do away with Christianity by force was not practicable—'So let us do it by cunning,' they said. 'We are all Christians, and so Christianity is *eo ipso* abolished.' And that is what we now are. The whole thing is a knavish trick; these 2,000 churches, or however many there are, are, Christianly considered, a knavish trick."

Kierkegaard's view was, to be sure, by no means typical of the theology of his time.

In the nineteenth and the early twentieth century many theologians and churches expended their energy in trying to come to terms with the advances being made by the culture. These advances, for example, the emergence of the modern historical consciousness and method and also of the new image of the world provided by the empirical sciences, had to be taken into account if the statement of the Christian message was to achieve new relevance or if it was to become disentangled from identification with mere traditionalism. To this end certain theologians "interrupted the meeting," particularly in the churches. Out of this effort came what has been called "Culture-Protestantism," the tendency to identify the Gospel with the highest ideals of the age.

The term is a misnomer in so far as it conceals the fact that the movement offered a critique of the prevalent piety that, despite its ostensible orthodoxy, was in its way a Culture-Protestantism of earlier vintage. It is a misnomer also in so far as it conceals the fact that the movement produced the Social Gospel, a prophetic critique of the economic patterns of the culture. Nevertheless, the new Culture-Protestantism was ill-prepared (as was orthodoxy) to confront "the storms of our times," the widespread economic distress, demonic nationalism and scientism, the World War, and the despairing nihilism born of disillusion. The religion that had appeared in the guise of Culture-Protestantism was now said to be merely a tinsel embellishment of the culture, a deceptive means of self-glorification, a systematic insulation of man from God. Karl Barth in *The Epistle to the Romans* (1918) sounded a thunderous protest against this sort of religion. What is "the Cause of the Night in which we are wandering"? he asked; and he answered: The Wrath of God is upon us. "'No-God' cannot seriously be named 'God.' When we set God upon the throne of the world, we mean by God ourselves. Our devotion consists of a solemn affirmation of ourselves and of the world and in a pious setting aside of the contradiction. Men fall a prey first to themselves and then to the 'No-God.' Under the banners of humility and emotion we rise in rebellion against God. Against such rebellion there can be revealed only the Wrath of God." What Kierkegaard had named "a knavish trick" was now being exposed anew. Indeed, the Barthian negative critique of the culture was so radical and complete that Adolph von Harnack with some exaggeration spoke of it as a new form of the Marcionite heresy, the assertion of a radical dualism between God and creation, between God and all culture.

Paul Tillich in the early Twenties set forth a more dialectical theology of culture than this, a theology that was able to say both Yes and No to the culture and that insisted upon a discriminating judgment and responsibility as over against merely bringing everything under an abstract negative cipher. Barth, to be sure, had claimed to maintain "subterranean connections" with the current Christian thrust towards social reform, and subsequently he modified his earlier near-dualism. But before Barth had done so, Tillich with others made specific and vigorous protest against the rising Nazism, and this protest was accompanied by a concrete analysis of economic maladjustments and idolatries, and of ecclesiastical alliances with political and economic demonries, and by efforts looking towards social-institutional as well as spiritual reconstruction. Accordingly, one of the members of Tillich's Kairos Circle in Berlin called for "a struggle against the church for the sake of the church."

In face of the easy conscience of Culture-Protestantism, an impressive number of theologians in Europe and America demanded a new self-understanding on the part of Protestantism. They raised afresh the question as to what is central in the Christian message. In connection with this question they asked also, What is the proper relation between Christian faith and the church and culture? The concern with these questions led to new approaches in Biblical study, to historical and systematic studies of the relation of Christian faith to politics, science, and culture, and to the search for new ways of making the response of Christian faith relevant to the contemporary situation. A common presupposition of this theological revival was the view that Christianity, properly understood, is not a culture-religion but rather a prophetic religion.

It is entirely fitting that this anthology should carry the subtitle, "Contemporary Prophetic Protestant Theology." What is the meaning of the term "prophetic theology" in this context? One of its decisive features has been indicated already—its intention to expose man's assistance, and particularly the religious man's assistance, "at the birth of 'no-God,' at the making of idols." Like the Old Testament prophets, it emphasizes the Commandment, "Thou shalt have no other gods before me." Neither Christianity as a historical phenomenon nor the Bible as a cultural creation, nor culture with all its "riches," nor anything that is of the order of creatures can be the proper "object" of faith. False faith places its trust in such idols. As Augustine observed, it gives to the creature that which belongs alone to the Creator. Thus it becomes a form of self-salvation, denying the need for grace from the invisible Origin. Prophetic theology, therefore, rejects the notion that Christian faith can provide sanction for a culture-religion. It holds that history and culture point beyond themselves to a commanding, judging, sustaining and transforming reality. Confidence in and response to this reality is the nerve of prophetic faith.

Such a confidence and such a response, however, issue in more than a warning and struggle against the idolatory of any attempt to domesticate this reality or power. Prophetic faith asserts that God through Jesus Christ is the Lord of history and of culture. This Lord of history calls men into a community of faith. In response to the Lord of history this community of faith takes time and culture seriously, so seriously as to hold that political and social institutions, the arts and the sciences, as well as the individual believer have a vocation from on high. Indeed, prophetic faith in its critical and formative power serves as the basis for the true and viable autonomy of these spheres. Redemption is for them as well as for individual persons. Accordingly, prophetic theology recognizes the obligation to interpret the signs of the times in the light of the End, that is, of the Kingdom of God. It aims to speak to the concrete situation in which man finds himself.

But prophetic theology in Protestantism does not presume to place limits upon the sovereignty of God by claiming that Protestantism possesses a monopoly on prophetic insight and action. To do so would be idolatry. Moreover, prophetic theology does not look for simple unanimity in the formulation or the understanding of the Christian message. It therefore carries on a dialogue with respect to the meaning of Christian faith in thought and action. This dialogue must be discerned in the present volume. For example, Barth rejects philosophical theology, Tillich insists upon its necessity. Barth speaks of the tension between eternity and time; Cullmann in criticism of Barth asserts that his conception of eternity is more Greek and philosophical than Biblical. H. Richard Niebuhr questions the validity of Kierkegaard's individualism on the ground that it is self-righteous and that it "gives up the cultural problem as irrelevant to faith." Bultmann, favoring Kierkegaard, assimilates Ernst Troeltsch to Culture-Protestantism; but H. Richard Niebuhr asserts that Troeltsch maintained better than Kierkegaard the tension between Christ and culture. Bultmann would "de-mythologize" the eschatological "framework" of the New Testament in order to grasp the kernel. Cullmann denies that the conception of redemptive history in the New Testament is merely framework, it *is* the kernel; and, besides, he says that what Bultmann calls the "kernel" is brought by him to the New Testament from Heidegger's existentialism. And so we could go on citing instances of rather fundamental disagreements among the theologians presented in this volume. H. Richard Niebuhr contends that each of the various major conceptions of the relation between Christ and culture has grasped an important facet of the meaning of Christian faith and thus should be kept in tension and in dialogue.

Through this dialogue of interpretation in response to the living God prophetic theology releases what is not ultimately within its power, the moving, reforming, transforming element in the history of religion and culture. It again and again "interrupts the meeting" in order not only to tell but also to listen. Viewed from from the human side this dialogue as it issues in responsible action is the process whereby Christians in each age achieve new self-understanding in the light of the

Gospel and in face of changing situations with their new demands and new possibilities. In this way prophetic theology acts out of faith in the Lord of history who moves in mysterious ways and in whose name men can prophesy only in part if they are not to assist at the birth of a Grand Inquisitor.

James Luther Adams
Harvard Divinity School

ACKNOWLEDGMENTS

The editors acknowledge with gratitude the helpful bibliographical suggestions given by William A. Clebsch of the Episcopal Theological Seminary of the Southwest.

We wish also to acknowledge with thanks the co-operation of the following publishers who have granted permission to quote from works copyrighted by them: Princeton University Press for a section of TRAINING IN CHRISTIANITY by Søren Kierkegaard, translated by Walter Lowrie, copyright 1944, and for passages from THE SICKNESS UNTO DEATH by Søren Kierkegaard, translated by Walter Lowrie, copyright 1941; Yale University Press for selections from THE COURAGE TO BE by Paul Tillich, copyright 1952; YMCA-Press for the chapter from Nicholas Berdyaev's THE MEANING OF THE CREATIVE ACT, translated by Donald A. Lowrie; Geoffrey Bles, Ltd. for the chapter from Nicholas Berdyaev's THE BEGINNING AND THE END, translated by R. M. French, copyright 1952; Random House, Inc. for the section from Feodor Dostoievsky's THE BROTHERS KARAMAZOV; Harper & Brothers for passages from H. R. Niebuhr, CHRIST AND CULTURE, copyright 1951.

TABLE OF CONTENTS

IV. THE ETHICAL-RELIGIOUS

INTRODUCTION

Suspect as the religious revival in our midst (measured by church attendance, etc.) is often found, interest in religion in academic circles has doubtless reached an intensity which a century ago hardly seemed possible, let alone probable. The intellectuals who gloried in man's progressive liberation from superstition and ignorance had—to be sure, with notable exceptions—done with religion, save as an alternately fascinating or embarrassing vestige of man's growing up. But now, it is clear, man's heightened power of manipulation over nature and society has sharpened his awareness of contingency and turned his attention back upon himself as a problematic being. All areas of thought in the twentieth century have undergone revolution, reëvaluation, and varying degrees of reconstruction, but in Protestant theology these developments are particularly pronounced and exciting. Unlike Roman Catholicism with its perennial philosophy, Protestantism must come to terms with prevailing currents of thought unless it fall into disuse and obscurantism. This, its essential nature, exposes it to the opposite danger of surrendering to the "kingdom of Caesar." In any event, the *Lebenswelt* of a true Protestant can never be the high Middle Ages of Luther's Wittenberg. His involvement in the world of his day and age is not merely an environmental necessity, but a vocation dictated by choice. Not all Protestants are prophets, by any means; nevertheless all prophetic writers have something Protestant in their makeup.

In praising the theological renaissance of the twentieth century as a desirable reaction against false and superficial ways of thinking, one should not evade the more serious criticisms levelled against the figures included in this anthology, both by orthodox believers and liberal humanists. The latter are prone to argue that the "neo-orthodox" theologian (using this term in its widest connotation) is too much the apologist predisposed to find in the intellectual landscape only those elements which fit his preconceived plan. Thus it has become commonplace to deny the Greeks a genuine sense of history, supposedly a Biblical contribution, although, as non-theologically-committed scholars would suggest, the evidence on which this estimate is reiterated appears flimsy indeed. It has also been felt that the theologians of our day with their fashionable pessimism and despair about the human condition are but sober secularists who, to underscore the "civilized barbarism" of man to man in contemporary civilization, profess the old sense of sin as a new discovery, leaving the grace of God and His redemptive activity to man's infinite capacity for self-delusion. These critics would assert that you don't have to become a Christian either to be "ultimately concerned" or to repudiate Condorcet's doctrine of human progress. (One eminent Harvard professor once was overheard remarking that he went a long way with Reinhold Niebuhr till God entered the picture.) Finally, some critics would contend with Freud that no degree of crisis justifies clinging to illusion, that in spite of everything the Protestant theologian tells us about human misery being true, this hardly warrants Barthian dualism or Tillichian "new being." On the contrary, man, however double-minded he may be, must learn to stand on his own feet, for there is in fact nothing else on which to lean. The "revelatory experience" is perhaps but another escape from reality.

From the Fundamentalist and orthodox side the criticisms are of quite a different sort. Here the uneasy alliance between modern science and theology is interpreted as a kind of surrender to the secular world. It has of course always been an inherent danger in Protestantism to sell out—either by leaving society to its own devices or by mixing with it to such an extent that all distinctions between the "holy" and the "profane" tend to disappear. The thinking of Barth and Tillich respectively exemplify these two possibilities. For Barth, God and man come close to having no access to each other, for Tillich, they often seem one and the same. Moreover, the religious critics of twentieth century Protestant theology question its claims for validity and authority. If the Church and Tradition are taken lightly (if not repudiated) as reliable mediators of the Word of God, what is left but the sovereignty of human reason, the very sovereignty the prophetic theologians seek to delimit and to subject to higher criticism? How can you be a Christian, these believers want to know, and not hold what Christians traditionally believed? how be religious in a general way while spurning all established forms of worship? If indeed there be no *real* conflict between science and religion, the Bible and world history, reason and revelation, if their intermittent warfare rests on mutual mistakes, why then the anxiousness to be up to date, to demythologize, to be sophisticated? The orthodox, in short, want to know whether you can eat your theological cake and have it too: the bread at Communion and the absence of all overbeliefs.

Both these lines of criticism must be taken seriously, more so than in the immediate past. But (for our purpose at hand) once it be granted that sheer apologetics are no substitute for the search for truth and that a dose of Kierkegaardian honesty has harmed no attempted theological synthesis, theology's status in the modern world emerges not appreciably different from that of the other arts and sciences. What we are witnessing is a momentous drama in which history, so to speak, is deciding about the nature of man and his situation. Within single disciplines and between the various branches of thought there are dramatic conflicts and claims, not only for validity and authority, but likewise for allegiance, enthusiasm, and priority. The ideological battle in the realm of politics is but a microscopic version of what can be traced everywhere, with the same questions constantly arising: how do you know? on what grounds trust the Bible or Karl Marx, or Lenin-Stalin, or the scientific method, or historical determinism, or the champions of Picasso and Shostakovitch? Should I die for my country, for the United Nations or for nuclear physics, wherever it might lead? and into what hierarchy, if any, do these diverse claims devolving upon me, fall? what deserves my primary commitment? how can I distinguish a true from a false absolute?

The last hundred years has witnessed an unprecedented relativization of knowledge and its departmentalization into highly specialized disciplines. Ultimately leading to a loss of common ground, this development first resulted in the attempt of each discipline to explain the others from its own premises. Accordingly, for a Marxist, economics explains history, politics, ethics, religion, art, in brief, the sum total of human activity; for a Freudian, the psychology of every subject matter tends to replace the subject matter itself. Sociology explains psychology, politics, religion, . . . ; anthropology explains sociology, and so on. That is, starting from one dimension—political man, economic man, social man—all other dimensions are accounted for from that single point of view. In the case of religion, for example, it is reduced either to the "opium of the masses" or an "illusion" or a response to whatever must be responded to in whatever happens to be called the environment, or cognitively speaking, something symbolically real though apparently imperceptible. All these descriptions contain germs of truth at the same time that they are distortions (one-sided accounts) of an immensely complex phenomenon. Nor is a compilation of many different views a genuine alternative to an embracing vision. Whereas Plato's dialogues imply a critique of themselves, the writings of Freud and Marx which have been so influential in our century are singularly devoid of dialectic. But the issue goes deeper than this. So far the sciences have glaringly failed to arrive at any unifying concept for correlating their respective bodies of data. Concede the imperfections of much current theology; nevertheless, in its prophetic manifestations it acknowledges these as among the "signs of the times" on which judgment must be passed. And this is more than can be said for the sciences.

Not only is the theologian by virtue of a high degree of self-criticism not any worse off than the psychologist, sociologist or historian, but a thinker like Tillich has been constructive to a degree for which duplicating examples from other areas would be difficult to cite. What twentieth century philosopher has even set out to produce a view of the whole? The acquiescence in perpetual fragmentation is one of the most telling indictments against the state of our sciences.

The ferment of creative thinking in theology should be seen contextually as part of a renewed interest in religious phenomena generally stimulated by the revolutionary findings of Freud, William James, Bergson, Emile Durkheim, and Max Weber. Whatever their personal intentions and beliefs may have been (Freud e.g. was an outspoken atheist), their theories proved instrumental in religion being taken seriously again. It should be remembered that from the death of Hegel to the birth of Tillich religion had not been taken seriously in the dominant academic circles. Nor can the theological ferment be dissociated from the great religious novels and poetry that began to appear towards the end of the nineteenth century. Particularly Tolstoy and Dostoievsky (very much read by their younger contemporaries) played a leading role in raising the old questions afresh and posing some new ones as well. To them one must also add Nietzsche with his prophetic "transvaluation of values," Schopenhauer with his anti-Enlightenment pessimism, and the hitherto virtually unknown Søren Kierkegaard whose explorations of the "daemonic" possibilities within man and the order of creation turned out to be a prophetic judgement on the horrors of World War I and subsequent waves of terror in this the most advanced century. Prophetic theology may have been dead just prior to its rejuvenation, but there certainly was no lack of proximate provocative influences. In perspective its revival is integral to the crisis of western man and his civilization.

The great body of theological thought emerging principally after World War I may be viewed from two points of view: one, as accounting for man in his situation on the same level as and parallel to the other disciplines. Like these it sets out, as it were, to explain everything from its special perspective and with its own principles, categories, and symbols. There is the implication of a religious interpretation of man side by side with the economic, sociological, and what have you. On this basis, however, religion becomes quite dispensable, since each of the other disciplines accounts more effectively for man's cognitive, moral, and aesthetic activities. As Schleiermacher already had remarked in his *On Religion, Speeches To Its Cultured Despisers* (1799), when theologians make claims for validity or adequacy in competition with *Wissenschaft,* they court disaster by losing sight of the autonomy of their subject matter. Conversely, whenever religion has been used to prop up a *Weltanschauung* or as a rigid system demanding intellectual assent, it has lost out in the long run to autonomous criticism.

From the other point of view, generally that of prophetic theologians, the religious dimension of experience is not one among other dimensions in which man comes to know himself and his situation; it is not at all a form of knowledge (*scientia*) commensurate with other forms, but rather the fundamental ground of experience out of which all other knowledge proceeds and which determines the form and character of a given culture —its modes of self-understanding in every branch of knowledge and field of endeavor. On this view there is an essential difference between theology and the various sciences of man (*Menschenwissenschaften*). Since the seventeenth century the latter have become more and more self-sufficient. Through rational analysis they explain man and culture out of culture itself. Imitating the methods of the natural and later also of the historical sciences, they seek general laws allowing for the predictability of the greatest number of particulars. Even the modern historian, with his categories of empathy and inner understanding as opposed to mere explanation, aspires to the exact and reliable knowledge of the scientist, aims to tell what would have happened if such and such had been thus and thus. The autonomy of the sovereign intellect first proclaimed by Descartes and reaffirmed in various guises through Kant and the German Idealists down to Positivism has continued to serve inquirers in almost every field as a model or primitive assumption.

The autonomy of theology, on the other hand, paradoxical as it may sound, is grounded in an attitude of dependency rather than self-sufficiency: in a conviction of the inability of man completely to understand himself and his situation and to determine his own destiny, but also in a faith that the possibility for such an understanding has uniquely been revealed in a source beyond time, intellect, and history. Those who have wanted to see Kant as the Thomas Aquinas of Protestantism were on the wrong track from the start. For Kant, notwithstanding his pietistic affinities and his famous discussion of radical evil in human nature, by his trust in man's ability to determine himself remained by and large an Enlightenment figure. Quite characteristically he had no use for revelation and measured all religious pronouncements by their degree of correspondence to rational precepts. Autonomous reason cannot believe in anything beyond its own limits, let alone surrender itself to paradox. The theologian's dependence on the Bible as the Word of God, however liberally that phrase be taken, was for Kant an abomination. It is on his own best humanity, the most perspicacious spokesman of modern rationalism teaches us, that man alone may depend. Schleiermacher's Protestant-theological critique of Kant was basically just, coming as it did from a spokesman of the Evangelical Church. His notion of an underlying piety potentially permeating everything we do, feel, and know, regardless of what we do, feel or know, constitutes a new life for the religious consciousness, although the heart of this life lies in its dependence on the Infinite.

Protestant theology (besides its immediate roots in the person of Luther) is rooted in a special historical event, when the inexhaustible source of meaning and value, the trans-historical, eternal source of creativity, power, life, and meaning was experienced in a unique and ecstatic encounter with the person of Jesus. The content of this encounter, embodied in the stories, images, metaphors and parables of the Bible, is the original and essential material which engages the theologian's mind. As material for meditation and devotion the scriptural narratives are self-communicative; as a *starting point* for theological thought they are beyond discussion, more basic than the theologian's understanding. However, for reason and understanding they demand interpretation. The role of the theologian, once his basic dependence on the Biblical sources is recognized, is that of interpreter. He returns perennially to this original scriptural source, itself an interpretation of certain events, and reappropriates it within history and culture. *Protestant theological interpretation may be considered to be either the continuous reinterpretation of the original substance in the language and forms of thought of each generation; or the continuous interpretation of historical human experience in the light of the original encounter with the trans-historical source of meaning.* Respectively, these two types of theological interpretation legitimize the Protestant emphasis on Biblical scholarship and exegesis as well as its inexhaustible literature on the relationship between culture and faith. Scripture becomes contemporaneous only when it is understood both in its abiding, eternal and its contingent, existential aspects. To paraphrase Kant: culture without faith is empty, and faith without culture is blind. The Protestant's dependence on Scripture must be tried through the agonies, doubts, temptations of his particular day and age, and those of his character. But dependence it must remain.

Even within Protestantism, to be sure, there can be found many types of theology—exegetical, systematic, critical, historical, philosophical as well as prophetic. That the present anthology is primarily drawn from the latter does indeed reflect on the anthologists. They may be said to hold the view that theology is innermost true to itself when judging, protesting, warning, and discerning the signs of the times. A prophetic theology will almost invariably recognize its own finite character and, so far as this is at all possible, avoid the *hybris* of self-infatuation. Apart from this value judgment of the anthologists, it is a matter of historical record that only this type of theological thinking still speaks authentically to modern man. Whether professing religion or not, like Hamlet he knows that something is rotten in his kingdom, and there are times when he continues to look for a cure as well as a diagnosis. What moves him then is not the history of the term *agapê,* for example —how it came to be, who first used it, what preceded it, etc.— but what truth it has for him now, what existential difference it makes. It is our conviction, moreover, that the best expressions of Protestant theology in the religious renaissance are in fact prophetic, including the writings of such non-Protestants (formally speaking) as Dostoievsky, Berdyaev, Romano Guardini, and Martin Buber. Prophetic theology cuts across all denominational lines although Protestantism in recent times seems to have produced more than its share. At the same time it would be unfair to underestimate the contributions of non-prophetic theologians within Protestantism though they be of an academic nature. Here we must invoke the anthologist's inalienable right to leave out what he has no room for and to put in what in his estimation warrants his particular enterprise. Obviously many other anthologies of modern theology are possible, so long as each is guided by an intelligible principle.

The selections chosen for the present anthology are representative of the central concerns of prophetic theology. The theological awakening was heralded by Kierkegaard with his violent attack upon Christendom (Selection 1). No longer can there be any doubt that Kierkegaard has been the keenest Protestant mind since Luther, one without whose work the twentieth century renaissance would be unthinkable. Humanistic theology, as represented by Adolph Harnack at the turn of the century, abandoned, along with original sin, the objective, trans-historical realities of traditional Christianity. It gave up the Logos character of Christ and concerned itself exclusively with the historical person of Jesus and with an ethic of good will analogous to Enlightenment optimism. It compromised itself with the frame of mind of a dominant middle class minority by reversing the accepted Protestant method of interpretation and interpreting the original substance in the light of the historical preferences of a given culture: instead of judging the finite under the aspect of the Infinite it set up the latter as the norm of the former. Thus the "kingdom of God" made its peace with the "kingdom of Caesar", and the "kingdom of Caesar" had no further need of religion for its self-understanding.

Twentieth-century theologians, stunned by the first world war and its aftermath, or by the crisis of modern culture, "discovered" Kierkegaard who only then entered the mainstream of western thought. Through him they were driven to self-examination and to a re-examination of the original substance (Albert Schweitzer's *Quest For The Historical Jesus* (1906) had already been a milestone in this direction), and eventually to a rediscovery of the theological venture. Since 1917 Protestant theologians have rediscovered the true meaning of "protest," that is, the protestation against every cultural claim for final validity with respect to man and his situation including the protestation against such claims on the part of Protestantism itself. In its most radical form the eternal "No" uttered against history and culture from the trans-historical judge of history has been voiced by Karl Barth (Selection 2) with his almost total separation of God from the kingdom of Caesar, and his denial of the possibility of self-understanding or self-fulfillment by man. Rudolph Bultmann (Selection 3) has devoted his efforts to peeling away the accretions and accumulations from traditional theology in order to rediscover the character of *Urchristentum* (the "primitive" or primordial interpretation of the original encounter) and to permit the underlying ecstatic experience to come to life again. The power of the revelation will be freed from the dead weight of images, concepts, and obsolete metaphysics that are no longer capable of communication. While Professor Bultmann's theological program has been challenged both from within and without the Church, notably by Karl Jaspers in a memorable controversy, the concept of demythologization is here to stay, with its foes as enthralled as its friends. Even the analytical philosophers who fancied themselves liberated once and for all from all metaphysical and religious questions have now turned their attention to the "special" nature of religious discourse. In this respect, like Bultmann, their aim is to disclose the characteristic features of the "language" of religion. Part One of our anthology may properly be called "rediscovery". Kierkegaard, Barth, and Bultmann each sets out to rediscover the core of the Christian faith.

Selections 4, 5, and 6 are interpretations of the Trinity or Three Persons of God, the central symbol of the Christian faith. Rudolph Otto's classic study of the *"numinous"* character of the Holy—the unnamable, unapproachable source of creativity—delineates the *deus absconditus* over against the empty abstractions of the philosophical scrutiny of religion or, just as bad, the sentimentalized concretions of Tiny Tim and the class of readers for whom Dickens intended his books. Dostoievsky's "Legend of the Grand Inquisitor" from *The Brothers Karamazov* is an epoch-making analysis of the daemonic, a re-examination of the ambiguous and self-destructive character of the creative power in existence. As Kierkegaard had already shown in his *Fear and Trembling,* everything, not excluding man's highest aspirations and God's commands, is subject to distortion. Dostoievsky's unforgettable story of the Christian Church crucifying its Founder for the sake of Christendom constitutes the most paradoxical instance of daemonic possession. Dostoievsky makes

Marx look childish as a critic of religious institutions. While the problem of the daemonic does not, of course, exhaust the meaning of the Second Person of the Trinity, it is certainly that dimension most akin to contemporary man's existential encounter with the hideous aberrations of civilization. The inclusion of Dostoievsky in this anthology testifies to the spread of theological concern beyond the confines of professional theology. Although he is not, strictly speaking, a theologian, his thought has had a profound influence upon virtually all major figures in twentieth century theology. Nicholas Berdyaev (6) has been rightly described as the theologian of the Spirit or Third Person because his thinking is rooted in the creative activity of freedom. The best human analogue to the creativity of God is the inspired artist whose spontaneity testifies to the presence of a power in him transcending the causal order. The "ideas" of Bach, Mozart, Schubert, and Beethoven are as fresh as the first dawn of creation, and it makes as little sense to ask where the one came from as the other.

These writings of Otto, Dostoievsky, and Berdyaev amplify the Kierkegaardian insight that the aesthetic genius and the apostle as well as the religious fanatic and the thrill killer have much in common with each other: a proneness to the unusual (none of them make good bourgeois) subject to the possibility of hideous distortion but also capable of profound self-transcendence. What is genuinely holy or genuinely possessed is always closer to God than what is conventionally tolerated. Part Two of our anthology may properly be called "the dynamics of creativity."

Selections 7 to 11 are studies in the relationship of Christian faith to history and human culture. Oscar Cullmann analyzes the problem of the relationship of eternity to time and of Biblical history to secular history. For him the central core of Christianity is its conception of time as the scene of redemptive history. He rejects the philosophical conception of a timeless eternity beyond time, the Hebraic conception of a future event which shall mark the end of time and of history, and all conceptions of a simultaneity of past, present and future times in a supra-temporal consciousness. Cullmann's brilliant analysis of New Testament time can already be regarded as a classic.

Richard Niebuhr (Selection 8) works out a typological approach to the various interpretations in history of the relationship between church and culture, the kingdom of God and that of Caesar. Christianity has judged the world, withdrawn from it almost entirely, mixed with it freely, struggled with it dualistically, or supplemented it supernaturally. What, if any of these roles, is its proper one? is there a choice between Christendom and a pure Christian community? can the Church serve God and man at once without loss of integrity? Needless to remark, these are perennially burning issues, not only in theory but in practice. Richard Kroner's philosophy of culture (Selection 9) attempts systematically rather than historically to comprehend the place of faith within the structures of post-Enlightenment western society. Part Three of our anthology might properly be called "the incarnation." The tensions in Christian faith between time and eternity, culture and faith, and the world and other-worldliness all center on the paradox of Spirit becoming flesh—the mystery of the Incarnation.

Reinhold Niebuhr's contribution here (10) is a characteristic examination of the morally ambiguous character of all social and political life. Over against the "do-gooders" Niebuhr, like Luther, delineates the Christian's unavoidable involvement in sin whatever his calling or profession: there is no place in the world which is immune from the world, and the best intentions are shot through with human pride. The goodness of man stands as much under the divine judgment as the evil he does. Particularly in the realm of the non-personal, guilt becomes the inescapable by-product of all action: a sobering thought for the Right as for the Left. Paul Tillich (11) analyzes the complex character of individual experience within a wider structure of being. It is Tillich's contention that a virtue or mood such as courage is not merely a subjective state through which we pass, but also something having its counterpart in the overall pattern or reality. Finally, Selection 12 from Tillich's ontological analysis of the structure of love in relation to power and justice, represents an interpretation of the central Christian message, the power of the New Being over the self-destructive aspects of existence. In this connection it is noteworthy that the last three decades have witnessed a renaissance in the philosophical-theological literature on love. As with the problem of time, the Greek and Biblical views of the matter are commonly contrasted. Must we choose between *eros* and *agapê* or are they but two aspects of the new light that John tells us came into the world with the Incarnation? Part Four of our anthology revolves around the Kierkegaardian category of the "ethical-religious." It is a kind of dialogue between the Greek virtues and the Christian task of responsibility.

Unfortunately this anthology (like all anthologies) leaves out a number of names deserving inclusion. Troeltsch, Brunner, Gogarten, William Temple, and John Baillie are conspicuous by their absence. Max Weber and Joachim Wach the sociologists, Heidegger, Jaspers and Bergson, philosophers, and poets such as Rilke and Peguy exerted great influence on the twentieth century theological renaissance. The same must be said for the work of Franz Kafka, Etienne Gilson, Romano Guardini, Martin Buber, Franz Rosenzweig, and Erich Frank. In spite of these omissions we hope to have given the reader insight into some modern dimensions of faith linked together by their common prophetic essence.

GEOFFREY CLIVE
WILLIAM KIMMEL

I. REDISCOVERY

"... unto the Jews a stumbling block, and unto the Greeks foolishness."

I Corinthians 1: 23.

One of the functions of the prophet in the life of religions is to prepare or clear a way for the self-manifestation of God to men. The inevitable tendency of religious life is to congeal, stagnate or disintegrate through the force of excessive rationalization or dogmatism or the lure of romantic-subjective mysticism or to fall under the sway of pseudo-religions in the form of philosophical, social or historical ideologies.

Protestantism is most true to itself when it protests against all cultural and religious forms which claim for themselves final or exclusive authority or validity or which demand unqualified loyalty and support. And the Protestant principle becomes most active in those periods when religious and cultural life have fallen into dogmatic confidence in, or liberal enthusiasm for, or complacent satisfaction with those forms of thought and action which claim to be adequate for the fulfillment of human needs.

The task of the prophet in every age is that of cutting through the superstructures of philosophical speculation, of undercutting the false presuppositions of spurious "isms," of "shaking the foundations" of both institutions and individuals, thereby reopening eyes and ears, mind and heart, for the possibility of spiritual renewal.

SØREN KIERKEGAARD

SØREN KIERKEGAARD was one of the most seminal thinkers of the 19th century. Largely overlooked by his own generation, his prophetic protest began to be heard and became a major historical influence upon human thought only in the 20th century. A student of Hegelian philosophy he used the master's dialectic to produce a most thoroughgoing destructive criticism of Hegelian rationalism. Nurtured in a Protestant Pietist atmosphere he voiced the most violent protest against Protestantism and, indeed, Christendom, which the modern world since Luther had heard.

Like Luther, he was acutely conscious of human alienation from God and of the fundamental "sickness" (sinfulness) of man. The experience of despair over one's existence becomes a central theological category which Kierkegaard develops dialectically in *The Sickness unto Death.* With all the penetrating subtlety of a modern psychologist he uncovers systematically every false refuge from despair, pursuing the despairing one further and further into despair with his every attempt to free himself from it until it becomes clear that despair is precisely the human condition from which man by his own efforts cannot escape.

But just as relentlessly as he pursues the individual through the subtle and devious forms of self-deception that mark modern man's attempts at self-justification, just so relentlessly in his *Attack Upon "Christendom"* does he attack the easy compromises made by the church and the Christian community with European middle-class ethics.

In *Training in Christianity* he attempts to describe what it would mean were one actually to become a Christian. Against the prevailing watered state of religious consciousness, reconciled to the pursuit of the "good life" and to individualistic egoistic strivings, he presents sharply, clearly and without compromise the ideal content of Christianity, revealing the great difficulty of becoming a Christian, the "unnaturalness" of becoming a Christian, and develops the Biblical concept of the Offense—Christianity an offense to common sense, to prudence, to "reason" and to all the virtues elaborated by "enlightened" culture. "It is nigh unto impossible not to be offended by Christianity, for there is only one alternative—faith."

The "shaking of the foundations" of man's autonomous intellectual fortress and of the church's liberal household which Kierkegaard began has been continued in every area of contemporary thought, but especially by those contemporary theologians whose minds were kindled by that of the Danish theologian.

SØREN KIERKEGAARD

from

The Sickness unto Death

THAT THE DEFINITION OF SIN CONTAINS THE POSSIBILITY OF THE OFFENSE —A GENERAL OBSERVATION ABOUT OFFENSE

THE OPPOSITION SIN/FAITH is the Christian one, which in a Christian way transforms the definition of all ethical concepts, giving them one distillation the more. At the bottom of this opposition lies the decisive Christian concept, "before God," a determinant which in turn stands in relation to the decisive criterion of Christianity: the absurd, the paradox, the possibility of offense. And that this should be indicated in every definition of Christianity is of the utmost importance, for the offense is Christianity's defense against all speculation. In this instance where is the possibility of the offense? It lies in the fact that a man, as a particular individual, should have such a reality as is implied by existing directly in the sight of God; and then again, and as a consequence of this, that a man's sin should concern God. This notion of the particular man . . . before God speculative philosophy never gets into its head, it can only universalize the particular man fantastically. It was just for this reason also that an incredulous Christianity made out that sin is sin, no matter whether it is directly in the sight of God or not. That is to say, they wanted to do away with the determinant "before God," and to this end they discovered a higher wisdom—which, however, strangely enough, was neither more nor less than what the higher wisdom no doubt generally is . . . the old paganism.

There is so much said now about people being offended at Christianity because it is so dark and gloomy, offended at it because it is so severe, etc. It is now high time to explain that the real reason why man is offended at Christianity is because it is too high, because its goal is not man's goal, because it would make of a man something so extraordinary that he is unable to get it into his head. A perfectly simple psychological investigation of what offense is will explain this, and at the same time it will show how infinitely silly their behavior has been who defended Christianity by taking away the offense, how stupidly or impudently they have ignored Christ's own instruction, who often and with such deep concern warns against the offense, that is, intimates that the possibility of the offense is present, and must be ever-present; for if it is not present, if it is not an eternally essential constituent of Christianity, it is nonsense, humanly speaking, for Christ, instead of taking it away, to be distressed about it and to give warning against it.

If I were to imagine to myself a day-laborer and the mightiest emperor that ever lived, and were to imagine that this mighty Emperor took a notion to send for the poor man, who never had dreamed, "neither had it entered into his heart to believe," that the Emperor knew of his existence, and who therefore would think himself indescribably fortunate if merely he was permitted once to see the Emperor, and would recount it to his children and children's children as the most important event of his life—but suppose the Emperor sent for him and informed him that he wished to have him for his son-in-law . . . what then? Then the laborer, humanly, would become somewhat or very much puzzled, shame-faced, and embarrassed, and it would seem to him, quite humanly (and this is the human element in it), something exceedingly strange, something quite mad, the last thing in the world about which he would say a word to anybody else, since he himself in his own mind was not far from explaining it by supposing (as his neighbors would be busily doing as soon as possible) that the Emperor wanted to make a fool of him, so that the poor man would be the laughing-stock of the whole town, his picture in the papers, the story of his espousal to the Emperor's daughter the theme of ballad-mongers. This thing, however, of becoming the Emperor's son-in-law might readily be subjected to the tests of reality, so that the laborer would be able to ascertain how far the Emperor was serious in this matter, or whether he merely wanted to make fun of the poor fellow, render him unhappy for the rest of his life, and help him to find his way to the mad-house; for the *quid nimis* is in evidence, which with such infinite ease can turn into its opposite. A small expression of favor the laborer would be able to get through his head; it would be understood in the market-town by "the highly respected cultured public," by all ballad-mongers, in short, by the 5 times 100,000 persons who dwelt in that market-town, which with respect to its population was even a very big city, but with respect to possessing understanding of and sense for the extraordinary was a very small market-town—but this thing of becoming the Emperor's son-in-law was far too much. And suppose now that this was not an external reality but an inward thing, so that factual proofs could not help the laborer to certitude, but faith itself was the facticity, and so it was all left to faith whether he possessed humble courage enough to dare to believe it (for impudent courage cannot help one to *believe*) —how many laboring men were there likely to be who possessed this courage? But he who had not this courage would be offended; the extraordinary would seem to him almost like mockery of him. He would then perhaps honestly and plainly admit, "Such a thing is too high for me, I cannot get it into my head; it seems to me, if I may blurt it straight out, foolishness."

And now for Christianity! Christianity teaches that this particular individual, and so every individual, whatever in other respects this individual may be, man, woman, serving-maid, minister of state, merchant, barber, student, etc.—this individual exists *before God*—this individual who perhaps would be vain for having once in his life talked with the King, this man who is not a little proud of living on intimate terms with that person or the other, this man exists before God, can talk with God any moment he will, sure to be heard by Him; in short, this man is invited to live on the most intimate terms with God! Furthermore, for this man's sake God came to the world, let himself be born, suffers and dies; and this suffering God almost begs and entreats this man to accept the help which is offered him! Verily, if there is anything that would make a man lose his understanding, it is surely this! Whosoever has not the humble courage to dare to believe it, must be offended at it. But why is he offended? Because it is too high for him, because he cannot get it into his head, because in the face of it he cannot acquire frank-heartedness, and therefore must have it done away with, brought to naught and nonsense, for it is as though it would stifle him.

For what is offense? Offense is unhappy admiration. It is therefore akin to envy, but it is an envy which is turned against oneself, or, more exactly, envy which is worst of all against oneself. The narrow-mindedness of the natural man cannot welcome for itself the extraordinary which God has intended for him; so he is offended.

The degree of the offense depends upon what passion a man has for admiration. The more prosaic men, devoid of imagination and passion, and who therefore are not apt to admire, they too may be offended, but they confine themselves to saying, "Such a thing I can't get through my head, I let it alone." These are the sceptics. But the more passion and imagination a man has, the nearer consequently he is in a certain sense (that is, in possibility) to being able to become a believer—*nota bene!* by adoringly humbling himself under the extraordinary—all the more passionate is the offense, which at last cannot be contented with less than getting this thing rooted out, annihilated and trodden in the dust.

If one would learn to understand offense, let him study human envy, a subject which I offer as an extra course, pluming myself upon having studied it profoundly. Envy is concealed admiration. An admirer who feels that he cannot be happy by surrendering himself elects to become envious of that which he admires. So he speaks another language, and in that language of his the thing which he really admires is called a stupid, insipid and queer sort of thing. Admiration is happy self-surrender; envy is unhappy self-assertion.

So also it is with offense: that which in the relation between man and man is known as admiration/envy, in the relation between man and God is adoration/offense. The *summa summarum* of all human wisdom is this "golden," or perhaps more properly the gilded, *ne quid nimis* [nothing to excess], too much or too little spoils the broth. This is given and taken between man and man as wisdom and is honored by admiration, its quotation never fluctuates, the whole of humanity guarantees its value. So if once in a while there lives a genius who goes a little bit beyond it, he is declared mad . . . by the wise. But Christianity takes a prodigious giant-stride beyond this *ne quid nimis,* a stride into the absurd—there Christianity begins . . . and the offense.

One sees now how extraordinarily (that there might be something extraordinary left)—how extraordinarily stupid it is to defend Christianity, how little knowledge of men this betrays, and how truly, even though it be unconsciously, it is working in collusion with the enemy, by making of Christianity a miserable something or another which in the end has to be rescued by a defense. Therefore it is certain and true that he who first invented the notion of defending Christianity in Christendom is *de facto* Judas No. 2; he also betrays with a kiss, only his treachery is that of stupidity. To defend anything is always to discredit it. Let a man have a storehouse full of gold, let him be willing to dispense every ducat to the poor—but let him besides that be stupid enough to begin this benevolent undertaking with a defense in which he advances three reasons to prove that it is justifiable—and people will be almost inclined to doubt whether he is doing any good. But now for Christianity! Yea, he who defends it has never believed in it. If he believes, then the enthusiasm of faith is . . . not defense, no, it is attack and victory. The believer is a victor.

Thus it stands with Christianity and the offense. The possibility of the offense is quite rightly included in the Christian definition of sin—in this phrase, "before God." A pagan, the natural man, is very willing to admit that sin exists, but this "before God," which really is what makes sin to be sin, is for him too much, it seems to him (though in a different sense from that pointed out here) to make too much of what it is to be a man; a little less, and then he is willing to agree to it—"but too much is too much."

The Socratic Definition of Sin

Sin is ignorance. This is the well-known Socratic definition of sin, which, like everything Socratic, is an opinion always worthy of attention. However, with respect to this Socratic position, as with respect to many other Socratic positions, how many men have felt a need of going further? What an innumerable number have felt the need of going further than the Socratic ignorance—presumably because they felt that it was impossible for them to stay there; for in every generation how many men are there that are capable, even for only a month, of enduring and existentially expressing ignorance about everything?

Therefore I do not by any means intend to dispose of the Socratic definition on the ground that one cannot stop with it; but, having the Christian definition *in mente* [in mind], I would make use of it to bring the other out sharply (just because the Socratic definition is so genuinely Greek), so that here as always the hollowness of every other definition which is not in the strictest sense Christian (that is, of every partial definition) may become manifest.

The difficulty with the Socratic definition is that it leaves undetermined how ignorance itself is to be more precisely understood, the question of its origin, etc. That is to say, even if sin be ignorance (or what Christianity would perhaps prefer to call stupidity), which in one sense cannot be denied, we have to ask, is this an original ignorance, is it always the case that one has not known and hitherto could not know anything about the truth, or is it a superinduced, a subsequent ignorance? If it is what the last question implies, then sin must properly have its ground in something else, it must have its ground in the activity with which a man has labored to obscure his intelligence. But also when this is assumed, the stiff-necked and tough-lived difficulty returns, prompting the question whether at the instant a man began to obscure his intelligence he was distinctly conscious of what he was doing. If he was not distinctly conscious of this, then his intelligence was already somewhat obscured before he began, and the question merely returns again. If it is assumed on the contrary that when he began to obscure his intelligence he was distinctly conscious of it, then sin (even though it be unconsciousness, seeing that this was an induced state) would not lie in the intelligence but in the will, and the question which must be raised is about the relation of the intelligence and the will to one another. With such questions as these (and one might continue to augment them for many a day) the Socratic definition does not deal. Socrates was certainly an ethical teacher (the Classical age claims him absolutely as the discoverer of ethics), he was the first one, as he is and remains the first in his class; but he begins with ignorance. Intellectually, it is toward ignorance he tends, toward the position of knowing nothing. Ethically, he understands by ignorance quite a different thing, and so he begins with that.

But on the other hand, as a matter of course, Socrates is not an essentially religious ethicist, still less a dogmatic one, as the Christian ethicist is. Hence he does not really enter into the whole investigation with which Christianity begins, into the *prius* [before] in which sin presupposes itself, and which is Christianly explained by the doctrine of original sin—a dogma to the border of which only we come in this investigation.

Socrates therefore never really gets to the determinant we know as sin, which is surely a defect in a definition of sin. Why is this? For if sin is indeed ignorance, then sin properly does not exist, since sin is definitely consciousness. If sin consists in being ignorant of what is right, so that one consequently does what is wrong, sin does not exist. If this is sin, then it must be assumed, as Socrates also assumed, that the case does not occur of a man knowing what is right and doing what is wrong, or knowing that a thing is wrong and doing the wrong. So then, if the Socratic definition is correct, sin does not exist. But, lo, precisely this is, Christianly understood, just as it should be, in a deeper sense it is quite correct, in the interest of Christianity it is *quod erat demonstrandum.* Precisely the concept by which Christianity distinguishes itself qualitatively and most decisively from paganism is the concept of sin, the doctrine of sin; and therefore Christianity also assumes quite consistently that neither paganism nor the natural man knows what sin is; yea, it assumes that there must be a revelation from God to make manifest what sin is. For it is not true, as a superficial view assumes, that the doctrine of the atonement is the qualitative difference between paganism and Christianity. No, the beginning must be made far deeper, with sin, with the doctrine of sin, as Christianity also does. What a dangerous objection therefore against Christianity if paganism had a definition of sin which Christianity must admit is correct!

What determinant is it then that Socrates lacks in determining what sin is? It is will, defiant will. The Greek intellectualism was too happy, too naïve, too aesthetic, too ironical, too witty . . . too sinful to be able to get it into its head that a person knowingly could fail to do the good, or knowingly, with knowledge of what was right, do what was wrong. The Greek spirit proposes an intellectual categorical imperative.

The truth in this definition must by no means be overlooked, and it needs to be enforced in times such as these which have gone astray in so much flatulent and unfruitful knowledge, so that doubtless now, just as in Socrates' age, only much more, it is advisable that people should be starved a little bit Socratically. It is enough to provoke both laughter and tears—not only all these protestations about having understood and comprehended the highest thought, but also the virtuosity with which many know how to present it *in abstracto,* and in a certain sense quite correctly—it is enough to provoke both laughter and tears when one sees then that all this knowing and understanding exercises no influence upon the lives of these men, that their lives do not in the remotest way express what they have understood, but rather the contrary. One involuntarily exclaims at the sight of a disproportion at once so sorrowful and so ludicrous. But how in the world is it possible that they have understood it? And is it true that they have understood? Here the ancient ironist and ethicist makes answer: "My dear man, never believe it, for if they truly had understood, their lives also would have expressed it, they would have done what they understood."

To understand/and to understand are therefore two things? Certainly they are; and he who has understood this (but not, be it noted, in the sense of the first sort of understanding) is initiated into all the secret mysteries of irony. It is with this contradiction irony is properly employed. To perceive the comic in the fact that a person is actually ignorant of something means a very low sort of comic, beneath the dignity of irony. There is properly no profound comic in the fact that people once lived who assumed that the earth stands still—

when nobody knew any better. The same thing will presumably befall our age in contrast with an age which knows more of physical law. The contradiction is one between two different ages, there is lacking a deeper point of coincidence; such a contradiction is not essential, and hence neither is it essentially comic. No, but that a man stands up and says the right thing . . . and so has understood it, and then when he has to act does the wrong thing . . . and so shows that he has not understood it—yes, that is comic. It is infinitely comic that a man, moved unto tears, so much moved that not only tears but sweat trickle from him, can sit and read, or hear, representations of self-denial, of the nobility of sacrificing one's life for the truth—and then the next instant—one, two, three, slap-dash, almost with the tears still in his eyes—is in full swing, in the sweat of his brow, with all his might and main, helping falsehood to conquer. It is infinitely comic that an orator, with truth in his voice and in the expression of his features, profoundly touched and profoundly touching, can present the truth in a heart-rending way, can tread all evil and all the powers of hell under his feet, with an aplomb in his attitude, an assurance in his glance, a resoluteness in his step, which is altogether admirable—it is infinitely comic that almost at the same moment, almost "with his dressing-gown still on," he can run cowardly and timidly out of the way of the least inconvenience. It is infinitely comic that a man can understand the whole truth about how wretched and petty this world is, etc.—that he can understand this, and then cannot recognize again what he understood; for almost in the same moment he himself goes off and takes part in the same pettiness and wretchedness, takes glory in it and receives glory from it, that is, accepts it. O when one beholds a man who protests that he has entirely understood how Christ went about in the form of a lowly servant, poor, despised, and, as the Scripture says, spat upon—when I see the same man so careful to betake himself thither where in a worldly sense it is good to be, and accommodate himself there in the utmost security, when I see him apprehensive of every puff of wind from right or left, as though his life depended upon it, and so blissful, so utterly blissful, so awfully glad—yes, to make the thing complete, so awfully glad that he is able to thank God for it—glad that he is held in honor by all men—then I have often said to myself and by myself, "Socrates, Socrates, Socrates, can it be possible that this man has understood what he says he has understood?" So I have said, and at the same time I have wished that Socrates might be right. For it seemed to me after all as though Christianity were too severe, nor can I bring it into accord with my experience to treat such a man as a hypocrite. No, Socrates, thee I can understand; thou dost treat him as a wag, as a sort of merry Andrew, thou dost treat him as a butt for laughter, thou has no objection, it has even thine approval, that I prepare and serve him up as a comic dish—provided I do it well.

Socrates, Socrates, Socrates! Yes, one may well call thy name thrice, it would not be too much to call it ten times, if that would do any good. People think that the world needs a republic, and they think that it needs a new social order, and a new religion—but it never occurs to anybody that what the world now needs, confused as it is by much knowing, is a Socrates. But that is perfectly natural, for if anybody had this notion, not to say if many were to have it, there would be less need of a Socrates. What a delusion most needs is the very thing it least thinks of—naturally, for otherwise it would not be a delusion.

So then, such an ironic-ethical correction might very well be what our age needs, and perhaps the only thing it really needs; for it is evident that this is the thing it least thinks of. It is highly important that, instead of going further than Socrates, we simply return to the Socratic dictum that to understand/and to understand are two things—not returning to it as a result [once for all acquired], for in the end that only helps men into the deepest wretchedness, since it simply abolishes the distinction between understanding/and understanding, but returning to it as the ethical interpretation of every-day life.

The Socratic definition helps itself out as follows. When a person doesn't do the right thing, why then, neither has he understood it; his understanding is a vain conceit, his assertion that he has understood it is a false indication of the way, his repeated assertion that the devil take him if he has not understood it is a prodigious remoteness along the greatest possible detour. But then indeed the definition is correct. If a man does the right thing, then surely he doesn't sin; and if he doesn't do the right thing, then neither has he understood it; if in truth he had understood it, this would at once have moved him to do it, would at once make him an echo of his understanding—*ergo* sin is ignorance.

But where does the difficulty lie? It is to be ascribed to a fact of which the Socratic view itself was aware (though only to a certain degree) and sought to remedy, that it lacks a dialectical determinant for the transition from having understood something to the doing of it. In this transition Christianity makes its start; by proceeding along this path it proves that sin lies in the will, thus attaining the concept of defiance; and then, in order to make the end thoroughly fast, it adjoins to this the dogma of original sin—for, alas, the secret of Speculation's success in comprehending is just this, of sewing without making the end fast and without knotting the thread, and therefore it can marvellously keep on sewing, i.e. keep on pulling the end through. Christianity, on the contrary, fastens the end by means of the paradox.

In pure ideality, where there is no question of the real individual man, the transition is accomplished by necessity (in the System indeed everything comes about by necessity), in other words, there is no difficulty at all connected with the transition from understanding to doing. This is purely in the Greek spirit—yet not Socratic, for Socrates was too much of an ethicist for that. And quite the same thing is really the secret of the whole of recent philosophy: *cogito ergo sum,* to think is to be. The Christian motto, on the contrary, is: As thou believest, so it comes to pass; or As though believest, so art thou; to believe is to be. So one can see that modern philosophy is neither more nor less than paganism. But this is not the worst, to be akin to Socrates is not the meanest position. But the entirely unsocratic trait of modern philosophy is that it wants to make itself and us believe that it is Christianity.

In the world of reality, on the other hand, where it is a question of the individual man, there is this little tiny transition from having understood to doing; it is not always *cito citissime* [as quickly as possible], not *geschwind wie der Wind* [fast as the wind], if I may speak German for lack of philosophic terms. On the contrary, here begins a very prolix story.

In the life of spirit, on the other hand, there is no stopping [*Stilstand*] (nor in reality is there any condition [*Tilstand*], everything is actuality): in case then a man the very same second he has known what is right does not do it—well then, first of all, the knowledge stops boiling. And next comes the question how the will likes this thing that is known. If it does not like it, it does not follow that the will goes ahead and does the opposite of that which the intelligence understood, such strong contrasts occur doubtless rather seldom; but the will lets some time pass, there is an interim, that means, "We'll see about that to-morrow." All this while the intelligence becomes more and more obscured, and the lower nature triumphs more and more. For, alas, the good must be done at once—at once, the moment it is known (and hence the transition goes so easily in the pure ideality where everything is "at once"), but the strength of the lower nature consists in dragging a thing out. The will has no particular objection to it—so it says with its fingers crossed. And then when the intelligence has become duly darkened, the intelligence and the will can understand one another better; at last they agree entirely, for now the intelligence has gone over to the side of the will and acknowledges that the thing is quite right as it would have it. And so there live perhaps a great multitude of men who labor off and on to obscure their ethical and religious understanding which would lead them out into decisions and consequences which the lower nature does not love, extending meanwhile their aesthetic and metaphysical understanding, which ethically is a distraction.

However, with all this we have not yet got any further than the Socratic position; for, as Socrates would say, if this comes about, then it only shows that such a man had not understood what is right. That is to say, the Greek spirit had not the courage to assert that a man knowingly does what is wrong, with knowledge of the right does what is wrong; so Socrates comes to its aid and says, When a man does wrong, he has not understood what is right.

Quite correct, and further than that no *man* can go: no man by himself and of himself can explain what sin is, precisely because he is in sin. All his talk about sin is at bottom palliation for sin, an excuse, a sinful mitigation. Hence Christianity begins also in another way, by declaring that there must be a revelation from God in order to instruct man as to what sin is, that sin does not consist in the fact that man has not understood what is right, but in the fact that he will not understand it, and in the fact that he will not do it.

With respect to the distinction between not being *able* to understand/and not being *willing* to understand, even Socrates furnishes no real enlightenment, whereas he is Grand Master above all ironists in operating by means of the distinction between understanding/and understanding. Socrates explains that he who does not do the right thing has not understood it; but Christianity goes a little further back and says, it is because he will not understand it, and this in turn is because he does not will the right. And in the next place, describing what properly is defiance, it teaches that a man does wrong although he understands what is right, or forbears to do right although he understands what is right; in short, the Christian doctrine of sin is pure impertinence against man, accusation upon accusation; it is the charge which the Deity as prosecutor takes the liberty of lodging against man.

But can anyone comprehend this Christian doctrine? By no means—this too is Christian, and so is an offense. It must be believed. Comprehension is conterminous with man's relation to the human, but faith is man's relation to the divine. How then does Christianity explain this incomprehensible? Quite consistently, in an equally incomprehensible way, by means of the fact that it is revealed.

So then, Christianly understood, sin lies in the will, not in the intellect; and this corruption of the will goes well beyond the consciousness of the individual. This is the perfectly consistent declaration, for otherwise the question how sin began must arise with respect to each individual.

Here again we have the criterion of the offense. The possibility of the offense consists in the fact that there has to be a revelation from God to enlighten man as to what sin is and how deep it lies. The natural man, the pagan, thinks thus: "O well, I admit that I have not understood everything in heaven and earth; if there is to be a revelation, let it inform us about the heavenly; but that there should be a revelation to explain what sin is, that is the most preposterous thing of all. I don't pretend to be a perfect man, far from it, but I know and I am willing to concede how far I am from perfection—ought I not then to know what sin is?" But Christianity makes answer, "No, that is what you know least about, how far you are from perfection, and what sin is." Behold, in this sense, in a Christian sense, sin doubtless is ignorance, it is ignorance of what sin is.

The definition of sin which was given in the preceding chapter therefore still needs to be completed: sin is, after having been informed by a revelation from God what sin is, then before God in despair not to will to be oneself, or before God in despair to will to be oneself.

Sin Is Not a Negation but a Position

For the truth of this affirmation the orthodox dogmatic as a whole has constantly contended, and it has rejected as pantheistic every definition of sin which makes it something negative—weakness, sensuality, finiteness, ignorance, etc. Orthodoxy has perceived very rightly that here is where the battle has to be fought, or (to recall the foregoing) that it is here the end must be made fast, that here is the place to put up resistance. Orthodoxy has rightly perceived that, if sin is defined negatively, all of Christianity totters. Therefore orthodoxy insists that there must be a revelation from God in order to teach fallen men what sin is, a revelation which, quite consistently, must be believed, since it is a dogma. And naturally paradox, faith, dogma, these three determinants, form an alliance and accord which is the firmest support and bulwark against pagan wisdom.

So it is with orthodoxy. By a strange misunderstanding, a so-called speculative dogmatic, which certainly has suspicious dealings with philosophy, has entertained the notion that it is able to *comprehend* this definition of sin as a position. But if this is true, then sin is a negation. The secret of all comprehending is that the very act of comprehension is higher than every position which it posits. The concept posits a position, but the fact that it is comprehended means precisely that it is negated. The speculative dogmatic, being itself aware of this to a certain degree, has known no other way to help itself but by the maneuver, not very seemly in a philosophic science, of throwing out a detachment of asseverations at the point where a movement is being made. One asseverates, each time more solemnly than the last, and with more and more oaths and curses, that sin is a position, that to say that it is merely a negation is pantheism and rationalism, and God knows what all, but altogether something which the speculative dogmatic renunciates and abhors —and then one goes on to comprehend what it means that sin is a position. That is to say that after all it is a position only up to a certain degree, not any more so than that one can after all comprehend it.

And the same duplicity of speculation is manifested also at another point, which is, however, related to the same subject. The interpretation of sin, or the way sin is defined, is decisive for the interpretation of repentance. Then since this thing of negating a negation is so speculative, there is nothing else to be done, repentance must be a negation of the negation—and so sin becomes the negation.

However, it is certainly very much to be desired that a sober thinker would for once explain how far this purely logical process, which recalls the grammatical rule that two negatives make an affirmative, and the mathematical rule that two minuses are a plus—how far, I say, this logical process is valid in the world of reality, in the world of qualities; whether after all the qualities are not subject to a different dialectic; whether in this case "transition" does not play a different rôle. *Sub specie aeterni, aeterno modo, etc.* the element of time is lacking in which things can be spaced out, hence everything *is,* and there is no transition at all. In this abstract medium to posit is *eo ipso* the same thing as to cancel or "resolve." But to regard reality in the same way is pretty close to madness. One can say also *in abstracto* that the perfect tense follows the imperfect. But if in the world of reality a man were to infer that it followed by itself and followed at once, that a work he had not completed (the imperfect) became complete (the perfect)—he surely would be crazy. But so it is too with the so-called "position" of sin when the medium in which it is posited is pure thinking; that medium is far too unstable to insure that this assertion that sin is a position can be taken seriously.

However, all such questions are aside from the issue which immediately concerns me here. I am merely keeping a steady hold upon the Christian dogma that sin is a position—not, however, as though it could be comprehended, but as a paradox which must be believed. To my way of thinking, this is the correct thing. If only one can get it made manifest that all attempts at comprehending are self-contradictory, then the thing assumes the correct position, and then it becomes clear that it must be left to faith whether one will believe or not.

I can well comprehend (this being not too divine a matter to be comprehended) that one who just simply has to comprehend, and only can think of such matters as offer themselves to comprehension, may find this material very scanty. But in case the whole of Christianity hinges upon this, that it must be believed, not comprehended, that it *either* must be believed *or* one must be offended at it—is it then so meritorious to be determined to comprehend it? Is it meritorious, or is it not rather insolence or thoughtlessness, to will to comprehend that which is not willing to be comprehended? When a King takes the notion of wishing to be entirely incognito, to be treated in all respects as a simple man, is it then, just because in general it seems to men a greater distinction to do him royal homage, is it then the correct thing to do it? Or is it not precisely to assert oneself and one's own way of thinking directly in opposition to the King's will? Is it not to do as one wilfully prefers to do, instead of deferring to the King's will? Or would it, I wonder, give pleasure to the King in proportion as such a man was more ingenious in displaying toward him the proper reverence of a subject when the King does not wish to be treated in that way—that is to say, the more ingenious such a man might be in acting contrary to the King's will?

So let others admire and extoll him who claims to be able to comprehend Christianity—I regard it as a plain ethical duty, which perhaps demands no little self-denial in such speculative times when all "the others" are busy about comprehending—I regard it then as a plain duty to admit that one neither can nor shall comprehend it. Just this, however, is doubtless what the age, what Christendom, needs, namely, a little Socratic ignorance in relation to Christianity—but I say emphatically *Socratic* ignorance. Let us never forget (yet after all how many are there that ever have known it or thought of it?)—let us never forget that the ignorance of Socrates was a kind of godly fear and divine worship, that his ignorance was the Greek rendering of the Jewish perception that the fear of God is the beginning of wisdom. Let us never forget that precisely out of reverence for the Deity he was ignorant, that, so far as a pagan could be, he kept watch as a *judge* on the border between God/and man, watching out to see that the deep gulf of qualitative distinction be firmly fixed between them, between God/and man, that God/and man may not in a way, *philosophice, poetice,* etc., coalesce into one. Lo, for this reason Socrates was the ignorant man, and for this reason the Deity recognized him as the most knowing.—But Christianity teaches that everything Christian exists only for faith; for this reason precisely it wills to be a Socratic, a Godfearing ignorance, which by ignorance defends faith against speculation, keeping watch to see that the deep gulf of qualitative distinction between God/and man may be firmly fixed, as it is in the paradox and in faith, lest God/and man, still more dreadfully than ever it occurred in paganism, might in a way, *philosophice, poetice,* etc., coalesce into one . . . in the System.

Only from one side can there be any question here of illuminating the fact that sin is a position. In the foregoing description of despair attention was constantly directed to an ascending scale. The expression for the scale was in part potentiation of consciousness of the self, in part potentiation as from passive suffering to conscious action. Both expressions in combination are in turn the expression for the fact that despair does not come from without but from within. And in the same degree despair is more and more positive [*ponerende*]. But according to the definition of sin we have formulated, a constituent of sin is the self as infinitely potentiated by the conception of God, and thus in turn it is the greatest possible consciousness of sin as a deed. This is the expression for the fact that sin is a position; the positive factor in it is precisely this, that it is *before God.*

Moreover, the determination of sin as a position involves also, in an entirely different sense, the possibility of offense, the paradox. For the paradox results from the doctrine of the atonement. First Christianity goes ahead and establishes sin so securely as a position that the human understanding never can comprehend it; and then it is the same Christian doctrine which in turn undertakes to do away with this position so completely that the human understanding never can comprehend it. Speculation, which chatters itself away from the paradoxes, lops a little bit off at both ends, and so it goes easier: it does not make sin so entirely positive—and in spite of this it cannot get it through its head that sin should be entirely forgotten. But Christianity, which is the first discoverer of the paradoxes, is in this case also as paradoxical as possible; it works directly against itself when it establishes sin so securely as a position that it seems a perfect impossibility to do away with it again—and then it is precisely Christianity which, by the atonement, would do away with it so completely that it is as though drowned in the sea.

BUT THEN IN A CERTAIN SENSE DOES NOT SIN BECOME A GREAT RARITY? (THE MORAL)

It was remarked in Part First that the more intense despair becomes, the more rare it is in the world. But now, as we have seen, sin is that despair which has been still further potentiated and qualitatively potentiated, and so this surely must be exceedingly rare! Marvellous objection! Christianity has concluded all under sin; we have endeavored to represent the Christian position as rigorously as possible—and from this results the strange conclusion that sin is not to be found at all in paganism, but only in Judaism and Christianity, and there again only very rarely!

And yet this is (but only in one sense) perfectly correct. "After having been informed by a revelation from God what sin is, then before God in despair not to will to be oneself, or before God in despair to will to be oneself," is to sin—and certainly it is rare for a man to be so developed, so transparent to himself, that this can fit his case. But what logically follows from this? Yea, one may well take heed of this, for here there is a peculiar dialectical turn. From the fact that a man is not in a more intense despair it did not follow that he is not in despair. On the contrary, it was proved precisely that most men, by far the majority of men, are in despair, despair in a lower form. There is no merit in being in despair in a higher degree. Aesthetically it is an advantage, for aesthetically one has regard merely to strength; but ethically the more intense kind of despair is further from salvation than is the lower.

And so it is also in the case of sin. The lives of most men, being determined by a dialectic of indifference, are so remote from the good (faith) that they are almost too spiritless to be called sin, yes, almost too spiritless to be called despair.

To be in the strictest sense a sinner is again very far from being meritorious. But then on the other hand how on earth can one expect to find an essential consciousness of sin (and after all that is what Christianity wants) in a life which is so retarded by triviality, by a chattering imitation of "the others," that one hardly can call it sin, that it is too spiritless to be so called, and fit only, as the Scripture says, to be "spewed out"?

But this is not the end of the matter, for the dialectic of sin merely catches one in another way. For how does it come about that a man's life becomes so spiritless that it is as if Christianity could not be brought into relation to it, as when a jack-screw (and like a jack-screw is the uplifting power of Christianity) cannot be employed because there is no solid ground but only moss and bog? Is this something that befalls a man? No, it is man's own fault. No man is born with spiritlessness, and however many there be who in death bring with them this as the only acquisition of their lives—this is not the fault of life.

But it must be said, and as outspokenly as possible, that the so-called Christendom (in which after a sort all men are Christians in a way, so that there are just as many, precisely as many Christians as there are men)—it must be said that not only is it a wretched edition of Christianity, full of misprints disturbing to the sense, and of senseless omissions and additions, but that it has abusively taken Christianity's name in vain. In a small country there are born hardly three poets in every generation, but of priests there are a plenty, many more than can get appointments. With regard to a poet people speak of his having a call; but as for becoming a priest, it seems enough to the generality of men (and that means of Christians) that one has taken an examination. And yet, alas, a true priest is even more rare than a true poet, and the word "call" originally was used in a religious sense. But with respect to being a poet people still retain a notion that it is something, and that there is something in it that a man is called. On the other hand, to be a priest is in the eyes of the generality of men (and so also of Christians) a thing bereft of every uplifting conception, lacking the least trace of the mysterious, *in puris naturalibus* [i.e., without mincing words] it is a career. "Call" means a benefice; people talk about getting a call; but about having a call—O yes, they talk about being "called" for trumps.

And, alas, the fate of this word in Christendom is like a motto for Christianity as a whole. The misfortune is not that

Christian truth is never uttered (just as it is not the misfortune that there are not priests enough), but that it is uttered in such a way that at last the generality of men attach to it no significance whatever (just as the generality of men attach to being a priest no other significance than that which goes with the week-day occupations of a merchant, attorney, book-binder, veterinary, etc.), so that the highest things make no impression at all, but sound out and are heard as something which somehow, God knows how, has become use and wont, like so many other things. What wonder then that certain people, instead of finding their own conduct indefensible, find it incumbent upon them to defend Christianity.

After all, a priest surely ought to be a believer. And think what a believer is! A believer is surely a lover, yea, of all lovers the most in love. With respect to enthusiasm a lover is after all only a stripling in comparison with a believer. Think now of a lover. He would be capable, would he not, day in and day out, as long as it was day and well into the night, of talking about his love. But dost thou believe it could occur to him, dost thou believe it would be possible for him, dost thou not believe that it would be an abomination to him, to talk in such a way as to try to prove by three reasons that there is after all something in this thing of being in love?—pretty much as when the parson proves by three reasons that it is profitable to pray, so that this thing of prayer has sunk so low in price that there must be three reasons alleged to bring it a little bit into repute. Or as when the parson (and this is the same thing, only still more laughable) proves by three reasons that to pray is a bliss surpassing all understanding. Oh, priceless anticlimax! The fact that something surpasses all understanding is proved by three . . . reasons, which, whatever else they may be good for, surely do not surpass the understanding, but precisely on the contrary make it evident to the understanding that this bliss does not surpass the understanding; for, after all, reasons certainly lie within the compass of the understanding. No, for that which surpasses the understanding, and for him who believes in it, the three reasons signify no more than three bottles or three red deer!—And now further. Dost thou believe it would occur to a lover to put up a defense for his love, that is, to admit that to him it was not the absolute, unconditionally the absolute, but that he thinks this thought of love along with objections against it, and from this proceeds the defense; that is to say, dost thou believe that he could or would concede that he was not in love, denounce himself as not being a lover? And in case a man were to propose to a lover to talk thus, dost thou not believe that he would regard that man as mad? And in case, besides being in love, he was something of an observer, dost thou not believe that he would suspect that the man who made to him this proposal had never known what it is to be in love, or would like to get him to betray and deny his love . . . by defending it?—Is it not evident that it could never occur to one who really is in love to want to prove it by three reasons or to defend it? For in fact he himself is that which is more than all reasons and more than every defense—he is a lover. And he who does this is not in love, he merely gives himself out [*udgiver*] to be that, and unfortunately—or fortunately—he does it so stupidly that he merely denounces [*angiver*] himself as one who is not in love.

But this is just the way Christianity is talked about . . . by believing priests. They either "defend" Christianity, or they translate it into "reasons"—if they are not at the same time dabbling in "comprehending" it speculatively. This is what is called preaching, and it is regarded in Christendom as already a big thing that such preaching is done and that some hear it. And it is precisely for this reason that Christendom (here is the proof of it) is so far from being what it calls itself that the lives of most men are, Christianly understoood, too spiritless even to be called in a strictly Christian sense sin.

SØREN KIERKEGAARD

from

Training in Christianity

Come hither, all ye that labor and are heavy laden, I will give you rest.

THE INVITER

THE INVITER, therefore, is Jesus Christ in His humiliation, and He it was who uttered these words of invitation. It was not from His glory that He uttered them. If such had been the case, Christianity is paganism and Christ is in vain—wherefore this supposition is not true. But supposing the case were such that He who sits in glory were disposed to utter this word, 'Come hither', as though it were an unambiguous invitation to rush straight into the arms of glory—what wonder then if a crowd were to come rushing up! But they who run in that fashion are on a wild-goose chase, vainly fancying that they *know* who Christ is. But that no one *knows*, and in order to believe, one must begin with the humiliation.

The Inviter who utters these words, consequently He whose words these are (whereas in the mouth of another these same words would be a falsehood), is the humiliated Jesus Christ, the lowly man, born of a despised maiden, His father a carpenter, His kindred people of the lowest class, the lowly man who at the same time (like pouring oil upon fire) declared that He was God.

It is this Jesus Christ in His humiliation who spoke these words. And you have no right to apply to yourself one word of Christ's, not one single word, you have not the least part in Him, no society with Him in the remotest way, unless you have become so contemporary with Him in His humiliation that, exactly like His immediate contemporaries, you must take heed of His warning: 'Blessed is he whosoever shall not be offended in me.' You have no right to appropriate Christ's words and mendaciously eliminate Him. You have no right to appropriate Christ's words and then transform Him fantastically into something other than He is, by means of the vain chatter of history, which while it chatters about Him really has no notion what it is chattering about.

It is Jesus Christ in His humiliation who speaks. It is historically true that *He* uttered these words. It is false that these words were uttered by *Him* the moment we alter His historical reality.

So then it is this lowly man, living in poverty, with twelve poor fellows as His disciples who were drawn from the simplest classes of society, who for a while was singled out as an object of curiosity, but later was to be found only in company with sinners, publicans, lepers, and madmen; for it might cost a man honour, life, and property, or at any rate expulsion from the synagogue (for this punishment we know was imposed), if he merely suffered himself to be helped by Him. Come now hither, all ye that labour and are heavy laden! Oh, my friend, though thou wert deaf and blind and lame and leprous, &c., though thou wert to unite (a thing never before seen or heard of) all human wretchedness in thy wretchedness, and though He stood ready to help thee by a miracle—it yet is possible that thou (for this is only human) wouldst fear more than all these sufferings the suffering imposed for letting oneself be helped by Him, the punishment of being banished from the society of other men, of being scorned and scoffed at day in and day out, of losing, perhaps, life itself. It would be human (only too human) if thou wert to say within thyself: No, I thank you; I had rather continue to be deaf, and dumb, and blind, &c., than to be helped in such a way.

'Come hither, hither, all ye that labour and are heavy laden; oh, come hither; behold how He bids you come, how He openeth His arms!' Oh, when these words are uttered by a fashionable man in a silk gown, with a pleasant and sonorous voice which resounds agreeably from the lovely, vaulted ceiling, a silken man who bestows honour and repute upon all who hear him; oh, when a king says this who is clothed in purple and velvet, with the Christmas tree in the background on which hang the splendid gifts he proposes to distribute—then indeed thou wilt agree that there is some sense in what he says. But make what sense out of it thou wilt, one thing is sure, it is not Christianity, it is exactly the opposite, as contrary to Christianity as could be—for remember who the Inviter is.

And now judge for thyself—for thou hast a right to do that, whereas on the other hand thou hast no right to do what people so commonly do, to deceive thyself. That a man who makes such an appearance as that, a man who is shunned by everybody who has the least particle of common sense in his noddle and has anything in the world to lose, that He (surely that is the absurdest and craziest thing of all—one hardly knows whether to laugh or to weep at it), that He (surely that is the very last thing one might expect to hear from Him—for if He had said, 'Come hither and help me', or 'Let me alone', or 'Spare me', or in a proud tone, 'I despise you all', that might be understandable), but that He says, 'Come hither to me!'—what an uninviting invitation! And then further: 'All ye that labour and are heavy laden'—just as if people like that hadn't already enough troubles to bear, and then in addition would expose themselves to all the consequences of associating with Him. And finally: 'I will give you rest.' That caps the climax—He will help them! It seems to me that even the most good-natured of the scoffers who were actually His contemporaries might well say, 'That is the very last thing He should undertake—to wish to help others when He Himself is in such a plight. It is as if a beggar were to notify the police that he had been robbed. For that one who does not own anything and never has owned anything declares that he has been robbed is self-contradictory, and so also it is if one offers to help others when he himself is in need of being helped.' Humanly speaking, this is indeed the craziest contradiction, that He who literally 'has nowhere to lay his head', that a person of whom (humanly) it was appropriately said, 'Behold the man!' that He says, 'Come hither to me, all ye that suffer—I will help!'

Now examine thyself—for that thou hast a right to do. On the other hand, thou hast properly no right, without self-examination, to let thyself be deluded by 'the others', or to delude thyself into the belief that thou art a Christian—therefore examine thyself. Suppose that thou wert contemporary with Him! True enough, He said—ah, it was *He* that said it—that He was God! Many a madman has done the same—and His whole generation was of the opinion that He 'blasphemed'. That, indeed, was the reason for the punishment imposed upon those who let themselves be helped by Him. On the part of the established order and of public opinion it was god-fearing care for souls, lest anyone be led astray. They persecuted Him thus out of godly fear. Therefore before a man resolves to let himself be helped he must consider that he has not only to expect the opposition of men, but consider this too, that even if thou couldst bear all the consequences of such a step, consider this too, that human punishment is God's punishment upon the blasphemer—the Inviter!

Now come hither, all ye that labour and are heavy laden!

Here obviously there is no call for haste. There is a brief halt which might appropriately be turned to account by going round by another street. And if thou, supposing that thou wert contemporary, wilt not sneak away thus by another street, or in present-day Christendom wilt not be one of the sham Christians—then truly there is occasion for a tremendous halt, for a halt which is the condition for the very existence of faith: thou art brought to a halt by the possibility of the offence.

In order, however, to make it quite clear and vivid that the halt is due to the Inviter, that it is the Inviter who brings one to a halt by making it evident that it is not just such a simple matter, but really quite an awkward thing, to follow the invitation, because it is not permissible to accept the invitation and reject the Inviter—to make this clear I shall briefly review His life in its two periods, which, though they exhibit a certain diversity, fall *essentially* under the concept of humiliation. For it is always a humiliation for God to be man, though He were Emperor of all emperors, and *essentially* He is not more humiliated by being a poor, lowly man, mocked and (as the Scripture adds) spat upon.

A.

The First Period of His Life

And let us now speak about Him quite freely, just as His contemporaries spoke about Him, and as we speak about a contemporary, a man like the rest of us, whom one encounters occasionally in the street, knowing where he lives, on what floor of the house, what his business is, what he has to live on, who his parents are, his family connexion, what he looks like and how he dresses, with whom he associates—'and there seems to be nothing extraordinary about him, he seems just like all the others'. In short, let us speak as one speaks of a contemporary about whom one makes no great ado. For in the situation of contemporaneousness, with these thousands and thousands of *real* people, there is no occasion to take account of such a difference as that of being remembered perhaps throughout the centuries and that of being *actually* a clerk in some shop, 'just as good a man as anybody else'.—So let us speak of Him the way contemporaries speak about a contemporary. I know well what I am doing; and believe me, the affected and formal reverence we indolently conform to in speaking of Christ always with a certain sort of reverence, seeing that from history one has acquired information of a sort, and has heard so much of a sort about Him, about His having been somehow some sort of a great person—this sort of reverence, I say, is not worth a straw, it is heedlessness and mock-holiness, and as such it is blasphemy; for it is blasphemous to have a heedless reverence for Him whom one must either believe in or be offended at.

It is Jesus Christ in His humiliation, a lowly man, born of a despised virgin, his father a carpenter. But for all that, He makes His appearance under circumstances which are bound to fix very especial attention upon Him. The little nation in which He appears—God's chosen people, as it calls itself—looks forward to an Expected One who will usher in a golden age for His land and nation. It is true that the form in which He appears upon the scene was as different as possibly could be from what most people expected. On the other hand, it corresponded better to the ancient prophecy with which the nation might be supposed to be acquainted. Thus He makes His appearance. A precursor had drawn attention to Him, and He too fixes attention upon Himself by signs and wonders which are talked about in the whole land—and He is the hero of the hour, a countless multitude surrounds Him wherever He goes or stops. The sensation he awakens is prodigious, all eyes are turned toward Him, everything that can walk, yea, what can only crawl, must see this wonder—and all must have a judgement about Him, form an opinion, so that the professional purveyors of opinions and judgements are wellnigh driven to bankruptcy because the demands are so pressing and the contradictions so glaring. Yet He, the miracle-worker, continues to be the lowly man who literally has nowhere to lay His head.—And let us not forget that in the situation of contemporaneousness signs and wonders have quite a different elasticity for repelling and attracting than has this vapid affair (still more vapid when the parsons, as they are accustomed to do, serve the thing up as a warmed-over dish) of dealing with signs and wonders of . . . 1,800 years ago. Signs and wonders in the situation of contemporaneousness are an exasperatingly impertinent thing, a thing which in a highly embarrassing way pretty nearly compels one to have an opinion, and which, if one is not in the humour to believe, may produce the utmost degree of exasperation at the misfortune of being contemporary with them, since they make life all too strenuous, and all the more so the more intelligent, educated, and cultured one is. It is an exceedingly delicate matter to find oneself obliged to give assent to signs and wonders performed by a contemporary. When one has Him at a distance, and when the upshot of His life helps one to entertain such a conceit, it is easy enough to fancy somehow that one believes.

So then the multitude is carried away by Him, follows Him jubilantly, beholds signs and wonders—not only such as He performs but such as he does not perform—exulting in the hope that the golden age will commence when He becomes King. But the crowd seldom can render a reason for its opinions; it thinks one thing to-day, another to-morrow. For this cause wise and prudent men are not in haste to adopt the opinions of the crowd. Let us see now what the judgement of the wise and prudent is so soon as the first impression of surprise and astonishment is past.

The wise and prudent man might say: 'Even assuming that this person is, as He gives Himself out to be, the Extraordinary (for all the talk of His being God I cannot but regard as an exaggeration, for which I should be quite ready to excuse and forgive Him if I really could regard Him as the Extraordinary, for I am not inclined to quarrel about words), assuming (though about this I have my doubts or at all events suspend my judgement) that the things He does are actually miracles, is it not then an inexplicable riddle that this same man can be so ignorant, so shallow, so totally unacquainted with human nature, so weak, so good-naturedly vain, or whatever one might prefer to call it, as to behave in such a way, almost forcing his benefits upon people! Instead of holding people at a distance with a proud and lordly mien, keeping them in the deepest subjection, and receiving their worship on the rare occasions when He permits Himself to be seen, that is to say, being instead approachable to all, or, more properly expressed, Himself approaching all, consorting with all, almost as if to be the Extraordinary meant to be the servant of all, as if to be the Extraordinary, as He Himself says He is, meant to be anxious whether people will derive profit from Him or not, in short, as if to be the Extraordinary were to be the most anxiously troubled of all men. On the whole, it is inexplicable to me what He wants, what His purpose is, what He is striving for, what He desires to accomplish, what the meaning of it all is. In many an individual utterance of His He discloses, as I cannot deny, so deep an insight into human nature that presumably He must know what I, with half my shrewdness, can tell Him in advance, that in such a fashion nobody can get on in the world—unless it might be that despising worldly prudence a man simple-heartedly aims at becoming a fool, or perhaps carries his simple-heartedness so far that He prefers to be put to death—but then a man is crazy, if that's what he wants. Having, as I said, a knowledge of human nature, He presumably knows that what one has to do is to deceive people and at the same time make one's deceit appear a benefaction to the whole race. In this way one stands to reap every advantage, including that which yields the most precious enjoyment of all, that of being called by one's contemporaries the benefactor of the human race—and when one is in the grave, a fig for what posterity may say. But to make such renunciation, not to take the least account of Himself, almost begging people to accept these benefactions—no, as for joining Him, such a thing could never enter my mind. And as a matter of fact He extends no invitation to me, for He invites only those who labour and are heavy laden.'

Or.—'His life is simply fantastic. Indeed this is the mildest expression one can use to describe it, for in passing that judgement one is good-humoured enough to ignore altogether this sheer madness of conceiving Himself to be God. It is fantastic. At the most one can live like that for a few years in one's youth. But He is already more than thirty years of age. And literally he is nothing. Moreover, no long time will elapse before He must lose all the popular respect and esteem He now enjoys—this being the only thing he can be said to have gained for himself hitherto. If in the long run a person would make sure of retaining popular favour (which I readily concede is quite the riskiest chance one can take), He must behave in a very different way. It will not be many months before the crowd is tired of a man who is thus at everybody's service; they will begin to regard Him as a ruined man, a sort of *mauvais sujet,* who might be thankful to end His days in some remote corner of the earth, forgetting the world and forgotten by it, provided at least that He does not obstinately hold his ground and, in conformity with the whole course of His life hitherto, want to be put to death, which is the inevitable consequence of holding His ground. What has He done to provide for His future? Nothing. Has He any definite job? No. What prospects has he? None. To speak only of a minor consideration—what will He do to pass the time when He grows older? The long winter nights, how will He occupy them? Why, He cannot even play cards. He enjoys some popular favour—verily, of all movable chattels the most movable, which in the twinkling of an eye can be transformed into popular disfavor.—To join myself to Him—no, I thank you. Praise God, I have not yet entirely lost my wits.'

Or.—'There is in fact something extraordinary about the man (though one may, on one's own behalf and on behalf of every sound human intelligence, reserve the right to refrain from any opinion with respect to His claim to be God), there is something extraordinary about Him; I have no doubt of that. In fact one might feel almost embittered at providence for entrusting to such a person what it has entrusted to Him, a person who Himself does the very opposite to that which He enjoins when He says not to cast your pearls before swine—wherefore the thing will end quite appropriately with their turning again and rending Him. This is what one can always expect of swine—but, on the other hand, one would not expect that He who Himself is aware of this truth would do exactly what He knew that other men should not do. If only one could craftily get possession of His wisdom—for as to His very peculiar personal notion that He is God, upon which He seems to set so much store, I will cheerfully leave it solely to Him as His undisputed personal possession—but if only one could craftily get possession of His wisdom . . . without becoming His disciple! If one could slyly visit Him by night and get that out of Him—for I am man enough to draft and edit it, and in quite a different fashion, I assure you. To the astonishment and admiration of the whole world, something very different shall come out of it, that I warrant you. For I can perceive well enough that there is something very profound concealed in what He says, the misfortune being that He is the man He is. But, who knows, perhaps in the end it may prove possible to cajole it out of Him. Perhaps in this respect also He is idiotically good-natured enough to impart it openly. That is not improbable, for it appears evident to me that the wisdom He is so plainly in possession of, being bestowed upon Him, has been bestowed upon a fool—such a contradiction is the very essence of His existence.—But to join myself to Him, to become His disciple; no, that would be to make a fool of myself.'

Or.—'In case (to advance an hypothesis which I leave undetermined) it is the Good and the True this man desires to further, it may be said at least that He is helpful in one respect, to young men especially, and to inexperienced youth in general, for whom it is so profitable to understand, the sooner the better, and to right good effect, in view of life's serious tasks, that all this high-flown talk about living for the Good and the True has a considerable admixture of the ludicrous. He proves how exactly the poets of our day have hit the mark when they always let the Good and the True be impersonated by a half-wit or by a blockhead who would serve for breaking down a door. To exert Himself as this man does, to renounce everything except troubles and hardships, to be at people's beck and call every hour of the day, more diligent than a practising physician—and why? Is it because this is His calling? No, not in the remotest sense. So far as one can judge, it has never occurred to Him to want to have any post. Is it then because He earns money thereby? No, not a penny. He doesn't own a penny; and if He owned it, he would at once give it away. Is it then to attain honour and prestige in the State? Quite the contrary: He abhors all worldly prestige. And He who, despising worldly prestige and practised in the art of living on nothing, seems qualified, if any man in the world is, to pass His life in the most agreeable *far niente* (a thing that has some sense in it after all)—why, it is precisely He that lives more laboriously than any government official who is rewarded with honour and prestige, more laboriously than any business man who makes money by the peck. Why does He exert Himself so strenuously, or (since it is vain to put a question which can have no answer), just remark with amazement that He exerts Himself thus to attain the good fortune of being laughed at and derided, &c.! A queer sort of pleasure, forsooth! That one should push through the crowd in order to get to the spot where money is dealt out, and honour, and glory—that one can understand. But to push oneself forward in order to be flogged—how sublime, how Christian, how stupid!'

Or.—'So many hasty judgements are expressed by people who understand nothing . . . and deify Him, and so many harsh judgements by those who perhaps misunderstand Him, that for my part I shall not give anyone occasion to charge me with a hasty judgement; I keep perfectly cool and calm, and what is more, I am conscious of being as indulgent and moderate as possible. Suppose it is true (which I concede, however, only up to a certain point) that even the understanding is not unimpressed by this man—what judgement then must I pass upon Him? My judgement is that at the outset I can form no judgement about Him. I do not mean with respect to the fact that He says he is God, for about that I can never to all eternity form any judgement at all. No, I mean an opinion about Him regarded as a man. Only the upshot of His life can determine whether He is the Extraordinary, or whether, deceived by His imagination, He has applied, not only to Himself but to mankind in general, a standard far too high for men. With the best will in the world I can do no more for Him than this; even if He were my only friend or my own son, I could not judge Him more indulgently or to any other effect. But hence it follows that I cannot on sufficient grounds reach any opinion about Him. For to have an opinion I must first see the upshot of His life, even up to the very end. That is to say He must be dead. Then I can (but still only perhaps) have an opinion about Him; and this being assumed, it is still only in a non-natural sense an opinion about Him, for then in fact He is no more. It follows as a matter of course that I cannot possibly join myself to Him as long as He lives. The *authority* with which He is said to teach cannot have for me decisive significance, for it is easy to see that it moves in a circle, appealing to the very fact He has to prove, which in turn can only be proved by the upshot, in so far as it does not derive from that fixed idea of His that He is God; for if it is *therefore* He possesses authority, because He is God, the rejoinder is . . . *if*. This much, however, I can concede to Him, that if I could fancy myself living in a later generation, and if then the upshot of His life, the consequences of it in history, were to make it evident that He was the Extraordinary—then it might not be altogether impossible that I might come very near to being His disciple.'

A clergyman might say.—'For an impostor and seducer of the people there is really something uncommonly honest about Him, and for this reason He can hardly be so absolutely dangerous as He appears to be. He appears now to be so dangerous while the storm lasts, appears so dangerous because of His immense popularity, until the storm has past over and the people—yes, precisely these people—overthrow Him. It is honesty that while desiring to make Himself out to be the Expected One, He resembles this figure so little as he does—the sort of honesty one can detect in a person who would issue false bank-notes, and makes them so badly that everyone who has any intelligence can easily detect the fraud.—True enough, we all look forward to an Expected One; but that it is God in His own person that should come is the expectation of no reasonable man, and every religious soul shudders at the blasphemy this person is guilty of. Nevertheless, we all look forward to an Expected One, in this we are all agreed. But the regiment of this world does not move forward tumultuously by leaps, the world development is (as the word itself implies) *evolutionary*, not *revolutionary*. The veritable Expected One will therefore appear totally different; He will come as the most glorious flower and the highest unfolding of the established order. Thus it is that the veritable Expected One will come; and He will act in a totally different way, He will recognize the established order as an authority, He will summon all the clergy to a council, lay before this body a report of what He has accomplished along with His credentials—and then, if by ballot He obtains a majority vote, He will be acclaimed as the extraordinary man He is, as the Expected One.

'But in this man's course of action there is an ambiguity. He is far too much the judge. It is as if He would be the judge which condemns the established order, and yet at the same time the Expected One. If it is not the former He wishes to be, to what purpose then His absolute isolation from the established order, His aloofness from everything that has to do with it! If He does not wish to be the judge, then to what purpose His fantastic flight outside reality and into the society of ignorant peasantry, to what purpose His proud contempt for all the intelligence and efficiency of the established order, and His resolution to begin entirely afresh and anew by the help of . . . fishermen and artisans! His whole mode of existence is aptly typified by the fact that He is an illegitimate child. If He wishes to be merely the Expected One, to what purpose His warning about putting a new piece of cloth upon an old garment? This is the watchword of every revolution, for it implies not merely the will to ignore the established order, but the will to do away with it—instead of joining forces with the establishment and as a reformer bettering it, or as the Expected One raising it to its highest potency. There is an ambiguity, and it is not feasible to be at once the judge and the Expected One. And this ambiguity must result in his downfall, which I have already calculated in advance. The catastrophe of the judge is rightly imagined by the dramatists as a violent death; but the thing looked forward to with hopeful expectation cannot possibly be downfall, and so He is *eo ipso* not the Expected One, that is to say, not Him whom the established order expects in order to deify Him. The people do not yet perceive this ambiguity; they regard Him as the Expected One, which the established order cannot possibly do, and the people can, the formless and fickle crowd, because they are at the farthest remove from being anything that can be called established. But as soon as the ambiguity is made manifest, it will be His downfall. Why, His precursor was a far more definitely defined figure. He was one thing only: the judge. But how confusing and bewildering to want to be both things at once, and what an extremity of confusion it is to recognize His precursor as the one who was to act as judge, which precisely means, of course, to make the established order receptive for the Expected One and to put it entirely in condition to receive Him, and then to want to be Himself the Expected One who follows close after the judge —and yet still not be willing to join hands with the established order!'

And the philosopher might say.—'Such dreadful, or, rather, insane vanity. For an individual man to want to be God is something hitherto unheard of. Never before has there been seen such an example of pure subjectivity and sheer negation carried to the utmost excess. He has no doctrine, no system, no fundamental knowledge; it is merely by detached aphoristic utterances, some bits of sententious wisdom, constantly repeated with variations, that He succeeds in dazzling the masses, for whom also He performs signs and wonders, so that they, instead of learning something and receiving instruction, come to believe in Him, who continues in the most odious manner possible to force his subjectivity upon people. There is absolutely nothing objective or positive in Him or in what He says. So far as this goes, one might say that He does not need to be brought to destruction, for philosophically considered He is already destroyed, perishableness being the very essence of subjectivity. One may concede that His is a remarkable subjectivity, and that regarded as a teacher (be it as it may with His other signs and wonders) He continually repeats the miracle of the five small loaves: by the aid of a little lyric and a few aphorisms He sets the whole land in commotion. But even if one would overlook the madness revealed in the fact that *He* thinks Himself to be God, it is an incomprehensible mistake, disclosing surely a lack of philosophic culture, to suppose that God could anyhow reveal Himself in the form of a single individual. The race, the universal, the totality, is God; but surely the race is not any single individual. In general it is characteristic of subjectivity that the individual desires to be something of importance. But this you can understand. Insanity is evinced by the fact that the individual desires to be God. If this insane thing were possible, that an individual was God, then logically one must worship this individual. A greater philosophical bestiality cannot be conceived.'

The statesman might say.—'That at the moment this man is a power, cannot be denied—leaving out of account, of course, the conceit He has that He is God. One can afford to ignore once for all a private hobby like that, which need not be reckoned with practically and concerns nobody else, least of all the statesman. A statesman is interested only in what power a man possesses, and, as has already been said, at this moment He is a power to be reckoned with. But what He wants, what He is heading for, it is not easy to make out. If this is shrewdness, it must be of an entirely new and peculiar order, not unlike what commonly is called madness. He has conspicuously strong points, but He seems to annul them instead of making use of them. He expends His forces, but gets nothing in return for *Himself*. I regard Him as a phenomenon, with which—as with every phenomenon—one does best not to ally oneself, since it is always impossible to calculate on Him or on the catastrophe which confronts Him. It is possible that He may become king—that is at least possible. But it is not impossible, or rather it is equally possible, that He may end on the scaffold. What is lacking in His whole effort is seriousness. With a vast spread of wing He hovers, merely hovers; He makes no end fast, makes no businesslike reckoning—He hovers. Would He fight for national interests, or is it a communistic revolution He aims after, is it a republic He wants or a kingdom, which party will He join or which oppose, will He try to stand well with all parties, or will He struggle against them all? Get into touch with Him? No, that is the very last thing I should want to do. I do even more than avoid Him; I keep perfectly still, make as if I did not exist; for it is impossible to reckon how He might intervene to confound one, if one were to take in hand the least thing, or how things might get tangled up in His hands. The man is dangerous, in a certain sense He is tremendously dangerous; but I calculate to catch Him, just by doing nothing. For He must be overthrown—and the surest way is to let Him do it Himself, by stumbling over Himself. At this moment at least I have not the power to overthrow Him, and I know of no one who has. To undertake the least thing against Him now would be merely to get oneself crushed. No, a steady negative resistance is the thing. To do nothing! then presumably He will involve Himself in the enormous consequences He drags after Him, He will finally trip on His own train—and fall.'

Or the solid citizen might express an opinion which in his own family would be received as a verdict.—'No, let us be men. Everything is good in moderation; too little and too much spoils all. And according to a French proverb which I heard from a travelling salesman, Every energy exerted to excess collapses—and as for this man, His downfall is obviously a sure thing. So I have seriously taken my son to task, warning and admonishing him that he should not drift into evil ways and join himself to that person. And why should he? Because all are running after Him. Yes, but who are these 'all'? Idle and unstable people, street loungers and vagabonds, who find it easy to run. But not very many who have their own houses and are well to do, and none of the wise and respected people after whom I always set my clock, not a one of them, neither Councillor Brown, nor Congressman Jones, nor the wealthy broker Robinson—nay, nay, these people know what's what. And if we look at the clergy, who surely must understand such matters best—they thank Him kindly. This is what Pastor Green said yesterday evening at the club: "That life will have a terrible ending." And he is a chap that doesn't only know how to preach. One should not hear him on Sundays in church, but on Mondays at the club—I only wish I had half of his knowledge of the world. He said quite rightly and as from his very heart, "it is only idle and unstable people that run after Him". And why do they run after Him? Because He is able to perform some miracles. But who knows whether they really are miracles, or whether He can confer the same power upon His disciples? In any case a miracle is a very uncertain thing, whereas certainty is certainty. Every serious father who has grown-up children must be truly concerned lest his sons be seduced and carried away to throw in their lot with Him and with the desperate men who follow Him, desperate men who have nothing to lose. And even these men—how does He help them? One must be mad to want to be helped in that fashion. It is true, even with regard to the poorest beggars, that He helps them out of the frying-pan into the fire, helps them into a new misery which the beggar could have avoided by remaining what he was, a mere beggar.'

And the mocker—not one who is despised by all for his malice, but one who is admired by all for his wit and liked for his good nature—the mocker might say.—'After all, that is a priceless idea, which must eventually inure to the advantage of all of us—that an individual man, just like the rest of us, says that He is God. If that is not to confer a benefit upon men, I do not know what benevolence and beneficence or beneficence and benevolence can mean. Granted that the criterion of being God is (I declare, who in all the world could hit upon such an idea! How true it is that such a thing never entered into the heart of man!), that it is just to look like all the rest of us, neither more nor less—hence we are all gods. *Quod erat demonstrandum.* Three cheers for Him, the discoverer of this invention so extraordinarily helpful to men! To-morrow I shall proclaim that I, the undersigned, am God—and the discoverer at least cannot deny it without contradicting Himself. All cats are grey in the dark—and if to be God is to look like all the rest, then it is dark, and we are all . . . or what was I about to say? we are all and every one of us God, and no one will have ground to be invidious of another. This is the most ludicrous thing imaginable; contradiction, which always is at the bottom of the comic, is here evident in the highest degree—but the credit for it is not mine, it belongs only and solely and exclusively to the discoverer of the fact that a man just like the rest of us, only not by any means so well dressed as the average, hence a shabbily dressed person who most nearly (at least more nearly than under the rubric God) comes under the attention of the Supervisor of the poor—that He is God. It is a pity, however, for the poor Supervisor of the poor, who with this general advancement of the human race will be out of a job.'

Oh, my friend, I know well what I am doing, and my soul is eternally assured of the rightness of what I do. Imagine thyself, therefore, contemporary with Him, the Inviter. Imagine that thou wast a sufferer—but reflect to what thou dost expose thyself by becoming His disciple, by following Him. Thou dost expose thyself to the loss of almost everything accounted precious in the eyes of people who are prudent, sensible, and held in esteem. He, the Inviter, requires of thee that thou give up everything, let all go—but the common sense which is contemporary with thee in thy generation will not easily let thee go, its verdict is that to join Him is madness. And cruel mockery will taunt thee. Whereas it almost spares Him out of pity, it accounts it a madder thing than the maddest to become His disciple. 'For', says common sense, 'a fanatic is a fanatic. Bad enough. But seriously to . . . become his disciple is the greatest possible madness. There is only one possible way of being madder than a madman: it is the higher madness of attaching oneself in all seriousness to a madman, regarding him as a wise man.'

Oh, say not that this whole treatment is an exaggeration. Thou knowest indeed (yet perhaps thou art not yet thoroughly sensible of it) that among all the men who were respected, enlightened, and wise, though some may have conversed with Him out of curiosity, yet there was only one, one single man, who seriously sought Him out, and he came to Him . . . by night. And thou knowest well that by night one treads forbidden paths, night is chosen as the time to go to a place one would not be seen frequenting. Think what a disparaging opinion of the Inviter this implies—to visit Him was a disgrace, something no respectable person, no man of honour, could openly do—no more than to go to . . . yet, no, I would not go on with what follows this 'no more than'.

Come *now* hither *to me,* all ye that labour and are heavy laden, I will give you rest.

B.

The Second Period of His Life

It has happened to Him now as all the shrewd and prudent men, the statesmen, and citizens, and mockers, &c., foretold. And like as it was said at a moment when it would seem that even the hardest hearts might be moved to sympathy, even stones to tears, 'He helped others, let him now help himself', so has it by this time been said thousands upon thousands of times by thousands upon thousands of people, 'What did he mean when he said that his time was not yet come; might it perhaps now be come?' Whereas, alas, 'that single individual',[1] the believer, must shudder every time he thinks of it, and yet cannot withhold his eyes from gazing into that abyss of (humanly speaking) senseless lunacy—that God in human form, that this divine doctrine, that these signs and wonders, which had they been performed in Sodom and Gomorrah, must have led to repentance, that in reality they produce the very opposite effect, seeing that the Teacher is shunned, hated, despised.

---

1 *Hiin Enkelte.* This, S. K. desired to have inscribed on his tomb. This, he said, is 'my category', the single individual, picked out from the crowd, isolated in the presence of God, and thus enabled to be an independent force in the world. I call attention here, once for all, to this significant word, about which S. K. wrote a whole chapter, which is appended to *The Point of View for my Life as an Author.* [Translator].

It is easier at this point to perceive what He is, since men of power and repute, the opposition of the establishment as a whole and the measures put in effect against Him have attenuated the impression He produced at the first, and the people have become impatient of waiting, seeing that His career, instead of going on to ever greater and greater renown, goes more and more backward to ever greater and greater degradation. It is a truism that every man is judged by the company he keeps. And what company does he keep? Well, that can be described by saying that he is an outcast from 'human society'. The company he keeps is the lowest class of the population, including, furthermore, sinners and tax-gatherers, who are shunned by every man of any importance who values his good name and reputation; and a good name and reputation is surely the last thing one would like to lose. His company consists, moreover, of lepers, who are shunned by everybody, madmen, who provoke only horror, of the sick and the needy, of poverty and wretchedness. Who then is this man that, being followed by such a train, He is still persecuted by the mighty? He is a man despised as a seducer, deceiver, blasphemer! It implies a sort of pity if any person of repute refrains from actually expressing his contempt for Him—the fact that they fear Him is another matter.—Such is now His appearance. For be on your guard not to be influenced by what you have come to learn later, to the effect that His exalted spirit, rising almost to divine majesty, never exhibited itself so evidently as just now. Oh, my friend, wert thou contemporary with a man who not only Himself was 'expelled from the synagogue', but—remember this!—a punishment was devised for everyone who let himself be helped by Him, and that punishment was 'expulsion from the synagogue'—wert thou contemporary with a man so despised, about whom everything seems correspondingly despicable (for there is nothing that cannot be interpreted in more than one way), art thou perhaps man enough to explain everything in a contrary way; or, what comes to the same thing, art thou 'that single individual', which as thou well knowest nobody wants to be, and which is regarded as a ludicrous eccentricity, perhaps as a crime?

And–to come to His principal companions, His Apostles! What madness–not to say new madness, for this is of a piece with the foregoing–His Apostles are a bunch of fishermen, who yesterday caught herring, and to-morrow (thus the logic of insanity expresses it) go out into all the world and change the face of the whole world. And it is He that says He is God, and these are His duly appointed Apostles! Is it He that is to assure respect for the Apostles, or is it perhaps the Apostles that are to ensure respect for Him? Is He, the Inviter, a crazy visionary? The procession which accompanies Him bears out this notion. No poet could invent it better. A teacher, a sage (or whatever you prefer to call Him), an ill-starred sort of genius who says of Himself that He is God–surrounded by a shouting mob, personally accompanied by a lot of publicans, criminals, and lepers, and closest to Him His chosen circle, the Apostles. And these persons, so competent to be judges of what truth is, these fishermen, tailors, and shoemakers, not only admire their teacher and master, taking every word of His for wisdom and truth, see not only what others do not see, His exalted character and holiness, no, they see God in Him and worship Him.–No poet could invent it better, indeed he might forget to mention the additional extraordinary fact that this same man is feared by the mighty, who lay their plans to destroy Him. His death is the only thing that can reassure and appease them. They have attached an ignominious penalty to the crime of joining Him, yes, even to that of letting oneself be helped by Him, and yet they cannot feel secure, they cannot feel quite certain that the whole thing is visionary madness. So much for the powerful. The people who idolized Him have more or less given Him up, only now and then for a moment does their old conception of Him flare up. There is not a single item in all the conditions of His existence that the most invidious of the envious could envy Him. And certainly the mighty did not envy Him, they require His death for the sake of their own security, that they may be at peace again when all has become as of old, only more securely settled by reason of his deterrent example.

These are the two periods of His life. It began with the people idolizing Him, whereas all who were implicated in the established order, all who had power and influence, hated Him, yet in a cowardly and underhand way spread their snare for Him. Into which He forthwith stepped? True, but He saw it clearly. Finally the people discovered that they were mistaken in Him, that the fulfilment He would consummate was at the farthest possible remove from the gold and the green gardens they were expecting. So the people fell away from Him, and the mighty drew the net closer . . . into which He forthwith stepped? True, but He saw it clearly. The mighty drew the net closer—and then the people, perceiving that they were completely deceived, turned their hate and the bitterness of their disillusionment against Him.

And (as the last straw) compassion might say, or in the society of compassion (for compassion is sociable, likes to get together, and in society with silly shallowness of feeling there is always to be found spite and envy, and even a pagan has remarked that none is so inclined to compassion as the envious), in that society the discourse might run as follows. 'And yet one really can be sorry for the poor man that He comes to such an end. He was a good sort of a chap after all. I grant that it was exorbitant of Him to want to be God, yet He really was good to the poor and needy, even though it was in the queer way of making Himself entirely one with the poor and going about with beggars. But all the same, there is something touching in the case, and one can't help being sorry for the poor man that he has to be put out of the way in such a pitiable fashion. For let them say what they will, and condemn Him as severely as they will, I can't help pitying

Him, I'm not hard-hearted enough for that, and I can't help showing my compassion.'

We have arrived at the last paragraph—not of sacred history, such as the Apostles and disciples who believed on Him recorded, but of the profane history which is the counterpart of it.

Come now hither, all ye that labour and are heavy laden—that is to say, if thou, of all sufferers the most miserable, still dost feel a desire to come, if thou still dost feel a desire to be helped in that fashion, that is, into still deeper misery, then come hither, He will help thee.

THE INVITATION AND THE INVITER

Let us now forget for a moment that in the strictest sense the offence lies in the fact that the Inviter said that He was God, and let us suppose that He represented Himself to be merely a man, and let us consider in this light the Inviter and the invitation.

The invitation is surely inviting enough; how then can one explain this incongruity in the event, this frightfully inverted proportion, that no one, or as good as none, accepted the invitation, that all, or as good as all (and, alas, it was 'all' that were expressly invited!), were at one in opposing the Inviter, in putting Him to death, yes, even in imposing a penalty for letting oneself be helped by Him. One might expect indeed that all, all sufferers especially, would come in throngs, and that all who were not sufferers but were moved by the thought of such loving-kindness and compassion would come in throngs, so that the whole race would be at one in admiring and praising the Inviter. How is the very opposite event to be explained? For that such a thing occurred is perfectly certain, and the fact that it occurred in this particular race must not be taken to signify that this race was worse than others. How could one be so thoughtless? Everyone who has any competence in such matters easily perceives that it occurred in this particular race because it was contemporary with Him. How then explain how it occurred, this frightful inversion of what it seems one might have expected?

The fact is that if the Inviter had (firstly) the aspect which the merely human conception of compassion would ascribe to His person; and if (secondly) He had had the merely human conception of what man's misery is, this surely would not have happened.

As for the first point: He should have been a thoroughly kindly and sympathetic man, who was in possession moreover of all the means for providing temporal and earthly relief, ennobling this relief with a deep and heart-felt sympathy. But he must be a man of distinction, not without a certain degree of human self-assertion, the consequence of which would be that he neither was able, in spite of his compassionate feeling, to stoop so low as to reach all sufferers, nor could clearly apprehend wherein man's misery, human misery, consists.

On the other hand, the divine compassion, its limitless *abandon* in its concern for the sufferer alone—not in the least for itself—and the absolute *abandon* with which it concerns itself for *every* sufferer—that cannot but be interpreted by men as a sort of insanity, which one hardly knows whether to laugh or to weep over. Even if there had been no other obstacle to the Inviter, this would have ensured that it would go ill with Him in the world.

Let a man merely experiment a little with divine compassion, that is to say, display some *abandon* in the practice of compassion, and then thou shalt see immediately what judgements men will form. Let one who might have a higher station in life—I do not say, let him, while maintaining the distinction of his station, give much to the poor, benevolently (i.e. as a superior) seek out the poor, and the sick, and the wretched—no, let him give up this distinction and seriously seek his society among the poor, live completely with the humble classes, with labourers, hod-carriers, mortar-mixers, and the like! Ah, in a quiet moment when one does not *see* him, most people perhaps may be touched by the thought of it; but as soon as they *see* him in this company and with this following, see him who might have been something great in the world coming along in close companionship with a bricklayer on his right and a broom-maker's apprentice on his left—what then? First of all they will have a thousand ways of explaining that it is by reason of his eccentricity and obstinacy and pride and vanity that he lives thus.[1] And even if they refrain from attributing to him such motives, they will not be able to reconcile themselves to the sight of him—in this company. Even the best men, generally speaking, will the moment they *see* it be tempted to laugh.

And though all the parsons, be they clothed in velvet, in silk, in broadcloth, or in bombasine, were to say otherwise, I would say, 'You lie, you merely deceive people with your Sunday discourses. For it will always be possible in the situation of contemporaneousness to say of such a compassionate one, who in this case therefore is a neighbour, "I believe it is vanity and hence I laugh at him. Quite a different matter if he were the truly compassionate one, or if I had lived contemporary with that noble figure!"' And as for these glorious ones 'who were misunderstood, &c.' (to quote the sermonizing phrase)—well, they are dead. In this way it is possible to play hide and seek. With regard to every compassionate man who ventures so far out,[2] one assumes that it is vanity—and as for the deceased, one takes it that they are deceased and that therefore they were glorious.

---

1 In his Journals S. K. was compelled to answer frequently to the common charge that his way of life was prompted by pride and vanity or was simply to be ascribed to his eccentricity.

2 'Venturing far out,' i.e. as a swimmer in the ocean, is the figure under which S. K. thought of the bold risk he was preparing to take.

This, however, must be remembered with regard to differences in human life, that everybody is for his own class. This partiality constitutes a fixed point, which explains why *human* compassion never goes beyond a certain degree. The greengrocer will be of the opinion that compassion descends too far when it extends to the inmates of the poor house and expresses equality with them. The greengrocer's compassion is entoiled in one sole reference, a reference first of all to the other greengrocers, and then to the alehouse keepers. Thus this compassion is not exercised with *abandon* (*hensynsløs*). And so with every class—the journalists who live off the pennies of the poor, under pretence of asserting and defending their rights, would be the first to render it ridiculous if anywhere there was manifested an example of this spirit of *abandon* in compassion.

To make oneself literally one with the most miserable (and this, this alone is *divine* compassion) is for men the 'too much', over which one weeps in the quiet hour on Sundays, and at which one bursts with laughter when one see it in *reality*. The fact is, this is so sublime that one cannot bear to see it in daily use; to bear it one must have it at a distance. Men are not on such intimate terms with the sublime that they really can believe in it. The contradiction therefore is this: This sublimity on the one hand; and, on the other, the fact that this is daily life, quite literally daily life, in which it manifests itself. When the poet or the orator illustrates this sublimity, that is, represents it with the Poet's aloofness from reality, people then are moved—but in reality, in the actuality of daily life, to perceive this sublimity in Copenhagen, in Amager market, in the midst of the week-day business life! Oh, when the poet or the orator does it, that lasts only an hour. Just for so long a time men are capable in a way of believing in this sublimity. But to behold it in reality *every day!* It is indeed a monstrous contradiction that the sublime has become the everyday thing.

In view of this, it was already decided beforehand what the fate of the Inviter must be, even if nothing else had contributed to His downfall. The unconditional, everything that applies the measuring-rod of the unconditional, is *eo ipso* a sacrifice. For though it is true enough that men wish to exercise compassion and self-denial and want to have wisdom, &c., yet they wish to determine for themselves the measure, insisting that it shall be only to *a certain degree;* they are not desirous of abolishing all these glorious virtues; on the contrary they would at a good bargain and without inconvenience have the appearance of practising them. Hence the true divine compassion is unconditionally a sacrifice as soon as it manifests itself in the world. It comes in compassion for man, and it is man who treads it under foot. And while it wanders about among men, even the sufferer will hardly dare to take refuge in it for fear of men. The fact is, it is for the world a matter of great consequence to preserve the appearance of being compassionate; this, then, the divine compassion reveals as falsehood —*ergo,* Away with this divine compassion!

But the Inviter was precisely the divine compassion—and therefore He was sacrificed, and therefore even the sufferers fled from Him; they understood (and, humanly speaking, quite rightly) that, as far as most human misery is concerned, it is better to remain what one is rather than be helped by Him.

As for the second point: The Inviter had also an entirely different conception than that which is purely human of what man's wretchedness is, and to help man in this respect was what He was intent upon—on the other hand, He had not brought with Him either money or medicaments or any such thing.

Thus the Inviter is so very far from having the appearance which human compassion would bestow upon His person that he is strictly an offence. Humanly speaking, there is actually something shocking, something at which one might become so embittered that he would have an inclination to kill the man—

at the thought of bidding the poor, and sick, and suffering to come to him, and then to be able to do nothing for them but only to promise them forgiveness of sins. 'Let us be men. A man is no spirit. And when a man is near to dying of hunger, then to say to him, "I promise thee the gracious forgiveness of thy sins"—that is shocking. Really, it is also ludicrous, but it is too serious a thing to laugh at.'

So then (for with these words in quotation we have merely wished to let the offence disclose the contradiction and exaggerate—we would not exaggerate) the Inviter really thought that *sin is man's ruin.* Behold now how that clears the ground! —and the Inviter did clear the ground, almost as if He had said, *procul, o procul este, profani,* or, even though He did not say this, it was as if a voice was heard which thus interpreted the Inviter's 'Come hither'. There remain not many sufferers to follow the invitation. Even if there had been one who, though he saw that there was no actual earthly help to be had from this Inviter, nevertheless followed, being touched by His compassion—now he too flees away from Him. 'It is indeed very close to being crafty of Him to pose as compassion in order to get a chance to talk about sin.'

Yes, indeed it is crafty, in case it is not clear to thee that thou art a sinner. In case it is only a toothache thou hast, or it is thy house that has burnt down, but it has escaped thy notice that thou art a sinner—then it is crafty of Him. It is crafty of the Inviter to say I have healing for all sicknesses; and then, when one comes, to tell him that there exists only one sickness, sin—for that and from that I have healing for all them that labour to labour themselves out of the power of sin, labour to resist the evil, to overcome their weakness, yet accomplish no more but to be heavy laden. From that sickness He heals 'all'; even if there were only one who on account of this sickness has recourse to Him, He heals all. On the other hand, to have recourse to Him on account of any other sickness, and on that account alone, is as if one who had broken his leg were to have recourse to a physician who employs himself only about eye diseases.

Other works by Kierkegaard:

Attack Upon "Christendom", 1854-55.
The Concept of Dread, 1844.
Concluding Unscientific Postscript, 1846.
De Omnibus Dubitandum, 1842-43.
Either/Or, 1843.
Stages on Life's Way, 1845.

Selected books on Kierkegaard:

Collins, James. *The Mind of Kierkegaard,* 1953.
Croxall, T. H. *Kierkegaard Commentary,* 1956.
Thomas, J. Haywood. *Subjectivity and Paradox; a Study of Kierkegaard,* 1957.

KARL BARTH

KARL BARTH, considered by some to be the uncontested giant of modern theology and vigorously criticized by others, is nevertheless recognized by all to have been one of the most powerful forces in modern Protestant thought. His first major work, *The Epistle to the Romans* (1921), strongly influenced by the insights of Kierkegaard, was the second "attack" upon Christendom which shattered the foundations of liberal theology and Christian humanism and forced a re-examination of religious life in all quarters.

Barth's theology is negative theology in so far as it separates radically the spheres of the human and the divine and denies to man the possibility of knowledge or understanding of God. God is the wholly Other, the Unknowable; the divine life is incommensurate with the human mind. All human attempts to bridge the gulf, including those of theologians and the church are met by the radical "No" of God's judgment against them.

His theology has been called "crisis" theology because of its interpretation of the relation of God to history. Liberal and natural theology had inclined toward the conception of history as the arena in which an immanent God brings about the progressive development of man's natural powers toward the good life. In Barth, on the contrary, the action of the wholly transcendent God in history is in the form of a radical invasion, an irruption into history which calls all historical life and cultural products to judgment.

Barth is one of the founders of neo-orthodox or neo-Protestant theology, so called because of its re-affirmation of the discontinuity between religion and culture, between man's knowledge of the world and his knowledge of God, and because of its renewed consciousness of the sinfulness of man and his powerlessness to achieve salvation for himself through his own acts.

In the light of the Eternal all mankind, including Christendom, is equally sinful.

Barth's theology is called "dialectical" because of the dialogic relationship it maintains for man's encounter with God. In the dialogue of the divine-human encounter man's self-affirmative "Yes" is answered by the "No" of God's judgment. In man's acceptance of the "No" in humility and obedience God's "Yes" becomes operative in forgiveness and acceptance. This tension between judgment and grace, sin and redemption, condemnation and justification in the divine-human encounter constitutes the dialectical life of faith.

Finally Barth's theology is Biblical because, for him, God reveals himself only in and through the Biblical word. Speculative knowledge of God is an impossibility. God is known only as he "speaks" to man out of the Holy Scriptures and the preaching of the Word.

The following excerpts from Barth's interpretation of Paul's *Epistle to the Romans* reveals the compelling power of Barth's thought and expression as well as his method of Biblical exegesis.

KARL BARTH

from

THE EPISTLE TO THE ROMANS*

THE NIGHT

ITS CAUSE

I. 18–21

v. 18. For the wrath of God is revealed from heaven against all ungodliness and unrighteousness of men, who hold the truth imprisoned in the chains of *their unrighteousness.*

IN THE NAME OF GOD! We know not what we should say to this. The believer knows our ignorance. With Job, he loves the God who in His unsearchable eminence is only to be feared: with Luther, he loves the DEUS ABSCONDITUS. To him is manifested the righteousness of God. He shall be saved, and he alone. 'Only the prisoner shall be free, only the poor shall be rich, only the weak strong, only the humble exalted, only the empty filled, only nothing shall be something' (Luther). But against the ungodliness and unrighteousness of men there is revealed the wrath of God.

"The wrath of God" is the judgement under which we stand in so far as we do not love the Judge; it is the 'No' which meets us when we do not affirm it; it is the protest pronounced always and everywhere against the course of the world in so far as we do not accept the protest as our own; it is the questionableness of life in so far as we do not apprehend it; it is our boundedness and corruptibility in so far as we do not acknowledge their necessity. The judgement under which we stand is a fact, quite apart from our attitude to it. Indeed, it is the fact most characteristic of our life. Whether it enters within the light of salvation and of the coming world depends upon the answer we

---

* Translated by E. C. Hoskyns, 1933. Reprinted by permission of Oxford University Press.

choose the scandal rather than faith (i. 16). That time is nothing when measured by the standard of eternity, that all things are semblance when measured by their origin and by their end, that we are sinners, and that we must die—all these things ARE, even though the barrier be not for us the place of exit. Life moves on its course in its vast uncertainty and we move with it, even though we do not see the great question-mark that is set against us. Men are lost, even though they know nothing of salvation. Then the barrier remains a barrier and does not become a place of exit. The prisoner remains a prisoner and does not become the watchman. Then is waiting not joyful but a bitter-sweet surrender to what is inevitable. Then is the contradiction not hope, but a sorrowful opposition. The fruitful paradox of our existence is then that which consumes it like a worm. And Negation is then—what is normally meant by the word. In the place of the Holy God there then appear Fate, Matter, the Universe, Chance, ANANKE. Indeed, a certain perception is betrayed when we begin to avoid giving the name 'God' to the 'No-God' of unbelief (i. 17). That which we, apart from faith in the resurrection, name 'God', is also a final consequence of the divine wrath. But the God who, contradicting His own name, affirms the course of this world, is God—God in His wrath, God who sorrows on our behalf, God who can only turn Himself from us and say only 'No'. And yet, for this very reason, no upright man can unreservedly name Him 'God'. For the wrath of God cannot be His last word, the true revelation of Him! 'Not-God' cannot seriously be named 'God'. Nevertheless, it is, in fact, always God against whom we are thrust. Even the unbeliever encounters God, but he does not penetrate through to the truth of God that is hidden from him, and so he is broken to pieces on God, as Pharaoh was (ix. 15-18). 'Everything that thwarts and damages the life that has been made by God, all the frailty and bondage of the creaturely life, including the sentence of death under which it lies, is a reaction of the power of God' (Zündel). Yes, but we must add that, if we do not make the apprehension of this divine reaction our own, we must perish at its hands. The whole world is the footprint of God; yes, but, in so far as we choose scandal rather than faith, the footprint in the vast riddle of the world is the footprint of His wrath. The wrath of God is to unbelief the discovery of His righteousness, for God is not mocked. The wrath of God is the righteousness of God—apart from and without Christ.

But what does 'apart from and without Christ' mean? *"The wrath of God is revealed against all ungodliness and unrighteousness of men."* These are the characteristic features of our relation to God, as it takes shape on this side resurrection. Our relation to God is *ungodly*. We suppose that we know what we are saying when we say 'God'. We assign to Him the highest place in our world: and in so doing we place Him fundamentally on one line with ourselves and with things. We assume that He *needs something*: and so we assume that we are able to arrange our relation to Him as we arrange our other relationships. We press ourselves into proximity with Him: and so, all unthinking, we make Him nigh unto ourselves. We allow ourselves an ordinary communication with Him, we permit ourselves to reckon with Him as though this were not extraordinary behaviour on our part. We dare to deck ourselves out as His companions, patrons, advisers, and commissioners. We confound time with eternity. This is the *ungodliness* of our relation to God. And our relation to God is *unrighteous*. Secretly we are ourselves the masters in this relationship. We are not concerned with God, but with our own requirements, to which God must adjust Himself. Our arrogance demands that, in addition to everything else, some super-world should also be known and accessible to us. Our conduct calls for some deeper sanction, some approbation and remuneration from another world. Our well-regulated, pleasurable life longs for some hours of devotion, some prolongation into infinity. And so, when we set God upon the throne of the world, we mean by God ourselves. In 'believing' on Him, we justify, enjoy, and adore ourselves. Our devotion consists in a solemn affirmation of ourselves and of the world and in a pious setting aside of the contradiction. Under the banners of humility and emotion we rise in rebellion against God. We confound time with eternity. That is our *unrighteousness.*—Such is our relation to God apart from and without Christ, on this side resurrection, and before we are called to order. God Himself is not acknowledged as God and what is called 'God' is in fact Man. By living to ourselves we serve the 'No-God'.

"Who hold the truth imprisoned in unrighteousness." This second characteristic is in point of time the first. Men fall a prey first to themselves and then to the 'No-God'. First is heard the promise —*ye shall be as God!*—and then men lose the sense for eternity. First mankind is exalted, and then men obscure the distance between God and man. The nodal point in the relation between God and man apart from and without Christ is the unrighteousness of slaves. Thinking of ourselves what can be thought only of God, we are unable to think of Him more highly than we think of ourselves. Being to ourselves what God ought to be to us, He is no more to us than we are to ourselves. This secret identification of ourselves with God carries with it our isolation from Him. The little god must, quite appropriately, dispossess the great God. Men have *imprisoned* and encased the *truth*—the righteousness of God; they have trimmed it to their own measure, and thereby robbed it both of its earnestness and of its significance. They have made it ordinary, harmless, and useless; and thereby transformed it into untruth. This has all been brought to light by their ungodliness, and this ungodliness will not fail to thrust them into ever new forms of unrighteousness. If mankind be itself God, the appearance of the idol is then inevitable. And whenever the idol is honoured, it is inevitable that men, feeling themselves to be the true God, should also feel that they have themselves fashioned the idol. This is the rebellion which makes it impos-

sible for us to see the new dimensional plane which is the boundary of our world and the meaning of our salvation. Against such rebellion there can be revealed only the wrath of God.

vv. 19–21. Because that which may be known of God is manifest to them; for God manifested it unto them. For the invisible things of him since the creation of the world are clearly seen, being perceived through the things that are made, even his everlasting power and divinity; so that they are without excuse: because that, in spite of *knowing God, they glorified him not as God, neither gave thanks; but became vain in their reasonings, and their senseless heart was darkened.*

"That which may be known of God is manifest unto them." The truth concerning the limiting and dissolving of men by the unknown God, which breaks forth in the resurrection, is a known truth: this is the tragic factor in the story of the passion of the truth. When our limitation is apprehended, and when He is perceived who, in bounding us, is also the dissolution of our limitation, the most primitive as well as the most highly developed forms of human self-consciousness become repeatedly involved in a 'despairing humiliation', in the 'irony of intelligence' (H. Cohen). We know that God is He whom we do not know, and that our ignorance is precisely the problem and the source of our knowledge. We know that God is the Personality which we are not, and that this lack of Personality is precisely what dissolves and establishes our personality. The recognition of the absolute heteronomy under which we stand is itself an autonomous recognition; and this is precisely *that which may be known of God.* When we rebel, we are in rebellion not against what is foreign to us but against that which is most intimately ours, not against what is removed from us but against that which lies at our hands. Our memory of God accompanies us always as problem and as warning. He is the hidden abyss; but

He is also the hidden home at the beginning and end of all our journeyings. Disloyalty to Him is disloyalty to ourselves.

"For the invisible things of God are clearly seen." This we have forgotten, and we must allow it to be brought once more to our minds. Our lack of humility, our lack of recollection, our lack of fear in the presence of God, are not in our present condition inevitable, however natural they may seem to us. Plato in his wisdom recognized long ago that behind the visible there lies the invisible universe which is the Origin of all concrete things. And moreover, the solid good sense of the men of the world had long ago perceived that the fear of the Lord is the beginning of wisdom. The clear, honest eyes of the poet in the book of Job and of the Preacher Solomon had long ago rediscovered, mirrored in the world of appearance, the archetypal, unobservable, undiscoverable Majesty of God. The speech of God can always be heard out of the whirlwind. Always it requires of us that we should perceive how unwisely we speak of that which is too high for us, too far beyond our understanding, when, in praising God or in complaining of Him, we plead with Him as with One who is like unto us. The insecurity of our whole existence, the vanity and utter questionableness of all that is and of what we are, lie as in a text-book open before us. What are all those enigmatic creatures of God—a zoological garden, for example—but so many problems to which we have no answer? But God only, God Himself, He is the Answer. And so the boundary which bars us in and which, nevertheless, points beyond itself, can *"since the creation of the world"* be clearly seen *"through the things that are made"* by God. By calm, veritable, unprejudiced religious contemplation the divine 'No' can be established and apprehended. If we do not ourselves hinder it, nothing can prevent our being translated into a most wholesome KRISIS by that which *may be known of God*. And indeed, we stand already in this KRISIS if we would but *see clearly*. And what is clearly seen to be indisputable reality is the invisibility of God, which is precisely and in strict agreement with the

gospel of the resurrection—*"His everlasting power and divinity."* And what does this mean but that we can know nothing of God, that we are not God, that the Lord is to be feared? Herein lies His pre-eminence over all gods; and here is that which marks Him out as God, as Creator, and as Redeemer (i. 16). And so through all history there runs the line of intersection between time and eternity, between the present and the future world (i. 4). Long ago it was proclaimed (i. 2); always it was visible. The wrath of God needed not to be revealed to those who stood already under His judgement, for they could have known and loved the Judge. *"So that,"* when they fail to see and fail to hear, *"they are without excuse."* Having eyes to see and ears to hear they are doing what they are doing. Inexcusable is their godlessness, for the *clearly seen* works of God speak of His *everlasting power* and they have already risen up in protest against the service of the 'No-God', by which God is ranged in the midst of the natural and 'spiritual' and other forces of this world. Inexcusable also is their unrighteousness, for the *clearly seen* facts bear witness to the *everlasting divinity* of God, and have already risen up in protest against the arrogance of religion, by which men, speaking of God from the welter of their experiences, mean in fact themselves. We have, therefore, encased the truth of God and evoked His wrath. But this was not because no alternative was open to us. God is not far from each one of us: *for in him we live, and move, and have our being* (Acts xvii. 27, 28). The situation might, therefore, have been very different.

But—*"in spite of knowing God."* The knowledge of God attainable through a simple observation of the incomprehensibility, the imperfection, the triviality of human life, was not taken advantage of. The invisibility of God seems to us less tolerable than the questionable visibility of what we like to call 'God'. We make of the eternal and ultimate presupposition of the Creator a 'thing in itself' above and in the midst of other things, of that which is living and abstracted from all concreteness a concrete thing—no doubt the highest—in the midst of other concrete things, of the Spirit a spirit, of what is inaccessible and therefore so nigh at hand an endlessly uncertain object of our experiences. Rather than see in His Light—eternal and which no man can approach unto—the Light, we allow Him to become a light—no doubt the most brilliant and, indeed, immaterial and supernatural—at which we kindle our OWN lights and then, quite consistently, seek to find in concrete things their OWN light. If, then, God is to us no longer the Unknown, what has become of the "*glory*" we owe Him? If God is to us no longer what we are not, what has become of the "*thanks*" which are due to Him? The revolt of Prometheus is wholly justified when once Zeus—the 'No-God'—has been exalted to the throne of God.

And so the light has become in us darkness, and the wrath of God is inevitable—*They became vain in their reasonings, and their senseless heart was darkened.* The barrier is now indeed a barrier, and the 'No' of God is now indeed negation. Bereft of understanding and left to themselves, men are at the mercy of the dominion of the meaningless powers of the world; for our life in this world has meaning only in its relation to the true God. But this relation can be re-established only through the—*clearly seen*—memory of eternity breaking in upon our minds and hearts. There is no other relation to God save that which appears upon the road along which Job travelled. If this 'breaking in' does not occur, our thought remains merely empty, formal, critical and unproductive, incapable of mastering the rich world of appearance and of apprehending each particular thing in the context of the whole. Unbroken thought thereby divests itself of any true relation to the concrete world, and, contrariwise, the unbroken heart, that is to say, that sensitiveness to things which is guarded by no final insight, divests itself of the control of thought. Dark, blind, uncritical, capricious, mankind becomes a thing in itself. Heartless, perceiving without observing and therefore empty, is our thought:

thoughtless, observing without perceiving and therefore blind, is our heart. Fugitive is the soul in this world and soulless is the world, when men do not find themselves within the sphere of the knowledge of the unknown God, when they avoid the true God in whom they and the world must lose themselves in order that both may find themselves again.

This is the Cause of the Night in which we are wandering: this also is the Cause of the Wrath of God which has been manifested over our heads.

ITS OPERATION

I. 22–32

v. 22. Professing themselves to be wise, they became fools.

The picture of a world without paradox and without eternity, of knowing without the background of not-knowing, of a religion without the unknown God, of a view of life without the memory of the 'No' by which we are encountered, has much to be said in its favour. It evokes confidence, for it is simple and straight-forward and uncramped; it provides considerable security and has few ragged edges; it corresponds, generally speaking, with what is required by the practical experiences of life; its standards and general principles are conveniently vague and flexible; and it possesses, moreover, a liberal prospect of vast future possibilities. Once the possibility that things can be *clearly seen* (i. 20) is abandoned, men are able against this background to profess that they are wise. The Night, too, has its wisdom. But, nevertheless, the vanity of the mind and the darkness of the heart still remain facts to be reckoned with. The brilliance of this unbroken wisdom cannot be maintained in the actual course of events, for they have passed inevitably under the wrath of God. That God is not known as God is due, not merely to some error of thought or to some gap in experience, but to a fundamentally wrong attitude to life. Vanity of mind and blindness of heart inevitably bring into being corrupt conduct. The more the unbroken man marches along his road secure of himself, the more surely does he make a fool of himself, the more certainly do that morality and that manner of life which are built up upon a forgetting of the abyss, upon a forgetting of men's true home, turn out to be a lie. It is indeed not difficult to show that this is so.

vv. 23, 24. And changed the glory of the incorruptible God for an image made like to corruptible man, and to birds, and fourfooted beasts, and creeping things. Wherefore God gave them up in the lusts of their hearts unto uncleanness, that their bodies should be dishonoured among themselves.

"They changed the glory of the incorruptible—for an image of the corruptible." That is to say, the understanding of what is characteristic of God was lost. They had lost their knowledge of the crevasse, the polar zone, the desert barrier, which must be crossed if men are really to advance from corruption to incorruption. The distance between God and man had no longer its essential, sharp, acid, and disintegrating ultimate significance. The difference between the incorruption, the pre-eminence and originality of God, and the corruption, the boundedness and relativity of men had been confused. Once the eye, which can perceive this distinction, has been blinded, there arises in the midst, between here and there, between us and the 'Wholly Other', a mist or concoction of religion in which, by a whole series of skilful assimilations and mixings more or less strongly flavoured with sexuality, sometimes the behaviour of men or of animals is exalted to be an experience of God, sometimes the Being and Existence of God is 'enjoyed' as a human or animal experience. In all this mist the prime factor is provided by the illusion that it is possible for men to hold communication with God or, at least, to enter into a covenant relationship with Him without miracle—vertical from

above, without the dissolution of all concrete things, and apart from THE truth which lies beyond birth and death. But, on whatever level it occurs, if the experience of religion is more than a void, or claims to contain or to possess or to 'enjoy' God, it is a shameless and abortive anticipation of that which can proceed from the unknown God alone. In all this busy concern with concrete things there is always a revolt against God. For in it we assist at the birth of the 'No-God', at the making of idols. Enveloped in mist, we forget not merely that all that passes to corruption is a parable, but also that it is ONLY a parable. The glory of the incorruptible God has been confused with the image (Ps. cvi. 20) of corruptible things. Some one of the relationships of men to the objects of their fear or of their desire, to some means of their subsistence, to some product of their own thought or action, to some impressive occurrence in nature or in history, is taken to be in itself significant and of supreme importance, as though even this selected relationship were not broken by the witness it bears to the unknown Creator whose glory cannot be confused with the known glory of an image, however pure and delicate. From such supposed direct communion with God—genuine only when it is not genuine, when it is not romanticized into an 'experience', when it is at once dissolved and claims to be merely an open space, a sign-post, an occasion, and an opportunity—there emerge precisely all those intermediary, collateral, lawless divinities and powers and authorities and principalities (viii. 38) that obscure and discolour the light of the true God. In the realm of romantic direct communion—in India, for example—these divinities are thrown up in the most extravagant numbers. Wherever the qualitative distinction between men and the final Omega is overlooked or misunderstood, that fetishism is bound to appear in which God is experienced in *"birds and fourfooted things,"* and finally, or rather primarily, in the *"likeness of corruptible man"*—Personality, the Child, the Woman—and the half-spiritual, half-material creations, exhibitions, and representations of His creative ability—Family, Nation, State, Church, Fatherland. And so the 'No-God' is set up, idols are erected, and God, who dwells beyond all this and that, is 'given up'.

"Wherefore God gave them up." The confusion avenges itself and becomes its own punishment. The forgetting of the true God is already itself the breaking loose of His wrath against those who forget Him (i. 18). The enterprise of setting up the 'No-God' is avenged by its success. Deified nature and deified spirits of men are, in truth, very gods; like Jupiter and Mars, Isis and Osiris, Cybele and Attis, they come to be the very breath of our life. Our conduct becomes governed precisely by what we desire. By a strict inevitability we reach the goal we have set before us. The images and likenesses, whose meaning we have failed to perceive, become themselves purpose and content and end. And now men have really become slaves and puppets of things, of 'Nature' and of 'Civilization', whose dissolution and establishing by God they have overlooked. And now there is no higher power to protect them from what they have set on high. And, moreover, the uncleanness of their relation to God submerges their lives also in uncleanness. When God has been deprived of His glory, men are also deprived of theirs. Desecrated within in their souls, they are desecrated also without in their bodies, for men are one. The concreteness of the creatureliness of their lives becomes now dishonour; and lust—sexuality both in the narrower and in the wider sense of the word—becomes, as the primary motive-power of their whole desire and striving, altogether questionable and open to suspicion. The whole ignominy of the course of the world they must now bear and bemoan and curse as ignominy; and further, in their separation from God they must continue to give it ever new birth. They have wished to experience the known god of this world: well! they have experienced him.

vv. 25–7. They exchanged the truth of God for a lie, and worshipped and served the creature rather than the Creator, who is blessed for ever. Amen. For this cause God gave them up unto vile passions: for their women changed the natural relation of sexes *into that which is against nature: and likewise also the men, leaving the natural use of the woman, burned in their lust one toward another, men with men working unseemliness, and receiving in* their own body *that recompense of their error which was due.*

"They exchanged the truth for a lie." Complete rebellion from God soon takes to itself more pronounced forms. It would not be unexpected were direct experience of God to have occasioned some occasional and rather humorous changes, some superficial errors, some dissolution of the Truth of God into a number of worldly-wise maxims. But though this is, no doubt, possible, it is not long before the Truth is quite seriously exchanged for a lie. The tiny mist between God and man, by which the far distance is obscured, soon becomes a veritable sea of clouds. Some half-conscious resentment at the unknown God very soon becomes fully conscious. The dazzled eye is soon damaged. Principalities and powers, formerly but seldom exalted to the throne, are soon established there, encircled with a halo of *everlasting power and divinity* (i. 20). The Creator, the eternal Archetype, meanwhile grows ever more and more 'abstract', 'theoretical', insignificant, and unloved. The completely concrete 'No-God' has won his victory, even though there may, perhaps, remain some bleak survival of the Unknown behind what is thought to be genuinely significant and magnificent, some occasional reference to a final secret in the midst of so much busy service of him whom we name 'God'. The only reality, the unknown, living God, appears nebulous, problematical, and unreal, whereas the world, separated from Him, and men, unbroken by any memory of Him, appear in a nimbus of security, necessity, and reality. The world is *"worshipped and served"*—if it be nec-

give to the problem of faith. But it is a fact, even should we essary, quite apart from its Creator. In their general view of the world scientists and historians are in far closer agreement with philosophers and theologians than is normally recognized. It is not merely that the world exists side by side with God: it has taken His place, and has itself become God, and demands 'the same devotion which the old-fashioned believer offered to His God' (Dr. F. Strauss). Contradictions within the deified world—Nature and Civilization, Materialism and Idealism, Capitalism and Socialism, Secularism and Ecclesiasticism, Imperialism and Democracy—are not so serious as they give themselves out to be. Such contradictions are contradictions within the world, and there is for them no paradox, no negation, no eternity.

"For this cause God gave them up." Unbroken naturalness is not pure. Nor are matters improved when 'naturalness' is penetrated by piety. In 'naturalness' there is always secreted that which is non-natural, and, indeed, that which actually contradicts nature. This contradictory factor awaits the hour when it will break forth. When, by allowing nature to run its course freely and uncontradicted, God and the world have become confused with one another, there comes into prominence a further confusion: what cannot be avoided or escaped from becomes confused with some necessity of nature, and this is in very truth a demonic caricature of the necessity of God. These two confusions stand altogether on one line, they belong together and cohere together. What is at first merely open to suspicion moves inexorably on to what is positively absurd. Everything then becomes Libido: life becomes totally erotic. When the frontier between God and man, the last inexorable barrier and obstacle, is not closed, the barrier between what is normal and what is perverse is opened.

vv. 28–31. A final and even sharper pointing of the whole situation is not only conceivable but actually takes place. In the perversity of this relation to God there still, however, remains a relic of clarity of sight, a last, warning recollection of the secret of God that withstands the arrogance of religion. A reflection of this secret lies even in the deified forces of the world, even in the deified universe itself. From time to time this bare relic of the Unknown reasserts itself in the presentiment of awe. But even this can cease. The damaged eye may become blind. Defective knowledge can become ignorance of God; it may become AGNOSIA (I Cor. xv. 34). *"Even as they refused to have God in their knowledge."*—That is to say, they became no longer capable of serious awe and amazement. They become unable to reckon with anything except feelings and experiences and events. They think only in terms of more or less spiritual sophistry, without light from above or from behind.—*"God gave them up to a reprobate mind, to do those things which are not fitting; being filled with all unrighteousness, wickedness, covetousness, maliciousness; full of envy, murder, strife, deceit, malignity; whisperers, backbiters, haters of God, insolent, haughty, boastful, inventors of evil things, disobedient to parents, without understanding, covenant-breakers, without natural affection, unmerciful."* Here is the final vacuity and disintegration. Chaos has found itself, and anything may happen. The atoms whirl, the struggle for existence rages. Even reason itself becomes irrational. Ideas of duty and of fellowship become wholly unstable. The world is full of personal caprice and social unrighteousness—this is not a picture merely of Rome under the Caesars! The true nature of our unbroken existence is here unrolled before us. Our ungodliness and unrighteousness stand under the wrath of God. His judgement now becomes judgement and nothing more; and we experience the impossibility of men as the real and final impossibility of God.

v. 32. It ought not to be difficult for us to perceive this sequence, but—*"Knowing the ordinance of God, that they which practise such things are worthy of death, not only do the same, but also consent with them that practise them."* This is the wisdom of the Night issuing in folly (i. 22): folly, because it holds firmly to a two-dimensional plane, a plane persistently contradicted by actual occurrence. The wisdom of the Night knows whither the unbroken road is leading. It understands quite clearly the meaning of its direction and of its goal. It knows the Cause; it see the Operation; but it dare not give the command to halt. The road of those who forget their Creator is accompanied always by a strange complaint against the frailty of human existence, and by indictments against human sinfulness. But in spite of all this, with their eyes fixed upon the earth, they affirm the edifice which is erected on it, concentrate their desire upon it, approve it, hope for its continued existence, and, regardless of every protest, constitute themselves its guardians. But why is it so difficult to remember what has been forgotten, though it is quite clear that the operation of this forgetfulness and the end of our wandering in the Night is—Death?

* * *

FAITH IS CREATION

IV. 13–17a

v. 13. For not through the law was the promise to Abraham or to his seed, that he should be heir of the world, but through the righteousness of faith.

"The promise that he should be heir of the world." The command that men should replenish and subdue the earth is here once more laid down. Permission is given to men to rule over all that God has made very good. Putting this in a reverse form: Abraham received the promise by anticipation. The blessedness of every creature is seen in a perspective which stretches beyond Isaac, Abraham's unexpected son, and beyond Jacob (Israel) to the Messiah, who, because He is the true Man from Heaven, is true humanity upon earth. This is the theme and meaning of the life of Abraham. Because he received the promise, he is the classic figure of the law (Gen. xviii. 17–19). He received the clear impression of revelation, and there-

fore Israel, as his seed, does him honour and claims spiritual kinship with him. Israel's peculiarity consists in readiness and longing to participate in the promise which he received; Israel's history is the story of the varieties of behaviour which this longing has occasioned; Israel's hope is the ceaseless desire to escape from the vicissitudes of history and to receive the promise.

Two questions now become urgent. In the first place, does the promise that, under the blessing of God, Israel should be the heir of the world, also constitute her the mediator of the blessing to the world? And secondly, has not Israel actually received the promise, and will she not always continue to receive it? No doubt a great possibility belongs to Israel. The real question, however, concerns the manner in which she participates in it. Does she participate—*"through the law"* or—*"through the righteousness of faith?"* The promise was made to Israel in the law by means of a series of impressions of revelation vouchsafed to Abraham and to others like him. It was, that is to say, made to a particular historical people. The problem is whether their peculiar status and history does or does not confer the promise positively and powerfully. Do the desire and readiness to reproduce Abraham's behaviour, which are the characteristic feature of Israel's history, constitute in themselves the ground of her peculiarity? Do the tradition and behaviour of Israel make her history the history of salvation? Does her fixity of hope create and appoint her children the true children of Abraham? Does Israel rightly understand the law, when she supposes that her status is conferred by her law, and by her history, and by her fixity of hope? Supposing, however, that we deny this altogether, and prefer to find the meaning of the law in its competence to testify and bear witness, rather than in any power conferred by it; do we thereby make the law of none effect (iii. 31)? Surely not; for does not the status conferred by the law point beyond itself to a creative power of a totally different kind? Does not the concrete likeness to Abraham, visible in his children, reflect a light which comes from elsewhere and which in no way belongs to Abraham? Is not the history of Israel the history of salvation, because it forms the boundary at which an unhistorical happening occurs, and because it is the audible answer to the inaudible voice of the divine call? Is not the hope of Israel the product of this peculiar situation? Nevertheless, when it is seen that the real meaning of the law is that, through the righteousness of God which is the righteousness of faith *apart from the law,* the children of Abraham are brought into being and established, the honour of the law is most surely vindicated.

v. 14. For if they which are of the law be heirs, faith is made void, and the promise is made of none effect.

In the book of Genesis it is written that Abraham received the promise *through faith.* This means that, through the creative efficacy of faith, he became the first expectant heir of the Messianic Kingdom (Gen. xv. 6). Faith, it is true, has also its 'legal' aspect, and may then be described as a positive status. But if faith be thought of from this legal and visible point of view, if it be regarded as a condition capable of human attainment, it is manifestly deprived of its dynamic power and remains insecure. If Abraham and his children are what they are *through the law,* faith is evacuated. But faith establishes certainty when it is the advance into what is invisible and eternal, and when it is itself invisible. Every visible status, every temporal road, every pragmatic approach to faith, is, in the end, the negation of faith. Faith is faith, only when it is an 'advance', possible and comprehensible because it comes from God alone, and from God Himself. Faith is creative, only in so far as it is light from light uncreated; living, only when it is life from death; positive, only if by it men are grounded upon the groundlessness of God. Only when it is thus understood is faith *reckoned for righteousness,* and can men through faith become recipients of the divine promise. Apart from this divine authentication of the visible and human impressions of revelation in the law, even the most deep-seated, most sincere, most fiery faith is—unbelief. When faith ceases to be faith, the promise, which can be received only by faith, is suspended also. For the promise which Abraham receives can be neither seen nor described; it is beyond all possibility and beyond all concrete reality. The world which has been blessed and made *good* by God is beyond our comprehending, nor is it possible to transform the dominion of men over this God-created world into an object of human historical endeavour. The Messiah who brings this sovereignty is, in any case, not man, as we understand humanity. The grace of redemption, like the grace of creation, is no concrete thing in the midst of other concrete things. Grace is the invisible relationship in which all things stand; and the knowledge of it remains always a dialectical knowledge. The promise has no point of contact with Abraham's 'Biblical outlook', or with Israel's disposition of hope, or, in fact, with any positive human status. The promise agrees with faith, since both involve the extremity of negation. If the promise be not received through faith, it is not received at all; it remains no more than an eschatological myth, which, like other myths, is suspended in mid-air. If it be not comprehended by faith, it can be comprehended by no substitute for faith: it cannot be experienced or seen in an 'ecstasy'; it can neither be heard nor seen nor felt. If we be heirs through the law, we are veritably dispossessed and excluded from all expectation of the promised heritage. We are not Abraham or his children.

v. 15. For the law apart from faith *worketh* for men not the promise but *the wrath* of God; *but where there is no law, neither is there transgression.*

"The law worketh wrath." By this we mean that the law, in itself and apart from faith, forms an actual obstacle to the inheritance of the Kingdom of God. This does not mean, of course, that the law is valueless apart from faith. Indeed, in assessing the value of the law, no regard need be paid to its

function of testifying and bearing witness to what lies beyond it. Regarded as a concrete experience from which there emerges a particular disposition and behaviour, it certainly has significance in itself, and possesses a brilliance of its own. But we must be careful to harbour no illusions here, lest we be tempted to define faith in terms of experience. Any attempt to stretch the relation between concrete and temporal things to cover their eternal Origin ends in destructive and incurable scepticism. The claim that the law *worketh* the promise breaks down on the plain truth that what is concrete and visible is incompatible with the promise. The only conspicuous element in the promise is that it is not coterminous with the actual and moral impressions in the world of God's revelation. Since the law shares in the corruptibility of the world, it *worketh* not the promise. And indeed, if it be regarded as possessing reality, rather than as testifying to it, it *worketh—wrath*. Hence, when the law claims to possess in itself ultimate reality and to be like God, it becomes *ungodliness* and *unrighteousness* (i. 18), and attracts to itself the wrath of God. This inevitability of judgement affects all religions in so far as their reality is merely the reality of temporal and concrete things. It affects religion, even when it is upright and sincere and genuine, even the religion of Abraham and of the Prophets, even the religion of the Epistle to the Romans—and it affects, of course, the religion of any one who undertakes to expound the Epistle. In this context the word 'law' embraces all who set out to experience the infinite, all who venture upon its contemplation or description or representation. This is always transgression. Whenever men suppose themselves conscious of the emotion of nearness to God, whenever they speak and write of divine things, whenever sermon-making and temple-building are thought of as an ultimate human occupation, whenever men are aware of divine appointment and of being entrusted with a divine mission, sin veritably abounds (v. 20)—unless the miracle of forgiveness accompanies such activity; unless, that is to say, the fear of the Lord maintains the distance by which God is separated from men (i. 22, 23). No human demeanour is more open to criticism, more doubtful, or more dangerous, than religious demeanour. No undertaking subjects men to so severe a judgement as the undertaking of religion. The whole rich abundance of the worship of God, from the grossest superstition to the most delicate spirituality, from naked rationalism to the most subtle mysticism of the metaphysician, is under suspicion both from above and from below. God treats it as arrogance, and men as illusion. But we must beware of running to the opposite misunderstanding. If religion is nebulous and lacking in security, so also is everything which is exalted to oppose religion. Anti-religious negation has no advantage over the affirmations of religion. To destroy temples is not better than to build them. The silence of devotion is not superior to the words of the preacher. Amaziah AND Amos, Martensen AND Kierkegaard, all the protestations against religion from Nietzsche down to the most degraded and loud-voiced anticlericals, the whole anti-theological romanticism of aestheticism, socialism, and the Youth Movement in its multifarious ramifications, are without exception enveloped in haze, and incompetent to provide security. And the haze solidifies into the cloud of the wrath of God. So long as religious as well as anti-religious activities fail to draw attention to that which lies beyond them, and so long as they attempt their own justification, either as faith, hope, and charity, or as the enthusiastic and dionysiac gestures of the Anti-Christ, they are assuredly mere illusion. Everything which seeks to justify itself, whether by affirmation or by negation, is under the sentence of judgement. Those who believe in immanent reality should ponder well the words—*the law worketh wrath.*

"But where there is no law, neither is there transgression." There is, however, a justification of the Prophet and of the Pharisee, of the practice of religion in its genuine and penetrating as well as in its less real and more superficial forms. It is also possible to justify anti-religious behaviour. But this

justification is by faith only. By faith—in so far as law, the whole concrete visibility of human behaviour, does not condition and control it. By faith—in so far as faith, as a positive or negative experience in this world, is rid of all arrogance and aware of its own emptiness before the pure 'No' of God. By faith—in so far as it stands on the critical line which divides the RELIGIOSUS Luther from the RELIGIOSUS Erasmus, and which separates the ANTI-RELIGIOSUS Overbeck from the ANTI-RELIGIOSUS Nietzsche; that is to say, in so far as faith is the relating of the whole content of human life to its eternal Origin and the awareness of the life which proceeds from death. If this invisible aspect of faith be paramount, *transgression,* affecting, as it does, its visible aspect, cannot be paramount. When therefore religion, or anti-religion, is concerned to point beyond itself, it loses its ambiguity, and absolute scepticism is deprived of all right. And so there appears, or at least can appear, the justification of sacrifice and prayer and preaching, of prophecy and mysticism and pharisaism, of theology and piety and churchmanship, of Catholicism and Protestantism, of books like the Epistle to the Romans where the paradox is clearly stated, and even of other books where the paradox is, to a greater or lesser extent, glossed over. But the justification appears only under the compulsion of the divine 'Nevertheless', in the recognition of the ever-recurring necessity of the forgiveness of sins, in a fearful and trembling consciousness that there is no human or pragmatic road which may be prolonged so far as to justify itself before God and man. Justification can be found only in the light of God's sincerity and of His irony. The use of the words 'in so far as' allows the possibility of clothing the divine in the garment of the human, and of the eternal in a temporal parable. But this can be permitted only when the possibility is recognized as the impossible possibility. We must not conclude from this that we have achieved a secure standing place. We have done no more than make room for the 'Moment' which has no before and no after, and for the decision which lies only in God's hands. We cannot claim that we have attained this possibility. We can only, in fear and trembling, assert the possibility of its occurrence. Apart from this fearful faith, the law remains a vast obstacle which renders it impossible for us to await the advent of the Kingdom of God.

vv. 16, 17a. For this cause we say that *it is of faith* that the heirs are what they are, *that it may be according to grace; to the end that the promise may be sure to all the seed; not to that only which is of the law, but to that also which is of the faith of Abraham, who is the father of us all (as it is written, A father of many nations have I made thee).*

"For this cause it is of faith." We say this after full consideration, since no other possibility is open to us. The Law, the History, and the Religion of Israel are the context in which men can await the heavenly inheritance; but they are not the effective power through which they enter it. In so far as the law has power, it is an earth-born and worldly and opposite power which actually makes the inheritance of Abraham impossible. The truly creative act by which men become the children of Abraham, by which stones are transformed into sons, does not lie in the possible possibility of the law, but in the impossible possibility of faith.

"That it may be according to grace; to the end that the promise may be to all the seed." The consideration of that which makes Abraham to be Abraham (iv. 1) forces us beyond the limit of what is concrete and visible, and directs us to a preceding relationship which, because it lies beyond his soul-and-sense experience, establishes the moral and actual course of his life. Abraham is Abraham according to grace. Law and History and Religion have significance and meaning—*according to grace*. Now, *grace* presupposes the line of death by which all concrete human conspicuousness is bounded absolutely. This line is, however, in God's sight the line of life, since it assumes the final negation which alone contains the affirmation of

God. It presupposes the last judgment apart from which there is no justification. In exposing this relationship, the history and experience of 'Abraham' and of 'Israel' have served their purpose, and the law is established (iii. 31). In speaking of Abraham, however, we necessarily speak of Christ; in speaking of Abraham's faith, we inevitably speak of that general KRISIS which we encounter in Him; in speaking of Abraham's sons, we speak with assurance of all those who, having first encountered the KRISIS of Christ, participate also in His Resurrection. Since the heirs are what they are not through the law but *of faith,* not as a consequence of moral and historical status but *according to grace,* it follows as a matter of course that participation in their company cannot be confined to those who have been made the children of Abraham according to the law, cannot be limited to the historical Israel, or to those who accept a particular and definite historical tradition and doctrine, or to those who are members of some particular 'movement'. Such limitation in the number of the heirs makes the inheritance itself more than insecure (iv. 14, 15). As the recipient of the promise, Abraham stands outside every historical and particular company of men; similarly his true seed, being the race of believers, likewise stand outside. Of course those who are, through the doctrine and tradition of the law, his children, can share with him the expectation of the Kingdom of the Messiah and of the blessing of God; the decisive and primal relation with God can be encountered within this particular company of men: but God is not the God of the Jews only (iii. 29). By the faithfulness of God, men who move in a different moral and historical environment can be directed to revelation. Sectarianism, whether crude or refined, is dissolved, if the children of Abraham are brought into being by faith only. The word delivered to Abraham *according to grace,* which he heard by faith, admits of no esoteric confinement; it is valid for all who have the form of a man. It cuts down vertically, from above, through every particular human status. Through the emergence of that status which men have in God, every human status is established by dissolution.

Are we, in saying that in Christ Abraham is the father of us all, and that this is the meaning by which the law is established, imposing an interpretation upon the Scriptures rather than expounding them? Assuredly not, for what do the Scriptures say? *"A father of many nations have I made thee"* (Gen. xvii. 5). Abraham is, of course, the father of the single nation, Israel; but we have seen that, because in Christ he is the father of this one nation, he is also, at the same time and in consequence, the father of many nations. The historical framework is broken through when the secret of history is laid bare. We have no occasion to deny the plain meaning of history, since it is history which bears witness to the many of the one forgiveness of sins: *And when they heard these things, they held their peace, and glorified God, saying, Then to the Gentiles also God hath granted repentance unto life* (Acts xi. 18).

* * *

THE REALITY OF RELIGION
VII. 14–25.

Apprehension of the meaning of religion depends upon the clarity with which the dominion of sin over the men of this world is disclosed to our view. When we recognize the peculiar sinfulness of the religious man and see sin *abounding* in him, we are able to understand the meaning of *grace more exceedingly abounding* (v. 20), and the necessity that the divine mercy should act in spite of sin. But, before turning our attention once more to the goal of our investigation, we must make sure whether religion, although incapable of providing a theoretical answer to the problem of sin, may not be perfectly competent to provide a practical answer. We may have established religion to be in theory no more than the last human possibility; but it may turn out to be in actual practice the sure and solid answer to guilt and destiny. The Psychology of Religion, concerned as it is with the reality of religion, with the religious man in the peculiarity of what he is and has, must now be allowed to say what it has to say. Will the religious man agree that sin celebrates its triumph in religion? Has he not something to say to all this? Will he admit that he is branded as a slave and handed over to death (vii. 13)—through the good, by means of the noblest, most necessary, most hopeful of all human possibilities? Yes, he does say this; he does agree with the theorist. The romantic psychologist may make many attempts to hush this up: he may represent religion as that human capacity by which 'all human occurrences are thought of as divine actions'; he may define it as 'the solemn music which accompanies all human experience' (Schleiermacher). Against such representations, however, religion is always on its guard. Religion, when it attacks vigorously, when it is fraught with disturbance, when it is non-aesthetic, non-rhetorical, non-pious, when it is the religion of the 39th Psalm, of Job and of Luther and of Kierkegaard, when it is the religion of Paul, bitterly protests against every attempt to make of its grim earnestness some trivial and harmless thing. Religion is aware that it is in no wise the crown and fulfilment of true humanity; it knows itself rather to be a questionable, disturbing, dangerous thing. It closes the circle of humanity completely; so completely that it completely opens it—covertly! Religion confronts every human competence, every concrete happening in this world, as a thing incomprehensible, which cannot be tolerated or accepted. Religion, so far from being the place where the healthy harmony of human life is lauded, is instead the place where it appears diseased, discordant, and disrupted. Religion is not the sure ground upon which human culture safely rests; it is the place where civilization and its partner, barbarism, are rendered fundamentally questionable. Nor does the frank judgement of honest men of the world disagree with the opinion of religion about itself.

The curtain is raised; the music must cease.
The temple is gone: and far in the distance
Appeareth the terrible form of the—Sphinx.

Fr. Schlegel on Schleiermacher's speeches.

Religion must beware lest it tone down in any degree the unconverted man's judgement. Conflict and distress, sin and death, the devil and hell, make up the reality of religion. So far from releasing men from guilt and destiny, it brings men under their sway. Religion possesses no solution of the problem of life; rather it makes of the problem a wholly insoluble enigma. Religion neither discovers the problem nor solves it: what it does is to disclose the truth that it cannot be solved. Religion is neither a thing to be enjoyed nor a thing to be celebrated: it must be borne as a yoke which cannot be removed. Religion is not a thing to be desired or extolled: it is a misfortune which takes fatal hold upon some men, and is by them passed on to others; it is the misfortune which assailed John the Baptist in the desert, and drove him out to preach repentance and judgement; which caused the writing of that long-drawn-out, harassed groan, which is the Second Epistle to the Corinthians; which laid upon Calvin's face that look which he bore at the end of his life. Religion is the misfortune which every human being has to endure, though it is, in the majority of cases, a hidden suffering.

The first piece of evidence is: *vv. 14–17. For I know*[1] *that the law is spiritual: but I am carnal, sold under sin. For that*

---

1 Adopting the reading *oida men,* because, in agreement with Hofmann and Zahn, I regard an appeal to a consensus of opinion among the Christian readers (*oidamen*) as unsuitable in the context. Nevertheless, the reading *oidamen* cannot be ruled out, for the passage is no biographical intermezzo! The contrasted *egô de,* which opponents of the reading *oida men* (for example, Kühl) think should in that case have been *eimi de,* is, however, intelligible, if it be borne in mind that the *egô* of the person dedicated to God is contrasted throughout with his knowledge and desire and action and achievement as *the* wholly ambiguous factor. Consequently, *sarkikos eimi* must not be unduly emphasized (against Beck).

which I do I know not: for not what I would, that do I practise; but what I hate, that I do. But if what I would not, that I do, I consent unto the law that it is good. So now it is no more I that do it, but sin which dwelleth in me.

"I know that the law is spiritual." To know this is the first requirement of a religious man. Whence does he come? And whither does he go? He comes from the realm of the Spirit; he passes relentlessly to death. When, therefore, he stands under the compelling impression of the Spirit, an intolerable tension is introduced into his life. He is engaged inevitably and hopefully in a conflict from which there is no escape, because it is the battle for his very existence. A demand is made upon him which he is bound to accept, because the vast inadequacy of his life in this world means that the demand is not only right but necessary. A question is asked him, to which he must find an answer. A call is given him, which he is bound to obey. The existence of God rises up in the midst of his life, like an immense boundary-wall shutting out some poor neighbour's view; or like a fortress occupied by the enemy; or like a boxer's closed fist. Yet he must stand up to it, come to terms with it, and live with it. Paul knows its meaning, when he calls himself elsewhere *a prisoner in bonds* (Eph. iii. 1, iv. 1; 2 Tim. i. 8; Philem. 9). *O Lord, thou hast persuaded me, and I was persuaded: thou art stronger than I, and hast prevailed* (Jer. xx. 7).

"But I am carnal, sold under sin." The tension becomes acute. If God be God, who then am I? If my human relation to Him be bondage and captivity, who then am I? The answer of experience to such questioning is quickly made. I see that the law which proceeds from the Spirit, compelling, necessary, and inevitable though it be, is excluded from my existence as a man. What form of human existence is competent to receive THIS impress, to arrange itself according to THIS misery and hope, and to accept THIS demand? Surely no human existence of which I have experience. What answer can I give? How

can I obey a call which has emerged from beyond the boundary of my existence? *I am carnal:* never can flesh become spirit, for that would mean the resurrection of the flesh. *I am sold under sin:* a transaction which may not be undone, save by the forgiveness of sin. I am a man: and no emotion or enthusiasm of religion can obscure what this means. Only a new man, only a victory over my humanity, only eternal life, can release me from the enigma of my being. What, then, doth the Spirit profit me? What advantage does the law which proceeds from the Spirit afford me? Of what use is my piety to me? How does the persuasive and prevailing power of God affect me? Is it not only too evident that I have no strength to bring forth? *Depart from me; for I am a sinful man, O Lord* (Luke v. 8). There is no bond of union between me, as I am, and God.

"For that which I do I know not: for not what I would, that do I practice; but what I hate, that I do." Yes, this is clearly the case. If the law of my religious being and having, were itself Spirit; if sensitive 'apprehension of the absolute'—'feeling and taste for eternity' (Schleiermacher)—could seriously be regarded as lying within the realm of human competence; if God and such a man as I am could be treated as co-partners; I should be in a proper position to contemplate and comprehend my words and acts and deeds from the point of view of eternity, or, at least, to think of them as the first stages of a movement in conformity with the movement of the Spirit of God. Then I should be led on to describe and comprehend myself quite properly as the answer to the problem of life, as obedient to the demand of God, and therefore as the new divinely inspired reality in the midst of other realities. I may, of course, be sufficiently humble and simple-minded only to make this claim occasionally. But facts are hard, and it is difficult for me to retain even this confidence for long. The more luminously clear it becomes that the demand requires my actual obedience to the will of God, and that His commandments are not grievous,

the more luminously clear it becomes to me that, even in the simplest occurrences of my life, His will has not been done, is not done, and never will be done. For not even at the most exalted moments of my life do I fulfil His commands. Does any single thought of mine express the all-compelling power of the Spirit? Does one single word of mine formulate the Word after which I am striving and which I long to utter in my great misery and hope? Does not each sentence I frame require another to dissolve its meaning? And are my actions any better? Does my lack of fidelity in little things make amends for my great infidelity, or vice versa? Take the case of any reputable and serious-minded philosopher, poet, statesman, or artist. Does he ever suppose his actual achievement to be identical with what he wished to achieve? When my piece of work is done, do I not take leave of it sorrowfully? Woe is me, if I have unduly celebrated what I have accomplished. If, then, my thoughts and words and actions are of such sort as this, can I seek refuge in the restless sea of my emotions? Can I find in the witches' cauldron of my unconscious achievements an adequate substitute for the failure of my conscious attainments? None but those who are past reclaiming really believe in the eternal significance of their emotions. No! there is no achievement of mine which I can recognize as legitimate. All my products are foreign bodies testifying to my inadequacy. I have no affection for them, no comprehension of them. If I could, I would deny them. They appear before me as hideous, evil-looking changelings. Fragmentary is our knowledge, and partial our understanding (1 Cor. xiii. 9). I am unable to apprehend what I have done. What I would, I do not; what I hate, that I do. Who then am I? for I stand betwixt and between, dragged hither by my desires and by my hates, and thither by my inability to do what I desire and by my ability to practise what I hate.

"If what I would not, that I do, I consent unto the law that it is good." We have just said: *what I hate, that I do.* It would

seem, therefore, that a point of contact has been established between myself and the incomprehensible, unapproachable, incommunicable, world of the Spirit. Surely, my hatred of my life as it is, my protesting against it, my dislike of my own behaviour, the disturbance which accompanies my passage through time, are points of contact. Is not such negation the means by which I am brought into harmony with myself? Am I not a doer of the law, at least in so far as I am aware of my deep-seated sinfulness and am disgusted at it? Can I not console myself with my own disconsolateness? 'If thou dost discover in thyself the conflict between the Spirit and the flesh, if thou doest often what thou willest not, thou dost declare thereby thy heart to be faithful. So long as a man maintains this conflict, he is not under the dominion of sin; so long as he struggles against sin and disapproves of it, sin is not reckoned unto him' (Joh. Arnd). These are perilous opinions. Who does not know this sunset glow, this quiet and secluded nook of pious dialectic? Who does not recognize here that middle way of compromise and resignation, where conscience is soothed by contemplating a conflict accepted and embraced?

"So now it is no more I that do it, but sin which dwelleth in me." What, then, is the meaning of my protesting hatred of myself and my actions? It has clearly no further meaning than that an abyss is disclosed between myself and—myself. Can this really be regarded as a satisfactory starting-point for answering the question: 'If God be God, who then am I?' The EGO which *practises* what I—the other EGO—contemplate with evident horror, cannot be an EGO capable of surviving the question. May not, however, the other EGO, that horrified, dissatisfied, ever-protesting EGO, survive the question? But what is this other EGO? Can this impotent outsider, this poor innocent, who merely shakes his head and disclaims what I am actually doing and practising, saying it is contrary to his will,—can such an EGO, with all his powers usurped, really survive

the question? Can my justification rest upon the claim that it is not I who am doing what I am doing, that another rules in my house, that I am no longer master of it, and that this other thinks, speaks, acts, feels, whilst I merely protest? This, surely, is no justification at all; my agreement with the law is simply my own condemnation of myself—the recognition that *sin dwelleth in me.* Faced by so vast a condemnation, I have no ground upon which I can stand; for who is able to entice me to the opinion that my EGO which acts as it wills is to be distinguished from my other EGO, in spite of its expressed disapproval? Is my onslaught upon myself more than a Münchhausen adventure,[2] which never gets beyond the four walls of that house of sin, which is my EGO? Then it is that religion is never competent to speak of that EGO whose existence lies beyond the boundary of the realm of sin. Religion speaks only of dissension: I practise perpetually what I do not will, and I will what I do not practise. Religion merely exposes the disunion of human knowledge and human life; for it speaks of one reality only—the reality of sin.

The second piece of evidence: *vv. 18–20. For I know that in me, that is, in my flesh, dwelleth no good thing: for to will is present with me, but to perform that which is good I find not. For the good that I would I do not: but the evil which I would not, that I practise. But if what I would not, that I do, it is no more I that do it, but sin which dwelleth in me.*

"I know that in me, that is, in my flesh, dwelleth no good thing." To know that *in me dwelleth no good thing* is the second requirement of the religious man. This knowledge follows at once from the first requirement. Here again we run up against the 'peculiarity' of all to whom the revelation of God is entrusted (iii. 1-20), namely, that they, as such, can and ought to know

---

2 *The Original Travels and Surprising Adventures of Baron Münchhausen* appeared first in England under the title of *Gulliver Revived; or, the Vice of Lying Exposed* (London: Printed for C. & G. Kearsley, 46 Fleet Street, 1786). [Tr.]

this. Into this sinister secret men are initiated also through the revelation which is in Christ Jesus, precisely because it is the revelation of Revelation. 'Paul, good man that he was, longed to be without sin, but to it he was chained. I too, in common with many others, long to stand outside it, but this cannot be. We belch forth the vapours of sin; we fall into it, rise up again, buffet and torment ourselves night and day; but, since we are confined in this flesh, since we have to bear about with us everywhere this stinking sack, we cannot rid ourselves completely of it, or even knock it senseless. We make vigorous attempts to do so, but the old Adam retains his power until he is deposited in the grave. The Kingdom of God is a foreign country, so foreign that even the saints must pray: "Almighty God, I acknowledge my sin unto thee. Reckon not unto me my guiltiness, O Lord." There is no sinless Christian. If thou chancest upon such a man, he is no Christian, but an anti-Christ. Sin stands in the midst of the Kingdom of Christ, and wherever the Kingdom is, there is sin; for Christ has set sin in the House of David' (Luther). *For I know* (vii. 14) is, then, not peculiar to some few men. Every religious man has this knowledge concerning himself. *I am flesh* (iii. 20), this is what he knows. We must, of course, bear in mind the meaning of the word *flesh:* unqualified, and finally unqualifiable, worldliness; a worldliness perceived by men, and especially by religious men; relativity, nothingness, non-sense. That is what I am! The man of property or of fashion may not be required to have this opinion of himself. How, indeed, could he, or ought he, to speak thus of himself? for his knowledge of himself may be a ray from the pity of God, which is more powerful than His wrath. No! it is rather the man dedicated to God who must speak of himself thus; the man of genuine and serious religious experience, the prophet, apostle, reformer; the man to whom the oneness of God's holiness and mercy has become the personal problem of his own existence. *Why callest thou me good? none is good save one, even God*

(Mark x. 18). So Jesus spake; and because He spake thus, we cannot dismiss the recognition that God and man, that is, the man that I am, do not cohere together, as though it proceeded from a purely pessimistic view of life. Indeed, we have already attained this perception from our knowledge of the Spirit (vii. 14). It is clear, then, that what we have established from the consideration of human experience corresponds with the real and logical situation, and that THIS knowledge about men is the proper rider to the knowledge of God.

"For to will is present with me, but to perform that which is good I find not. For the good that I would I do not: but the evil which I would not, that I practise." My will merely reminds me of the good which is not in me, and agrees with my knowledge that the law is divine (vii. 14); for I cannot know what is divine without willing it. *To will is present with me.* But what is meant by *to will?* It means, presumably, to strive after, desire, demand, question, seek, pray, knock; in other words, it constitutes the theme and purpose of all preaching and of all pastoral work. Appealing to the cloud of witnesses in all ages, preachers and pastors breathlessly repeat this theme with every conceivable variation and with all manner of emphasis. How desperately simple the theme is! and, because of its simplicity, it is the final word of religion. If it does not entice men, what can? And they are assuredly attracted by it. The exhortation to 'seek God' does not fall on deaf ears; for it is the final exhortation which the human ear is able to receive. It is certain that the number of those who genuinely *will* and who genuinely *seek after God* is far greater than the casual observer would suppose. Who can be deprived of this earnest *will?* Do I not also perhaps *seek after God? To will is present with me.* Maybe it is so! but the comfortable nook into which I am tempted to creep, when I have said this, is no more comfortable than that other place over which is inscribed the words: *What I would not, that I do* (vii. 16). As there, so here, everything depends upon action, upon the per-

formance of *that which is good.* I require that the good should exist in me. But it is quite certain that the most sincere, most upright, most deep-seated vigour of *will* remains uncrowned by the performance of *that which is good.* Consider once again that vast cemetery where lies the history of the Church and of Christian piety. Surely there was there no lack of upright *will!* What is it, then, which distinguishes the *doing* of Jeremiah from the *doing* of the false prophets, with whom he is so sharply contrasted? What distinguishes the 'success' of Primitive Christianity which reached its zenith with Constantine —untheologically-minded historians please understand!—from the contemporary 'success' of the worship of Mithras and of Cybele? What distinguishes the 'success' of the Reformers of Wittenberg, Zürich, and Geneva, from the 'success' of the Roman Pontiffs and of the architects of the loftiest towers of Babel? What distinguishes the 'achievement' in delineating the inner piety which shines out of the eyes of the Sistine Madonna from the 'achievement' in delineating the bigotry which peers out of the eyes of the Madonnas of El Greco? May we not conclude that we should be right in setting every human achievement upon one single ladder, although perhaps upon different rungs of that ladder? Are they not, at best, parables of an achievement which lies on a wholly different plane? Yes, no doubt; but nevertheless, must we not also say that the Lord permits to some human achievements a maturity which is lacking in others, even though the distinction which we note and with which we are satisfied cannot be identified with a human will-to-achieve? Are we not bound to own that the path which leads from our will-to-achieve to the 'success' bestowed by the Lord lies wholly beyond our comprehension? We know nothing beyond the frontier which bounds our work and renders it fragmentary and incomplete: *the good that I would I do not: but the evil I would not, that I practise.* The religious man must answer questions concerning human 'success', by saying that, so far as he succeeds, his success lies beyond the competence of his will. I cannot identify my will to do good with the good itself. The characteristic mark of the good is that it persistently demands realization, for action is the end of knowledge and of will. But this end is foreign to me. I do not practise what is good; I perform all manner of evil that I would not. And so the question arises once again: Who then am I? I am he that wills and he that does not perform: I am intolerably both at once. When my will is most steadfast, it does but remind me that the good is—not in me.

"But if what I would not, that I do, it is no more I that do it, but sin which dwelleth in me." Seen from the standpoint of my will, there is, then, no performance of *that which is good* (vii. 18b, 19). We return therefore to the decisive question: What is performed? Answer: *I do what I would not.* I am therefore no more justified by the nobility of my desire to do good than I am by my desire not to do evil (vii. 16, 17). For the second time the judgment pronounced by myself upon myself is wholly justified: *it is no more I that do it.* Excluded from responsibility for what is happening in my house, I am thrust up against the wall merely as an observer. An appeal to my goodwill only proves that *sin dwelleth in me.* It is sin that acts, sin that performs, and to sin that the 'success' belongs. And yet, this does not mean that I am, in fact, released from all responsibility: it means, rather, that I stand self-condemned. I have no reason to suppose that the EGO which performs and the EGO which disapproves can escape identification. Reality, even the reality of religion, knows but one man, and I, and not some other, am that man. It is one man that wills and does not perform; one man that does not will, and yet performs: within the four walls of the house of sin dwells but one man. Religious experience, then, simply bears witness to the fact that sin is all-embracing.

Conclusion from the evidence: *vv. 21–3. I find then the* reality of *the law* exposed in that, *to me who would do good, evil is present. For I delight in the law of God after the inward man: but I see a different law in my members, warring against the law of my mind, and bringing me into captivity under the law of sin which is in my members.*

Religion spells disruption, discord, and the absence of peace. A man at one with himself is a man still unacquainted with the great problem of his union with God. Our whole behaviour proves us to be in no way at one with ourselves; and for this reason, our relation to God is a disturbed relation. Happy the man who is able to deny this evident truth! May he long remain innocent of his own questionableness! The reality of religion, however, lies precisely in the utter questionableness of my EGO, confronted, as it is, by my inability to do what I would and by my ability to do what I would not. The subject of these contrasted predicates—my EGO—becomes an *x,* capable neither of life nor of death. By the law, through which I know God, I am enabled *to will to do good:* by the same law, through which I am known by God, my success in *doing evil* is clearly exposed. Thus my noblest capacity becomes my deepest perplexity; my noblest opportunity, my uttermost distress; my noblest gift, my darkest menace. It is almost incredible that, on the day when Schleiermacher finished writing his 'Lectures about Religion', his joy in creation, apparently suddenly, was crossed by the fear of death. 'What a shame it would be', he said, 'were I to die to-night!' One would have supposed that, whilst writing so many beautiful and moving words 'about religion' (!) he would have been faced continually by the fact of death. Is it possible to recommend religion to men who long sincerely and simply for peace? Can religion be presented, not merely as a tolerable thing, but as a thing of such absorbing interest that it may be welcomed as an enrichment of life, a valuable addition to civilization, or even as a substitute for it? When men are already sufficiently burdened by the inner uncertainty which attaches both to civilization and to barbarism, is it credible that religion should be brought triumphantly into connexion with science, art, ethics, socialism, the State, Youth Movements and Race, as though we had not had abundant experience of the waste land of 'Religion and . . .'? Is it possible to justify these strange prophets, when we see hosts of men and women flocking to enlist willingly under their banners, eager to lay hold of religion, in order that their complacent capacities may be sanctioned, developed, and consecrated; when we behold them zealous to add to their passions one further emotion, the emotion of eternity, and to their other capacities yet one more good thing, the capacity for piety? We may be surprised that all this should go on before our eyes; but surprise cannot alter the fact that all of them, teachers and taught alike, are busily engaged in sawing off the branch upon which they are sitting, in setting fire to the house in which they dwell, and in scuttling the ship in which they are sailing into the 'maelstrom'. Those who are genuinely concerned to preserve their own peace of mind, to retain humanism on an even keel, and to assist the steady progress of culture—or of barbarism!—will, with Lessing, Lichtenberg, and Kant, so long as they are able, do their best to prevent the intrusion of religion into this world. They will lift up their voices to warn those careless ones, who, for aesthetic or historical or political or romantic reasons, dig through the dam and open up a channel through which the flood of religion may burst into the cottages and palaces of men, after first overwhelming those thoughtless pioneers! Such warning guardians of humanity will, at any rate, have displayed more sense for reality than the futile amateurs in piety—How cruel, in fact, these dilettantes are!—who, without knowing what they are doing, with romantic enthusiasm conjure up the spirits of religion but are powerless to exorcize them. But such warning wisdom is unavailing, since the capacity for religion is deep-seated and cannot be disregarded. Even our western civilization is powerless to protect men from it. The watchman at the gate of humanity has only to take care lest, at the eleventh hour, he too may be compelled to conclude a short armistice with the adversary of whom he is so terrified. Religion, though it come disguised as the most intimate friend of men, be they Greeks or barbarians, is nevertheless the adversary. Religion is the KRISIS of culture and of barbarism. Apart from God, it is the most dangerous enemy a man has on this side of the grave. For religion is the human possibility of remembering that we must die: it is the place where, in the world of time and of things and of men, the intolerable question is clearly formulated—Who, then, art thou? 'The Law of God brings men under condemnation; for, in so far as they are under law, they are slaves of sin, and consequently guilty of death' (Calvin).

"For I delight in the law of God after the inward man: but I see a different law in my members, warring against the law of my mind, and bringing me into captivity under the law of sin which is in my members." In religion, dualism makes its appearance. The man who conceals this with the fine-sounding phrases of monism is the 'supreme betrayer of religion' (Overbeck), and does the greatest possible disservice to those who are satisfied with them. But the secret he endeavours to conceal cannot be hidden. The bomb, which he has so carefully decked out with flowers, will sooner or later explode. Religion breaks men into two halves. One half is the *spirit* of the inward man, which delights in the law of God.—Am I to identify myself with this *spirit?* Am I merely *inward?* But no one dares to make this claim. The other half is the *natural* world of my members; a world swayed by a wholly different law, by a quite different vitality and possibility. This latter wards against the *law of my mind,* and denies what it affirms. This corporeality, this essential second factor, this emergent opposition to my soul, is manifestly the supreme law and the supreme human possibility; and here undoubtedly is the sin by which I am imprisoned. Am I to be identified with this sin-laden *nature?*—Who dares to claim this? The contrast may be defined as inwardness

and outwardness, idealism and materialism, that side and this side. But to which dost thou belong? Who art thou? Art thou 'Spirit' or 'Nature'? Thou canst not deny 'Spirit', and hold thee only to 'Nature'; for, as a religious man, thou hast knowledge of God, and thy most particular perception is that 'Nature' desires to be altogether 'Spirit'. Neither canst thou deny 'Nature', and hold thee only to 'Spirit'; for, as a religious man, thou hast knowledge of God, and thou knowest only too well that 'Spirit' desires to be altogether 'Nature'. Am I then both together?! Well, try: Art thou 'Spirit-Nature' or 'Nature-Spirit' . . . ?! Once attempt any such arrogant anticipation, and thou wilt soon perceive that the desired union cannot be manœuvred merely by ranging the two alongside one another, or by amalgamating them, or by conglomerating them. The more thou dost madly endeavour to synthesize things which are directly opposed to one another, the more surely do they break apart and become manifestly antithetic. And thou thyself art harried hither and thither, from one to the other, but never wholly attaining the one or the other. At one moment one has excluded the other—and yet not finally or mortally; for, when the banished one seems weakest, there always remains a way for it to return in the fullness of its power.

vv. 24, 25a. O wretched man that I am! who shall deliver me out of this body of death? I thank God through Jesus Christ our Lord.

And so we retrace our steps to the place from which we set out at the beginning of the chapter. We know only the religious man, the man of human possibilities, the man of this world, the man *as long as he liveth* (vii. 1). Such a one can never be what he is, and he is not what he ought to be. Indissolubly and undistinguishably one with his mortal body, he bears about with him always the reminder that he—yes, precisely he—must die. Yet, once the reality of religion is established, there arises an ultimate ambiguity concerning the future of the man of the earth. He can neither live nor die! In his piety he is suspended between heaven and earth. But what does this ambiguity profit me? In spite of all the contortions of my soul, of all the gymnastics of my dialectic, the brutal fact remains that *I am*—a man. And it is precisely my religion which compels me to recognize this so clearly. No other possibility is open to me except the possibility of being a man of the earth—*"O wretched man that I am!"* We have seen at last the reality of religion; we have recognized what men are. How vast a gulf separates the nineteenth-century conquering-hero attitude to religion from that disgust of men at themselves, which is the characteristic mark of true religion!—But Jesus Christ is the new man, standing beyond all piety, beyond all human possibility. He is the dissolution of the man of this world in his totality. He is the man who has passed from death to life. He is—what I am not—my existential I—I—the I which in God, in the freedom of God—I am! Thanks be to God: through Jesus Christ our Lord I am not the wretched man that I am.

v. 25b. So then I myself, as a man, *with the mind serve the law of God; but with the flesh the law of sin.*

Wretched man that I am! We must not deprive this *am* of its heavy significance. Paul is not describing the situation before his conversion! If conversion means the dissolution of the man of the earth, what relevance has this preposition 'before'? What Paul is here asserting was well understood by the Reformers; but it is misunderstood by those modern theologians who read him through the spectacles of their own piety. Paul describes his past, present, and future existence. He portrays a situation as real after the episode on the road to Damascus as before it. He is writing about a man, broken in two by the law, but who, according to the law, cannot be thus broken. Paul is thrust into a dualism which contradicts itself. He is shattered on God, without the possibility of forgetting Him.

Do we now understand the meaning of the Grace of God and of His Freedom?

* * *

AN EPISODE.

vv. 19–21. Thou wilt say then unto me, Why doth he still find fault? For who hath resisted his will? Nay but, O man, who art thou that repliest against God? Shall the thing formed say to him that formed it, Why didst thou make me thus? Or hath not the potter a right over the clay, from the same lump to make one part a vessel unto honour, and another unto dishonour?

"Why doth he still find fault? For who has resisted his will?" This is no new objection (iii. 8; vi. 1, 15). Human action neither assists the victory of God nor hinders it. It must follow, then, from His freedom and sole-dominion, that men are irresponsible, and, from His overcoming of sin by grace, that men are free to do both good and evil. Yes, when men undertake seriously to consider the thought of God, this deduction does follow inevitably. But, the deduction once made, we must tremble with fear, for we are close to the Burning Bush, we are nigh unto God. The Church ought not to be prevented by its responsibility for human conduct from pondering seriously over this conclusion; it ought not to be dissuaded by fear lest those who dare to reckon with it may find themselves within the domain of crime and immorality, of insanity and suicide, or by the dread lest the Church's responsibility for the moral stability of society may thereby be jeopardized. The appalling disturbances which can occur on the frontier where the Gospel is proclaimed, and which indeed have actually occurred on the loftiest summits which run along that frontier, do not constitute an argument against the Truth, but against men who are unable to bear the Truth—not, of course, merely against particular individuals, but against all men. It is by

no means irrelevant that certain particular men—as, for example, Nietzsche—should, just because of their strength or their weakness, demonstrate in their body and in their general view of life, that the Truth is intolerable. For such disturbances show that, when mankind and the world approach the ordering of God too nearly, they are thrown out of gear. The conclusion of Dostoevsky's 'Idiot', the end of men like Hölderlin and Nietzsche, the inevitable catastrophes in the history of the 'Baptists'—Muck-Lamberty![3]—make it only too clear that, in spite of its supposed richness and healthiness and righteousness, humanity has no alternative but death when confronted by the Truth. These catastrophes serve as significant parables to those who, perhaps not to their credit, are spared so great temptations, and therefore escape so great a fall. The sufferings of such men do, at any rate, make clear how grievous is the sickness which men suffer at God's hands. It is not fitting that we should refuse to think the thought of God because of the objections which may be brought against it, or because the symptoms of the sickness terrify us. We do all suffer from the sickness, and the most terrible aberrations and disasters which befall the few or the many are after all no more than symptoms. We engage with safety in active love of men only when it is the love of God; and love of God will not permit us for fear of men, or because of our anxiety on their behalf, to silence the fear which we owe to Him. And so we think we understand the danger which threatens us at the point where the objection arises: *Why doth he still find fault?* The danger lies in the possibility of our speaking of the freedom and power and grace of God in such a way that, instead of leading men to apprehend His will, we encourage them to discard all sense of responsibility. For this reason it is impossible for us com-

3 The allusion is to a scandal which took place on the frontier of religion and the Youth Movement in the immediately post-war period in Germany. The episode is now forgotten, and the allusion is therefore best left in its obscurity. [Tr.]

fortably to repose in the thought of the sacrifice demanded of us by the indirect road of the Truth. Rather, we are compelled to abandon directness and unbrokenness at all points, and precisely when we most earnestly undertake to think the thought of God. We must maintain quite firmly that the objection against God is untruth and must be rejected. Once again, therefore, we proceed to reject it (iii. 5, 6, vi. 1, 2, 15, 16).

"Nay but, O man, who art thou that repliest against God?" All that must be said about the objection is comprehended in the words—*O man.* The objector overlooks the infinite qualitative distinction between God and man. He proceeds as though God and man were two things. He speaks of men as though they were God's partners, junior partners perhaps, but nevertheless competent to conduct an argument with Him. Regarding human conduct as an operation of which the will of God is the efficient cause, he sets both within a single chain of causality in such a manner that human conduct confronts the will of God as a second thing. But this is preposterous. Human conduct is related to the will of God neither as cause nor as effect. Between human responsibility and the freedom of God there is no direct observable relation, but only the indirect, underivable, unexecutable relation between time and eternity, between the creature and the Creator. The freedom of God confronts men neither as a mechanism imposed upon them from outside nor as their own active and creative life (see the 1st edition of this book!). The freedom of God is the pure and primal Origin of men: the Light, the presence or absence of which renders their eyes brightness or darkness—the Infinite, by the twofold measurement of which they are great or little—the Decision, by which they stand or fall. Men are competent by their action neither to increase nor to decrease, neither to assist nor to obstruct, God's freedom. In fact, so little is their action relevant that it is precisely the indirectness of the relation between their freedom and God's freedom that establishes and sanctions the relative necessity, the relative seriousness,

the relative ordering, of their freedom. And so it is precisely the knowledge of God's freedom and power and grace which does NOT throw men wholly out of gear, because such knowledge is indissolubly one with the knowledge that they are men and not God. It is precisely the man who respects God as God who will have no occasion to object, for he will neither fear nor desire the dissolution of his responsibility: such a man will become NOT insane, NOT immoral, NOT a criminal, NOT a suicide. And should he, in spite of this, become one of these, he certainly will not make of it a 'sacrament' (Blüher),[4] but rather, like the murdered Raskolnikoff in Dostoievsky's novel,[5] will take it as a warning monument to the possibility of a final misunderstanding of the command that men should fear and love God above all things. The catastrophes of religion warn us how strange to men is the honouring of God, how incapable we are of watching but one hour with Christ, how difficult we find it to support the paradox of life without attempting to satisfy our need for an equilibrium by falling into some kind of Titanism! But when it is recognized that God is the tribulation of His people, it will at once become evident that, whether moral or immoral, men are blameworthy and opposed to the will of God (ix. 19); that they can achieve no equilibrium; and that neither moral uprightness nor immoral depravity provides them with an opportunity of arguing with God, of justifying themselves before Him, and so of escaping the tribulation. If, on the other hand, the tribulation be accepted, men will discover that their relative sense of responsibility is thereby guaranteed—'These things have not been said in order that we might by our lethargy checkmate the Holy Spirit, who hath given us a spark of His brightness, but in order

---

4 Hans Blüher was formerly a leading exponent of the ideals of the German Youth Movement. In his book — *Die Rolle der Erotik in der männlichen Gesellschaft* (1921)—he maintained that suicide is a sacrament. Blüher is now a supporter of the German Nationalist Party. [Tr.]

5 *Crime and Punishment.* [Tr.]

that we might perceive that what we have comes from Him, and in order that we may learn to hope in Him, to surrender ourselves to Him, and to pursue our salvation with fear and trembling' (Calvin).

"Shall the thing formed say to him that formed it, Why didst thou make me thus? Or hath not the potter a right over the clay, from the same lump to make one part a vessel unto honour, and another unto dishonour?" Such is the relation between God and man. We introduce at this point the familiar prophetic parable (Isa. xxix. 16, xlv. 9, lxiv. 7; Wisd. of Sol. xv. 7), for it is relevant to the problem we are considering. Men are related to God as the thing formed is related to him that formed it, as clay to the potter. Who now dares to speak of partners or of links in a chain of causality? On the one side stands the purpose-full master, on the other side the material which serves his purpose and becomes his work. No bridge, no continuity, links the potter and the clay, the master and his work. They are incommensurable. The distinction between them is infinite and qualitative; the link which connects them is altogether indirect and unobservable—or so, at least, it is in the parable. 'Here' is confronted by 'There'. And this situation remains, when we have said all that can be said about the state of the material or about the requirements, skill, temper, and success of the master. The freedom of the master to propose this or that remains intact, even when we have investigated the complicated process which is involved in any kind of creative work, even when we have explained how it is possible for the same hand to fashion flower-vases and chamber-pots out of the same material, and how the master can change from this work to that, and from this purpose to that. In spite of all observations, which may so easily be stretched to appear as a chain of causation, there remains the freedom of the master. And so it is with God and men. God confronts men as their Primal Origin, not as their immediate cause. Are men righteous?—It is before Him that they are so. Are men

sinners?—It is against Him that they sin. Are men alive?—It is in His life that they participate. Do men die?—It is at His hands. Men are not merely conditioned in the course of their lives: they are, like everything which does, or can, condition them—even though it bear the name of 'god'—created. The parable of the master and his work, the potter and his clay, is not, of course, adequate to explain what 'creation' means. But it does point the way to the proper understanding of it. Men are related to God as a visible and concrete thing is related to what is invisible and immaterial, as existence is related to non-existence. Whenever it is possible for us to point to the existence of human independence or freedom, we are, in fact, simply deferring the problem of primal origin, of the right and freedom of God, the problem of beginning and end, creation and redemption. The thought of predestination is, however, the final abandonment of this deferring of the problem. Its abandonment is bound to occur when God is known to be God in His relation to the being and having and doing of men. God must be apprehended as the God of Jacob and of Esau; otherwise we shall not understand that, whilst He is, in every moment of time, the God of Esau, He is in eternity the God of Jacob. How could the conception of human responsibility—the undermining of which the objectors either feared or desired (ix. 19)—be more securely protected, than by the complete relativity (relatedness!) of men when they are confronted by God?

Other books by Karl Barth:

The Christian Life, 1926 (Engl. trans. 1930).
Church Dogmatics, 1932-55 (Engl. trans. 1936–).
Come Holy Spirit, 1924 (Engl. trans. 1934).
The Knowledge of God and the Service of God (Gifford Lectures, 1937-8), 1938.
Protestant Thought from Rousseau to Ritschl, 1952 (Engl. trans. 1959).
The Word of God and the Word of Man, 1925 (Engl. trans. 1928).

Other books on the same problem:

Brunner, Emil. *The Theology of Crisis,* 1929.
Keller, Adophe. *Karl Barth and Christian Unity,* 1933.
Lowrie, Walter. *Our Concern with the Theology of Crisis,* 1932.

RUDOLPH BULTMANN

Rudolph Bultmann is primarily a Biblical scholar whose major concern is the problem of interpretation. If, as Barth and Biblical theology maintain, our knowledge of God is confined to his self-revelation through the Biblical word, in what sense does the Bible "communicate" that revelation to modern man? Many theologians admit the very real fact that Biblical language, as well as traditional religious concepts, images and symbols, are no longer capable of communicating to contemporary man. Applying all the modern techniques of text, style and form criticism to the Bible as a historical document, Bultmann arrives at a position with respect to this problem which places him at the center of a major theological controversy.

For him the New Testament is not a document that records past events, nor a ready made body of theological concepts but rather an *interpretation* of the religious encounter of a group of men with the person and life of Jesus, an encounter in which God revealed himself in a unique way. As an interpretation of a religious encounter, the New Testament is subject to the limitations of every historical document, that is, it is cast in the forms of thought and language of a special historical group in a particular time in history. These forms of thought contain many mythical elements which, while they spoke meaningfully to the first generations of Christians, now stand in the way of our re-experiencing the original encounter which they interpret. It is against these mythical elements that Bultmann directs his criticism. They are opaque encumbrances that must be cleared away if the New Testament is to speak to our generation. Demythologization of the New Testament means, for Bultmann, the peeling off of these mythical elements from the Biblical narration in order to make possible a rediscovery of the original revelation, the living "Word" of God.

This is a highly problematical thesis and has many opponents. Where Bultmann claims that modern man is incapable of mythical thinking, Karl Jaspers, for example, would say that man's thinking is always mythical, or better, symbolical. For Jaspers, man's thinking founders whenever he forgets this fact. To demythologize the New Testament would deprive it of the very symbols through which alone man is capable of encountering Transcendence. Rather than demythologizing the New Testament one should remythologize it, that is, overcome the limits imposed upon our minds by an exclusive scientific literalism and re-read the Bible as the "cypher script", the symbolic communication that it is. Tillich takes a more moderate position. With Bultmann he admits the Biblical narration of the revelation to be itself an interpretation, its forms and images derived from first century culture. These forms and images, however, are adequate symbolic bearers of the original substance of the revelation. Here he agrees with Jaspers. Nevertheless, their power to communicate anew from generation to generation depends not upon a fixed meaning they might possess for man in general but upon the continual process of re-interpretation in the language and thought forms of each generation as answers to the urgent questions that arise from particular men in their specific existential situation.

For all, however, the Biblical formulation of God's self-disclosure presents a problem, an obstacle, and each in his way attempts to "clear the way" for a renewal of the divine-human encounter.

RUDOLPH BULTMANN

from

NEW TESTAMENT AND MYTHOLOGY*

THE MYTHOLOGICAL ELEMENT IN THE MESSAGE OF THE NEW TESTAMENT AND THE PROBLEM OF ITS RE-INTERPRETATION

I

THE TASK OF DEMYTHOLOGIZING THE NEW TESTAMENT PROCLAMATION

A. The Problem

1. *The Mythical View of the World and the Mythical Event of Redemption*

THE COSMOLOGY OF THE NEW TESTAMENT is essentially mythical in character. The world is viewed as a three-storied structure, with the earth in the centre, the heaven above, and the underworld beneath. Heaven is the abode of God and of celestial beings—the angels. The underworld is hell, the place of torment. Even the earth is more than the scene of natural, everyday events, of the trivial round and common task. It is the scene of the supernatural activity of God and his angels on the one hand, and of Satan and his daemons on the other. These supernatural forces intervene in the course of nature and in all that men think and will and do. Miracles are by no means rare. Man is not in control of his own life. Evil spirits may take possession of him. Satan may inspire him with evil thoughts. Alternatively, God may inspire his thought and guide his purposes. He may grant him heavenly visions. He may allow

* From *Kerygma and Myth,* edited by Hans Werner Bartsch, translated by Reginald H. Fuller, copyright 1953. Reprinted by permission of The Macmillan Company.

him to hear his word of succour or demand. He may give him the supernatural power of his Spirit. History does not follow a smooth unbroken course; it is set in motion and controlled by these supernatural powers. This aeon is held in bondage by Satan, sin, and death (for "powers" is precisely what they are), and hastens towards its end. That end will come very soon, and will take the form of a cosmic catastrophe. It will be inaugurated by the "woes" of the last time. Then the Judge will come from heaven, the dead will rise, the last judgement will take place, and men will enter into eternal salvation or damnation.

This then is the mythical view of the world which the New Testament presupposes when it presents the event of redemption which is the subject of its preaching. It proclaims in the language of mythology that the last time has now come. "In the fulness of time" God sent forth his Son, a pre-existent divine Being, who appears on earth as a man.[1] He dies the death of a sinner[2] on the cross and makes atonement for the sins of men.[3] His resurrection marks the beginning of the cosmic catastrophe. Death, the consequence of Adam's sin, is abolished,[4] and the daemonic forces are deprived of their power.[5] The risen Christ is exalted to the right hand of God in heaven[6] and made "Lord" and "King".[7] He will come again on the clouds of heaven to complete the work of redemption, and the resurrection and judgment of men will follow.[8] Sin, suffering and death will then be finally abolished.[9] All this is to happen very soon; indeed, St Paul thinks that he himself will live to see it.[10]

---

1 Gal. 4. 4; Phil. 2. 6ff.; 2 Cor. 8. 9; John 1. 14, etc.

2 2 Cor. 5. 21; Rom. 8. 3.

3 Rom. 3. 23-26; 4. 25; 8. 3; 2 Cor. 5. 14, 19; John 1. 29; I John 2. 2, etc.

4 I Cor. 15. 21f.; Rom. 5. 12ff.

5 I Cor. 2. 6; Col. 2. 15; Rev. 12. 7ff., etc.

6 Acts 1. 6f.; 2. 33; Rom. 8. 34, etc.

7 Phil. 2. 9-11; I Cor. 15. 25.

8 I Cor. 15. 23f., 50ff., etc.

9 Rev. 21. 4, etc.

10 I Thess. 4. 15ff.; I Cor. 15. 51f.; cf. Mark 9. 1.

All who belong to Christ's Church and are joined to the Lord by Baptism and the Eucharist are certain of resurrection to salvation,[11] unless they forfeit it by unworthy behaviour. Christian believers already enjoy the first instalment of salvation, for the Spirit[12] is at work within them, bearing witness to their adoption as sons of God,[13] and guaranteeing their final resurrection.[14]

2. *The Mythological View of the World Obsolete*

All this is the language of mythology, and the origin of the various themes can be easily traced in the contemporary mythology of Jewish Apocalyptic and in the redemption myths of Gnosticism. To this extent *the kerygma is incredible to modern man, for he is convinced that the mythical view of the world is obsolete.* We are therefore bound to ask whether, when we preach the Gospel to-day, we expect our converts to accept not only the Gospel message, but also the mythical view of the world in which it is set. If not, does the New Testament embody a truth which is quite independent of its mythical setting? If it does, theology must undertake the task of stripping the Kerygma from its mythical framework, of "demythologizing" it.

Can Christian preaching expect modern man *to accept the mythical view of the world as true?* To do so would be both senseless and impossible. It would be senseless, because there is nothing specifically Christian in the mythical view of the world as such. It is simply the cosmology of a pre-scientific age. Again, it would be impossible, because no man can adopt a view of the world by his own volition—it is already determined for him by his place in history. Of course such a view is not absolutely unalterable, and the individual may even contribute

---

11 Rom. 5. 12ff.; I Cor. 15. 21ff., 44b, ff.

12 *Aparkê*: Rom. 8. 23, *arrabôn*: 2 Cor. 1. 22; 5. 5.

13 Rom. 8. 15; Gal. 4. 6.

14 Rom. 8. 11.

to its change. But he can do so only when he is faced by a new set of facts so compelling as to make his previous view of the world untenable. He has then no alternative but to modify his view of the world or produce a new one. The discoveries of Copernicus and the atomic theory are instances of this, and so was romanticism, with its discovery that the human subject is richer and more complex than enlightenment or idealism had allowed, and nationalism, with its new realization of the importance of history and the tradition of peoples.

It may equally well happen that truths which a shallow enlightenment had failed to perceive are later rediscovered in ancient myths. Theologians are perfectly justified in asking whether this is not exactly what has happened with the New Testament. At the same time it is impossible to revive an obsolete view of the world by a mere fiat, and certainly not a mythical view. For all our thinking to-day is shaped for good or ill by modern science. A blind acceptance of the New Testament mythology would be irrational, and to press for its acceptance as an article of faith would be to reduce Christian faith to the level of a human achievement. Wilhelm Herrmann pointed this out many years ago, and one would have thought that his demonstration was conclusive. It would involve a sacrifice of the intellect which could have only one result—a curious form of schizophrenia and insincerity. It would mean accepting a view of the world in our faith and religion which we should deny in our everyday life. Modern thought as we have inherited it provides us with *a motive for criticizing the New Testament view of the world.*

Man's knowledge and mastery of the world have advanced to such an extent through science and technology that it is no longer possible for anyone seriously to hold the New Testament view of the world—in fact, there is hardly anyone who does. What meaning, for instance, can we attach to such phrases in the creed as "descended into hell" or "ascended into heaven"? We no longer believe in the three-storied universe which the creeds take for granted. The only honest way of reciting the creeds is to strip the mythological framework from the truth they enshrine—that is, assuming that they contain any truth at all, which is just the question that theology has to ask. No one who is old enough to think for himself supposes that God lives in a local heaven. There is no longer any heaven in the traditional sense of the word. The same applies to hell in the sense of a mythical underworld beneath our feet. And if this is so, we can no longer accept the story of Christ's descent into hell or his Ascension into heaven as literally true. We can no longer look for the return of the Son of Man on the clouds of heaven or hope that the faithful will meet him in the air (1 Thess. 4. 15ff.).

Now that the forces and the laws of nature have been discovered, we can no longer believe in *spirits, whether good or evil.* We know that the stars are physical bodies whose motions are controlled by the laws of the universe, and not daemonic beings which enslave mankind to their service. Any influence they may have over human life must be explicable in terms of the ordinary laws of nature; it cannot in any way be attributed to their malevolence. Sickness and the cure of disease are likewise attributable to natural causation; they are not the result of daemonic activity or of evil spells.[15] The *miracles of the New Testament* have ceased to be miraculous, and to defend their historicity by recourse to nervous disorders or hypnotic effects

---

15 It may of course be argued that there are people alive to-day whose confidence in the traditional scientific view of the world has been shaken, and others who are primitive enough to qualify for an age of mythical thought. And there are also many varieties of superstition. But when belief in spirits and miracles has degenerated into superstition, it has become something entirely different from what it was when it was genuine faith. The various impressions and speculations which influence credulous people here and there are of little importance, nor does it matter to what extent cheap slogans have spread an atmosphere inimical to science. What matters is the world view which men imbibe from their environment, and it is science which determines that view of the world through the school, the press, the wireless, the cinema, and all the other fruits of technical progress.

only serves to underline the fact. And if we are still left with certain physiological and psychological phenomena which we can only assign to mysterious and enigmatic causes, we are still assigning them to causes, and thus far are trying to make them scientifically intelligible. Even occultism pretends to be a science.

It is impossible to use electric light and the wireless and to avail ourselves of modern medical and surgical discoveries, and at the same time to believe in the New Testament world of daemons and spirits.[16] We may think we can manage it in our own lives, but to expect others to do so is to make the Christian faith unintelligible and unacceptable to the modern world.

The mythical eschatology is untenable for the simple reason that the parousia of Christ never took place as the New Testament expected. History did not come to an end, and, as every schoolboy knows, it will continue to run its course. Even if we believe that the world as we know it will come to an end in time, we expect the end to take the form of a natural catastrophe, not of a mythical event such as the New Testament expects. And if we explain the parousia in terms of modern scientific theory, we are applying criticism to the New Testament, albeit unconsciously.

But natural science is not the only challenge which the mythology of the New Testament has to face. There is the still more serious challenge presented by *modern man's understanding of himself.*

Modern man is confronted by a curious dilemma. He may regard himself as pure nature, or as pure spirit. In the latter case he distinguishes the essential part of his being from nature. In either case, however, *man is essentially a unity.* He bears the sole responsibility for his own feeling, thinking, and willing.[17] He is not, as the New Testament regards him, the victim of a strange dichotomy which exposes him to the interference of powers

---

16 Cp. the observations of Paul Schütz on the decay of mythical religion in the East through the introduction of modern hygiene and medicine.

17 Cp. Gerhardt Krüger, *Einsicht und Leidenschaft, Das Wesen des platonischen Denkens,* Frankfort, 1939, p. 11 f.

outside himself. If his exterior behaviour and his interior condition are in perfect harmony, it is something he has achieved himself, and if other people think their interior unity is torn asunder by daemonic or divine interference, he calls it schizophrenia.

Although biology and psychology recognize that man is a highly dependent being, that does not mean that he has been handed over to powers outside of and distinct from himself. This dependence is inseparable from human nature, and he needs only to understand it in order to recover his self-mastery and organize his life on a rational basis. If he regards himself as spirit, he knows that he is permanently conditioned by the physical, bodily part of his being, but he distinguishes his true self from it, and knows that he is independent and responsible for his mastery over nature.

In either case he finds *what the New Testament has to say about the "Spirit"* (pneuma) *and the sacraments utterly strange and incomprehensible.* Biological man cannot see how a supernatural entity like the *pneuma* can penetrate within the close texture of his natural powers and set to work within him. Nor can the idealist understand how a *pneuma* working like a natural power can touch and influence his mind and spirit. Conscious as he is of his own moral responsibility, he cannot conceive how baptism in water can convey a mysterious something which is henceforth the agent of all his decisions and actions. He cannot see how physical food can convey spiritual strength, and how the unworthy receiving of the Eucharist can result in physical sickness and death (1 Cor. 11. 30). The only possible explanation is that it is due to suggestion. He cannot understand how anyone can be baptized for the dead (1 Cor. 15. 29).

We need not examine in detail the various forms of modern *Weltanschauung,* whether idealist or naturalist. For the only criticism of the New Testament which is theologically relevant is that which arises *necessarily* out of the situation of modern man. The biological *Weltanschauung* does not, for instance, arise necessarily out of the contemporary situation. We are still free to adopt it or not as we choose. The only relevant question for the theologian is the basic assumption on which the adoption of a biological as of every other *Weltanschauung* rests, and that assumption is the view of the world which has been moulded by modern science and the modern conception of human nature as a self-subsistent unity immune from the interference of supernatural powers.

Again, the biblical doctrine that *death is the punishment of sin* is equally abhorrent to naturalism and idealism, since they both regard death as a simple and necessary process of nature. To the naturalist death is no problem at all, and to the idealist it is a problem for that very reason, for so far from arising out of man's essential spiritual being it actually destroys it. The idealist is faced with a paradox. On the one hand man is a spiritual being, and therefore essentially different from plants and animals, and on the other hand he is the prisoner of nature, whose birth, life, and death are just the same as those of the animals. Death may present him with a problem, but he cannot see how it can be a punishment for sin. Human beings are subject to death even before they have committed any sin. And to attribute human mortality to the fall of Adam is sheer nonsense, for guilt implies personal responsibility, and the idea of original sin as an inherited infection is sub-ethical, irrational, and absurd.

The same objections apply to *the doctrine of the atonement*. How can the guilt of one man be expiated by the death of another who is sinless—if indeed one may speak of a sinless man at all? What primitive notions of guilt and righteousness does this imply? And what primitive idea of God? The rationale of sacrifice in general may of course throw some light on the theory of the atonement, but even so, what a primitive mythology it is, that a divine Being should become incarnate, and atone for the sins of men through his own blood! Or again, one might adopt an analogy from the law courts, and explain the death of Christ as a transaction between God and man through which God's claims on man were satisfied. But that would make sin a juridical matter; it would be no more than an external transgression of a commandment, and it would make nonsense of all our ethical standards. Moreover, if the Christ who died such a death was the pre-existent Son of God, what could death mean for him? Obviously very little, if he knew that he would rise again in three days!

The *resurrection of Jesus* is just as difficult, if it means an event whereby a supernatural power is released which can henceforth be appropriated through the sacraments. To the biologist such language is meaningless, for he does not regard death as a problem at all. The idealist would not object to the idea of a life immune from death, but he could not believe that such a life is made available by the resuscitation of a corpse. If that is the way God makes life available for man, his action is inextricably involved in a nature miracle. Such a notion he finds intolerable, for he can see God at work only in the life of the spirit (which is for him the only real life) and in the transformation of his personality. But, quite apart from the incredibility of such a miracle, he cannot see how an event like this could be the act of God, or how it could affect his own life.

Gnostic influence suggests that this Christ, who died and rose again, was not a mere human being but a God-man. His death and resurrection were not isolated facts which concerned him alone, but a cosmic event in which we are all involved.[18] It is only with effort that modern man can think himself back into such an intellectual atmosphere, and even then he could never accept it himself, because it regards man's essential being as nature and redemption as a process of nature. And as for the pre-existence of Christ, with its corollary of man's translation into a celestial realm of light, and the clothing of the human

18 Rom. 5. 12ff.; 1 Cor. 15. 21ff., 44b.

personality in heavenly robes and a spiritual body—all this is not only irrational but utterly meaningless. Why should salvation take this particular form? Why should this be the fulfilment of human life and the realization of man's true being?

B. The Task before Us

1. *Not Selection or Subtraction*

Does this drastic criticism of the New Testament mythology mean the complete elimination of the kerygma?

Whatever else may be true, we cannot save the kerygma by selecting some of its features and subtracting others, and thus reduce the amount of mythology in it. For instance, it is impossible to dismiss St Paul's teaching about the unworthy reception of Holy Communion or about baptism for the dead, and yet cling to the belief that physical eating and drinking can have a spiritual effect. If we accept *one* idea, we must accept everything which the New Testament has to say about Baptism and Holy Communion, and it is just this one idea which we cannot accept.

It may of course be argued that some features of the New Testament mythology are given greater prominence than others: not all of them appear with the same regularity in the various books. There is for example only one occurrence of the legends of the Virgin birth and the Ascension; St Paul and St John appear to be totally unaware of them. But, even if we take them to be later accretions, it does not affect the mythical character of the event of redemption as a whole. And if we once start subtracting from the kerygma, where are we to draw the line? The mythical view of the world must be accepted or rejected in its entirety.

At this point absolute clarity and ruthless honesty are essential both for the academic theologian and for the parish priest. It is a duty they owe to themselves, to the Church they serve, and to those whom they seek to win for the Church. They must make it quite clear what their hearers are expected to accept and what they are not. At all costs the preacher must not leave his people in the dark about what he secretly eliminates, nor must he be in the dark about it himself. In Karl Barth's book *The Resurrection of the Dead* the cosmic eschatology in the sense of "chronologically final history" is eliminated in favour of what he intends to be a non-mythological "ultimate history". He is able to delude himself into thinking that this is exegesis of St Paul and of the New Testament generally only because he gets rid of everything mythological in 1 Corinthians by subjecting it to an interpretation which does violence to its meaning. But that is an impossible procedure.

If the truth of the New Testament proclamation is to be preserved, the only way is to demythologize it. But our motive in so doing must not be to make the New Testament relevant to the modern world at all costs. The question is simply whether the New Testament message consists exclusively of mythology, or whether it actually demands the elimination of myth if it is to be understood as it is meant to be. This question is forced upon us from two sides. First there is the nature of myth in general, and then there is the New Testament itself.

2. *The Nature of Myth*

The real purpose of myth is not to present an objective picture of the world as it is, but to express man's understanding of himself in the world in which he lives. Myth should be interpreted not cosmologically, but anthropologically, or better still, existentially.[19] Myth speaks of the power or the powers which man supposes he experiences as the ground and limit of his world and of his own activity and suffering. He describes these powers in terms derived from the visible world, with its tangible objects and forces, and from human life, with its

19 Cf. Gerhardt Krüger, *Einsicht und Leidenschaft,* esp. p. 17f., 56f.

feelings, motives, and potentialities. He may, for instance, explain the origin of the world by speaking of a world egg or a world tree. Similarly he may account for the present state and order of the world by speaking of a primeval war between the gods. He speaks of the other world in terms of this world, and of the gods in terms derived from human life.[20]

Myth is an expression of man's conviction that the origin and purpose of the world in which he lives are to be sought not within it but beyond it—that is, beyond the realm of known and tangible reality—and that this realm is perpetually dominated and menaced by those mysterious powers which are its source and limit. Myth is also an expression of man's awareness that he is not lord of his own being. It expresses his sense of dependence not only within the visible world, but more especially on those forces which hold sway beyond the confines of the known. Finally, myth expresses man's belief that in this state of dependence he can be delivered from the forces within the visible world.

Thus myth contains elements which demand its own criticism —namely, its imagery with its apparent claim to objective validity. The real purpose of myth is to speak of a transcendent power which controls the world and man, but that purpose is impeded and obscured by the terms in which it is expressed.

Hence the importance of the New Testament mythology lies not in its imagery but in the understanding of existence which it enshrines. The real question is whether this understanding of existence is true. Faith claims that it is, and faith ought not to be tied down to the imagery of New Testament mythology.

---

20 Myth is here used in the sense popularized by the 'History of Religions' school. Mythology is the use of imagery to express the other worldly in terms of this world and the divine in terms of human life, the other side in terms of this side. For instance, divine transcendence is expressed as spatial distance. It is a mode of expression which makes it easy to understand the cultus as an action in which material means are used to convey immaterial power. Myth is not used in that modern sense, according to which it is practically equivalent to ideology.

3. *The New Testament Itself*

The New Testament itself invites this kind of criticism. Not only are there rough edges in its mythology, but some of its features are actually contradictory. For example, the death of Christ is sometimes a sacrifice and sometimes a cosmic event. Sometimes his person is interpreted as the Messiah and sometimes as the Second Adam. The kenosis of the pre-existent Son (Phil. 2. 6ff.) is incompatible with the miracle narratives as proofs of his messianic claims. The Virgin birth is inconsistent with the assertion of his pre-existence. The doctrine of the Creation is incompatible with the conception of the "rulers of this world" (1 Cor. 2. 6ff.), the "god of this world" (2 Cor. 4. 4) and the "elements of this world" *otoicheia tou chosmou*, Gal. 4. 3). It is impossible to square the belief that the law was given by God with the theory that it comes from the angels (Gal. 3. 19f.).

But the principal demand for the criticism of mythology comes from a curious contradiction which runs right through the New Testament. Sometimes we are told that human life is determined by cosmic forces, at others we are challenged to a decision. Side by side with the Pauline indicative stands the Pauline imperative. In short, man is sometimes regarded as a cosmic being, sometimes as an independent "I" for whom decision is a matter of life or death. Incidentally, this explains why so many sayings in the New Testament speak directly to modern man's condition while others remain enigmatic and obscure. Finally, attempts at demythologization are sometimes made even within the New Testament itself. But more will be said on this point later.

4. *Previous Attempts at Demythologizing*

How then is the mythology of the New Testament to be reinterpreted? This is not the first time that theologians have approached this task. Indeed, all we have said so far might have been said in much the same way thirty or forty years ago, and it is a sign of the bankruptcy of contemporary theology that it has been necessary to go all over the same ground again. The reason for this is not far to seek. The liberal theologians of the last century were working on the wrong lines. They threw away not only the mythology but also the kerygma itself. Were they right? Is that the treatment the New Testament itself required? That is the question we must face to-day. The last twenty years have witnessed a movement away from criticism and a return to a naïve acceptance of the kerygma. The danger both for theological scholarship and for the Church is that this uncritical resuscitation of the New Testament mythology may make the Gospel message unintelligible to the modern world. We cannot dismiss the critical labours of earlier generations without further ado. We must take them up and put them to constructive use. Failure to do so will mean that the old battles between orthodoxy and liberalism will have to be fought out all over again, that is assuming that there will be any Church or any theologians to fight them at all! Perhaps we may put it schematically like this: whereas the older liberals used criticism to *eliminate* the mythology of the New Testament, our task to-day is to use criticism to *interpret* it. Of course it may still be necessary to eliminate mythology here and there. But the criterion adopted must be taken not from modern thought, but from the understanding of human existence which the New Testament itself enshrines.[21]

To begin with, let us review some of these earlier attempts at demythologizing. We need only mention briefly the allegorical interpretation of the New Testament which has dogged the Church throughout its history. This method spiritualizes the mythical events so that they become symbols of processes going on in the soul. This is certainly the most comfortable

---

21 As an illustration of this critical re-interpretation of myth cf. Hans Jonas, *Augustin und das paulinische Freiheitsproblem*, 1930, pp. 66-76.

way of avoiding the critical question. The literal meaning is allowed to stand and is dispensed with only for the individual believer, who can escape into the realm of the soul.

It was characteristic of the older liberal theologians that they regarded mythology as relative and temporary. Hence they thought they could safely eliminate it altogether, and retain only the broad, basic principles of religion and ethics. They distinguished between what they took to be the essence of religion and the temporary garb which it assumed. Listen to what Harnack has to say about the essence of Jesus' preaching of the Kingdom of God and its coming: "The kingdom has a triple meaning. Firstly, it is something supernatural, a gift from above, not a product of ordinary life. Secondly, it is a purely religious blessing, the inner link with the living God; thirdly, it is the most important experience that a man can have, that on which everything else depends; it permeates and dominates his whole existence, because sin is forgiven and misery banished." Note how completely the mythology is eliminated: "The kingdom of God comes by coming to the individual, by entering into his *soul* and laying hold of it." [22]

It will be noticed how Harnack reduces the kerygma to a few basic principles of religion and ethics. Unfortunately this means that *the kerygma has ceased to be kerygma:* it is no longer the proclamation of the decisive act of God in Christ. For the liberals the great truths of religion and ethics are timeless and eternal, though it is only within human history that they are realized, and only in concrete historical processes that they are given clear expression. But the apprehension and acceptance of these principles does not depend on the knowledge and acceptance of the age in which they first took shape, or of the historical persons who first discovered them. We are all capable of verifying them in our own experience at whatever period

22 *What is Christianity?* Williams and Norgate, 1904, pp. 63-4 and 57.

we happen to live. History may be of academic interest, but never of paramount importance for religion.

But the New Testament speaks of an *event* through which God has wrought man's redemption. For it, Jesus is not primarily the teacher, who certainly had extremely important things to say and will always be honoured for saying them, but whose person in the last analysis is immaterial for those who have assimilated his teaching. On the contrary, his person is just what the New Testament proclaims as the decisive event of redemption. It speaks of this person in mythological terms, but does this mean that we can reject the kerygma altogether on the ground that it is nothing more than mythology? That is the question.

Next came the History of Religions school. Its representatives were the first to discover the extent to which the New Testament is permeated by mythology. The importance of the New Testament, they saw, lay not in its teaching about religion and ethics but in its actual religion and piety; in comparison with that all the dogma it contains, and therefore all the mythological imagery with its apparent objectivity, was of secondary importance or completely negligible. The essence of the New Testament lay in the religious life it portrayed; its high-water mark was the experience of mystical union with Christ, in whom God took symbolic form.

These critics grasped one important truth. Christian faith is not the same as religious idealism; the Christian life does not consist in developing the individual personality, in the improvement of society, or in making the world a better place. The Christian life means a turning away from the world, a detachment from it. But the critics of the History of Religions school failed to see that in the New Testament this detachment is essentially eschatological and not mystical. Religion for them was an expression of the human yearning to rise above the world and transcend it: it was the discovery of a supramundane sphere where the soul could detach itself from all earthly care and find its rest. Hence the supreme manifestation of religion was to be found not in personal ethics or in social idealism but in the cultus regarded as an end in itself. This was just the kind of religious life portrayed in the New Testament, not only as a model and pattern, but as a challenge and inspiration. The New Testament was thus the abiding source of power which enabled man to realize the true life of religion, and Christ was the eternal symbol for the cultus of the Christian Church.[23] It will be noticed how the Church is here defined exclusively as a worshipping community, and this represents a great advance on the older liberalism. This school rediscovered the Church as a *religious* institution. For the idealist there was really no place for the Church at all. But did they succeed in recovering the meaning of the Ecclesia in the full, New Testament sense of the word? For in the New Testament the Ecclesia is invariably a phenomenon of salvation history and eschatology.

Moreover, if the History of Religions school is right, the kerygma has once more ceased to be kerygma. Like the liberals, they are silent about a decisive act of God in Christ proclaimed as the event of redemption. So we are still left with the question whether this event and the person of Jesus, both of which are described in the New Testament in mythological terms, are nothing more than mythology. Can the kerygma be interpreted apart from mythology? Can we recover the truth of the kerygma for men who do not think in mythological terms without forfeiting its character as kerygma?

5. *An Existentialist Interpretation the Only Solution*

The theological work which such an interpretation involves can be sketched only in the broadest outline and with only a few examples. We must avoid the impression that this is a

23 Cf. e.g. Troeltsch, *Die Bedeutung der Geschichtlichkeit Jesu für den Glauben,* Tübingen, 1911.

light and easy task, as if all we have to do is to discover the right formula and finish the job on the spot. It is much more formidable than that. It cannot be done single-handed. It will tax the time and strength of a whole theological generation.

The mythology of the New Testament is in essence that of Jewish apocalyptic and the Gnostic redemption myths. A common feature of them both is their basic dualism, according to which the present world and its human inhabitants are under the control of daemonic, satanic powers, and stand in need of redemption. Man cannot achieve this redemption by his own efforts; it must come as a gift through a divine intervention. Both types of mythology speak of such an intervention: Jewish apocalyptic of an imminent world crisis in which this present aeon will be brought to an end and the new aeon ushered in by the coming of the Messiah, and Gnosticism of a Son of God sent down from the realm of light, entering into this world in the guise of a man, and by his fate and teaching delivering the elect and opening up the way for their return to their heavenly home.

The meaning of these two types of mythology lies once more not in their imagery with its apparent objectivity but in the understanding of human existence which both are trying to express. In other words, they need to be interpreted existentially. A good example of such treatment is to be found in Hans Jonas's book on Gnosticism.[24]

Our task is to produce an existentialist interpretation of the dualistic mythology of the New Testament along similar lines. When, for instance, we read of daemonic powers ruling the world and holding mankind in bondage, does the understanding of human existence which underlies such language offer a solution to the riddle of human life which will be acceptable even to the non-mythological mind of to-day? Of course we must not take this to imply that the New Testament presents

---

24 *Gnosis und Spätantiker Geist. I. Die mythologische Gnosis,* 1934.

us with an anthropology like that which modern science can give us. It cannot be proved by logic or demonstrated by an appeal to factual evidence. Scientific anthropologies always take for granted a definite understanding of existence, which is invariably the consequence of a deliberate decision of the scientist, whether he makes it consciously or not. And that is why we have to discover whether the New Testament offers man an understanding of himself which will challenge him to a genuine existential decision.

II

DEMYTHOLOGIZING IN OUTLINE

A. The Christian Interpretation of Being

1. *Human Existence apart from Faith*

What does the New Testament mean when it talks of the "world", of "this world" (*ho chosmos outos*), or of "this aeon" (*outos ho aiôn*)? In speaking thus, the New Testament is in agreement with the Gnostics, for they too speak of "this world", and of the princes, prince, or god of this world; and moreover they both regard man as the slave of the world and its powers. But there is one significant difference. In the New Testament one of these powers is conspicuously absent—viz., *matter,* the physical, sensual part of man's constitution. Never does the New Testament complain that the soul of man, his authentic self, is imprisoned in a material body: never does it complain of the power of sensuality over the spirit. That is why it never doubts the responsibility of man for his sin. God is always the Creator of the world, including human life in the body. He is also the Judge before whom man must give account. The part played by Satan as the Lord of this world must therefore be limited in a peculiar way, or else, if he is the lord or god of world, "this world" must stand in a peculiar dialectical relation to the world as the creation of God.

"This world" is the world of corruption and death. Clearly, it was not so when it left the hands of the Creator, for it was only in consequence of the fall of Adam that death entered into the world (Rom. 5. 12). Hence it is sin, rather than matter as such, which is the cause of corruption and death. The Gnostic conception of the soul as a pure, celestial element imprisoned by some tragic fate in a material body is entirely absent. Death is the wages of sin (Rom. 6. 23; cf. 1 Cor. 15. 56). True, St Paul seems to agree with the Gnostics as regards the effects which he ascribes to the fall of Adam as the ancestor of the human race. But it is clear that he later returns to the idea of individual responsibility when he says that since Adam death came to all men "for that all sinned" (Rom. 5. 12), a statement which stands in formal contradiction to the Adam theory. Perhaps he means to say that with Adam death became possible rather than inevitable. However that may be, there is another idea which St Paul is constantly repeating and which is equally incompatible with the Adam theory, and that is the theory that sin, including death, is derived from the flesh (*sarx,* Rom. 8. 13; Gal. 6. 8, etc.). But what does he mean by "flesh"? Not the bodily or physical side of human nature, but the sphere of visible, concrete, tangible, and measurable reality, which as such is also the sphere of corruption and death. When a man chooses to live entirely in and for this sphere, or, as St Paul puts it, when he "lives after the flesh", it assumes the shape of a "power". There are indeed many different ways of living after the flesh. There is the crude life of sensual pleasure and there is the refined way of basing one's life on the pride of achievement, on the "works of the law" as St. Paul would say. But these distinctions are ultimately immaterial. For "flesh" embraces not only the material things of life, but all human creation and achievement pursued for the sake of some tangible reward, such as for example the fulfilling of the law (Gal. 3. 3). It includes every passive quality, and every advantage a man can have, in the sphere of visible, tangible reality (Phil. 3. 4ff.).

St Paul sees that the life of man is weighed down by anxiety (*merimnan,* 1 Cor. 7. 32ff.). Every man focuses his anxiety upon some particular object. The natural man focuses it upon security, and in proportion to his opportunities and his success in the visible sphere he places his "confidence" in the "flesh" (Phil. 3. 3f.), and the consciousness of security finds its expression in "glorying" (*chauchasthai*).

Such a pursuit is, however, incongruous with man's real situation, for the fact is that he is not secure at all. Indeed, this is the way in which he loses his true life and becomes the slave of that very sphere which he had hoped to master, and which he hoped would give him security. Whereas hitherto he might have enjoyed the world as God's creation, it has now become "this world", the world in revolt against God. This is the way in which the "powers" which dominate human life come into being, and as such they acquire the character of mythical entities.[25] Since the visible and tangible sphere is essentially transitory, the man who bases his life on it becomes the prisoner and slave of corruption. An illustration of this may be seen in the way our attempts to secure visible security for ourselves bring us into collision with others; we can seek security for ourselves only at their expense. Thus on the one hand we get envy, anger, jealousy, and the like, and on the other compromise, bargainings, and adjustments of conflicting interests. This creates an all-pervasive atmosphere which controls all our judgements; we all pay homage to it and take it for granted. Thus man becomes the slave of anxiety (Rom. 8. 15). Everybody tries to hold fast to his own life and property, because he has a secret feeling that it is all slipping away from him.

---

25 Terms like "the spirit of the age" or "the spirit of technology" provide some sort of modern analogy.

The Life of Faith

The authentic life, on the other hand, would be a life based on unseen, intangible realities. Such a life means the abandonment of all self-contrived security. This is what the New Testament means by "life after the Spirit" or "life in faith".

For this life we must have faith in *the grace of God.* It means faith that the unseen, intangible reality actually confronts us as love, opening up our future and signifying not death but life.

The grace of God means *the forgiveness of sin,* and brings deliverance from the bondage of the past. The old quest for visible security, the hankering after tangible realities, and the clinging to transitory objects, is sin, for by it we shut out invisible reality from our lives and refuse God's future which comes to us as a gift. But once we open our hearts to the grace of God, our sins are forgiven; we are released from the past. This is what is meant by "faith": to open ourselves freely to the future. But at the same time faith involves obedience, for faith means turning our backs on self and abandoning all security. It means giving up every attempt to carve out a niche in life for ourselves, surrendering all our self-confidence, and resolving to trust in God alone, in the God who raises the dead (2 Cor. 1. 9) and who calls the things that are not into being (Rom. 4. 17). It means radical self-commitment to God in the expectation that everything will come from him and nothing from ourselves. Such a life spells deliverance from all worldly, tangible objects, leading to complete detachment from the world and thus to freedom.

This detachment from the world is something quite different from asceticism. It means preserving a distance from the world and dealing with it in a spirit of "as if not" (*hôs mê,* 1 Cor. 7. 29–31). The believer is lord of all things (1 Cor. 3. 21–3). He enjoys that power (*exousia*) of which the Gnostic boasts, but with the proviso: "All things are lawful for me, but I will not be brought under the power of any" (1 Cor. 6. 12; cf. 10. 23f.). The believer may "rejoice with them that do rejoice, and weep with them that weep" (Rom. 12. 15), but he is no longer in bondage to anything in the world (1 Cor. 7. 17–24). Everything in the world has become indifferent and unimportant. "For though I was free from all men, I brought myself under bondage to all" (1 Cor. 9. 19–23). "I know how to be abased, and I know also how to abound in everything, and in all things I have learned the secret both to be filled and to be hungry, both to abound and to be in want" (Phil. 4. 12). The world has been crucified to him, and he to the world (Gal. 6. 14). Moreover, the power of his new life is manifested even in weakness, suffering, and death (2 Cor. 4. 7–11; 12. 9f.). Just when he realizes that he is nothing in himself, he can have and be all things through God (2 Cor. 12. 9f.; 6. 8–10).

Now, this is eschatological existence; it means being a "new creature" (2 Cor. 5. 17). The eschatology of Jewish apocalyptic and of Gnosticism has been emancipated from its accompanying mythology, in so far as the age of salvation has already dawned for the believer and the life of the future has become a present reality. The fourth gospel carries this process to a logical conclusion by completely eliminating every trace of apocalyptic eschatology. The last judgement is no longer an imminent cosmic event, for it is already taking place in the coming of Jesus and in his summons to believe (John 3. 19; 9. 39; 12. 31). The believer has life here and now, and has passed already from death into life (5. 24 etc.). Outwardly everything remains as before, but inwardly his relation to the world has been radically changed. The world has no further claim on him, for faith is the victory which overcometh the world (1 John 5. 4).

The eschatology of Gnosticism is similarly transcended. It is not that the believer is given a new nature (*physis*) or that his pre-existent nature is emancipated, or that his soul is assured of a journey to heaven. The new life in faith is not an assured possession or endowment, which could lead only to libertinism. Nor is it a possession to be guarded with care and vigilance, which could lead only to asceticism. Life in faith is not a possession at all. It cannot be exclusively expressed in indicative terms; it needs an imperative to complete it. In other words, the decision of faith is never final; it needs constant renewal in every fresh situation. Our freedom does not excuse us from the demand under which we all stand as men, for it is freedom for obedience (Rom. 6. 11ff.). To believe means not to have apprehended but to have been apprehended. It means always to be travelling along the road between the "already" and the "not yet", always to be pursuing a goal.

For Gnosticism redemption is a cosmic process in which the redeemed are privileged to participate here and now. Although essentially transcendent, faith must be reduced to an immanent possession. Its outward signs are freedom (*eleutheria*), power (*exousia*), pneumatic phenomena, and above all ecstasy. In the last resort the New Testament knows no phenomena in which transcendent realities become immanent possessions. True, St. Paul is familiar with ecstasy (2 Cor. 5. 13; 12. 1ff.). But he refuses to accept it as a proof of the possession of the Spirit. The New Testament never speaks of the training of the soul in mystical experience or of ecstasy as the culmination of the Christian life. Not psychic phenomena but faith is the hallmark of that life.

Certainly St. Paul shares the popular belief of his day that the Spirit manifests itself in miracles, and he attributes abnormal psychic phenomena to its agency. But the enthusiasm of the Corinthians for such things brought home to him their questionable character. So he insists that the gifts of the Spirit must be judged according to their value for "edification", and in so doing he transcends the popular view of the Spirit as an agency that operates like any other natural force. True, he regards the Spirit as a mysterious entity dwelling in man and guaranteeing his resurrection (Rom. 8. 11). He can even speak of the Spirit as if it were a kind of supernatural material (1 Cor. 15. 44ff.). Yet in the last resort he clearly means by "Spirit" the possibility of a new life which is opened up by faith. The Spirit does not work like a supernatural force, nor is it the permanent possession of the believer. It is the possibility of a new life which must be appropriated by a deliberate resolve. Hence St. Paul's paradoxical injunction: "If we live by the Spirit, by the Spirit also let us walk." (Gal. 5. 25). "Being led by the Spirit" (Rom. 8. 14) is not an automatic process of nature, but the fulfilment of an imperative: "live after the Spirit, not after the flesh". Imperative and indicative are inseparable. The possession of the Spirit never renders decision superfluous. "I say, Walk by the Spirit and ye shall not fulfil the lust of the flesh" (Gal. 5. 16). Thus the concept "Spirit" has been emancipated from mythology.

The Pauline catalogue of the fruits of the Spirit ("love, joy, peace, long-suffering, kindness, goodness, faithfulness, temperance", Gal. 5. 22) shows how faith, by detaching man from the world, makes him capable of fellowship in community. Now that he is delivered from anxiety and from the frustration which comes from clinging to the tangible realities of the visible world, man is free to enjoy fellowship with others. Hence faith is described as "working through love" (Gal. 5. 6). And this means being a new creature (cf. Gal. 5. 6 with 6. 15).

B. The Event of Redemption

1. *Christianity without Christ?*

We have now suggested an existentialist unmythological interpretation of the Christian understanding of Being. But is this interpretation true to the New Testament? We seem to have overlooked one important point, which is that in the New Testament faith is always *faith in Christ.* Faith, in the strict sense of the word, was only there at a certain moment in history. It had to be *revealed;* it *came* (Gal. 3. 23, 25). This might of course be taken as part of the story of man's spiritual evolution. But the New Testament means more than that. It claims that faith only became possible at a definite point in history in consequence of an *event*—viz., the event of Christ. Faith in the sense of obedient self-commitment and inward detachment from the world is only possible when it is faith in Jesus Christ.

Here indeed is the crux of the matter—have we here a remnant of mythology which still requires restatement? In fact it comes to this: can we have a Christian understanding of Being without Christ?

The reader will recall our criticism of the History of Religions school for eliminating the decisive event of Christ. Is our re-interpretation of Christianity in existentialist terms open to precisely the same objection?

It might well appear as though the event of Christ were a relic of mythology which still awaits elimination. This is a serious problem, and if Christian faith is to recover its self-assurance it must be grappled with. For it can recover its certainty only if it is prepared to think through to the bitter end the possibility of its own impossibility or superfluity.

It might well appear possible to have a Christian understanding of Being without Christ, as though what we had in the New Testament was the first discovery and the more or less clear expression, in the guise of mythology, of an understanding of Being which is at bottom man's natural understanding of his Being, as it has been given clear expression in modern existentialist philosophy. Does this mean that what existentialism has done is simply to remove the mythological disguise and to vindicate the Christian understanding of Being as it is found in the New Testament and to carry it to more logical conclusion? Is theology simply the precursor of existentialism? Is it no more than an antiquated survival and an unnecessary incubus?

Such is the impression we might derive from a consideration of the recent developments in philosophy. Might we not say that the New Testament lays bare what the existentialists call "the historicity of Being"?

Count Yorck von Wartenburg[26] wrote to Dilthey on 15 December 1892: "Dogmatics was an attempt to formulate an ontology of the higher historic life. Christian dogmatics was inevitably the antithesis of intellectualism, because Christianity is the supreme vitality." [26a] Dilthey agrees: ". . . all dogmas need to be translated so as to bring out their universal validity for all human life. They are cramped by their connection with the situation in the past in which they arose. Once they have been freed from this limitation they become . . . the consciousness of the supra-sensual and supra-intelligible nature of historicity pure and simple. . . . Hence the principal Christian dogmas, which include such symbols as "Son of God", "satisfaction", "sacrifice", and the like, are, in so far as they are limited to the facts of the Christian story, untenable. But once they are re-interpreted as statements of universal validity they express the highest living form of all history. They thus lose their rigid and exclusive reference to the person of Jesus, which deliberately excludes all other references." [27]

Yorck gives by way of illustration a re-interpretation of the doctrines of original sin and the atonement. He finds them intelligible in the light of what he calls the "virtual connection" which runs like a thread right through history. "Jesus is the historical demonstration of a universal truth. The child profits from the self-sacrifice of its mother. This involves a conveyance of virtue and power from one person to another, without which history is impossible. [Note the corollary—*all* history, not only Christian history, involves transference of power.] This is why

---

26 *Briefwechsel zwischen Wilhelm Dilthey und dem Grafen Paul Yorck von Wartenburg*, 1877-97. Halle, Niemeyer, 1923.

26a P. 154.

27 P. 158.

rationalism is blind to the concept of history. And sin—not specific acts of wrong-doing, but man's sinfulness in general—is, as the religious man knows from his own experience, quite unpredictable. Is it less 'monstrous and repulsive' [as Dilthey had stigmatized the doctrine of original sin] that sickness and misery are inherited from generation to generation? These Christian symbols are drawn from the very depths of nature, for religion itself—I mean Christianity—is supernatural, not unnatural." [28]

The development of philosophy since Dilthey's day has, it would seem, amply justified these contentions. Karl Jaspers has found no difficulty in transposing Kierkegaard's interpretation of Christian Being to the sphere of philosophy. Above all, Heidegger's existentialist analysis of the ontological structure of being would seem to be no more than a secularized, philosophical version of the New Testament view of human life. For him the chief characteristic of man's Being in history is anxiety. Man exists in a permanent tension between the past and the future. At every moment he is confronted with an alternative. Either he must immerse himself in the concrete world of nature, and thus inevitably lose his individuality, or he must abandon all security and commit himself unreservedly to the future, and thus alone achieve his authentic Being. Is not that exactly the New Testament understanding of human life? Some critics have objected that I am borrowing Heidegger's categories and forcing them upon the New Testament. I am afraid this only shows that they are blinding their eyes to the real problem, which is that the philosophers are saying the same thing as the New Testament and saying it quite independently.

The whole question has been posed afresh in the recent book by Wilhelm Kamlah.[29] It is true that Kamlah expressly attacks

---

28 P. 155.

29 *Christentum und Selbstbehauptung,* Frankfort, 1940

the eschatological character of the Christian understanding of Being, but that is because he misinterprets the detachment from the world which is consequent upon faith. He understands it undialectically as a simple negation of the world, and so fails to do justice to the element of "as if not" which is so characteristic of the Pauline Epistles. But the understanding of Being which Kamlah develops philosophically is manifestly a secularized version of that which we find in Christianity. For the Christian concept of faith he substitutes "self-commitment", by which he means "surrender to the universal reality", or to God as the source of all Being. Self-commitment is the antithesis of autonomy. It brings with it a revelation of the meaning of universal reality. Further, it is emancipation, bringing inward freedom through detachment from all sensual objects of desire. Kamlah himself is aware how close this is to the Christian conception of faith. He says: "The theologians have often observed the paradoxical character of this ability to trust, at least so far as the inception of faith is concerned. It has often been asked how the individual can come to believe at all if faith is the gift of God and is not to be won through human effort, and how faith can be demanded if it is outside the limit of human capacity. The question has often been left unanswered because the theologians have failed to see that this is a problem which is not peculiar to Christianity, but which belongs to the fundamental structure of our natural Being." [30]

Christian faith, properly understood, would seem to be identical with natural self-commitment. "Since it offers the true understanding of Being, philosophy emancipates natural self-commitment and enables it to become what it was meant to be." [31] Thus it has no need of any revelation.

---

30 P. 321.

31 P. 326.

Christian love, through which faith operates, is open to a similar interpretation. It is equivalent to committing ourselves to our familiar surroundings. Indeed, Kamlah thinks he can correct the New Testament at this point. As he sees it, the Christian conception of love interrupts what he calls the smooth flow of history. It infringes the priority of the immediate environment in which we have been placed by history. It dissipates love by universalizing it instead of directing it to our true neighbours, those who are nigh to us. Kamlah would have us see as our neighbours those who are tied to us by the inexorable bonds of history. In this way he would emancipate the true naturalness of man.[32]

But is it really true that in the last resort the New Testament means by faith the natural disposition of man? Clearly "natural" in this context means not "empirical" but "proper to man's authentic Being". This Being has first to be set free. But according to Kamlah this does not require revelation. All that is necessary is philosophical reflection. Is faith in this sense the natural disposition of man?

Yes and no. Yes, because faith is not a mysterious supernatural quality, but the disposition of genuine humanity. Similarly, love is not the effect of mysterious supernatural power, but the "natural" disposition of man. The New Testament goes part of the way with Kamlah when it calls man-in-faith a "new creation". Its implication is that by faith man enters upon the life for which he was originally created.

The question is not whether the nature of man can be *discovered* apart from the New Testament. As a matter of fact it has not been discovered without the aid of the New Testament, for modern philosophy is indebted both to it and to Luther and to Kierkegaard. But this merely indicates the place of existentialism in the intellectual history of man, and as far as its content is concerned it owes little to its historical

32 P. 337.

origin. On the contrary, the very fact that it is possible to produce a secularized version of the New Testament conception of faith proves that there is nothing mysterious or supernatural about the Christian life.

No; the question is whether the "nature" of man is realizable. Is it enough simply to show man what he ought to be? Can he achieve his authentic Being by a mere act of reflection? It is clear that philosophy, no less than theology, has always taken it for granted that man has to a greater or lesser degree erred and gone astray, or at least that he is always in danger of so doing. Even the idealists try to show us what we *really* are—namely, that we are really spirit, and that it is therefore wrong to lose ourselves in the world of things. Become what you are! For Heidegger man has lost his individuality, and therefore he invites him to recover his true selfhood. Kamlah again realizes that what he calls "genuine historical existence" may lie hidden and buried beneath the rubble of unreality, and that this is especially the case to-day when we are suffering from the after-effects of the Enlightenment. Kamlah also is aware that self-commitment is not the natural disposition of modern man, but a demand continually imposed upon him from without. There can be no emancipation without obedience.[33]

At the same time, however, these philosophers are convinced that all we need is to be told about the "nature" of man in order to realize it. "Since it is the true understanding of Being, philosophy emancipates that self-commitment which is proper to man and enables it to attain to its full stature" [34]—evidently, that means: it emancipates man for true self-commitment. Philosophy seeks to "liberate" [35] the true naturalness of man.

Is this self-confidence of the philosophers justified? Whatever the answer may be, it is at least clear that this is the point

33 P. 403.

34 P. 326.

35 P. 337.

where they part company with the New Testament. For the latter affirms the total incapacity of man to release himself from his fallen state. That deliverance can come only by an act of God. The New Testament does not give us a doctrine of "nature", a doctrine of the authentic nature of man; it proclaims the event of redemption which was wrought in Christ.

That is why the New Testament says that without this saving act of God our plight is desperate, an assertion which existentialism repudiates. What lies behind this difference?

The philosophers and the New Testament agree that man can be only what he already is. For instance, the idealists believed that the life of the spirit was possible only because they regarded man as essentially spirit. Become what you *are!* Similarly Heidegger can summon us to the resolve to exist as selves in face of death because he opens our eyes to our situation as one of "thrownness" [36] into Nothing. Man has to undertake to be what he already is. Similarly it is reasonable for Kamlah to invite us to emancipate ourselves by an act of self-commitment, because he sees that our empirical life is already a life of self-commitment—we are already members of society, we already receive its benefits and contribute to its maintenance.

The New Testament also sees that man can be only what he already is. St. Paul exhorts Christians to be holy because they have already been made holy (1 Cor. 6. 11, cp. 5. 7), and to walk in the Spirit because they are already in the spirit (Gal. 5. 25), and to mortify sin because they are already dead unto sin (Rom. 6. 11ff.); or in Johannine language, because they are not "of the world" (*tou chosmou,* John 17. 16); they can overcome the world, and because they are born of God they do not sin (1 John 3. 9). Eschatological existence is an attainable ideal because "the fulness of time has come" and God has

---

36 *Geworfenheit:* see "Existence and Being" Vision Press, 1949, p. 49f. (Translator).

sent his Son "that he might deliver us out of this present evil world" (Gal. 4. 4; 1. 4).

Thus the New Testament and the philosophers agree that the authentic life is possible only because in some sense it is already a present possession. But there is one difference—the New Testament speaks only to Christian believers, only to those who have opened their hearts to the redemptive action of God. It never speaks thus to natural man, for he does not possess life, and *his* plight is one of despair.

Why does the New Testament take this line? Because it knows that man can become only what he already is, and it sees that natural man, man apart from Christ, is not as he ought to be—he is not alive, but dead.

The point at issue is how we understand the fall. Even the philosophers are agreed about the fact of it. But they think that all man needs is to be shown his plight, and that then he will be able to escape from it. In other words, the corruption resulting from the fall does not extend to the core of the human personality. The New Testament, on the other hand, regards the fall as total.

How then, if the fall be total, can man be aware of his plight? He certainly is aware of it, as the philosophers themselves testify. How can man be aware that his fall is total and that it extends to the very core of his personality? As a matter of fact, it is the other way round: it is only because man is a fallen being, only because he knows he is not what he really ought to be and what he would like to be, that he can be aware of his plight. That awareness of his authentic nature is essential to human life, and without it man would not be man. But his authentic nature is not an endowment of creation or a possession at his own disposal. The philosophers would agree thus far, for they also know that man's authentic nature has to be apprehended by a deliberate resolve. But they think that all man needs is to be told about his authentic nature. This nature is what he never realizes, but what at every moment he is capable of realizing—you can because you ought. But the philosophers are confusing a theoretical possibility with an actual one. For, as the New Testament sees it, man has lost that actual possibility, and even his awareness of his authentic manhood is perverted, as is shown by his deluded belief that it is a possession he can command at will.

Why then has the fall destroyed this actual possibility? The answer is that in his present plight every impulse of man is the impulse of a fallen being. St. Paul demonstrates this in the case of the Jews. In their search for righteousness they missed the very object of their quest. They looked for justification from their own works; they wanted to have a ground for glorying before God. Here is a perfect illustration of the plight of man, of his bondage to the flesh, which the Jews were trying so frantically to escape. This bondage leads to self-glorying and self-assertion, to a desperate attempt to control our own destiny. If the authentic life of man is one of self-commitment, then that life is missed not only by the blatantly self-assertive but also by those who try to achieve self-commitment by their own efforts. They fail to see that self-commitment can be received only as a gift from God.

The glorying of the Jew over his faithfulness to the law and the glorying of the Gnostic in his wisdom are both illustrations of the dominant attitude of man, of his independence and autonomy which lead in the end to frustration. We find the same thing in idealism with its *deus in nobis:*

> Lay hold on divinity; make it your own:
> Down it will climb from its heavenly throne.

In Heidegger's case the perversity of such an attitude is less obvious because he does not characterize resolve as self-commitment. But it is clear that the shouldering of the accident of his destiny in the facing of death is really the same radical self-assertion on man's part. Kamlah is relatively nearer to the Christian position when he asserts that the commandment of self-commitment is capable of fulfilment because God grants an understanding of himself[37] or because "Reality" makes self-commitment possible to man by disclosing its own meaning to him,[38] or because self-commitment receives an indication of its own intelligibility from "Reality" itself.[39] But to assert the intelligibility of Reality is to my mind a counsel of despair. Is it not a desperate act of self-assertion when Kamlah says: "It is not possible to doubt altogether in the intelligibility of Reality"?[40] This surely goes to prove that the only reasonable attitude for man to adopt apart from Christ is one of despair, to despair of the possibility of his ever achieving authentic Being.

This at any rate is what the New Testament asserts. Of course it cannot prove its case any more than the philosophers can prove the intelligibility of Reality. It is a matter for decision. The New Testament addresses man as one who is through and through a self-assertive rebel who knows from bitter experience that the life he actually lives is not his authentic life, and that he is totally incapable of achieving that life by his own efforts. In short, he is a totally fallen being.

This means, in the language of the New Testament, that man is a sinner. The self-assertion of which we have spoken is identical with sin. Sin is self-assertion, self-glorying, for "No flesh should glory before God. . . . He that glorieth, let him glory in the Lord" (1 Cor. 1. 29, 31; 2 Cor. 10. 17). Is that no more than an unnecessary mythologizing of an ontological proposition? Can man as he is perceive that self-assertion involves guilt, and that he is personally responsible to God for it? Is sin a mythological concept or not? The answer will depend on what we make of St. Paul's words to the

37 Pp. 341, 353.

38 P. 298.

39 P. 336.

40 P. 358.

Corinthians: "What hast thou that thou didst not receive? but if thou didst receive it, why dost thou glory, as if thou hadst not received it?" (1 Cor. 4. 7). Does this apply to all men alike, or only to Christians? This much at any rate is clear: self-assertion is guilt only if it can be understood as ingratitude. If the radical self-assertion which makes it impossible for man to achieve the authentic life of self-commitment is identical with sin, it must obviously be possible for man to understand his existence altogether as a gift of God. But it is just this radical self-assertion which makes such an understanding impossible. For self-assertion deludes man into thinking that his existence is a prize within his own grasp. How blind man is to his plight is illustrated by that pessimism which regards life as a burden thrust on man against his will, or by the way men talk about the "right to live" or by the way they expect their fair share of good fortune. Man's radical self-assertion then blinds him to the fact of sin, and this is the clearest proof that he is a fallen being. Hence it is no good telling man that he is a sinner. He will only dismiss it as mythology. But it does not follow that he is right.

Sin ceases to be mere mythology when the love of God meets man as a power which embraces and sustains him even in his fallen, self-assertive state. Such a love treats man as if he were other than he is. By so doing, love frees man from himself as he is.

For as a result of his self-assertion man is a totally fallen being. He is capable of knowing that his authentic life consists in self-commitment, but is incapable of realizing it because however hard he tries he still remains what he is, self-assertive man. So in practice authentic life becomes possible only when man is delivered from himself. It is the claim of the New Testament that this is exactly what has happened. This is precisely the meaning of that which was wrought in Christ. At the very point where man can do nothing, God steps in and acts—indeed he has acted already—on man's behalf.

St. Paul is endeavouring to express this when he speaks of the expiation of sin, or of "righteousness" created as a gift of God rather than as a human achievement. Through Christ, God has reconciled the world to himself, not reckoning to it its trespasses (2 Cor. 5. 19). God made Christ to be sin for us, that we through him might stand before God as righteous (2 Cor. 5. 21). For everyone who believes, his past life is dead and done with. He is a new creature, and as such he faces each new moment. In short, he has become a free man.

It is quite clear from this that forgiveness of sins is not a juridical concept. It does not mean the remission of punishment.[41] If that were so, man's plight would be as bad as ever. Rather, forgiveness conveys freedom from sin, which hitherto had held man in bondage. But this freedom is not a static quality: it is freedom *to obey.* The indicative implies an imperative. Love is the fulfilment of the law, and therefore the forgiveness of God delivers man from himself and makes him free to devote his life to the service of others (Rom. 13. 8–10; Gal. 5. 14).

Thus eschatological existence has become possible. God has *acted,* and the world—"this world"—has come to an end. *Man himself has been made new.* "If any man is in Christ, he is a new creature: the old things are passed away; behold, they are become new" (2 Cor. 5. 17). So much for St. Paul. St. John makes the same point in his own particular language. The knowledge of the "truth" as it is revealed in Jesus makes men free (8. 32), free from the bondage of sin (8. 34). Jesus calls the dead to life (5. 25) and gives sight to the blind (9. 39). The believer in Christ is "born again" (3. 3ff.); he is given a fresh start in life. He is no longer a worldling, for he has overcome the world through faith (1 John 5. 4).

---

41 It is worth noting that St. Paul never uses the term *aphesis ton hamartian,* though it reappears in the deutero-Pauline literature; see e.g. Col. 1, 14; Eph. 1. 7.

The event of Jesus Christ is therefore the revelation of the love of God. It makes a man free from himself and free to be himself, free to live a life of self-commitment in faith and love. But faith in this sense of the word is possible only where it takes the form of faith in the love of God. Yet such faith is still a subtle form of self-assertion so long as the love of God is merely a piece of wishful thinking. It is only an abstract idea so long as God has not revealed his love. That is why faith for the Christian means faith in Christ, for it is faith in the love of God revealed in Christ. Only those who are loved are capable of loving. Only those who have received confidence as a gift can show confidence in others. Only those who know what self-commitment is by experience can adopt that attitude themselves. We are free to give ourselves to God because he has given up himself for us. "Herein is love, not that we loved God, but that he loved us, and sent his Son to be the propitiation for our sins" (1 John 4. 10). "We love, because he first loved us." (1 John 4. 19).

The classic statement of this self-commitment of God, which is the ground of our own self-commitment, is to be found in Rom. 8. 32: "God spared not his Son, but delivered him up for us; how shall he not also with him freely give us all things?" Compare the Johannine text: "God so loved the world, that he gave his only-begotten Son, that whosoever believeth in him should not perish, but have eternal life" (John 3. 16). There are also similar texts which speak of Jesus' giving up himself for us: ". . . who gave himself for our sins, that he might deliver us out of this present evil world" (Gal. 1. 4); "I have been crucified with Christ; yet I live; and yet no longer I, but Christ liveth in me: and the life which I live in the flesh I live in faith, the faith which is in the Son of God, who loved me and gave himself up for me" (Gal. 2. 19f.).

Here then is the crucial distinction between the New Testament and existentialism, between the Christian faith and the natural understanding of Being. The New Testament speaks and faith knows of an act of God through which man becomes capable of self-commitment, capable of faith and love, of his authentic life.

Have we carried our demythologizing far enough? Are we still left with a myth, or at least an event which bears a mythical character? It is possible, as we have seen, to restate in non-mythological terms the New Testament teaching on human existence apart from faith and in faith. But what of the point of transition between the old life and the new, authentic life? Can it be understood otherwise than as an act of God? Is faith genuine only when it is faith in the love of God revealed in Christ?

2. *The Event of Jesus Christ*

Anyone who asserts that to speak of an act of God at all is mythological language is bound to regard the idea of an act of God in Christ as a myth. But let us ignore this question for a moment. Even Kamlah thinks it philosophically justifiable to use "the mythological language of an act of God" (p. 353). The issue for the moment is whether that particular event in which the New Testament sees the act of God and the revelation of his love—that is, the event of Jesus Christ—is essentially a mythical event.

(a) The Demythologizing of the Event of Jesus Christ

Now, it is beyond question that the New Testament presents the event of Jesus Christ in mythical terms. The problem is whether that is the only possible presentation. Or does the New Testament itself demand a restatement of the event of Jesus Christ in non-mythological terms? Now, it is clear from the outset that the event of Christ is of a wholly different order from the cult-myths of Greek or Hellenistic religion. Jesus Christ is certainly presented as the Son of God, a pre-existent divine being, and therefore to that extent a mythical figure. But he is also a concrete figure of history—Jesus of Nazareth. His life is more than a mythical event; it is a human life which ended in the tragedy of crucifixion. We have here a unique combination of history and myth. The New Testament claims that this Jesus of history, whose father and mother were well known to his contemporaries (John 6. 42) is at the same time the pre-existent Son of God, and side by side with the historical event of the crucifixion it sets the definitely non-historical event of the resurrection. This combination of myth and history presents a number of difficulties, as can be seen from certain inconsistencies in the New Testament material. The doctrine of Christ's pre-existence as given by St. Paul and St. John is difficult to reconcile with the legend of the Virgin birth in St. Matthew and St. Luke. On the one hand we hear that "he emptied himself, taking the form of a servant, being made in the likeness of men: and being found in fashion as a man . . ." (Phil. 2. 7), and on the other hand we have the gospel portraits of a Jesus who manifests his divinity in his miracles, omniscience, and mysterious elusiveness, and the similar description of him in Acts as "Jesus of Nazareth, a man approved of God unto you by mighty works and wonders and signs" (Acts 2. 22). On the one hand we have the resurrection as the exaltation of Jesus from the cross or grave, and on the other the legends of the empty tomb and the ascension.

We are compelled to ask whether all this mythological language is not simply an attempt to express the meaning of the historical figure of Jesus and the events of his life; in other words, significance of these as a figure and event of salvation. If that be so, we can dispense with the objective form in which they are cast.

It is easy enough to deal with the doctrine of Christ's pre-existence and the legend of the Virgin birth in this way. They are clearly attempts to explain the meaning of the Person of Jesus for faith. The facts which historical criticism can verify cannot exhaust, indeed they cannot adequately indicate, all that Jesus means to me. How he actually originated matters little, indeed we can appreciate his significance only when we cease to worry about such questions. Our interest in the events of his life, and above all in the cross, is more than an academic concern with the history of the past. We can see meaning in them only when we ask what God is trying to say to each one of us through them. Again, the figure of Jesus cannot be understood simply from his context in human evolution or history. In mythological language, this means that he stems from eternity, his origin transcends both history and nature.

We shall not, however, pursue the examination of the particular incidents of his life any further. In the end the crux of the matter lies in the cross and resurrection.

(b) The Cross

Is the cross, understood as the event of redemption, exclusively mythical in character, or can it retain its value for salvation without forfeiting its character as history?

It certainly has a mythical character as far as its objective setting is concerned. The Jesus who was crucified was the pre-existent, incarnate Son of God, and as such he was without sin. He is the victim whose blood atones for our sins. He bears vicariously the sin of the world, and by enduring the punishment for sin on our behalf he delivers us from death. This mythological interpretation is a hotch-potch of sacrificial and juridical analogies, which have ceased to be tenable for us to-day. And in any case they fail to do justice to what the New Testament is trying to say. For the most they can convey is that the cross effects the forgiveness of all the past and future sins of man, in the sense that the punishment they deserved has been remitted. But the New Testament means more than this. The cross releases men not only from the guilt, but also from the power of sin. That is why, when the author of

Colossians says "He [God] . . . having forgiven us all our trespasses, having blotted out the bond written in ordinances that was against us, which was contrary to us; and he hath taken it out of the way, nailing it to the cross" he hastens to add: "having put off from himself the principalities and powers, he made a show of them openly, triumphing over them in it" (Col. 2. 13–15).

The historical event of the cross acquires cosmic dimensions and so its full significance is brought into sharper relief. For if we see in the cross the judgement of the world and the defeat of the rulers of this world (1 Cor. 2. 6ff.), the cross becomes the judgement of ourselves as fallen creatures enslaved to the powers of the "world".

By giving up Jesus to be crucified, God has set up the cross for us. To believe in the cross of Christ does not mean to concern ourselves with a mythical process wrought outside of us and our world, or with an objective event turned by God to our advantage, but rather to make the cross of Christ our own, to undergo crucifixion with him. The cross in its redemptive aspect is not an isolated incident which befell a mythical personage, but an event of "cosmic" importance. Its decisive, revolutionary significance is brought out by the eschatological framework in which it is set. In other words, the cross is not just an event of the past which can be contemplated in detachment, but the eschatological event in and beyond time, for as far as its meaning—that is, its meaning for faith—is concerned, it is an ever-present reality.

The cross becomes a present reality in the sacraments. In baptism men and women are baptized into Christ's death (Rom. 6. 3) and crucified with him (Rom. 6. 6). At every celebration of the Lord's Supper the death of Christ is proclaimed (1 Cor. 11. 26). The communicants thereby partake of his crucified body and his blood outpoured (1 Cor. 10. 16). Again, the cross of Christ is an ever-present reality in the everyday life of the Christians. "They that are of Christ Jesus have crucified the flesh with the passions and the lusts thereof" (Gal. 5. 24). That is why St. Paul can speak of "the cross of our Lord Jesus Christ, through which the world hath been crucified unto me, and I unto the world" (Gal. 6. 14). That is why he seeks to know "the fellowship of his sufferings", as one who is "conformed to his death" (Phil. 3. 10).

The crucifying of the affections and lusts includes the overcoming of our natural dread of suffering and the perfection of our detachment from the world. Hence the willing acceptance of sufferings in which death is already at work in man means: "always bearing about in our body the dying of Jesus" and "always being delivered unto death for Jesus' sake" (2 Cor. 4. 10f.).

Thus the cross and passion are ever-present realities. How little they are confined to the events of the first Good Friday is amply illustrated by the words which a disciple of St. Paul puts into his master's mouth: "Now I rejoice in my sufferings for your sake, and fill up on my part that which is lacking of the afflictions of Christ in my flesh for his body's sake, which is the Church" (Col. 1. 24).

In its redemptive aspect the cross of Christ is no mere mythical event, but a permanent historical fact originating in the past historical event which is the crucifixion of Jesus. The abiding significance of the cross is that it is the judgement of the world, the judgement and the deliverance of man. In this sense Christ is crucified "for us", a phrase which does not necessarily imply any theory of sacrifice or satisfaction. This interpretation of the cross as a permanent fact rather than a mythological event does far more justice to the redemptive significance of the event of the past than any of the traditional interpretations. In the last resort mythological language is only a medium for conveying the meaning of the past event. The real meaning of the cross is that it has created a new and permanent situation in history. The preaching of the cross as the event of redemption challenges all who hear it to appropriate the significance for themselves, to be willing to be crucified with Christ.

But, it will be asked, is this significance to be discerned in the actual event of past history? Can it, so to speak, be read off from that event? Or does the cross bear this significance because it is the cross of *Christ?* In other words, must we first be convinced of the significance of Christ and believe in him in order to discern the real meaning of the cross? If we are to perceive the real meaning of the cross, must we understand it as the cross of Jesus as a figure of past history? Must we go back to the Jesus of history?

As far as the first preachers of the gospel are concerned this will certainly be the case. For them the cross was the cross of him with whom they had lived in personal intercourse. The cross was an experience of their own lives. It presented them with a question and it disclosed to them its meaning. But for us this personal connection cannot be reproduced. For us the cross cannot disclose its own meaning: it is an event of the past. We can never recover it as an event in our own lives. All we know of it is derived from historical report. But the New Testament does not proclaim Jesus Christ in this way. The meaning of the cross is not disclosed from the life of Jesus as a figure of past history, a life which needs to be reproduced by historical research. On the contrary, Jesus is not proclaimed merely as the crucified; he is also risen from the dead. The cross and the resurrection form an inseparable unity.

(c) The Resurrection

But what of the resurrection? Is it not a mythical event pure and simple? Obviously it is not an event of past history with a self-evident meaning. Can the resurrection narratives and every other mention of the resurrection in the New Testament be understood simply as an attempt to convey the meaning of the cross? Does the New Testament, in asserting that

Jesus is risen from the dead, mean that his death is not just an ordinary human death, but the judgement and salvation of the world, depriving death of its power? Does it not express this truth in the affirmation that the Crucified was not holden of death, but rose from the dead?

Yes indeed: the cross and the resurrection form a single, indivisible cosmic event. "He was delivered up for our trespasses, and was raised for our justification" (Rom. 4. 25). The cross is not an isolated event, as though it were the end of Jesus, which needed the resurrection subsequently to reverse it. When he suffered death, Jesus was already the Son of God, and his death by itself was the victory over the power of death. St. John brings this out most clearly by describing the passion of Jesus as the "hour" in which he is glorified, and by the double meaning he gives to the phrase "lifted up", applying it both to the cross and to Christ's exaltation into glory.

Cross and resurrection form a single, indivisible cosmic event which brings judgement to the world and opens up for men the possibility of authentic life. But if that be so, the resurrection cannot be a miraculous proof capable of demonstration and sufficient to convince the sceptic that the cross really has the cosmic and eschatological significance ascribed to it.

Yet it cannot be denied that the resurrection of Jesus is often used in the New Testament as a miraculous proof. Take for instance Acts 17. 31. Here we are actually told that God substantiated the claims of Christ by raising him from the dead. Then again the resurrection narratives: both the legend of the empty tomb and the appearances insist on the physical reality of the risen body of the Lord (see especially Luke 24. 39–43). But these are most certainly later embellishments of the primitive tradition. St. Paul knows nothing about them. There is however one passage where St. Paul tries to prove the miracle of the resurrection by adducing a list of eye-witnesses (1 Cor. 15. 3–8). But this is a dangerous procedure, as Karl Barth has involuntarily shown. Barth seeks to explain away the real meaning of 1 Cor. 15 by contending that the list of eye-witnesses was put in not to prove the fact of the resurrection, but to prove that the preaching of the apostle was, like the preaching of the first Christians, the preaching of Jesus as the risen Lord. The eye-witnesses therefore guarantee St. Paul's preaching, not the fact of the resurrection. An historical fact which involves a resurrection from the dead is utterly inconceivable!

Yes indeed: the resurrection of Jesus cannot be a miraculous proof by which the sceptic might be compelled to believe in Christ. The difficulty is not simply the incredibility of a mythical event like the resuscitation of a corpse—for that is what the resurrection means, as is shown by the fact that the risen Lord is apprehended by the physical senses. Nor is it merely the difficulty of establishing the objective historicity of the resurrection no matter how many witnesses are cited, as though once it was established it might be believed beyond all question and faith might have its unimpeachable guarantee. No; the real difficulty is that the resurrection is itself an article of faith, and you cannot establish one article of faith by invoking another. You cannot prove the redemptive efficacy of the cross by invoking the resurrection. For the resurrection is an article of faith because it is far more than the resuscitation of a corpse —it is the eschatological event. And so it cannot be a miraculous proof. For, quite apart from its credibility, the bare miracle tells us nothing about the eschatological fact of the destruction of death. Moreover, such a miracle is not otherwise unknown to mythology.

It is however abundantly clear that the New Testament is interested in the resurrection of Christ simply and solely because it is the eschatological event *par excellence*. By it Christ abolished death and brought life and immortality to light (2 Tim. 1. 10). This explains why St. Paul borrows Gnostic language to clarify the meaning of the resurrection. As in the death of Jesus all have died (2 Cor. 5. 14f.), so through his resurrection all have been raised from the dead, though naturally this event is spread over a long period of time (1 Cor. 15. 21f.). But St Paul does not only say: "In Christ shall all be made alive"; he can also speak of rising again with Christ in the present tense, just as he speaks of our dying with him. Through the sacrament of baptism Christians participate not only in the death of Christ but also in his resurrection. It is not simply that we *shall* walk with him in newness of life and be united with him in his resurrection (Rom. 6. 4f.); we are doing so already here and now. "Even so reckon ye yourselves to be dead indeed unto sin, but alive unto God in Jesus Christ" (Rom. 6. 11).

Once again, in everyday life the Christians participate not only in the death of Christ but also in his resurrection. In this resurrection-life they enjoy a freedom, albeit a struggling freedom, from sin (Rom. 6. 11ff.). They are able to "cast off the works of darkness", so that the approaching day when the darkness shall vanish is already experienced here and now. "Let us walk honestly as in the day" (Rom. 13. 12f.): "we are not of the night, nor of the darkness. . . . Let us, since we are of the day, be sober . . . (1 Thess. 5. 5–8). St. Paul seeks to share not only the sufferings of Christ but also "the power of his resurrection" (Phil. 3. 10). So he bears about in his body the dying of Jesus, "that the life also of Jesus may be manifested in our body" (2 Cor. 4. 10f.). Similarly, when the Corinthians demand a proof of his apostolic authority, he solemnly warns them: "Christ is not weak, but is powerful in you: for he was crucified in weakness, yet he liveth in the power of God. For we also are weak ın him, but we shall live with him through the power of God toward you" (2 Cor. 13. 3f.).

In this way the resurrection is not a mythological event adduced in order to prove the saving efficacy of the cross, but an article of faith just as much as the meaning of the cross itself. Indeed, *faith in the resurrection is really the same thing as faith in the saving efficacy of the cross,* faith in the cross as the cross of Christ. Hence you cannot first believe in Christ and then in the strength of that faith believe in the cross. To believe in Christ means to believe in the cross as the cross of Christ. The saving efficacy of the cross is not derived from the fact that it is the cross of Christ: it is the cross of Christ because it has this saving efficacy. Without that efficacy it is the tragic end of a great man.

We are back again at the old question. How do we come to believe in the cross as the cross of Christ and as the eschatological event *par excellence?* How do we come to believe in the saving efficacy of the cross?

There is only one answer. This is the way in which the cross is proclaimed. It is always proclaimed together with the resurrection. Christ meets us in the preaching as one crucified and risen. He meets us in the word of preaching and nowhere else. The faith of Easter is just this–faith in the word of preaching.

It would be wrong at this point to raise again the problem of how this preaching arose historically, as though that could vindicate its truth. That would be to tie our faith in the word of God to the results of historical research. The word of preaching confronts us as the word of God. It is not for us to question its credentials. It is we who are questioned, we who are asked whether we will believe the word or reject it. But in answering this question, in accepting the word of preaching as the word of God and the death and resurrection of Christ as the eschatological event, we are given an opportunity of understanding ourselves. Faith and unbelief are never blind, arbitrary decisions. They offer us the alternative between accepting or rejecting that which alone can illuminate our understanding of ourselves.

The real Easter faith is faith in the word of preaching which brings illumination. If the event of Easter Day is in any sense an historical event additional to the event of the cross, it is nothing else than the rise of faith in the risen Lord, since it was this faith which led to the apostolic preaching. The resurrection itself is not an event of past history. All that historical criticism can establish is the fact that the first disciples came to believe in the resurrection. The historian can perhaps to some extent account for that faith from the personal intimacy which the disciples had enjoyed with Jesus during his earthly life, and so reduce the resurrection appearances to a series of subjective visions. But the historical problem is scarcely relevant to Christian belief in the resurrection. For the historical event of the rise of the Easter faith means for us what it meant for the first disciples—namely, the self-manifestation of the risen Lord, the act of God in which the redemptive event of the cross is completed.[42]

We cannot buttress our own faith in the resurrection by that of the first disciples and so eliminate the element of risk which faith in the resurrection always involves. For the first disciples' faith in the resurrection is itself part and parcel of the eschatological event which is the article of faith.

In other words, the apostolic preaching which originated in the event of Easter Day is itself a part of the eschatological event of redemption. The death of Christ, which is both the judgement and the salvation of the world, inaugurates the "ministry of reconciliation" or "word of reconciliation" (2 Cor. 5. 18f.). This word supplements the cross and makes its saving efficacy intelligible by demanding faith and confronting men with the question whether they are willing to understand themselves as men who are crucified and risen with Christ. Through the word of preaching the cross and the resurrection are made present: the eschatological "now" is here, and the promise of Isa. 49. 8 is fulfilled: "Behold, now is the acceptable time; behold, now is the day of salvation" (2 Cor. 6. 2). That is

42 This and the following paragraphs are also intended as an answer to the doubts and suspicions which Paul Althaus has raised against me in *Die Wahrheit des kirchlichen Osterglaubens,* 1941, p. 90ff. Cf. also my discussion of Emanuel Hirsch's "Die Auferstehungsgeschichten und der christliche Glaube", 1940, in *Theol. Lit.-Ztg.,* 1940, pp. 242-6.

why the apostolic preaching brings judgement. For some the apostle is "a saviour from death unto death" and for others a "saviour from life unto life" (2 Cor. 2. 16). St. Paul is the agent through whom the resurrection life becomes effective in the faithful (2 Cor. 4. 12). The promise of Jesus in the Fourth Gospel is eminently applicable to the preaching in which he is proclaimed: "Verily I say unto you, He that heareth my words and believeth on him that sent me, hath eternal life, and cometh not unto judgement, but hath passed out of death into life. . . . The hour cometh and now is, when the dead shall hear the voice of the Son of God; and they that hear shall live" (John 5. 24f.). In the word of preaching and there alone we meet the risen Lord. "So belief cometh of hearing, and hearing by the word of Christ" (Rom. 10. 17).

Like the word itself and the apostle who proclaims it, so the Church where the preaching of the word is continued and where the believers or "saints" (i.e., those who have been transferred to eschatological existence) are gathered is part of the eschatological event. The word "Church" (*ecclêsia*) is an eschatological term, while its designation as the Body of Christ emphasizes its cosmic significance. For the Church is not just a phenomenon of secular history, it is phenomenon of significant history, in the sense that it realizes itself in history.

Conclusion

We have now outlined a programme for the demythologizing of the New Testament. Are there still any surviving traces of mythology? There certainly are for those who regard all language about an act of God or of a decisive, eschatological event as mythological. But this is not mythology in the traditional sense, not the kind of mythology which has become antiquated with the decay of the mythical world view. For the redemption of which we have spoken is not a miraculous supernatural event, but an historical event wrought out in time and space.

We are convinced that this restatement does better justice to the real meaning of the New Testament and to the paradox of the kerygma. For the kerygma maintains that the eschatological emissary of God is a concrete figure of a particular historical past, that his eschatological activity was wrought out in a human fate, and that therefore it is an event whose eschatological character does not admit of a secular proof. Here we have the paradox of Phil. 2. 7: "He emptied himself"; of 2 Cor. 8. 9: ". . . though he was rich, yet for your sakes he became poor"; of Rom. 8. 3: "God, sending his Son in the likeness of sinful flesh"; of 1 Tim. 3. 16: "He was manifested in the flesh"; and above all of the classic formula of John 1. 14: "The Word became flesh."

The agent of God's presence and activity, the mediator of his reconciliation of the world unto himself, is a real figure of history. Similarly the word of God is not some mysterious oracle, but a sober, factual account of a human life, of Jesus of Nazareth, possessing saving efficacy for man. Of course the kerygma may be regarded as part of the story of man's spiritual evolution and used as a basis for a tenable *Weltanschauung*. Yet this proclamation claims to be the eschatological word of God.

The apostles who proclaim the word may be regarded merely as figures of past history, and the Church as a sociological and historical phenomenon, part of the history of man's spiritual evolution. Yet both are eschatological phenomena and eschatological events.

All these assertions are an offence (*skandalon*), which will not be removed by philosophical discussion, but only by faith and obedience. All these are phenomena subject to historical, sociological and psychological observation, yet for faith they are all of them eschatological phenomena. It is precisely its immunity from proof which secures the Christian proclamation against the charge of being mythological. The transcendence of God is not as in myth reduced to immanence. Instead, we have the paradox of a transcendent God present and active in history: "The Word became flesh".

Other books by Rudolph Bultmann:

Jesus and the Word, 1934.
Jesus Christ and Mythology, 1958.
The Presence of Eternity (Gifford Lectures, 1955), 1957.
Primitive Christianity in its Contemporary Setting, 1956.
The Theology of the New Testament, 1951–55.

Other books on the same problem:

Bartsch, Hans Werner. *Kerygma and Myth; a Theological Debate,* 1957.
Dillistone, F. W. *Christianity and Symbolism,* 1955.
Jaspers, Karl and Rudolph Bultmann. *Myth and Christianity: an Inquiry into the Possibility of Religion without Myth,* 1953 (Engl. trans. 1958).
Jaspers, Karl. *Truth and Symbol,* trans. from *Von der Wahrheit,* 1959.
Macquarrie, John. *An Existentialist Theology,* 1955.
Minnear, Paul S. *Eyes of Faith,* 1946.
Tillich, Paul. *The Religious Situation,* 1932.

II. THE DYNAMICS OF CREATIVITY

4. The Holiness of the Holy: Rudolph Otto
   from *The Idea of the Holy*

5. The Distortion of the Holy: Feodor Dostoievsky
   from *The Brothers Karamazov*

6. Creativity and the Spirit: Nicholas Berdyaev
   from *The Beginning and the End* and *The Meaning of the Creative Act*

> "*. . . for the Spirit searcheth all things, yea, the deep things of God.*"
>
> *I Corinthians 2: 12.*

The doctrine of the Trinity seeks to comprehend the mystery of creativity within the Godhead itself in terms of the interrelationship between Father, Son and Holy Spirit as designations for phases in the action of divine creativity. Enlightened rationalism and humanistic liberalism had reduced God the Father to a philosophical concept—the Absolute, God the Son to the ethical teacher Jesus—a superior example of human moral excellence, and the Holy Spirit to a principle of evolutionary development in nature and of moral growth in man.

From this pursuit of a religion "within the limits of reason" man became the measure of God. But, if God is a philosophical concept and the religious life equated with moral striving, then the specifically religious has disappeared, and with it the need for religion.

In protest against this shallow and empty concept of God the three "prophets" in Part II of our anthology, like the authors of Job and of the apocalyptic books, seek to penetrate into the mysteries of Creativity itself and, in the light of God's self-manifestation in the career of Christ, to free the mind for a consciousness of the ungraspable magnitude, power and purpose of the creative-destructive dynamics in the life of God, man and the universe.

All three possessed in a high degree what has been called "ecstatic reason", reason which reaches out beyond the limits of the finite categories of thought while still not contradicting them. All three use image, metaphor or parable in order to reveal that which eludes the logical categories of conceptualization. All three reveal the inadequacy of intellectual, institutional or ethical categories in the encounter with the creative source of all being (Otto), with the demonic distortions of creative power in individual and institutional life (Dostoievsky), or with the infinite potentiality of freedom and creativity in the historical and cultural destiny of man (Berdyaev).

RUDOLPH OTTO

RUDOLPH OTTO's creative scholarship was directed primarily toward the philosophy of religion. This required a broad and critical examination and comparison of the many and varied forms in which the religious consciousness of mankind has articulated itself, both in the East and in the West. As a consequence he was not only aware of that which was specific and unique in each but also of that which was common to all, even though expressed in diverse forms.

Foremost in this second group is what he calls the "numinous" experience, that is, the experience of the holiness of divinity. A systematic exploration of the dimensions of this experience resulted in his major, now classic, study, *The Idea of the Holy*.

In his concept of the numinous Otto brings into consciousness again that which belongs to religion *sui generis*—an awareness of the "holiness of the Holy" which is experienced in terms of awe, wonder, fascination and terror precisely because it eludes the grasp of philosophical reason and wells out in power and meaning beyond the limits of conceptualization. In this Presence, like Moses before the burning bush and Job in response to the voice out of the whirlwind, man can only lay his hand upon his mouth and proceed no further.

Behind all concepts and images of God is the *mysterium tremendum*, in the presence of which reason falters, the tongue ceases, the creature becomes aware of his creatureliness and religious consciousness is born.

RUDOLPH OTTO

from

THE IDEA OF THE HOLY*

'NUMEN' AND THE 'NUMINOUS'

'HOLINESS'—'THE HOLY'—is a category of interpretation and valuation peculiar to the sphere of religion. It is, indeed, applied by transference to another sphere—that of ethics—but it is not itself derived from this. While it is complex, it contains a quite specific element or 'moment', which sets it apart from 'the rational' in the meaning we gave to that word above, and which remains inexpressible—an *arrêton* or *ineffabile*—in the sense that it completely eludes apprehension in terms of concepts. The same thing is true (to take a quite different region of experience) of the category of the beautiful.

Now these statements would be untrue from the outset if 'the holy' were merely what is meant by the word, not only in common parlance, but in philosophical, and generally even in theological usage. The fact is we have come to use the words 'holy', 'sacred' *(heilig)* in an entirely derivative sense, quite different from that which they originally bore. We generally take 'holy' as meaning 'completely good'; it is the absolute moral attribute, denoting the consummation of moral goodness. In this sense Kant calls the will which remains unwaveringly obedient to the moral law from the motive of duty a 'holy' will; here clearly we have simply the *perfectly moral* will. In the same way we may speak of the holiness or sanctity of duty or law, meaning merely that they are imperative upon conduct and universally obligatory.

But this common usage of the term is inaccurate. It is true that all this moral significance is contained in the word 'holy', but it includes in addition—as even we cannot but

---

* Translated by J. W. Harner, second edition 1950. A Galaxy Book. Reprinted by permission of Oxford University Press.

feel—a clear overplus of meaning, and this it is now our task to isolate. Nor is this merely a later or acquired meaning; rather, 'holy', or at least the equivalent words in Latin and Greek, in Semitic and other ancient languages, denoted first and foremost *only* this overplus: if the ethical element was present at all, at any rate it was not original and never constituted the whole meaning of the word. Any one who uses it to-day does undoubtedly always feel 'the morally good' to be implied in 'holy'; and accordingly in our inquiry into that element which is separate and peculiar to the idea of the holy it will be useful, at least for the temporary purpose of the investigation, to invent a special term to stand for 'the holy' *minus* its moral factor or 'moment', and, as we can now add, minus its 'rational' aspect altogether.

It will be our endeavour to suggest this unnamed Something to the reader as far as we may, so that he may himself feel it. There is no religion in which it does not live as the real innermost core, and without it no religion would be worthy of the name. It is pre-eminently a living force in the Semitic religions, and of these again in none has it such vigour as in that of the Bible. Here, too, it has a name of its own, viz. the Hebrew *qadôsh,* to which the Greek *hagios* and the Latin *sanctus,* and, more accurately still, *sacer,* are the corresponding terms. It is not, of course, disputed that these terms in all three languages connote, as part of their meaning, *good, absolute goodness,* when, that is, the notion has ripened and reached the highest stage in its development. And we then use the word 'holy' to translate them. But this 'holy' then represents the gradual shaping and filling in with ethical meaning, or what we shall call the 'schematization', of what was a unique original feeling-response, which can be in itself ethically neutral and claims consideration in its own right. And when this moment or element first emerges and begins its long development, all those expressions (*quadôsh, hagios, sacer,* &c.) mean beyond all question something quite other than 'the good'. This is universally agreed by contemporary criticism, which rightly explains the rendering of *quadôsh* by 'good' as a mistranslation and unwarranted 'rationalization' or 'moralization' of the term.

Accordingly, it is worth while, as we have said, to find a word to stand for this element in isolation, this 'extra' in the meaning of 'holy' above and beyond the meaning of goodness. By means of a special term we shall the better be able, first, to keep the meaning clearly apart and distinct, and second, to apprehend and classify connectedly whatever subordinate forms or stages of development it may show. For this purpose I adopt a word coined from the Latin *numen*. *Omen* has given us 'ominous', and there is no reason why from *numen* we should not similarly form a word 'numinous'. I shall speak, then, of a unique 'numinous' category of value and of a definitely 'numinous' state of mind, which is always found wherever the category is applied. This mental state is perfectly *sui generis* and irreducible to any other; and therefore, like every absolutely primary and elementary datum, while it admits of being discussed, it cannot be strictly defined. There is only one way to help another to an understanding of it. He must be guided and led on by consideration and discussion of the matter through the ways of his own mind, until he reach the point at which 'the numinous' in him perforce begins to stir, to start into life and into consciousness. We can co-operate in this process by bringing before his notice all that can be found in other regions of the mind, already known and familiar, to resemble, or again to afford some special contrast to, the particular experience we wish to elucidate. Then we must add: 'This *X* of ours is not precisely *this* experience, but akin to this one and the opposite of that other. Cannot you now realize for yourself what it is?' In other words our *X* cannot, strictly speaking, be taught, it can only be evoked, awakened in the mind; as everything that comes 'of the spirit' must be awakened.

THE ELEMENTS IN THE 'NUMINOUS'

Creature-Feeling

The reader is invited to direct his mind to a moment of deeply-felt religious experience, as little as possible qualified by other forms of consciousness. Whoever cannot do this, whoever knows no such moments in his experience, is requested to read no farther; for it is not easy to discuss questions of religious psychology with one who can recollect the emotions of his adolescence, the discomforts of indigestion, or, say, social feelings, but cannot recall any intrinsically religious feelings. We do not blame such an one, when he tries for himself to advance as far as he can with the help of such principles of explanation as he knows, interpreting 'aesthetics' in terms of sensuous pleasure, and 'religion' as a function of the gregarious instinct and social standards, or as something more primitive still. But the artist, who for his part has an intimate personal knowledge of the distinctive element in the aesthetic experience, will decline his theories with thanks, and the religious man will reject them even more uncompromisingly.

Next, in the probing and analysis of such states of the soul as that of solemn worship, it will be well if regard be paid to what is unique in them rather than to what they have in common with other similar states. To be *rapt* in worship is one thing; to be morally *uplifted* by the contemplation of a good deed is another; and it is not to their common features, but to those elements of emotional content peculiar to the first that we would have attention directed as precisely as possible. As Christians we undoubtedly here first meet with feelings familiar enough in a weaker form in other departments of experience, such as feelings of gratitude, trust, love, reliance, humble submission, and dedication. But this does not by any means exhaust the content of religious worship. Not in any of these have we got the special features of the quite unique and incomparable experience of solemn worship. In what does this consist?

Schleiermacher has the credit of isolating a very important element in such an experience. This is the 'feeling of dependence'. But this important discovery of Schleiermacher is open to criticism in more than one respect.

In the first place, the feeling or emotion which he really has in mind in this phrase is in its specific quality not a 'feeling of dependence' in the 'natural' sense of the word. As such, other domains of life and other regions of experience than the religious occasion the feeling, as a sense of personal insufficiency and impotence, a consciousness of being determined by circumstances and environment. The feeling of which Schleiermacher wrote has an undeniable analogy with these states of mind: they serve as an indication to it, and its nature may be elucidated by them, so that, by following the direction in which they point, the feeling itself may be spontaneously felt. But the feeling is at the same time also qualitatively different from such analogous states of mind. Schleiermacher himself, in a way, recognizes this by distinguishing the feeling of pious or religious dependence from all other feelings of dependence. His mistake is in making the distinction merely that between 'absolute' and 'relative' dependence, and therefore a difference of degree and not of intrinsic quality. What he overlooks is that, in giving the feeling the name 'feeling of dependence' at all, we are really employing what is no more than a very close analogy. Anyone who compares and contrasts the two states of mind introspectively will find out, I think, what I mean. It cannot be expressed by means of anything else, just because it is so primary and elementary a datum in our psychical life, and therefore only definable through itself. It may perhaps help him if I cite a well-known example, in which the precise 'moment' or element of religious feeling of which we are speaking is most actively present. When Abraham ventures to plead with God for the men of Sodom, he says (Gen. xviii. 27): 'Behold now, I have taken upon me to speak unto the Lord, which am but dust and ashes.' There you have a self-confessed 'feeling of dependence', which is yet at the same time far more than, and something other than, *merely* a feeling of dependence. Desiring to give it a name of its own, I propose to call it 'creature-consciousness' or creature-feeling. It is the emotion of a creature, submerged and overwhelmed by its own nothingness in contrast to that which is supreme above all creatures.

It is easily seen that, once again, this phrase, whatever it is, is not a *conceptual* explanation of the matter. All that this new term, 'creature-feeling', can express, is the note of submergence into nothingness before an overpowering, absolute might of some kind; whereas everything turns upon the *character* of this overpowering might, a character which cannot be expressed verbally, and can only be suggested indirectly through the tone and content of a man's feeling-response to it. And this response must be directly experienced in oneself to be understood.

We have now to note a second defect in the formulation of Schleiermacher's principle. The religious category discovered by him, by whose means he professes to determine the real content of the religious emotion, is merely a category of *self*-valuation, in the sense of self-depreciation. According to him the religious emotion would be directly and primarily a sort of *self*-consciousness, a feeling concerning oneself in a special, determined relation, viz. one's dependence. Thus, according to Schleiermacher, I can only come upon the very fact of God as the result of an inference, that is, by reasoning to a cause beyond myself to account for my 'feeling of dependence'. But this is entirely opposed to the psychological facts of the case. Rather, the 'creature-feeling' is itself a first subjective concomitant and effect of another feeling-element, which casts it like a shadow, but which in itself indubitably has immediate and primary reference to an object outside the self.[1]

Now this object is just what we have already spoken of as 'the numinous'. For the 'creature-feeling' and the sense of dependence to arise in the mind the 'numen' must be experienced as present, a *numen praesens,* as is in the case of Abraham. There must be felt a something 'numinous', something bearing the character of a 'numen', to which the mind turns spontaneously; or (which is the same thing in other words) these feelings can only arise in the mind as accompanying emotions when the category of 'the numinous' is called into play.

The numinous is thus felt as objective and outside the self. We have now to inquire more closely into its nature and the modes of its manifestation.

---

1 This is so manifestly borne out by experience that it must be about the first thing to force itself upon the notice of psychologists analysing the facts of religion. There is a certain naïveté in the following passage from William James's *Varieties of Religious Experience* (p. 58), where, alluding to the origin of the Grecian representations of the gods, he says: 'As regards the origin of the Greek gods, we need not at present seek an opinion. But the whole array of our instances leads to a conclusion something like this: It is as if there were in the human consciousness *a sense of reality, a feeling of objective presence, a perception* of what we may call *"something there"*, more deep and more general than any of the special and particular "senses" by which the current psychology supposes existent realities to be originally revealed.' (The italics are James's own.) James is debarred by his empiricist and pragmatist standpoint from coming to a recognition of faculties of knowledge and potentialities of thought in the spirit itself, and he is therefore obliged to have recourse to somewhat singular and mysterious hypotheses to explain this fact. But he grasps the fact itself clearly enough and is sufficient of a realist not to explain it away. But this 'feeling of reality', the feeling of a 'numinous' *object* objectively given, must be posited as a primary immediate datum of consciousness, and the 'feeling of dependence' is then a consequence, following very closely upon it, viz. a depreciation of the *subject* in his own eyes. The latter presupposes the former.

'MYSTERIUM TREMENDUM'

The Analysis of 'Tremendum'

We said above that the nature of the numinous can only be suggested by means of the special way in which it is reflected in the mind in terms of feeling. 'Its nature is such that it grips or stirs the human mind with this and that determinate affective state.' We have now to attempt to give a further indication of these determinate states. We must once again endeavour, by adducing feelings akin to them for the purpose of analogy or contrast, and by the use of metaphor and symbolic expressions, to make the states of mind we are investigating ring out, as it were, of themselves.

Let us consider the deepest and most fundamental element in all strong and sincerely felt religious emotion. Faith unto salvation, trust, love—all these are there. But over and above these is an element which may also on occasion, quite apart from them, profoundly affect us and occupy the mind with a wellnigh bewildering strength. Let us follow it up with every effort of sympathy and imaginative intuition wherever it is to be found, in the lives of those around us, in sudden, strong ebullitions of personal piety and the frames of mind such ebullitions evince, in the fixed and ordered solemnities of rites and liturgies, and again in the atmosphere that clings to old religious monuments and buildings, to temples and to churches. If we do so we shall find we are dealing with something for which there is only one appropriate expression, '*mysterium tremendum*'. The feeling of it may at times come sweeping like a gentle tide, pervading the mind with a tranquil mood of deepest worship. It may pass over into a more set and lasting attitude of the soul, continuing, as it were, thrillingly vibrant and resonant, until at last it dies away and the soul resumes its 'profane', non-religious mood of everyday experience. It may burst in sudden eruption up from the depths of the soul with spasms and convulsions, or lead to the strangest excitements, to intoxicated frenzy, to transport, and to ecstasy. It has its wild and demonic forms and can sink to an almost grisly horror and shuddering. It has its crude, barbaric antecedents and early manifestations, and again it may be developed into something beautiful and pure and glorious. It may become the hushed, trembling, and speechless humility of the creature in the presence of—whom or what? In the presence of that which is a *mystery* inexpressible and above all creatures.

It is again evident at once that here too our attempted formulation by means of a concept is once more a merely negative one. Conceptually *mysterium* denotes merely that which is hidden and esoteric, that which is beyond conception or understanding, extraordinary and unfamiliar. The term does not define the object more positively in its qualitative character. But though what is enunciated in the word is negative, what is meant is something absolutely and intensely positive. This pure positive we can experience in feelings, feelings which our discussion can help to make clear to us, in so far as it arouses them actually in our hearts.

1. *The Element of Awefulness*

To get light upon the positive *'quale'* of the object of these feelings, we must analyse more closely our phrase *mysterium tremendum,* and we will begin first with the adjective.

Tremor is in itself merely the perfectly familiar and 'natural' emotion of *fear*. But here the term is taken, aptly enough but still only by analogy, to denote a quite specific kind of emotional response, wholly distinct from that of being afraid, though it so far resembles it that the analogy of fear may be used to throw light upon its nature. There are in some languages special expressions which denote, either exclusively or in the first instance, this 'fear' that is more than fear proper.

The Hebrew *hiqdish* (hallow) is an example. To 'keep a thing holy in the heart' means to mark it off by a feeling of peculiar dread, not to be mistaken for any ordinary dread, that is, to appraise it by the category of the numinous. But the Old Testament throughout is rich in parallel expressions for this feeling. Specially noticeable is the *'emah* of Yahweh ('fear of God'), which Yahweh can pour forth, dispatching almost like a daemon, and which seizes upon a man with paralysing effect. It is closely related to the *deima panikon* of the Greeks. Compare Exod. xxiii. 27: 'I will send my fear before thee, and will destroy all the people to whom thou shalt come . . .', also Job ix. 34; xiii. 21 ('let not his fear terrify me'; 'let not thy dread make me afraid'). Here we have a terror fraught with an inward shuddering such as not even the most menacing and overpowering created thing can instil. It has something spectral in it.

In the Greek language we have a corresponding term in *sebastos*. The early Christians could clearly feel that the title *sebastos* (*augustus*) was one that could not fittingly be given to any creature, not even to the emperor. They felt that to call a man *sebastos* was to give a human being a name proper only to the *numen*, to rank him by the category proper only to the *numen*, and that it therefore amounted to a kind of idolatry. Of modern languages English has the words 'awe', 'aweful', which in their deeper and most special sense approximate closely to our meaning. The phrase, 'he stood aghast', is also suggestive in this connexion. On the other hand, German has no native-grown expression of its own for the higher and riper form of the emotion we are considering, unless it be in a word like *erschauern*, which does suggest it fairly well. It is far otherwise with its cruder and more debased phases, where such terms as *grausen* and *Schauer*, and the more popular and telling *gruseln* ('grue'), *gräsen*, and *grässlich* ('grisly'), very clearly designate the numinous element. In my examination of Wundt's Animism I suggested the term *Scheu* (dread); but the special 'numinous' quality (making it 'awe' rather than 'dread' in the ordinary sense) would then, of course, have to be denoted by inverted commas. 'Religious dread' (or 'awe') would perhaps be a better designation. Its antecedent stage is 'daemonic dread' (cf. the horror of Pan) with its queer perversion, a sort of abortive offshoot, the 'dread of ghosts'. It first begins to stir in the feeling of 'something uncanny', 'eerie', or 'weird'. It is this feeling which, emerging in the mind of primeval man, forms the starting-point for the entire religious development in history. 'Daemons' and 'gods' alike spring from this root, and all the products of 'mythological apperception' or 'fantasy' are nothing but different modes in which it has been objectified. And all ostensible explanations of the origin of religion in terms of animism or magic or folk-psychology are doomed from the outset to wander astray and miss the real goal of their inquiry, unless they recognize this fact of our nature—primary, unique, underivable from anything else—to be the basic factor and the basic impulse underlying the entire process of religious evolution.[2]

Not only is the saying of Luther, that the natural man cannot fear God perfectly, correct from the standpoint of psychology, but we ought to go farther and add that the natural man is quite unable even to 'shudder' *(grauen)* or feel horror in the real sense of the word. For 'shuddering' is something more than 'natural', ordinary fear. It implies that the mysterious is already beginning to loom before the mind, to touch the

---

2 Cf. my papers in *Theologische Rundschau,* 1910, vol. i, on 'Myth and Religion in Wundt's *Völkerpsychologie*', and in *Deutsche Literaturzeitung,* 1910, No. 38. I find in more recent investigations, especially those of R. R. Marett and N. Söderblom, a very welcome confirmation of the positions I there maintained. It is true that neither of them calls attention quite as precisely as, in this matter, psychologists need to do, to the unique character of the religious 'awe' and its qualitative distinction from all 'natural' feelings. But Marett more particularly comes within a hair's breadth of what I take to be the truth about the matter. Cf. his *Threshold of Religion* (London, 1909), and N. Söderblom's *Das Werden des Gottesglaubens* (Leipzig, 1915), also my review of the latter in *Theol. Literaturzeitung,* Jan. 1915.

feelings. It implies the first application of a category of valuation which has no place in the everyday natural world of ordinary experience, and is only possible to a being in whom has been awakened a mental predisposition, unique in kind and different in a definite way from any 'natural' faculty. And this newly-revealed capacity, even in the crude and violent manifestations which are all it at first evinces, bears witness to a completely new function of experience and standard of valuation, only belonging to the spirit of man.

Before going on to consider the elements which unfold as the '*tremendum*' develops, let us give a little further consideration to the first crude, primitive forms in which this 'numinous dread' or *awe* shows itself. It is the mark which really characterizes the so-called 'religion of primitive man', and there it appears as 'daemonic dread'. This crudely naïve and primordial emotional disturbance, and the fantastic images to which it gives rise, are later overborne and ousted by more highly developed forms of the numinous emotion, with all its mysteriously impelling power. But even when this has long attained its higher and purer mode of expression it is possible for the primitive types of excitation that were formerly a part of it to break out in the soul in all their original naïveté and so to be experienced afresh. That this is so is shown by the potent attraction again and again exercised by the element of horror and 'shudder' in ghost stories, even among persons of high all-round education. It is a remarkable fact that the physical reaction to which this unique 'dread' of the uncanny gives rise is also unique, and is not found in the case of any 'natural' fear or terror. We say: 'my blood ran icy cold', and 'my flesh crept'. The 'cold blood' feeling may be a symptom of ordinary, natural fear, but there is something non-natural or supernatural about the symptom of 'creeping flesh'. And any one who is capable of more precise introspection must recognize that the distinction between such a 'dread' and natural fear is not simply one of degree and intensity. The awe or 'dread' *may* indeed be so overwhelmingly great that it seems to penetrate to the very marrow, making the man's hair bristle and his limbs quake. But it may also steal upon him almost unobserved as the gentlest of agitations, a mere fleeting shadow passing across his mood. It has therefore nothing to do with intensity, and no natural fear passes over into it merely by being intensified. I may be beyond all measure afraid and terrified without there being even a trace of the feeling of uncanniness in my emotion.

We should see the facts more clearly if psychology in general would make a more decisive endeavour to examine and classify the feelings and emotions according to the qualitative differences. But the far too rough division of elementary feelings in general into pleasures and pains is still an obstacle to this. In point of fact 'pleasures' no more than other feelings are differentiated merely by degrees of intensity: they show very definite and specific differences. It makes a specific difference to the condition of mind whether the soul is merely in a state of pleasure, or joy, or aesthetic rapture, or moral exaltation, or finally in the religious bliss that may come in worship. Such states certainly show resemblances one to another, and on that account can legitimately be brought under a common class-concept ('pleasure'), which serves to cut them off from other psychical functions, generically different. But this class-concept, so far from turning the various subordinate species into merely different degrees of the same thing, can do nothing at all to throw light upon the essence of each several state of mind which it includes.

Though the numinous emotion in its completest development shows a world of difference from the mere 'daemonic dread', yet not even at the highest level does it belie its pedigree or kindred. Even when the worship of 'daemons' has long since reached the higher level of worship of 'gods', these gods still retain as *numina* something of the 'ghost' in the impress they make on the feelings of the worshipper, viz. the peculiar quality of the 'uncanny' and 'aweful', which survives with the quality of exaltedness and sublimity or is symbolized by means of it. And this element, softened though it is, does not disappear even on the highest level of all, where the worship of God is at its purest. Its disappearance would be indeed an essential loss. The 'shudder' reappears in a form ennobled beyond measure where the soul, held speechless, trembles inwardly to the farthest fibre of its being. It invades the mind mightily in Christian worship with the words: 'Holy, holy, holy'; it breaks forth from the hymn of Tersteegen:

> God Himself is present:
> Heart, be stilled before Him:
> Prostrate inwardly adore Him.

The 'shudder' has here lost its crazy and bewildering note, but not the ineffable something that holds the mind. It has become a mystical awe, and sets free as its accompaniment, reflected in self-consciousness, that 'creature-feeling' that has already been described as the feeling of personal nothingness and submergence before the awe-inspiring object directly experienced.

The referring of this feeling numinous *tremor* to its object in the numen brings into relief a property of the latter which plays an important part in our Holy Scriptures, and which has been the occasion of many difficulties, both to commentators and to theologians, from its puzzling and baffling nature. This is the *orgê,* the Wrath of Yahweh, which recurs in the New Testament as *orgê theou,* and which is clearly analogous to the idea occurring in many religions of a mysterious *ira deorum.* To pass through the Indian Pantheon of gods is to find deities who seem to be made up altogether out of such an *orgê;* and even the higher Indian gods of grace and pardon have frequently, beside their merciful, their 'wrath' form. But as regards the 'wrath of Yahweh', the strange features about it have for long been a matter for constant remark. In the first place, it is patent from many passages of the Old Testament that this 'wrath' has no concern whatever with moral qualities. There is something very baffling in the way in which it 'is kindled' and manifested. It is, as has been well said, 'like a hidden force of nature', like stored-up electricity, discharging itself upon anyone who comes too near. It is 'incalculable' and 'arbitrary'. Anyone who is accustomed to think of deity only by its rational attributes must see in this 'wrath' mere caprice and wilful passion. But such a view would have been emphatically rejected by the religious men of the Old Covenant, for to them the Wrath of God, so far from being a diminution of His Godhead, appears as a natural expression of it, an element of 'holiness' itself, and a quite indispensable one. And in this they are entirely right. This *orgê* is nothing but the *tremendum* itself, apprehended and expressed by the aid of a naïve analogy from the domain of natural experience, in this case from the ordinary passional life of men. But naïve as it may be, the analogy is most disconcertingly apt and striking; so much so that it will always retain its value and for us no less than for the men of old be an inevitable way of expressing one element in the religious emotion. It cannot be doubted that, despite the protest of Schleiermacher and Ritschl, Christianity also has something to teach of the 'wrath of God'.

It will be again at once apparent that in the use of this word we are not concerned with a genuine intellectual 'concept', but only with a sort of illustrative substitute for a concept. 'Wrath' here is the 'ideogram' of a unique emotional moment in religious experience, a moment whose singularly *daunting* and awe-inspiring character must be gravely disturbing to those persons who will recognize nothing in the divine nature but goodness, gentleness, love, and a sort of confidential intimacy, in a word, only those aspects of God which turn towards the world of men.

This *orgê* is thus quite wrongly spoken of as 'natural' wrath: rather it is an entirely non- or super-natural, i.e. numinous, quality. The rationalization process takes place when it begins to be filled in with elements derived from the moral reason: righteousness in requital, and punishment for moral transgression. But it should be noted that the idea of the wrath of God in the Bible is always a synthesis, in which the original is combined with the later meaning that has come to fill it in. Something supra-rational throbs and gleams, palpable and visible, in the 'wrath of God', prompting to a sense of 'terror' that no 'natural' anger can arouse.

Beside the 'wrath' or 'anger' of Yahweh stands the related expression 'jealousy of Yahweh'. The state of mind denoted by the phrase 'being jealous *for* Yahweh' is also a numinous state of mind, in which features of the *tremendum* pass over into the man who has experience of it.

2. *The element of 'Overpoweringness' ('majestas')*

We have been attempting to unfold the implications of that aspect of the *mysterium tremendum* indicated by the adjective, and the result so far may be summarized in two words, constituting, as before, what may be called an 'ideogram', rather than a concept proper, viz. 'absolute unapproachability'.

It will be felt at once that there is yet a further element which must be added, that, namely, of 'might', 'power', 'absolute overpoweringness'. We will take to represent this the term *majestas,* majesty—the more readily because anyone with a feeling for language must detect a last faint trace of the numinous still clinging to the word. The *tremendum* may then be rendered more adequately *tremenda majestas,* or 'aweful majesty'. This second element of majesty may continue to be vividly preserved, where the first, that of unapproachability, recedes and dies away, as may be seen, for example, in mysticism. It is especially in relation to this element of majesty or absolute overpoweringness that the creature-consciousness, of which we have already spoken, comes upon the scene, as a sort of shadow or subjective reflection of it. Thus, in contrast to 'the overpowering' of which we are conscious as an object over against the self, there is the feeling of one's own submergence, of being but 'dust and ashes' and nothingness. And this forms the numinous raw material for the feeling of religious humility.[3]

Here we must revert once again to Schleiermacher's expression for what we call 'creature-feeling', viz. the 'feeling of dependence'. We found fault with this phrase before on the ground that Schleiermacher thereby takes as basis and point of departure what is merely a secondary effect; that he sets out to teach a consciousness of the religious *object* only by way of an inference from the shadow its casts upon *self*-consciousness. We have now a further criticism to bring against it, and it is this. By 'feeling of dependence' Schleiermacher means consciousness of *being conditioned* (as effect by cause), and so he develops the implications of this logically enough in his sections upon Creation and Preservation. On the side of the deity the correlate to 'dependence' would thus be 'causality', i.e. God's character as all-causing and all-conditioning. But a sense of this does not enter at all into that immediate and first-hand religious emotion which we have in the moment of worship, and which we can recover in a measure for analysis; it belongs on the contrary decidedly to the *rational* side of the idea of God; its implications admit of precise conceptual determination; and it springs from quite a distinct source. The difference between the 'feeling of dependence' of Schleiermacher and that which finds typical utterance in the words of Abraham already cited might be expressed as that between the consciousness of *createdness*[4] and the consciousness of *creaturehood*.[5] In the one case you have the creature as the work of the divine

3 Cf. R. R. Marett, 'The Birth of Humility', in *The Threshold of Religion*, 2nd ed., 1914. [Tr.]

4 *Geschaffenheit.*

5 *Geschöpflichkeit.*

creative act; in the other, impotence and general nothingness as against overpowering might, dust and ashes as against 'majesty'. In the one case you have the fact of having been created; in the other, the status of the creature. And as soon as speculative thought has come to concern itself with this latter type of consciousness—as soon as it has come to analyse this 'majesty'—we are introduced to a set of ideas quite different from those of creation or preservation. We come upon the ideas, first, of the annihilation of self, and then, as its complement, of the transcendent as the sole and entire reality. These are the characteristic notes of mysticism in all its forms, however otherwise various in content. For one of the chiefest and most general features of mysticism is just this *self-depreciation* (so plainly parallel to the case of Abraham), the estimation of the self, of the personal 'I', as something not perfectly or essentially real, or even as mere nullity, a self-depreciation which comes to demand its own fulfilment in practice in rejecting the delusion of selfhood, and so makes for the annihilation of the self. And on the other hand mysticism leads to a valuation of the transcendent object of its reference as that which through plenitude of being stands supreme and absolute, so that the finite self contrasted with it becomes conscious even in its nullity that 'I am naught, Thou art all'. There is no thought in this of any causal relation between God, the creator, and the self, the creature. The point from which speculation starts is not a 'consciousness of absolute dependence'—of myself as result and effect of a divine cause—for that would in point of fact lead to insistence upon the reality of the self; it starts from a consciousness of the absolute superiority or supremacy of a power other than myself, and it is only as it falls back upon ontological terms to achieve its end—terms generally borrowed from natural science—that that element of the *tremendum,* originally apprehended as 'plenitude of power', becomes transmuted into 'plenitude of being'.

This leads again to the mention of mysticism. No mere inquiry into the genesis of a thing can throw any light upon its essential nature, and it is hence immaterial to us how mysticism historically arose. But essentially mysticism is the stressing to a very high degree, indeed the overstressing, of the non-rational or supra-rational elements in religion; and it is only intelligible when so understood. The various phases and factors of the non-rational may receive varying emphasis, and the type of mysticism will differ according as some or others fall into the background. What we have been analysing, however, is a feature that recurs in all forms of mysticism everywhere, and it is nothing but the 'creature-consciousness' stressed to the utmost and to excess, the expression meaning, if we may repeat the contrast already made, not 'feeling of our createdness' but 'feeling of our creaturehood', that is, the consciousness of the littleness of every creature in face of that which is above all creatures.

A characteristic common to all types of mysticism is the *Identification,* in different degrees of completeness, of the personal self with the transcendent Reality. This identification has a source of its own, with which we are not here concerned, and springs from 'moments' of religious experience which would require separate treatment. 'Identification' alone, however, is not enough for mysticism; it must be Identification with the Something that is at once absolutely supreme in power and reality and wholly non-rational. And it is among the mystics that we most encounter this element of religious consciousness. Récéjac has noticed this in his *Essai sur les fondements de la connaissance mystique* (Paris, 1897). He writes (p. 90):

> Le mysticisme commence par la crainte, par le sentiment d'une *domination* universelle, *invincible,* et devient plus tard un désir d'union avec ce qui domine ainsi.

And some very clear examples of this taken from the religious experience of the present day are to be found in W. James *(op. cit.,* p. 66):

> The perfect stillness of the night was thrilled by a more solemn silence. The darkness held a presence that was all the more felt because it was not seen. I could not any more have doubted that *He* was there than that I was. Indeed, I felt myself to be, if possible, the less real of the two.

This example is particularly instructive as to the relation of mysticism to the 'feelings of identification', for the experience here recounted was on the point of passing into it.[6]

3. *The Element of 'Energy' or Urgency*

There is, finally, a third element comprised in those of *tremendum* and *majestas,* awefulness and majesty, and this I venture to call the 'urgency' or 'energy' of the numinous object. It is particularly vividly perceptible in the *orgê* or 'wrath'; and it everywhere clothes itself in symbolical expressions—vitality, passion, emotional temper, will, force, movement,[7] excitement, activity, impetus. These features are typical and recur again and again from the daemonic level up to the idea of the 'living' God. We have here the factor that has everywhere more than any other prompted the fiercest opposition to the 'philosophic' God of mere rational speculation, who can be put into a definition. And for their part the philosophers have condemned these expressions of the energy of the numen, whenever they are brought on to the scene, as sheer anthropomorphism. In so far as their opponents have for the most part themselves failed to recognize that the terms they have borrowed from the sphere of human conative and

---

6 Compare too the experience on p. 70: '. . . What I felt on these occasions was a temporary loss of my own identity'.

7 The 'mobilitas Dei' of Lactantius.

affective life have merely value as analogies, the philsophers are right to condemn them. But they are wrong, in so far as, this error notwithstanding, these terms stood for a genuine aspect of the divine nature—its non-rational aspect—a due consciousness of which served to protect religion itself from being 'rationalized' away.

For wherever men have been contending for the 'living' God or for voluntarism, there, we may be sure, have been non-rationalists fighting rationalists and rationalism. It was so with Luther in his controversy with Erasmus; and Luther's *omnipotentia Dei* in his *De Servo Arbitrio* is nothing but the union of 'majesty'—in the sense of absolute supremacy—with this 'energy', in the sense of a force that knows not stint nor stay, which is urgent, active, compelling, and alive. In mysticism, too, this element of 'energy' is a very living and vigorous factor, at any rate in the 'voluntaristic' mysticism, the mysticism of love, where it is very forcibly seen in that 'consuming fire' of love whose burning strength the mystic can hardly bear, but begs that the heat that has scorched him may be mitigated, lest he be himself destroyed by it. And in this urgency and pressure the mystic's 'love' claims a perceptible kinship with the *orgê* itself, the scorching and consuming wrath of God; it is the same 'energy', only differently directed. 'Love', says one of the mystics, 'is nothing else than quenched wrath.'

The element of 'energy' reappears in Fichte's speculations on the Absolute as the gigantic, never-resting, active world-stress, and in Schopenhauer's daemonic 'Will'. At the same time both these writers are guilty of the same error that is already found in myth; they transfer 'natural' attributes, which ought only to be used as 'ideograms' for what is itself properly beyond utterance, to the non-rational as real qualifications of it, and they mistake symbolic expressions of feelings for adequate concepts upon which a 'scientific' structure of knowledge may be based.

In Goethe, as we shall see later, the same element of energy is emphasized in a quite unique way in his strange descriptions of the experience he calls 'daemonic'.

THE ANALYSIS OF 'MYSTERIUM'

Ein begriffener Gott ist kein Gott.
'A God comprehended is no God.' (TERSTEEGEN.)

We gave to the object to which the numinous consciousness is directed the name *mysterium tremendum,* and we then set ourselves first to determine the meaning of the adjective *tremendum*—which we found to be itself only justified by analogy—because it is more easily analysed than the substantive idea *mysterium.* We have now to turn to this, and try, as best we may, by hint and suggestion, to get to a clearer apprehension of what it implies.

4. *The 'Wholly Other'*

It might be thought that the adjective itself gives an explanation of the substantive; but this is not so. It is not merely analytical; it is a synthetic attribute to it; i.e. *tremendum* adds something not necessarily inherent in *mysterium.* It is true that the reactions in consciousness that correspond to the one readily and spontaneously overflow into those that correspond to the other; in fact, anyone sensitive to the use of words would commonly feel that the idea of 'mystery' *(mysterium)* is so closely bound up with its synthetic qualifying attribute 'aweful' *(tremendum)* that one can hardly say the former without catching an echo of the latter, 'mystery' almost of itself becoming 'aweful mystery' to us. But the passage from the one idea to the other need not by any means be always so easy. The elements of meaning implied in 'awefulness' and 'mysteriousness' are in themselves definitely different.

The latter may so far preponderate in the religious consciousness, may stand out so vividly, that in comparison with it the former almost sinks out of sight; a case which again could be clearly exemplified from some forms of mysticism. Occasionally, on the other hand, the reverse happens, and the *tremendum* may in turn occupy the mind without the *mysterium.*

This latter, then, needs special consideration on its own account. We need an expression for the mental reaction peculiar to it; and here, too, only one word seems appropriate, though, as it is strictly applicable only to a 'natural' state of mind, it has here meaning only by analogy: it is the word 'stupor'. *Stupor* is plainly a different thing from *tremor;* it signifies blank wonder, an astonishment that strikes us dumb, amazement absolute.[8] Taken, indeed, in its purely natural sense, *mysterium* would first mean merely a secret or a mystery in the sense of that which is alien to us, uncomprehended and unexplained; and so far *mysterium* is itself merely an ideogram, an analogical notion taken from the natural sphere, illustrating, but incapable of exhaustively rendering, our real meaning. Taken in the religious sense, that which is 'mysterious' is—to give it perhaps the most striking expression—the 'wholly other' (*thateron, anyad, alienum*), that which is quite beyond the sphere of the usual, the intelligible, and the familiar, which therefore falls quite outside the limits of the 'canny', and is contrasted with it, filling the mind with blank wonder and astonishment.

---

8 Compare also *obstupefacere.* Still more exact equivalents are the Greek *thambos* and *thambein.* The sound *thamb* excellently depicts this state of mind of blank, staring wonder. And the difference between the moments of *stupor* and *tremor* is very finely suggested by the passage, Mark x. 32. On the other hand, what was said above of the facility and rapidity with which the two moments merge and blend is also markedly true of *thambos,* which then becomes a classical term for the (ennobled) awe of the numinous in general. So Mark xvi. 5 is rightly translated by Luther 'und sie entsetzten sich', and by the English Authorized Version 'and they were affrighted'.

This is already to be observed on the lowest and earliest level of the religion of primitive man, where the numinous consciousness is but an inchoate stirring of the feelings. What is really characteristic of this stage is *not*—as the theory of Animism would have us believe—that men are here concerned with curious entities, called 'souls' or 'spirits', which happen to be invisible. Representations of spirits and similar conceptions are rather one and all early modes of 'rationalizing' a precedent experience, to which they are subsidiary. They are attempts in some way or other, it little matters how, to guess the riddle it propounds, and their effect is at the same time always to weaken and deaden the experience itself. They are the source from which springs, not religion, but the rationalization of religion, which often ends by constructing such a massive structure of theory and such a plausible fabric of interpretation, that the 'mystery' is frankly excluded.[9] Both imaginative 'myth', when developed into a system, and intellectualist Scholasticism, when worked out to its completion, are methods by which the fundamental fact of religious experience is, as it were, simply rolled out so thin and flat as to be finally eliminated altogether.

Even on the lowest level of religious development the essential characteristic is therefore to be sought elsewhere than in the appearance of 'spirit' representations. It lies rather, we repeat, in a peculiar 'moment' of consciousness, to wit, the *stupor* before something 'wholly other', whether such an other be named 'spirit' or 'daemon' or 'deva', or be left without any name. Nor does it make any difference in this respect whether, to interpret and preserve their apprehension of this 'other', men coin original imagery of their own or adapt imaginations drawn from the world of legend, the fabrications of fancy apart from and prior to any stirrings of daemonic dread.

---

9 A spirit or soul that has been conceived and comprehended no longer prompts to 'shuddering', as is proved by Spiritualism. But it thereby ceases to be of interest for the psychology of religion.

In accordance with laws of which we shall have to speak again later, this feeling or consciousness of the 'wholly other' will attach itself to, or sometimes be indirectly aroused by means of, objects which are already puzzling upon the 'natural' plane, or are of a surprising or astounding character; such as extraordinary phenomena or astonishing occurrences or things in inanimate nature, in the animal world, or among men. But here once more we are dealing with a case of association between things specifically different—the 'numinous' and the 'natural' moments of consciousness—and not merely with the gradual enhancement of one of them—the 'natural'—till it becomes the other. As in the case of 'natural fear' and 'daemonic dread' already considered, so here the transition from natural to daemonic amazement is not a mere matter of degree. But it is only with the latter that the complementary expression *mysterium* perfectly harmonizes, as will be felt perhaps more clearly in the case of the adjectival form 'mysterious'. No one says, strictly and in earnest, of a piece of clockwork that is beyond his grasp, or of a science that he cannot understand: 'That is "mysterious" to me.'

It might be objected that the mysterious is something which is and remains absolutely and invariably beyond our understanding, whereas that which merely eludes our understanding for a time but is perfectly intelligible in principle should be called, not a 'mystery', but merely a 'problem'. But this is by no means an adequate account of the matter. The truly 'mysterious' object is beyond our apprehension and comprehension, not only because our knowledge has certain irremovable limits, but because in it we come upon something inherently 'wholly other', whose kind and character are incommensurable with our own, and before which we therefore recoil in a wonder that strikes us chill and numb.[10]

---

10 In *Confessions,* ii 9. 1, Augustine very strikingly suggests this stiffening, benumbing element of the 'wholly other' and its contrast to the rational aspect of the numen; the *dissimile* and the *simile:*

This may be made still clearer by a consideration of that degraded offshoot and travesty of the genuine 'numinous' dread or awe, the fear of ghosts. Let us try to analyse this experience. We have already specified the peculiar feeling-element of 'dread' aroused by the ghost as that of 'grue', grisly horror.[11] Now this 'grue' obviously contributes something to the attraction which ghost-stories exercise, in so far, namely, as the relaxation of tension ensuing upon our release from it relieves the mind in a pleasant and agreeable way. So far, however, it is not really the ghost itself that gives us pleasure, but the fact that we are rid of it. But obviously this is quite insufficient to explain the ensnaring attraction of the ghost-story. The ghost's real attraction rather consists in this, that of itself and in an uncommon degree it entices the imagination, awakening strong interest and curiosity; it is the weird thing itself that allures the fancy. But it does this, not because it is 'something long and white' (as someone once defined a ghost), nor yet through any of the positive and conceptual attributes which fancies about ghosts have invented, but because it is a thing that 'doesn't really exist at all', the 'wholly other', something which has no place in our scheme of reality but belongs to an absolutely different one, and which at the same time arouses an irrepressible interest in the mind.

But that which is perceptibly true in the fear of ghosts, which is, after all, only a caricature of the genuine thing, is in a far stronger sense true of the 'daemonic' experience itself, of which the fear of ghosts is a mere off-shoot. And while, following this main line of development, this element in the numinous consciousness, the feeling of the 'wholly other', is

---

'Quid est illud, quod interlucet mihi et percutit cor meum sine laesione? Et inhorresco et inardesco. *Inhorresco,* in quantum *dissimilis* ei sum. Inardesco, in quantum similis ei sum.'

('What is that which gleams through me and smites my heart without wounding it? I am both a-shudder and a-glow. A-shudder, in so far as I am unlike it, a-glow in so far as I am like it.')

11 *gruseln, gräsen.*

heightened and clarified, its higher modes of manifestation come into being, which set the numinous object in contrast not only to everything wonted and familiar (i.e. in the end, to nature in general), thereby turning it into the 'supernatural', but finally to the world itself, and thereby exalt it to the 'supramundane', that which is above the whole world-order.

In mysticism we have in the 'beyond' (*epekeina*) again the strongest stressing and over-stressing of those non-rational elements which are already inherent in all religion. Mysticism continues to its extreme point this contrasting of the numinous object (the numen), as the 'wholly other', with ordinary experience. Not content with contrasting it with all that is of nature or this world, mysticism concludes by contrasting it with Being itself and all that 'is', and finally actually calls it 'that which is nothing'. By this 'nothing' is meant not only that of which nothing can be predicated, but that which is absolutely and intrinsically other than and opposite of everything that is and can be thought. But while exaggerating to the point of paradox this *negation* and contrast—the only means open to conceptual thought to apprehend the *mysterium* —mysticism at the same time retains the *positive quality* of the 'wholly other' as a very living factor in its over-brimming religious emotion.

But what is true of the strange 'nothingness' of our mystics holds good equally of the *sunyam* and the *sunyata,* the 'void' and 'emptiness' of the Buddhist mystics. This aspiration for the 'void' and for becoming void, no less than the aspiration of our western mystics for 'nothing' and for becoming nothing, must seem a kind of lunacy to anyone who has no inner sympathy for the esoteric language and ideograms of mysticism, and lacks the matrix from which these come necessarily to birth. To such an one Buddhism itself will be simply a morbid sort of pessimism. But in fact the 'void' of the eastern, like the 'nothing' of the western, mystic is a numinous ideogram of the 'wholly other'.

These terms 'supernatural' and 'transcendent'[12] give the appearance of positive attributes, and, as applied to the mysterious, they appear to divest the *mysterium* of its originally negative meaning and to turn it into an affirmation. On the side of conceptual thought this is nothing more than appearance, for it is obvious that the two terms in question are merely negative and exclusive attributes with reference to 'nature' and the world or cosmos respectively. But on the side of the feeling-content it is otherwise; that *is* in very truth positive in the highest degree, though here too, as before, it cannot be rendered explicit in conceptual terms. It is through this positive feeling-content that the concepts of the 'transcendent' and 'supernatural' become forthwith designations for a unique 'wholly other' reality and quality, something of whose special character we can *feel,* without being able to give it clear conceptual expression.

5. THE ELEMENT OF FASCINATION

The qualitative *content* of the numinous experience, to which 'the mysterious' stands as *form,* is in one of its aspects the element of daunting 'awefulness' and 'majesty', which has already been dealt with in detail; but it is clear that it has at the same time another aspect, in which it shows itself as something uniquely attractive and *fascinating.*

These two qualities, the daunting and the fascinating, now combine in a strange harmony of contrasts, and the resultant dual character of the numinous consciousness, to which the entire religious development bears witness, at any rate from the level of the 'daemonic dread' onwards, is at once the strangest and most noteworthy phenomenon in the whole history of religion. The daemonic-divine object may appear to the mind an object of horror and dread, but at the same time it is no less something that allures with a potent charm,

---

12 Literally, supramundane: *überweltlich.*

and the creature, who trembles before it, utterly cowed and cast down, has always at the same time the impulse to turn to it, nay even to make it somehow his own. The 'mystery' is for him not merely something to be wondered at but something that entrances him; and beside that in it which bewilders and confounds, he feels a something that captivates and transports him with a strange ravishment, rising often enough to the pitch of dizzy intoxication; it is the Dionysiac-element in the numen.

The ideas and concepts which are the parallels or 'schemata' on the rational side of this non-rational element of 'fascination' are love, mercy, pity, comfort; these are all 'natural' elements of the common psychical life, only they are here thought as absolute and in completeness. But important as these are for the experience of religious bliss or felicity, they do not by any means exhaust it. It is just the same as with the opposite experience of religious infelicity—the experience of the *orgê* or 'wrath' of God:—both alike contain fundamentally non-rational elements. Bliss or beatitude is more, far more, than the mere natural feeling of being comforted, of reliance, of the joy of love, however these may be heightened and enhanced. Just as 'wrath', taken in a purely rational or a purely ethical sense, does not exhaust that profound element of *awefulness* which is locked in the mystery of deity, so neither does 'graciousness' exhaust the profound element of *wonderfulness* and rapture which lies in the mysterious beatific experience of deity. The term 'grace' may indeed be taken as its aptest designation, but then only in the sense in which it is really applied in the language of the mystics, and in which not only the 'gracious intent' but 'something more' is meant by the word. This 'something more' has its antecedent phases very far back in the history of religions.

It may well be possible, it is even probable, that in the first stage of its development the religious consciousness started with only one of its poles—the 'daunting' aspect of the numen

—and so at first took shape only as 'daemonic dread'. But if this did not point to something beyond itself, if it were not but one 'moment' of a completer experience, pressing up gradually into consciousness, then no transition would be possible to the feelings of positive self-surrender to the numen. The only type of worship that could result from this 'dread' alone would be that of *apaiteisthai* and *apotrepein,* taking the form of expiation and propitiation, the averting or the appeasement of the 'wrath' of the numen. It can never explain how it is that 'the numinous' is the object of search and desire and yearning, and that too for its own sake and not only for the sake of the aid and backing that men expect from it in the natural sphere. It can never explain how this takes place, not only in the forms of 'rational' religious worship, but in those queer 'sacramental' observances and rituals and procedures of communion in which the human being seeks to get the numen into his possession.

Religious practice may manifest itself in those normal and easily intelligible forms which occupy so prominent a place in the history of religion, such forms as propitiation, petition, sacrifice, thanksgiving, &c. But besides these there is a series of strange proceedings which are constantly attracting greater and greater attention, and in which it is claimed that we may recognize, besides mere religion in general, the particular roots of mysticism. I refer to those numerous curious modes of behaviour and fantastic forms of mediation, by means of which the primitive religious man attempts to master 'the mysterious', and to fill himself and even to identify himself with it. These modes of behaviour fall apart into two classes. On the one hand the 'magical' identification of the self with the numen proceeds by means of various transactions, at once magical and devotional in character—by formula, ordination, adjuration, consecration, exorcism, &c.: on the other hand are the 'shamanistic' ways of procedure, possession, indwelling, self-fulfilment in exaltation and ecstasy. All these have, indeed, their starting-points simply in magic, and their intention at first was certainly simply to appropriate the prodigious force of the numen for the natural ends of man. But the process does not rest there. Possession of and by the numen becomes an end in itself; it begins to be sought for its own sake; and the wildest and most artificial methods of asceticism are put into practice to attain it. In a word, the *vita religiosa* begins; and to remain in these strange and bizarre states of numinous possession becomes a good in itself, even a way of salvation, wholly different from the profane goods pursued by means of magic. Here, too, commences the process of development by which the experience is matured and purified, till finally it reaches its consummation in the sublimest and purest states of the 'life within the Spirit' and in the noblest mysticism. Widely various as these states are in themselves, yet they have this element in common, that in them the *mysterium* is experienced in its essential, positive, and specific character, as something that bestows upon man a beatitude beyond compare, but one whose real nature he can neither proclaim in speech nor conceive in thought, but may know only by a direct and living experience. It is a bliss which embraces all those blessings that are indicated or suggested in positive fashion by any 'doctrine of salvation', and it quickens all of them through and through; but these do not exhaust it. Rather by its all-pervading, penetrating glow it makes of these very blessings more than the intellect can conceive in them or affirm of them. It gives the peace that passes understanding, and of which the tongue can only stammer brokenly. Only from afar, by metaphors and analogies, do we come to apprehend what it is in itself, and even so our notion is but inadequate and confused.

'Eye hath not seen, nor ear heard, neither have entered into the heart of man, the things which God hath prepared for them that love him.' Who does not feel the exalted sound of these words and the 'Dionysiac' element of transport and fervour in them? It is instructive that in such phrases as these, in which consciousness would fain put its highest consummation into words, 'all images fall away' and the mind turns from them to grasp expressions that are purely negative. And it is still more instructive that in reading and hearing such words their merely negative character simply is not noticed; that we can let whole chains of such negations enrapture, even intoxicate us, and that entire hymns—and deeply impressive hymns—have been composed, in which there is really nothing positive at all! All this teaches us the independence of the positive content of this experience from the implications of its overt conceptual expression, and how it can be firmly grasped, thoroughly understood, and profoundly appreciated, purely in, with, and from the feeling itself.

Mere love, mere trust, for all the glory and happiness they bring, do not explain to us that moment of rapture that breathes in our tenderest and most heart-felt hymns of salvation, as also in such eschatological hymns of longing as that Rhyme of St. Bernard in which the very verses seem to dance.

> Urbs Sion unica, mansio mystica, condita coelo,
> Nunc tibi gaudeo, nunc tibi lugeo, tristor, anhelo,
> Te, quia corpore non queo, pectore saepe penetro;
> Sed caro terrea, terraque carnea, mox cado retro.
> Nemo retexere, nemoque promere sustinet ore,
> Quo tua moenia, quo capitolia plena nitore.
> Id queo dicere, quo modo tangere pollice coelum,
> Ut mare currere, sicut in aere figere telum.
> Opprimit omne cor ille tuus decor, O Sion, O Pax.
> Urbs sine tempore nulla potest fore laus tibi mendax.
> O nova mansio, te pia concio, gens pia munit,
> Provehit, excitat, auget, identitat, efficit, unit.[13]

13 'O Sion, thou city sole and single, mystic mansion hidden away in the heavens, now I rejoice in thee, now I moan for thee and mourn and yearn for thee; thee often I pass through in the heart, as I cannot in the body, but being but earthly flesh and fleshly earth soon I fall back. None can disclose or utter in speech what plenary radiance fills thy walls and thy citadels. I can as little

This is where the living 'something more' of the *fascinans*, the element of fascination, is to be found. It lives no less in those tense extollings of the blessing of salvation, which recur in all religions of salvation, and stand in such remarkable contrast to the relatively meagre and frequently childish import of that which is revealed in them by concept or by image. Everywhere salvation is something whose meaning is often very little apparent, is even wholly obscure, to the 'natural' man; on the contrary, *so far as he understands it,* he tends to find it highly tedious and uninteresting, sometimes downright distasteful and repugnant to his nature, as he would, for instance, find the beatific vision of God in our own doctrine of salvation, or the *henôsis* of 'God all in all' among the mystics. 'So far as he understands', be it noted; but then he does not understand it in the least. Because he lacks the inward teaching of the Spirit, he must needs confound what is offered him as an expression for the experience of salvation—a mere ideogram of what is felt, whose import it hints at by analogy—with 'natural' concepts, as though it were itself just such an one. And so he 'wanders ever farther from the goal'.

It is not only in the religious feeling of longing that the moment of fascination is a living factor. It is already alive and present in the moment of 'solemnity', both in the gathered concentration and humble submergence of private devotion, when the mind is exalted to the holy, and in the common worship of the congregation, where this is practised with earnestness and deep sincerity, as, it is to be feared, is with us a thing rather desired than realized. It is this and nothing else that in the solemn moment can fill the soul so full and keep

---

tell of it as I can touch the skies with my finger, or run upon the sea or make a dart stand still in the air. This thy splendour overwhelms every heart, O Sion, O Peace! O timeless City, no praise can belie thee. O new dwelling-place, thee the concourse and people of the faithful erects and exalts, inspires and increases, joins to itself, and makes complete and one.'

it so inexpressibly tranquil. Schleiermacher's assertion[14] is perhaps true of it, as of the numinous consciousness in general, viz. that it cannot really occur alone on its own account, or except combined and penetrated with rational elements. But, if this be admitted, it is upon other grounds than those adduced by Schleiermacher; while, on the other hand, it may occupy a more or less predominant place and lead to states of calm (*hêsuchia*) as well as of transport, in which it *almost* of itself wholly fills the soul. But in all the manifold forms in which it is aroused in us, whether in eschatological promise of the coming kingdom of God and the transcendent bliss of Paradise, or in the guise of an entry into that beatific reality that is 'above the world'; whether it come first in expectancy or pre-intimation or in a present experience ('When I but *have* Thee, I ask no question of heaven and earth'); in all these forms, outwardly diverse but inwardly akin, it appears as a strange and mighty propulsion towards an ideal good known only to religion and in its nature fundamentally non-rational, which the mind knows of in yearning and presentiment, recognizing it for what it is behind the obscure and inadequate symbols which are its only expression. And this shows that above and beyond our rational being lies hidden the ultimate and highest part of our nature, which can find no satisfaction in the mere allaying of the needs of our sensuous, psychical, or intellectual impulses and cravings. The mystics called it the basis or ground of the soul.

We saw that in the case of the element of the mysterious the 'wholly other' led on to the supernatural and transcendent and that above these appeared the 'beyond' (*epekeina*) of mysticism, through the non-rational side of religion being raised to its highest power and stressed to excess. It is the same in the case of the element of 'fascination'; here, too, is possible a transition into mysticism. At its highest point of stress the

14 *Glaubenslehre,* § 5.

fascinating becomes the 'overabounding', 'exuberant',[15] the mystical 'moment' which exactly corresponds upon this line to the *epekeina* upon the other line of approach, and which is to be understood accordingly. But while this feeling of the 'overabounding' is specially characteristic of mysticism, a trace of it survives in all truly felt states of religious beatitude, however restrained and kept within measure by other factors. This is seen most clearly from the psychology of those great experiences—of grace, conversion, second birth—in which the religious experience appears in its pure intrinsic nature and in heightened activity, so as to be more clearly grasped than in the less typical form of piety instilled by education. The hard core of such experiences in their Christian form consists of the redemption from guilt and bondage to sin, and we shall have presently to see that this also does not occur without a participation of non-rational elements. But leaving this out of account, what we have here to point out is the unutterableness of what has been yet genuinely experienced, and how such an experience may pass into blissful excitement, rapture, and exaltation verging often on the bizarre and the abnormal.[16] This is vouched for by the autobiographical testimony of the 'converted' from St. Paul onward. William James has collected a great number of these, without, however, himself noticing the non-rational element that thrills in them.

Thus, one writes

> . . . For the moment nothing but an ineffable joy and exaltation remained. It is impossible fully to describe the

15 *das Überschwengliche.*

16 This may be found fatal to the attempt to construct a 'religion within the limits of pure reason', or 'of humanity'; but, none the less, the matter is as we have described it, as far as concerns the psychological inquiry into religion, which asks, not what it is within the aforementioned limits, but what it is in its own essential nature. And for that matter this proceeding of constructing a 'humanity' prior to and apart from the most central and potent of human capacities is like nothing so much as the attempt to frame a standard idea of the human body after having previously cut off the head.

> experience. It was like the effect of some great orchestra, when all the separate notes have melted into one swelling harmony, that leaves the listener conscious of nothing save that his soul is being wafted upwards and almost bursting with its own emotion. (*Varieties of Religious Experience*, p. 66.)

And another:

> . . . The more I seek words to express this intimate intercourse, the more I feel the impossibility of describing the thing by any of our usual images. (Ibid., p. 68.)

And almost with the precision of dogma, a third (Jonathan Edwards) indicates the qualitative difference of the experience of beatitude from other 'rational' joy:

> The conceptions which the saints have of the loveliness of God and that kind of delight which they experience in it are quite peculiar and entirely different from anything which a natural man can possess or of which he can form any proper notion. (Ibid., p. 229.)

Cf. also pp. 192, 225; and the testimony of Jacob Boehme given on p. 417. Also this of Boehme:

> But I can neither write nor tell of what sort of Exaltation the triumphing in the Spirit is. It can be compared with nought, but that when in the midst of death life is born, and it is like the resurrection of the dead.

With the mystics these experiences pass up wholly into the 'over-abounding'. 'O that I could tell you what the heart feels, how it burns and is consumed inwardly! Only, I find no words to express it. I can but say: Might but one little drop of what I feel fall into Hell, Hell would be transformed into a Paradise.' So says St. Catherine of Genoa; and all the multitude of her spiritual kindred testify to the same effect.

What we Christians know as the experiences of grace and the second birth have their parallels also in the religions of high spiritual rank beyond the borders of Christianity. Such are the breaking out of the saving 'Bodhi', the opening of the 'heavenly eye', the *Jnâna,* by *Isvaras prasâda,* which is victorious over the darkness of nescience and shines out in an experience with which no other can be measured. And in all these the entirely non-rational and specific element in the beatific experience is immediately noticeable. The qualitative character of it varies widely in all these cases, and is again in them all very different from its parallels in Christianity; still in all it is very similar in intensity, and in all it is a 'salvation' and an absolute 'fascination', which in contrast to all that admits of 'natural' expression or comparison is deeply imbued with the 'over-abounding' ('exuberant') nature of the numen.

And this is also entirely true of the rapture of Nirvana, which is only in appearance a cold and negative state. It is only conceptually that 'Nirvana' is a negation; it is felt in consciousness as in the strongest degree positive; it exercises a 'fascination' by which its votaries are as much carried away as are the Hindu or the Christian by the corresponding objects of their worship. I recall vividly a conversation I had with a Buddhist monk. He had been putting before me methodically and pertinaciously the arguments for the Buddhist 'theology of negation', the doctrine of Anatman and 'entire emptiness'. When he had made an end, I asked him, what then Nirvana itself is; and after a long pause came at last the single answer, low and restrained: 'Bliss—unspeakable'. And the hushed restraint of that answer, the solemnity of his voice, demeanour, and gesture, made more clear what was meant than the words themselves.

And so we maintain, on the one hand, following the *via eminentiae et causalitatis,* that the divine is indeed the highest, strongest, best, loveliest, and dearest that man can think of; but we assert on the other, following the *via negationis,* that God is not *merely* the ground and superlative of all that can be thought; He is in Himself a subject on His own account and in Himself.

* * * * *

In the adjective *deinos* the Greek language possesses a word peculiarly difficult to translate, and standing for an idea peculiarly difficult to grasp in all its strange variations. And if we ask whence this difficulty arises, the answer is plain; it is because *deinos* is simply the numinous (mostly of course at a lower level, in an arrested form, attenuated by rhetorical or poetic usage). Consequently *deinos* is the equivalent of *dirus* and *tremendus.* It may mean evil or imposing, potent and strange, queer and marvellous, horrifying and fascinating, divine and daemonic, and a source of 'energy'. Sophocles means to awaken the feeling of 'numinous awe' through the whole gamut of its phases at the contemplation of man, the creature of marvel, in the choric song of the *Antigone:*

polla ta deina k'ouden anthrôpou deinoteron pelei

This line defies translation, just because our language has no term that can isolate distinctly and gather into one word the total numinous impression a thing may make on the mind. The nearest that German can get to it is in the expression *das Ungeheuere* (monstrous), while in English 'weird' is perhaps the closest rendering possible. The mood and attitude represented in the foregoing verse might then be fairly well rendered by such a translation as:

Much there is that is weird; but nought
is weirder than man.

The German *ungeheuer* is not by derivation simply 'huge', in quantity or quality;—this, its common meaning, is in fact a rationalizing interpretation of the real idea; it is that which is not *geheuer,* i.e. approximately, the *uncanny*—in a word, the numinous. And it is just this element of the uncanny in man that Sophocles has in mind. If this, its fundamental meaning, be really and thoroughly felt in consciousness, then the word could be taken as a fairly exact expression for the numinous in its aspects of mystery, awefulness, majesty, augustness, and 'energy'; nay, even the aspect of fascination is dimly felt in it.

The variations of meaning in the German word *ungeheuer* can be well illustrated from Goethe.[17] He, too, uses the word first to denote the huge in size—what is too vast for our faculty of space-perception, such as the immeasurable vault of the night sky. In other passages the word retains its original non-rational colour more markedly; it comes to mean the uncanny, the fearful, the dauntingly 'other' and incomprehensible, that which arouses in us *stupor* and *thambos;* and finally, in the wonderful words of Faust which I have put at the beginning of this book, it becomes an almost exact synonym for our 'numinous' under all its aspects.

> Das Schaudern ist der Menschheit bestes Teil.
> Wie auch die Welt ihm das Gefühl verteuere,
> Ergriffen fühlt er tief das Ungeheuere.[18]

---

17 Cf. *Wilhelm Meisters Wanderjahre,* Bk. I, ch. 10; *Wahlverwandtschaften,* 2. 15; *Dichtung und Wahrheit,* 2. 9: 4. 20.

18 Awe is the best of man: howe'er the world's
Misprizing of the feeling would prevent us,
Deeply we feel, once gripped, the weird Portentous.
(GOETHE, *Faust,* Second Part, Act I, Sc. v.)

Other books by Rudolph Otto:

India's Religion of Grace and Christianity, 1932.
The Kingdom of God and the Son of Man, 1943.
Mysticism East and West, 1932.
Naturalism and Religion, 1905.
The Philosophy of Religion Based on Kant and Friess, 1931.

Other books on the same problem:

Brunner, Emil. *The Christian Doctrine of God,* 1946.
Tillich, Paul. *Systematic Theology,* Vol. I, 1951.
Horton, Walter Marshall. *The Objective Element in the Experience of God,* 1927.
Dillenberger, John. *God Hidden and Revealed,* 1953.

FEODOR DOSTOIEVSKY

FEODOR DOSTOIEVSKY, the classical modern novelist, is, of course, in the strict sense of the term, not a theologian. In a broader sense, however, he is fundamentally nothing else, since he seeks ultimate answers for the ultimate questions of human experience. A Slavophile, he was permeated by an intense belief in the spiritual destiny of Russia as the historically necessary counter to Western materialism. His religious roots were in the mystical tradition of Russian Orthodoxy. But it is in his keen psychological analyses of the devious ambiguous and labyrinthean sources of human behavior, in which man and his existence become problematic, that Dostoievsky has entered into the mainstream of western theology as a major influence. In contrast to the humanist's image of well-intentioned man caught in a network of social and institutional evils Dostoievsky presents the tragic image of man who bears in himself monstrous potentialities for evil, self-deception and crime as well as for super-human goodness, self-abnegation and saintliness.

In this dialectical duality of man's nature, but especially in the ambiguous character of the dynamic interplay of creative forces in his spiritual development, an interplay in which the positive transforms itself into the negative and the negative into the positive, in which the good becomes a mask of Satanic intention and evil an area in which the divine reveals itself—in this dialectical drama of the human spirit Dostoievsky develops a doctrine of man that is closer to Christian anthropology than that found in any modern literature before his time. Fulfilled man is not "enlightened" man, self-perfected through intellectual, moral or cultural striving, but broken and defeated man redeemed through sources outside of and in spite of himself, that is, through Grace.

In the episode of "The Grand Inquisitor" the crucifixion—the possibility (inevitability?) in life of a demonic distortion of truth in the name of truth, of the good in the name of goodness, of freedom in the name of freedom—is given its most powerful modern expression.

FEODOR DOSTOIEVSKY

"The Grand Inquisitor"
from
The Brothers Karamazov

AND BEHOLD, He deigned to appear for a moment to the people, to the tortured, suffering people, sunk in iniquity, but loving Him like children. My story is laid in Spain, in Seville, in the most terrible time of the Inquisition, when fires were lighted every day to the glory of God, and 'in the splended *auto da fé* the wicked heretics were burnt.' Oh, of course, this was not the coming in which He will appear according to His promise at the end of time in all His heavenly glory, and which will be sudden 'as lightning flashing from east to west.' No, He visited His children only for a moment, and there where the flames were crackling round the heretics. In His infinite mercy He came once more among men in that human shape in which He walked among men for three years fifteen centuries ago. He came down to the 'hot pavement' of the southern town in which on the day before almost a hundred heretics had, *ad majorem gloriam Dei,* been burnt by the cardinal, the Grand Inquisitor, in a magnificent *auto da fé,* in the presence of the king, the court, the knights, the cardinals, the most charming ladies of the court, and the whole population of Seville.

"He came softly, unobserved, and yet, strange to say, every one recognised Him. That might be one of the best passages in the poem. I mean, why they recognised Him. The people are irresistibly drawn to Him, they surround Him, they flock about Him, follow Him. He moves silently in their midst with a gentle smile of infinite compassion. The sun of love burns in His heart, light and power shine from His eyes, and their radiance, shed on the people, stirs their hearts with responsive love. He holds out His hands to them, blesses them, and a healing virtue comes from contact with Him, even with His garments. An old man in the crowd, blind from childhood, cries out, 'O Lord, heal me and I shall see Thee!' and, as it were, scales fall from his eyes and the blind man sees Him. The crowd weeps and kisses the earth under His feet. Children throw flowers before Him, sing, and cry hosannah. 'It is He—it is He!' all repeat. 'It must be He, it can be no one but Him!' He stops at the steps of the Seville cathedral at the moment when the weeping mourners are bringing in a little open white coffin. In it lies a child of seven, the only daughter of a prominent citizen. The dead child lies hidden in flowers. 'He will raise your child,' the crowd shouts to the weeping mother. The priest, coming to meet the coffin, looks perplexed, and frowns, but the mother of the dead child throws herself at His feet with a wail. 'If it is Thou, raise my child!' she cries, holding out her hands to Him. The procession halts, the coffin is laid on the steps at His feet. He looks with compassion, and His lips once more softly pronounce, 'Maiden, arise!' and the maiden arises. The little girl sits up in the coffin and looks around, smiling with wide-open wondering eyes, holding a bunch of white roses they had put in her hand.

"There are cries, sobs, confusion among the people, and at that moment the cardinal himself, the Grand Inquisitor, passes by the cathedral. He is an old man, almost ninety, tall and erect, with a withered face and sunken eyes, in which there is still a gleam of light. He is not dressed in his gorgeous cardinal's robes, as he was the day before, when he was burning the enemies of the Roman Church—at that moment he was wearing his coarse, old, monk's cassock. At a distance behind him come his gloomy assistants and slaves and the 'holy guard.' He stops at the sight of the crowd and watches it from a distance. He sees everything; he sees them set the coffin down at His feet, sees the child rise up, and his face darkens. He knits his thick grey brows and his eyes gleam with a sinister fire. He holds out his finger and bids the guards take Him. And such is his power, so completely are the people cowed into submission and trembling obedience to him, that the crowd immediately makes way for the guards, and in the midst of deathlike silence they lay hands on Him and lead Him away. The crowd instantly bows down to the earth, like one man, before the old inquisitor. He blesses the people in silence and passes on. The guards lead their prisoner to the close, gloomy vaulted prison in the ancient palace of the Holy Inquisition and shut Him in it. The day passes and is followed by the dark, burning 'breathless' night of Seville. The air is 'fragrant with laurel and lemon.' In the pitch darkness the iron door of the prison is suddenly opened and the Grand Inquisitor himself comes in with a light in his hand. He is alone; the door is closed at once behind him. He stands in the doorway and for a minute or two gazes into His face. At last he goes up slowly, sets the light on the table and speaks.

" 'Is it Thou? Thou?' but receiving no answer, he adds at once, 'Don't answer, be silent. What canst Thou say, indeed? I know too well what Thou wouldst say. And Thou hast no right to add anything to what Thou hadst said of old. Why, then, art Thou come to hinder us? For Thou hast come to hinder us, and Thou knowest that. But dost Thou know what will be to-morrow? I know not who Thou art and care not to know whether it is Thou or only a semblance of Him, but to-morrow I shall condemn Thee and burn Thee at the stake as the worst of heretics. And the very people who have to-day kissed Thy feet, to-morrow at the faintest sign from me will rush to heap up the embers of Thy fire. Knowest Thou that? Yes, maybe Thou knowest it,' he added with thoughtful penetration, never for a moment taking his eyes off the Prisoner."

"I don't quite understand, Ivan. What does it mean?" Alyosha, who had been listening in silence, said with a smile. "Is it simply a wild fantasy, or a mistake on the part of the old man—some impossible *quiproquo?*"

"Take it as the last," said Ivan, laughing, "if you are so corrupted by modern realism and can't stand anything fantastic. If you like it to be a case of mistaken identity, let it be so. It is true," he went on laughing, "the old man was ninety, and he might well be crazy over his set idea. He might have been struck by the appearance of the Prisoner. It might, in fact, be simply his ravings, the delusion of an old man of ninety, over-excited by the *auto da fé* of a hundred heretics the day before. But does it matter to us after all whether it was a mistake of identity or a wild fantasy? All that matters is that the old man should speak out, should speak openly of what he has thought in silence for ninety years."

"And the Prisoner too is silent? Does He look at him and not say a word?"

"That's inevitable in any case," Ivan laughed again. "The old man has told Him He hasn't the right to add anything to what He has said of old. One may say it is the most fundamental feature of Roman Catholicism, in my opinion at least. 'All has been given by Thee to the Pope,' they say, 'and all, therefore, is still in the Pope's hands, and there is no need for Thee to come now at all. Thou must not meddle for the time, at least.' That's how they speak and write too—the Jesuits, at any rate. I have read it myself in the works of their theologians. 'Hast Thou the right to reveal to us one of the mysteries of that world from which Thou hast come?' my old man asks Him, and answers the question for Him. 'No, Thou hast not; that Thou mayest not add to what has been said of old and mayest not take from men the freedom which Thou didst exalt when Thou wast on earth. Whatsoever Thou revealest anew will encroach on men's freedom of faith; for it will be manifest as a miracle, and the freedom of their faith was dearer to Thee than anything in those days fifteen hundred years ago. Didst Thou not often say then, "I will make you free"? But now Thou hast seen these "free" men,' the old man adds suddenly, with a pensive smile. 'Yes, we've paid dearly for it,' he goes on, looking sternly at Him, 'but at last we have completed that work in Thy name. For fifteen centuries we have been wrestling with Thy freedom, but now it is ended and over for good. Dost Thou not believe that it's over for good? Thou lookest meekly at me and deignest not even to be wroth with me. But let me tell Thee that now, to-day, people are more persuaded than ever that they have perfect freedom, yet they have brought their freedom to us and laid it humbly at our feet. But that has been our doing. Was this what Thou didst? Was this Thy freedom?' "

"I don't understand again," Alyosha broke in. "Is he ironical, is he jesting?"

"Not a bit of it! He claims it as a merit for himself and his Church that at last they have vanquished freedom and have done so to make men happy. 'For now' (he is speaking of the Inquisition, of course) 'for the first time it has become possible to think of the happiness of men. Man was created a rebel; and how can rebels be happy? Thou wast warned,' he says to Him. "Thou hast had no lack of admonitions and warnings, but Thou didst not listen to those warnings; Thou didst reject the only way by which men might be made happy. But, fortunately, departing Thou didst hand on the work to us. Thou has promised, Thou hast established by Thy word, Thou hast given to us the right to bind and to unbind, and now, of course, Thou canst not think of taking it away. Why, then, has Thou come to hinder us?' "

"And what's the meaning of 'no lack of admonitions and warnings'?" asked Aloshya.

"Why, that's the chief part of what the old man must say."

" 'The wise and dread spirit, the spirit of self-destruction and non-existence,' the old man goes on, 'the great spirit talked with Thee in the wilderness, and we are told in the books that he "tempted" Thee. Is that so? And could anything truer be said than what he revealed to Thee in three questions and what Thou didst reject, and what in the books is called "the temptation"? And yet if there has ever been on earth a real stupendous miracle, it took place on that day, on the day of the three temptations. The statement of those three questions was itself the miracle. If it were possible to imagine simply for the sake of argument that those three questions of the dread spirit had perished utterly from the books, and that we had to restore them and to invent them anew, and to do so had gathered together all the wise men of the earth—rulers, chief priests, learned men, philosophers, poets—and had set them the task to invent three questions, such as would not only fit the occasion, but express in three words, three human phrases, the whole future history of the world and of humanity—dost Thou believe that all the wisdom of the earth united could have invented anything in depth and force equal to the three questions which were actually put to Thee then by the wise and mighty spirit in the wilderness? From those questions alone, from the miracle of their statement, we can see that we have here to do not with the fleeting human intelligence, but with the absolute and eternal. For in those three questions the whole subsequent history of mankind is, as it were, brought together into one whole, and foretold, and in them are united all the unsolved historical contradictions of human nature. At the time it could not be so clear, since the future was unknown; but now that fifteen hundred years have passed, we see that everything in those three questions was so justly divined and foretold, and has been so truly fulfilled, that nothing can be added to them or taken from them.

"'Judge Thyself who was right—Thou or he who questioned Thee then? Remember the first question; its meaning, in other words, was this: "Thou wouldst go into the world, and art going with empty hands, with some promise of freedom which men in their simplicity and their natural unruliness cannot even understand, which they fear and dread—for nothing has ever been more insupportable for a man and a human society than freedom. But seest Thou these stones in this parched and barren wilderness? Turn them into bread, and mankind will run after Thee like a flock of sheep, grateful and obedient, though for ever trembling, lest Thou withdraw Thy hand and deny them Thy bread." But Thou wouldst not deprive man of freedom and didst reject the offer, thinking, what is that freedom worth, if obedience is bought with bread? Thou didst reply that man lives not by bread alone. But dost Thou know that for the sake of that earthly bread the spirit of the earth will rise up against Thee and will strive with Thee and overcome Thee, and all will follow him, crying, "Who can compare with this beast? He has given us fire from heaven!" Dost Thou know that the ages will pass, and humanity will proclaim by the lips of their sages that there is no crime, and therefore no sin; there is only hunger? "Feed men, and then ask of them virtue!" that's what they'll write on the banner, which they will raise against Thee, and with which they will destroy Thy temple. Where Thy temple stood will rise a new building; the terrible tower of Babel will be built again, and though, like the one of old, it will not be finished, yet Thou mightest have prevented that new tower and have cut short the sufferings of men for a thousand years; for they will come back to us after a thousand years of agony with their tower. They will seek us again, hidden underground in the catacombs, for we shall be again persecuted and tortured. They will find us and cry to us, "Feed us, for those who have promised us fire from heaven haven't given it!" And then we shall finish building their tower, for he finishes the building who feeds them. And we alone shall feed them in Thy name, declaring falsely that it is in Thy name. Oh, never, never can they feed themselves without us! No science will give them bread so long as they remain free. In the end they will lay their freedom at our feet, and say to us, "Make us your slaves, but feed us." They will understand themselves, at last, that freedom and bread enough for all are inconceivable together, for never, never will they be able to share between them! They will be convinced, too, that they can never be free, for they are weak, vicious, worthless and rebellious. Thou didst promise them the bread of Heaven, but, I repeat again, can it compare with earthly bread in the eyes of the weak, ever sinful and ignoble race of man? And if for the sake of the bread of Heaven thousands and tens of thousands shall follow Thee, what is to become of the millions and tens of thousands of millions of creatures who will not have the strength to forego the earthly bread for the sake of the heavenly? Or dost Thou care only for the tens of thousands of the great and strong, while the millions, numerous as the sands of the sea, who are weak but love Thee, must exist only for the sake of the great and strong? No, we care for the weak too. They are sinful and rebellious, but in the end they too will become obedient. They will marvel at us and look on us as gods, because we are ready to endure the freedom which they have found so dreadful and to rule over them—so awful it will seem to them to be free. But we shall tell them that we are Thy servants and rule them in Thy name. We shall deceive them again, for we will not let Thee come to us again. That deception will be our suffering, for we shall be forced to lie.

" 'This is the significance of the first question in the wilderness, and this is what Thou hast rejected for the sake of that freedom which Thou hast exalted above everything. Yet in this question lies hid the great secret of this world. Choosing "bread," Thou wouldst have satisfied the universal and everlasting craving of humanity—to find some one to worship. So long as man remains free he strives for nothing so incessantly and so painfully as to find some one to worship. But man seeks to worship what is established beyond dispute, so that all men would agree at once to worship it. For these pitiful creatures are concerned not only to find what one or the other can worship, but to find something that all would believe in and worship; what is essential is that all may be *together* in it. This craving for *community* of worship is the chief misery of every man individually and of all humanity from the beginning of time. For the sake of common worship they've slain each other with the sword. They have set up gods and challenged one another, "Put away your gods and come and worship ours, or we will kill you and your gods!" And so it will be to the end of the world, even when gods disappear from the earth; they will fall down before idols just the same. Thou didst know, Thou couldst not but have known, this fundamental secret of human nature, but Thou didst reject the one infallible banner which was offered Thee to make all men bow down to Thee alone—the banner of earthly bread; and Thou hast rejected it for the sake of freedom and the bread of Heaven. Behold what Thou didst further. And all again in the name of freedom! I tell Thee that man is tormented by no greater anxiety than to find some one quickly to whom he can hand over that gift of freedom with which the ill-fated creature is born. But only one who can appease their conscience can take over their freedom. In bread there was offered Thee an invincible banner; give bread, and man will worship Thee, for nothing is more certain than bread. But if some one else gains possession of his conscience—oh! then he will cast away Thy bread and follow after him who has ensnared his conscience. In that Thou wast right. For the secret of man's being is not only to live but to have something to live for. Without a stable conception of the object of life, man would not consent to go on living, and would rather destroy himself than remain on earth, though he had bread in abundance. That is true. But what happened? Instead of taking men's freedom from them, Thou didst make it greater than ever! Didst Thou forget that man prefers peace, and even death, to freedom of choice in the knowledge of good and evil? Nothing is more seductive for man than his freedom of conscience, but nothing is a greater cause of suffering. And behold, instead of giving a firm foundation for setting the conscience of man at rest for ever, Thou didst choose all that is exceptional, vague and enigmatic; Thou didst choose what was utterly beyond the strength of men, acting as though Thou didst not love them at all—Thou who didst come to give Thy life for them! Instead of taking possession of men's freedom, Thou didst increase it, and burdened the spiritual kingdom of mankind with its sufferings for ever. Thou didst desire man's free love, that he should follow Thee freely, enticed and taken captive by Thee. In place of the rigid ancient law, man must hereafter with free heart decide for himself what is good and what is evil, having only Thy image before him as his guide. But didst Thou not know he would at last reject even Thy image and Thy truth, if he is weighed down with the fearful burden of free choice? They will cry aloud at last that the truth is not in Thee, for they could not have been left in greater confusion and suffering than Thou hast caused, laying upon them so many cares and unanswerable problems.

" 'So that, in truth, Thou didst Thyself lay the foundation for the destruction of Thy kingdom, and no one is more to blame for it. Yet what was offered Thee? There are three powers, three powers alone, able to conquer and to hold captive for ever the conscience of these impotent rebels for their happiness—those forces are miracle, mystery and authority. Thou hast rejected all three and hast set the example for doing so. When the wise and dread spirit set Thee on the pinnacle of the temple and said to Thee, "If Thou wouldst know whether Thou art the Son of God then cast Thyself down, for it is written: the angels shall hold him up lest he fall and bruise himself, and Thou shalt know then whether Thou art the Son of God and shalt prove then how great is Thy faith in Thy Father." But Thou didst refuse and wouldst not cast Thyself down. Oh! of course, Thou didst proudly and well, like God; but the weak, unruly race of men, are they gods? Oh, Thou didst know then that in taking one step, in making one movement to cast Thyself down, Thou wouldst be tempting God and have lost all Thy faith in Him, and wouldst have been dashed to pieces against that earth which Thou didst come to save. And the wise spirit that tempted Thee would have rejoiced. But I ask again, are there many like Thee? And couldst Thou believe for one moment that men, too, could face such a temptation? Is the nature of men such, that they can reject miracle, and at the great moments of their life, the moments of their deepest, most agonising spiritual difficulties, cling only to the free verdict of the heart? Oh, Thou didst know that Thy deed would be recorded in books, would be handed down to remote times and the utmost ends of the earth, and Thou didst hope that man, following Thee, would cling to God and not ask for a miracle. But Thou didst not know that when man rejects miracle he rejects God too; for man seeks not so much God as the miraculous. And as man cannot bear to be without the miraculous, he will create new miracles of his own for himself, and will worship deeds of sorcery and witchcraft, though he might be a hundred times over a rebel, heretic and infidel. Thou didst not come down from the Cross when they shouted to Thee, mocking and reviling Thee, "Come down from the cross and we will believe that Thou art He." Thou didst not come down, for again Thou wouldst not enslave man by a miracle, and didst crave faith given freely, not based on miracle. Thou didst crave for free love and not the base raptures of the slave before the might that has overawed him for ever. But Thou didst think too highly of men therein, for they are slaves, of course, though rebellious by nature. Look round and judge; fifteen centuries have passed, look upon them. Whom hast Thou raised up to Thyself? I swear, man is weaker and baser by nature than Thou hast believed him! Can he, can he do what Thou didst? By showing him so much respect, Thou didst, as it were, cease to feel for him, for Thou didst ask far too much from him—Thou who hast loved him more than Thyself! Respecting him less, Thou wouldst have asked less of him. That would have been more like love, for his burden would have been lighter. He is weak and vile. What though he is everywhere now rebelling against our power, and proud of his rebellion? It is the pride of a child and a schoolboy. They are little children rioting and barring out the teacher at school. But their childish delight will end; it will cost them dear. They will cast down temples and drench the earth with blood. But they will see at last, the foolish children, that, though they are rebels, they are impotent rebels, unable to keep up their own rebellion. Bathed in their foolish tears, they will recognise at last that He who created them rebels must have meant to mock at them. They will say this in despair, and their utterance will be a blasphemy which will make them more unhappy still, for man's nature cannot bear blasphemy, and in the end always avenges it on itself. And so unrest, confusion and unhappiness—that is the present lot of man after Thou didst bear so much for their freedom! Thy great prophet tells in vision and in image, that he saw all those who took part in the first resurrection and that there were of each tribe twelve thousand. But if there were so many of them, they must have been not men but gods. They had borne Thy cross, they had endured scores of years in the barren, hungry wilderness, living upon locusts and roots—and Thou mayest indeed point with pride at those children of freedom, of free love, of free and splendid sacrifice for Thy name. But remember that they were only some thousands; and what of the rest? And how are the other weak ones to blame, because they could not endure what the strong have endured? How is the weak soul to blame that it is unable to receive such terrible gifts? Canst Thou have simply come to the elect and for the elect? But if so, it is a mystery and we cannot understand it. And if it is a mystery, we too have a right to preach a mystery, and to teach them that it's not the free judgment of their hearts, not love that matters, but a mystery which they must follow blindly, even against their conscience. So we have done. We have corrected Thy work and have founded it upon *miracle, mystery* and *authority*. And men rejoiced that they were again led like sheep, and that the terrible gift that had brought them such suffering, was, at last, lifted from their hearts. Were we right teaching them this? Speak! Did we not love mankind, so meekly acknowledging their feebleness, lovingly lightening their burden, and permitting their weak nature even sin with our sanction? Why hast Thou come now to hinder us? And why dost Thou look silently and searchingly at me with Thy mild eyes? Be angry. I don't want Thy love, for I love Thee not. And what use is it for me to hide anything from Thee? Don't I know to Whom I am speaking? All that I can say is known to Thee already. And is it for me to conceal from Thee our mystery? Perhaps it is Thy will to hear it from my lips. Listen, then. We are not working with Thee, but with *him*—that is our mystery. It's long—eight centuries—since we have been on *his* side and not on Thine. Just eight centuries ago, we took from him what Thou didst reject with scorn, that last gift he offered Thee, showing Thee all the kingdoms of the earth. We took from him Rome and the sword of Cæsar, and proclaimed ourselves sole rulers of the earth, though hitherto we have not been able to complete our work. But whose fault is that? Oh, the work is only beginning, but it has begun. It has long to await completion and the earth has yet much to suffer, but we shall triumph and shall be Cæsars, and then we shall plan the universal happiness of man. But Thou mightest have taken even then the sword of Cæsar. Why didst Thou reject that last gift? Hadst Thou accepted that last counsel of the mighty spirit, Thou wouldst have accomplished all that man seeks on earth—that is, some one to worship, some one to keep his conscience, and some means of uniting all in one unanimous and harmonious ant-heap, for the craving for universal unity is the third and last anguish of men. Mankind as a whole has always striven to organise a universal state. There have been many great nations with great histories, but the more highly they were developed the more unhappy they were, for they felt more acutely than other people the craving for worldwide union. The great conquerors, Timours and Ghenghis-Khans, whirled like hurricanes over the face of the earth striving to subdue its people, and they too were but the unconscious expression of the same craving for universal unity. Hadst Thou taken the world and Cæsar's purple, Thou wouldst have founded the universal state and have given universal peace. For who can rule men if not he who holds their conscience and their bread in his hands? We have taken the sword of Cæsar, and in taking it, of course, have rejected Thee and followed *him*. Oh, ages are yet to come of the confusion of free thought, of their science and cannibalism. For having begun to build their tower of Babel without us, they will end, of course, with cannibalism. But then the beast will crawl to us and lick our feet and spatter them with tears of blood. And we shall sit upon the beast and raise the cup, and on it will be written, "Mystery." But then, and only then, the reign of peace and happiness will come for men. Thou art proud of Thine elect, but Thou has only the elect, while we give rest to all. And besides, how many of those elect, those mighty ones who could become elect, have grown weary waiting for Thee, and have transferred and will transfer the powers of their spirit and the warmth of their heart to the other camp, and end by raising their *free* banner against

Thee. Thou didst Thyself lift up that banner. But with us all will be happy and will no more rebel nor destroy one another as under Thy freedom. Oh, we shall persuade them that they will only become free when they renounce their freedom to us and submit to us. And shall we be right or shall we be lying? They will be convinced that we are right, for they will remember the horrors of slavery and confusion to which Thy freedom brought them. Freedom, free thought and science, will lead them into such straits and will bring them face to face with such marvels and insoluble mysteries, that some of them, the fierce and rebellious, will destroy themselves, others, rebellious but weak, will destroy one another, while the rest, weak and unhappy, will crawl fawning to our feet and whine to us: "Yes, you were right, you alone possess His mystery, and we come back to you, save us from ourselves!"

" 'Receiving bread from us, they will see clearly that we take the bread made by their hands from them, to give it to them, without any miracle. They will see that we do not change the stones to bread, but in truth they will be more thankful for taking it from our hands than for the bread itself! For they will remember only too well that in old days, without our help, even the bread they made turned to stones in their hands, while since they have come back to us, the very stones have turned to bread in their hands. Too, too well they know the value of complete submission! And until men know that, they will be unhappy. Who is most to blame for their not knowing it, speak? Who scattered the flock and sent it astray on unknown paths? But the flock will come together again and will submit once more, and then it will be once for all. Then we shall give them the quiet humble happiness of weak creatures such as they are by nature. Oh, we shall persuade them at last not to be proud, for Thou didst lift them up and thereby taught them to be proud. We shall show them that they are weak, that they are only pitiful children, but that childlike happiness is the sweetest of all. They will become timid and will look to us and huddle close to us in fear, as chicks to the hen. They will marvel at us and will be awe-stricken before us, and will be proud at our being so powerful and clever, that we have been able to subdue such a turbulent flock of thousands of millions. They will tremble impotently before our wrath, their minds will grow fearful, they will be quick to shed tears like women and children, but they will be just as ready at a sign from us to pass to laughter and rejoicing, to happy mirth and childish song. Yes, we shall set them to work, but in their leisure hours we shall make their life like a child's game, with children's songs and innocent dance. Oh, we shall allow them even sin, they are weak and helpless, and they will love us like children because we allow them to sin. We shall tell them that every sin will be expiated, if it is done with our permission, that we allow them to sin because we love them, and the punishment for these sins we take upon ourselves. And we shall take it upon ourselves, and they will adore us as their saviours who have taken on themselves their sins before God. And they will have no secrets from us. We shall allow or forbid them to live with their wives and mistresses, to have or not to have children—according to whether they have been obedient or disobedient—and they will submit to us gladly and cheerfully. The most painful secrets of their conscience, all, all they will bring to us, and we shall have an answer for all. And they will be glad to believe our answer, for it will save them from the great anxiety and terrible agony they endure at present in making a free decision for themselves. And all will be happy, all the millions of creatures except the hundred thousand who rule over them. For only we, we who guard the mystery, shall be unhappy. There will be thousands of millions of happy babes, and a hundred thousand sufferers who have taken upon themselves the curse of the knowledge of good and evil. Peacefully they will die, peacefully they will expire in Thy name, and beyond the grave they will find nothing but death. But we shall keep the secret, and for their happiness we shall allure them with the reward of heaven and eternity. Though if there were anything in the other world, it certainly would not be for such as they. It is prophesied that Thou wilt come again in victory, Thou wilt come with Thy chosen, the proud and strong, but we will say that they have only saved themselves, but we have saved all. We are told that the harlot who sits upon the beast, and holds in her hands the *mystery,* shall be put to shame, that the weak will rise up again, and will rend her royal purple and will strip naked her loathsome body. But then I will stand up and point out to Thee the thousand millions of happy children who have known no sin. And we who have taken their sins upon us for their happiness will stand up before Thee and say: "Judge us if Thou canst and darest." Know that I fear Thee not. Know that I too have been in the wilderness, I too have lived on roots and locusts, I too prized the freedom with which Thou hast blessed men, and I too was striving to stand among Thy elect, among the strong and powerful, thirsting "to make up the number." But I awakened and would not serve madness. I turned back and joined the ranks of those *who have corrected Thy work.* I left the proud and went back to the humble, for the happiness of the humble. What I say to Thee will come to pass, and our dominion will be built up. I repeat, to-morrow Thou shalt see that obedient flock who at a sign from me will hasten to heap up the hot cinders about the pile on which I shall burn Thee for coming to hinder us. For if any one has ever deserved our fires, it is Thou. To-morrow I shall burn Thee. Dixi.' "

Ivan stopped. He was carried away as he talked and spoke with excitement; when he had finished, he suddenly smiled.

Alyosha had listened in silence; towards the end he was greatly moved and seemed several times on the point of interrupting, but restrained himself. Now his words came with a rush.

"But . . . that's absurd!" he cried, flushing. "Your poem is in praise of Jesus, not in blame of Him—as you meant it to be. And who will believe you about freedom? Is that the way to understand it? That's not the idea of it in the Orthodox Church . . . That's Rome, and not even the whole of Rome, it's false—those are the worst of the Catholics, the Inquisitors, the Jesuits! . . . And there could not be such a fantastic creature as your Inquisitor. What are these sins of mankind they take on themselves? Who are these keepers of the mystery who have taken some curse upon themselves for the happiness of mankind? When have they been seen? We know the Jesuits, they are spoken ill of, but surely they are not what you describe? They are not that at all, not at all. . . . They are simply the Romish army for the earthly sovereignty of the world in the future, with the Pontiff of Rome for Emperor . . . that's their ideal, but there's no sort of mystery or lofty melancholy about it. . . . It's simple lust of power, of filthy earthly gain, of domination—something like a universal serfdom with them as masters—that's all they stand for. They don't even believe in God perhaps. Your suffering inquisitor is a mere fantasy."

"Stay, stay," laughed Ivan, "how hot you are! A fantasy you say, let it be so! Of course it's a fantasy. But allow me to say: do you really think that the Roman Catholic movement of the last centuries is actually nothing but the lust of power, of filthy earthly gain? Is that Father Païssy's teaching?"

"No, no, on the contrary, Father Païssy did once say something rather the same as you . . . but of course it's not the same, not a bit the same," Alyosha hastily corrected himself.

"A precious admission, in spite of your 'not a bit the same.' I ask you why your Jesuits and Inquisitors have united simply for vile material gain? Why can there not be among them one martyr oppressed by great sorrow and loving humanity? You see, only suppose that there was one such man among all those who desire nothing but filthy material gain—if there's only one like my old inquisitor, who had himself eaten roots in the desert and made frenzied efforts to subdue his flesh to make himself free and perfect. But yet all his life he loved humanity, and suddenly his eyes were opened, and he saw that it is no great moral blessedness to attain perfection and freedom, if at the same time one gains the conviction that millions of God's creatures have been created as a mockery, that they will never be capable of using their freedom, that these poor rebels can never turn into giants to complete the tower, that it was not for such geese that the great idealist dreamt his dream of harmony. Seeing all that he turned back and joined—the clever people. Surely that could have happened?"

"Joined whom, what clever people?" cried Alyosha, completely carried away. "They have no such great cleverness and no mysteries and secrets. . . . Perhaps nothing but Atheism, that's all their secret. Your inquisitor does not believe in God, that's his secret!"

"What if it is so! At last you have guessed it. It's perfectly true that that's the whole secret, but isn't that suffering, at least for a man like that, who has wasted his whole life in the desert and yet could not shake off his incurable love of humanity? In his old age he reached the clear conviction that nothing but the advice of the great dread spirit could build up any tolerable sort of life for the feeble, unruly, 'incomplete, empirical creatures created in jest.' And so, convinced of this, he sees that he must follow the counsel of the wise spirit, the dread spirit of death and destruction, and therefore accept lying and deception, and lead men consciously to death and destruction, and yet deceive them all the way so that they may not notice where they are being led, that the poor blind creatures may at least on the way think themselves happy. And note, the deception is in the name of Him in Whose ideal the old man had so fervently believed all his life long. Is not that tragic? And if only one such stood at the head of the whole army 'filled with the lust of power only for the sake of filthy gain'—would not one such be enough to make a tragedy? More than that, one such standing at the head is enough to create the actual leading idea of the Roman Church with all its armies and Jesuits, its highest idea. I tell you frankly that I firmly believe that there has always been such a man among those who stood at the head of the movement. Who knows, there may have been some such even among the Roman Popes. Who knows, perhaps the spirit of that accursed old man who loves mankind so obstinately in his own way, is to be found even now in a whole multitude of such old men, existing not by chance but by agreement, as a secret league formed long ago for the guarding of the mystery, to guard it from the weak and the unhappy, so as to make them happy. No doubt it is so, and so it must be indeed. I fancy that even among the Masons there's something of the same mystery at the bottom, and that that's why the Catholics so detest the Masons as their rivals breaking up the unity of the idea, while it is so essential that there should be one flock and one shepherd. . . . But from the way I defend my idea I might be an author impatient of your criticism. Enough of it."

"You are perhaps a Mason yourself!" broke suddenly from Alyosha. "You don't believe in God," he added, speaking this time very sorrowfully. He fancied besides that his brother was looking at him ironically. "How does your poem end?" he asked, suddenly looking down. "Or was it the end?"

"I meant to end it like this. When the Inquisitor ceased speaking he waited some time for his Prisoner to answer him. His silence weighed down upon him. He saw that the Prisoner had listened intently all the time, looking gently in his face and evidently not wishing to reply. The old man longed for Him to say something, however bitter and terrible. But He suddenly approached the old man in silence and softly kissed him on his bloodless aged lips. That was all his answer. The old man shuddered. His lips moved. He went to the door, opened it, and said to Him: 'Go, and come no more. . . . come not at all, never, never!' And he let Him out into the dark alleys of the town. The Prisoner went away."

Other books by Dostoievsky:

The Idiot, 1869.
The Journal of an Author, 1877.
Notes From the Underworld, 1864.
The Possessed, 1871.

Other books on the same problem:

Berdyaev, Nicholas. *Slavery and Freedom,* 1944.
Haroutunian, Joseph. *Lust for Power,* 1949.
Kierkegaard, Søren. *Fear and Trembling,* 1843.
Lewis, C. S. *The Problem of Pain,* 1940.
de Rougemont, Denis. *The Devil's Share,* 1944.
Tillich, Paul. *The Interpretation of History,* 1926 (Engl. trans. 1936).
Tillich, Paul. *Systematic Theology,* Vol. II, 1957.

NICHOLAS BERDYAEV

NICHOLAS BERDYAEV has been called the "philosopher of spirit", and indeed, no one has been more "intoxicated with spirit" than he. One of the most scintillating, flamelike minds in Europe between the two wars, he illuminated every problem he approached with original insights, bringing new life to that which seemed dead, new light to intellectual fires that seemed burned out, new hope and expectations to Europe's broken and exhausted spirit. Even his literary style reflects a mind functioning always in the ecstasy of creative inspiration, ideas leaping freely like sparks rather than developing systematically and logically under the sober control of the disciplined intellect. He does not demonstrate; he illuminates. He does not confine thought in logical conclusions; he opens it to unexplored intellectual vistas. Herein lies both his strength and his weakness.

Uniting in himself widely divergent cultural traditions he serves as a catalytic agent which fuses together and integrates elements of Russian oriental mysticism and western rationalism, of Old Testament Prophetism and Greek Idealism, of Protestant individualism and Catholic universalism, of Romantic subjectivism, Marxian socialism etc., not in eclectic synthesis but in the uniqueness of his own spiritual perspective.

But wherever his mind moves, its point of departure and of return is always spirit, freedom and creativity which seem almost like three names for that which to Berdyaev is the sole reality. Burdened with the dead weight of all that is, all that has become "objectified" and therefore congealed, opaque, lifeless and unreal, he lives only for the *possibility* of the new man, the new world, the new cosmos, the New Being which the creativity of spirit in freedom can bring about. He is therefore primarily eschatologically oriented toward final ends, toward the ultimate fulfillment of history, the total transfiguration of the cosmos through the power of the creative spirit which man essentially is. Human creativity in symbolic forms, in art, is a clue to the nature of creativity, but such *transformations* of the world in aesthetic forms are not enough. Only that activity of the spirit which *transfigures* the "broken and distorted world" itself is true creativity, and it is toward this end that Spirit, operative in human creativity, strives. Perhaps in no other contemporary have the eschatological, apocalyptic and pneumatic elements of Christianity been more alive and articulate.

But this eschatological expectation is not the only theme of Berdyaev. In the opposite direction, the direction of depth, he penetrates below surface manifestations for the source of creativity and freedom which he indicates in his concept of pre-ontic freedom. With this term he establishes freedom and creativity below the level of being itself as the *prius* of all being and beings, the infinite, unformed potentiality of all being, out of which all things are generated and from which they derive their power to be. So freedom, creativity and spirit are from the beginning, absolutely original, derived from nothing else, that without which nothing else would be.

Thus from the abysmal depths of the source of creativity in pre-ontic freedom to the extremest point of its creative possibility in the transfiguration of the cosmos Berdyaev glimpses the depth and the height of divine creativity in which the human spirit participates. Between these extremes is the broad area in which freedom is actualized in human creativity throughout the entire realm of historical cultural life. Whether in intellectual, socio-political, aesthetic or religious contexts, wherever problems of freedom or creativity may be encountered Berdyaev has contributed new ways of looking at old problems or established new problems that demand new ways of looking.

NICHOLAS BERDYAEV

from

The Beginning and the End

1.

TO BE AWARE OF THE FACT that man does not exist within a finished and stabilized system of being is fundamental to the philosophy of creativeness, and it is only on that understanding that the creative act of man is possible and intelligible. Another fundamental position consists in the realization that the creative act of man is not simply a regrouping and redistribution of the matter of the world. Nor is it merely an emanation, an outflowing of the primary matter of the world. Nor again is it just a shaping of the material in the sense of imposing ideal forms upon it. In the creative act of man, a new element is introduced, something which was not there before, which is not contained in the given world, and is not part of its make-up, but which breaks through from another scheme of the world, not out of the eternally given ideal forms, but out of freedom; and not out of a dark freedom, but out of an illuminated freedom.

The fact that creativity is possible in the world testifies to the inadequacy of this world, to a continual overcoming of it and to the existence of a power to achieve that purpose which issues from another world, or from a deeper level than this flat world. At the same time the creativeness of man is evidence of the fact that he belongs to two worlds and that he is called to assume a ruling position in the world. Pascal made the very profound observation that man's awareness of his insignificance is a sign of his greatness.

I have already said that the appearance of men of great creative power is not to be attributed to their environment nor to be explained by causal relations. The environment of the times in which he lived was incapable of giving birth to Pushkin; from that point of view his appearance must be regarded as a miracle. And this is true of every act of creativeness that is conceived, in it the old world always comes to an end.

Nor is it only that which the ego creates, but the very existence of the ego itself is a creative effort, a synthesizing creative act. Hundolph says with truth that creative power is an expression of the whole life of a man. Man creates his personality and in the act of doing so expresses his personality. In the self-creation of the ego, of the personality, the human spirit accomplishes a creative act of synthesis. A creative effort is needed in order to avoid any disintegration of the ego, any division of the personality, to prevent its breaking up into parts. Man is not only called to creativeness, as an activity which operates in the world and is exerted upon the world, but he is himself creative power and without that creative power his human countenance is lacking.

Man is a microcosmos and a microtheos. And it is only when he refuses to acquiesce in being part of anything whatever or in being himself made up of parts, that he is a person. The true image and form of man is a creative unity. It is difficult to understand Gilson's assertion, in terms of traditional Thomism, that it is impossible to imagine creative activity in man.[1] To my mind that amounts to the same thing as saying that it is impossible to imagine man. Man is a being who masters and surmounts himself and overcomes the world; it is in that that his value and dignity consist. But this securing of the mastery is creative power. The mystery of creativeness is the mystery of achieving the mastery over given reality, over the determinism of the world, over the locking of its closed circle. In this sense creative activity is an act of transcending; in a deeper sense it is the victory over non-being.

1 See E. Gilson: *L'Esprit de la philosophie médiévale.*

The philosophy of creativeness is not a philosophy of finitism, which, as Bergson justly observes, is based upon the assumption that everything is included in the datum. In regard to creativeness what needs to be established is a doctrine analogous to the teaching of Kant and Fichte, that is to say we must assert the creative activity of the subject, a creative activity which is not deducible from objective being. Fichte calls contemplation the productive power of imagination. But this is to recognize the character of intuition as creative and not passive. It is commonly said of art that it is concrete creative power as compared with the abstract nature of philosophy. But this may give rise to misunderstanding and requires elucidation.

Creativeness in art, like every other form of creative activity, consists in triumph over given, determined, concrete life, it is a victory over the world. Objectification knows a humdrum day-to-day concreteness of its own, but creative power finds its way out from this imposed concreteness, into concreteness of another kind. Creative activity does not consist merely in the bestowal of a more perfect form upon this world; it is also liberation from the burden and bondage of this world. Creativeness cannot be merely creation out of nothing, it presupposes the material which the world supplies. But the element of 'out of nothing' does enter into creative activity. For it is creativeness out of the freedom of the other world. This means that what is most important, most mysterious and most creatively new, comes not from 'the world' but from spirit.

There is something miraculous about the transformation of matter which takes place in art. This miraculous element exists also in images of beauty in nature, that nature in which the forces of enmity, ruin and chaos are at work. From a shapeless stone or lump of clay the beautiful form of a statue is given to us; out of a chaos of sounds we have one of Beethoven's symphonies; out of a chaos of words, the verses of Pushkin with all their power to charm. From sensations and impressions all unaware of meaning, knowledge is derived, from elemental subconscious instincts and attractions the beauty of moral form takes shape, out of an ugly world beauty is captured. In all this there is something miraculous from the point of view of the world, this given empirical world. Creative power anticipates the transfiguration of the world. This is the meaning of art, of art of any kind. And creative power has an eschatological element in it. It is an end of this world and a beginning of the new world. The world is created not by God only, but also by man. Creation is a divine-human work. And the crowning point of world creation is the end of this world. The world must be turned into an image of beauty, it must be dissolved in creative ecstasy.

The creative act is by its very nature ecstatic; it involves movement out beyond the boundaries; there is an act of transcendence in it. Creativeness is not an immanent process, nor susceptible of explanation in terms of immanence. There is always more in it than in any of the clauses by which it is sought to explain creative power; that is to say, the forcing of a way through within the realm of fettering determinism. Creative activity will not come to terms with the given state of the world, it desires another. The creative act always calls up the image of something different; it imagines something higher, better and more beautiful than this—than the 'given'. This evoking of the image of something different, something better and more beautiful, is a mysterious power in man and it cannot be explained by the action of the world environment. The world environment is full of the results of creative power in the past, which have grown cold and rigid. How is the rekindling of a new creative fire out of them to be explained?

Creative fancy and the rise of images of something better are of fundamental significance in human life. The relation between the real and what can be imagined is more complex than is commonly thought. That which appears to be a solid reality in the realm of things might be the stabilized, lignified, petrified, ossified result of very ancient imagination. I have already pointed out that Jacob Boehme regarded evil as a result of vicious imagination. A bright serene imagination, directed towards divine beauty can create a bright serene world. It is interesting to note that positivists, agnostics, materialists and sceptics ascribe extraordinary power to human imagination and thereby deny the primary foundation of their own *Weltanschauung*. Man, a pitiful product of his natural environment, and wholly determined from without, has, it would appear, discovered within himself the power to invent a spiritual world, God, and eternity! There is something wildly improbable about this.

Productive imagination is a metaphysical force which wages war against the objective and determinate world, against the realm of the commonplace and dull. The creative imagination builds up realities. The forms which are constructed by the creators of works of art lead a real existence and they are active in the world. Imagination is a way out from an unendurable reality. But a lying imagination, and it is not rare for it to be lying, precipitates a man into a reality which is a nightmare. It is always to be remembered that the imagination can be creative of falsehood, it can cast man into a world which, for all that it is a world of things, is fictitious. Present day psychopathology reveals much truth in this connection. Books on the spiritual life had formerly a great deal to say on this same subject. The creative imagination may construct a true idealization and a false; it can be an act of real love or an act which is unreal and brings terrible disillusionment with it. This is a source of the deep sense of tragedy in human existence.

It is possible for man to become the victim of his own imagination, despite the fact that the imagination is capable of being a way out towards a higher world. The antithesis between image and thing is fundamental. The primary reality is not the thing, it belongs to the image. Man finds it intolerable to live in the midst of things which have no image or which have lost it. Imagination brings feeling and thought to bear upon the complete image. The concrete reality which has an image is apprehended through the imagination, not through sensation. The imagination has played an enormous part in the very creation of objects which appear to be stable realities and exert their force from without. But the image is an act not a thing.[2]

The theme of creative power leads to a question which is fundamental in metaphysics: what is the primary reality, the thing, the object, including even spirit if it be understood in that way, or the act, the subject, the creative life? If the former is the case, the world cannot be changed and the situation of man in the world is hopeless. If the latter is the truth, then the world can be changed and man can find a way out from the realm of necessity into the realm of freedom. It is, therefore, necessary to draw a distinction between rational metaphysics and the metaphysics of images. The philosophy of the Spirit is the metaphysics of images.

Ribot, who has a positivist frame of mind, says that the creative imagination corresponds to the will, that it moves from the internal to the external and that images are the material of creative imagination.[3] In Ribot's view creative activity depends upon the power of the images to incite and prompt. The myth-creating process which belongs to the fountain head of human nature and from which human nature has not emancipated itself even today, is a product of imagination and personification. And there has been a greater element of truth in mythology than in the undivided power of concept and thing. Beauty is connected with the image, not with concepts. Kant says that if objects are regarded through concepts, every presentment of beauty disappears.[4]

---

2 See Sartre: *L'imagination,* Husserl's influence is to be seen in the fact that the image is regarded as the recognition of whatever it may be.

3 See Ribot: *Essai sur l'imagination créatrice.*

4 See *Kritik der Urteilskraft.*

The image of something different, something better, the image of beauty is brought into being out of the mysterious depth, out of freedom, not out of necessity, it arises from the noumenon, not from the phenomenon. And the creative act is, as it were, a link between the noumenal and phenomenal worlds, a way out beyond the confines of the phenomenal world, it is ecstasy, an experience of transcendence. The choice between the two orientations of metaphysics depends upon the line of direction which the spirit takes. The recognition of things and objects as the primary reality, has a very great deal behind it in which it can find a basis, and the metaphysics which correspond to this is movement in the line of least resistance.

On the other hand, to regard the act, the subject and spirit as the primary reality requires an effort of spirit and the exercise of faith, it means a fight against the power of necessity. What is in question is not merely two ways of cognition, but also two ways of existence. It would be absurd to say—is there any meaning in making an effort of the spirit, if there is even a possibility that spirit, as a reality, does not exist? If I am able to make an effort of spirit, then spirit does exist. It is in this that the particular reality of the spirit lies, and it is not the same sort of reality as that of the world of things.[5]

To picture oneself as a free spirit in a consistent and thoroughgoing manner, and to act as a free spirit, means to *be* a free spirit. Creative fancy is capable of producing real and vital consequences. Creative ecstasy is a way out from the time of this world, historical time and cosmic time, it takes place in existential time. Those who have experienced creative ecstasy are well aware that in it man is, as it were, in the grip of a higher power. It is possession by a god, by a daemon (in the Greek sense of the word). In Plato's *Phaedrus* there is an amazing story about the growth of wings on a man. Ecstasy is akin to delirium. Genius is a daemon which has taken

5 See my *Spirit and Reality*.

up its abode in a man and assumed control of him. Creative power is always of an individually personal character, but the man is not alone in it. Human creative power is not human only, it is divine-human. The mystery of creative power lies in that fact. An act of transcending takes place in it, in it the closed circle of human existence is broken open. The creative act is an act which is achieved by man, and in achieving it man has a feeling within that he is going beyond his strength. The genius of Pushkin has put this into words. There is a kinship between the poet and the prophet.

There is an element of gracious beneficence in creative activity. It is bound up with the nature of all gifts which are freely bestowed–*gratia gratis data.* The creative act is gracious and beneficent, creative freedom is clarified and serene. This does not hinder the fact that man can put his gift to evil use. The contradictory and paradoxical aspect of the creative condition consists in this that man at the moment of creative impulse feels himself, as it were, possessed by a higher power, by a daemon, and yet at the same time has a sense of extraordinary freedom, of scope for the expression of his own will. In creative activity, and especially in art and poetry, there is a suggestion of the remembrance of a lost Paradise. The poetry of Pushkin in particular calls up such memories. But the memory of a lost Paradise, a memory which never abandons man, and to which the most gracious moments of creative power draw his attention, is no mere turning to the past, which has withdrawn beyond the boundaries of this empirical world. Such reminiscences of a lost Paradise are also a turning to the future which likewise lies beyond the bounds of this empirical world. The creative act cannot but turn to face the future. But beyond the confines of the objectified time of our world, the distinction and the opposition we make between past and future are taken away. It is a distinction which holds good only for the intervening state, not for the boundaries, or to put it more exactly, not for what lies beyond the confines of world life.

Messianic thought was characteristic of the ancient Hebrews, and it faced towards the future. The ancient Greeks also faced their Golden Age, but in their case it meant looking to the past. Still, there is a sphere in which the messianic kingdom of the future and the Golden Age of the past draw together and are compressed into a single hope. Thus if one looks more deeply into creative activity we can say that there is a prophetic element in it. It speaks prophetically of a different world, of another, a transformed state of the world. But that means that the creative act is eschatological. In it the impossibility of resting content with this given world is proclaimed, in it this world comes to an end, and another world begins.

This is true in every case of the creative condition in man, even though no creative product should result from it. The significance of the creative state for the inner life of man lies in this, that it shows he is overcoming the state of subjection and humiliation which is imposed by the burden of this world; it shows he has attained the experience of an exalting impulse. Creative power, therefore, proclaims that this world is superable, that congealed being can be overcome. It tells of the possibility of setting it free from its chains, it speaks of liberation and transformation.

The romantics have been fond of connecting the creative artistic process with the fruitful imagination experienced in dreams.[6] This cannot be accepted in the form in which the romantics assert it, but it does contain a certain amount of truth. The images which arise in dreams are not called up by impressions received from the external empirical world immediately, but are due to those that have been preserved in the depth of the subconscious.[7] The state of dreaming is not

6 See A. Beguin: *L'Ame romantique et le rêve.*

7 See Lafargue: *Le Rêve et la psychanalyse.*

dependent upon the perception of images of the world of sense at the given moment, it is a passive condition, not active. Consciousness is suppressed and almost paralyzed. When a man is dreaming he may be absolutely overwhelmed by the past. In creative activity, on the other hand, images arise which are not determined by the empirical world, or if they are determined by it, it is through the medium of creative transformation. And they bring with them liberation from subjection to the past, from impressions and injuries which have accumulated in the subconscious, and from the wounds which the past has inflicted. There occur, it is true, radiant, luminous visions, and there are dreams which are prophetic (though such conditions are comparatively rare), and in them the creative exalting impulse has a place. It is not only the subconscious which is operating in creative activity but the supra-conscious also; there is a movement upwards.

2

There are two sides and two meanings to the creative impulse. There is an inward creative act, and there is the created product, the outward disclosure of the creative act. I have written a great deal on this subject.[8] Here I shall say what is necessary on a new aspect of the matter. It is most important to elucidate the question whether the created embodiment is an objectification or whether we ought to distinguish between embodiment and objectification. It is necessary also to draw a distinction between embodiment and materialization, for bodily form and materiality are not one and the same: the bodily form may be illuminated, whereas the material thing is to be overcome. The creative impulse is realized along a line which ascends, and along a line which descends. The primary creative act is a flight upwards, towards another world. But within the matter of this world it meets with difficulty and oppo-

8 See as especially important my *The Meaning of the Creative Act.*

sition, from its formlessness, its solidity and its weight, from its evil infinitude which surrounds the creator on all sides. Man is a demiurge, he creates, working upon the matter of this world, shaping it and illuminating it. There is in the creative state much that is easy, wings grow ready for the flight, but there is much difficulty also, much suffering, and much that hinders and hampers the flight. The creative subject stands face to face with a world of objectification, and the results of the creative act have to enter into that world of objectification. It is in this that the tragedy of creative activity consists.

The primary creative impulse takes place outside the objectified world, outside the time of this world; it happens in existential time, in a flash of the present; it knows neither past nor future. A creative act is a noumenal act, but the product which is created by it belongs to the phenomenal world. Beethoven makes a symphony and thereupon in this creation of his people discover 'objective' regulating principles. But the creative activity of Beethoven ought to have led to the whole world's breaking into sound like a symphony. And in the same way the creative power of a genuine philosopher should have led to the changing of the world and not merely to the enrichment of it by new and expensive books.

The Greeks already drew a distinction between acting (*praxis*), the aim of which is the activity of the acting subject itself, and making (*poiêsis*) the aim of which is in the object which has been made and possesses being.[9] The creating mind which is in a state of creative upward flight is in actual fact not bent upon the realization of an end, but of expressing the condition it is in. Benedetto Croce is to a notable degree right when he sees the essence of art in self-expression.[10] But in any case the creating mind cannot remain within itself, it

---

9 See Jacques Maritain: *L'art et la scholastique.*

10 See Benedetto Croce: *Esthétique comme science de l'expression et linguistique générale.*

must issue out of itself. This going out from the self is usually called embodiment and a character in the highest degree objective is ascribed to it. It is precisely in such embodiment that the creating mind strives after perfection of form. In creativeness there is no matter and no content without form. The creative act is bent upon the infinite, whereas the form of the created product is always finite. And the whole matter in question is this: does the infinite shine through in the finite image?

The whole creative process takes place between the infinite and the finite, between the flight and the image which enters into this objectified world. The initial creative act along an ascending line is creative ecstasy, an upward flight, primary intuition, discovery. It is a marvellous evocation of images, a great project, a great love; it is an attraction which draws upward to the heights, an ascent into the mount, creative fire. At such a time the creating mind stands before God, face to face with Mystery, before the primordial source of all life.

Knowledge, for example, is not a written book, not a system, nor a body of proof, nor the objectification into the external world of what has been discovered. It is the dawn of inward light, entry into communion, an experience of transcending. One must speak in exactly the same way about a projected purpose in the sphere of art or about a design for a new social order; and, in absolutely the same way again, about the love which has taken fire and constitutes the creative condition of a man.

But creative activity is not only all this, it is also a turning towards men and women, towards society, towards this world, it is the attraction of the creative act downwards. And here a man must display dexterity, he must be a master of artistry in every respect, not merely in 'art' in the strict sense of the word, but in science as well, and in creativeness in the social and moral spheres, and again in the technical side of life. Art strives after perfection, but it is a movement which goes downwards, not in an ascending line. The art of a man comes to light as a result of the resistance which the creative act meets with in the world, in the matter of the world. It is the duty of art to convert this force which resists man into an instrument for the use of the creative power which produces results. There is a paradox in this, and it consists in the fact that creative power and art (not merely that of the painter) are inseparably linked with each other, and at the same time find themselves, so to speak, in conflict and not rarely hostile to one another. In methodically elaborated scientific knowledge creative intuition may vanish, in the finished classical form of works of art the creative fire of the artist may have cooled down, in elaborated social forms of human community the initial thirst for righteousness and the brotherhood of men may disappear. There are forms of family life which have become cold and rigid and from which the flame of love may have vanished away. Faith and the prophetic spirit may become weak and disappear in traditional ecclesiastical institutions. The embodiment of spirit may be an objectification of spirit and in that case it is impossible to recognize the spirit in its embodiments. Objective spirit is a *contradictio in adjecto,* it is the exhaustion of spirit, spirit which is drained of its life.[11] And this holds good for the organizations of human society and civilization. And every time that the will to power lays its grip upon a man in this world he enters upon the path which means that spirit is chilled and drained of life, upon the way of servitude to this world. It is essential to underline the truth that the bestowal of form, with which all creative power is connected, is an absolutely different thing from objectification, that is to say, it quite certainly does not denote alienation from the core of existence, a process of cooling, or subjugation to the power of determinism.

Creative impulse is at its first beginning connected with dissatisfaction with this world. It is an end of this world and

11 See N. Hartmann: *Das Problem des geistigen Seins.*

in its original outburst, it desires the end of this world, it is the beginning of a different world. Creative activity is, therefore, eschatological. It is a matter for surprise that no attention has been given to the eschatological side of creative activity. The explanation of this may be in fact that there are two views which open out before the creative act. The first is the end of this world and the beginning of a new; and the second is the process of strengthening and perfecting this world. They are respectively the outlook of revolutionary eschatology and that of evolutionary construction. The creative act, both initially and finally, is eschatological, it is an upward flight towards a different world. But in its medial aspect it produces works which count upon a long continued existence in this world.

The embodiment achieved by creative power is not the same thing as objectification, but the results of creative power may equally well be objectified, just as the whole of human existence may be in this world of objects. The very possibility of creation presupposes an infusion of the Spirit into man, and that we call inspiration. And this raises the action of creative power above the world. But the world demands that the creating mind should conform to it, the world seeks to make its own use of creative acts which count upon the end of this world.

Great creators produce great works. And this success is at the same time a failure of creative power. What does the world do with what is made in the world, what happens to all the creative acts which are for ever flaming up from their source? The creative fire cools down, and the load of the world bears heavily upon it. A new life does not advance to meet us. The transformation of the world does not take place, nor a new heaven and a new earth appear. Every act of love, of eros-love and of the love which is compassion is a creative act. In it something which is new arrives in the world, that which had not been comes to light, and in it there is hope of the transformation of the world. A genuine act of love is eschatological, it marks an end of this world, this world of hatred and enmity, and the beginning of a new world. But within its existence in the world love grows cold, it becomes objectified and it is robbed of its eschatological character. And so it is with everything.

The creative act of knowing has an eschatological character; it points to the coming of an end, the end of this world of darkness and the rise of the world of light. But knowledge also in its existence in this world cools down and is objectified in just the same way. Every creative moral act, which always presupposes its own mental images, is an end of this world (which is founded upon the abuse of the good and the persecution of good men) and the beginning of a world of true godlike humanity. But moral acts, in their existence in the world are objectified and turned into an oppressive realm of legalism and an inhuman systematization of virtue.[12]

Every creative act, whether moral or social, whether in the sphere of art or in the realm of knowledge, is an act which has its share in the coming of the end of the world, it is a flight upwards towards a different world, it makes a new plan for existence. But for the sake of the world and in the interests of other men the creating mind must give bodily form to its images of the other world, to its ecstasy, its fire, its transcending experience, its communion with another life; and it is obliged to do this in accordance with the laws of this world. The creative freedom of man is strengthened and tempered by the resistance of this world and by the weight of it. Man is sometimes a victor and at times he suffers defeat. Freedom which is too easily won has a demoralizing effect. Creative power is noumenal in its origin but it is in the phenomenal world that it reveals itself. The product of creative power belongs to phenomena, but the noumenal also shines through in those phenomena, the eternal also is in them.

---

12 See my *Slavery and Freedom,* and *The Destiny of Man,* An Essay in Paradoxical Ethics.

The embodiment has a noumenal significance, it reveals the ideal image, it is disclosed in an experience shared with others, with other subjects, that is to say, but it is distorted by objectification in which the initial fire of its life is spent. This world does not come to an end. It is held back from doing so. But it ought to come to an end. The creative act of man is an answer to the call of God, it ought to prepare the way for the end of this world and the beginning of another. It is very important to establish the truth that there is an antithesis between teleology and eschatology, as there is between teleology and creativeness. A consistent teleological view of the world recognizes a definite aim to which everything is subordinated, but it excludes an end, it makes an end unnecessary. The world ought to come to an end precisely because there is in the world no perfect conformity of purpose, in other words there is no complete conformity with the Kingdom of God.

Creative genius is rarely content with its own creations. Eternal discontent of spirit is indeed one of the marks of genius. The inward fire of natural genius is not completely transferred to the work it produces. The perfection of created work is something different from creative fire. The fate of a genius is tragic. He is frequently not recognized in his lifetime, he is dissatisfied with himself and he is misrepresented after his death, the productions of his genius are utilized for purposes which are alien to him.

There is something prophetic in creative power, in the genius which creates. But there is nothing more painful and tragic than the fate of prophets. The voice of God which is heard through them arouses the hatred which is felt for an inconvenient and unwelcome reminder. The prophets are stoned to death. It has been said of the genius, that he focuses within him the spirit of his time and expresses it. This is a most inaccurate saying and one which distorts the truth. The genius is a man who does not belong to his own day, he is one who is not adjusted to his own time and throws out a challenge to it.

But the genius is a vehicle of the Spirit which moves within him. He looks forward into ages that are coming in the future. He plucks off the mask from the falsehood of his own day. In this respect the spirit of genius comes close to the spirit of prophecy. For the rest there are several types of genius. A creative man who has produced a most perfect work is called a genius. But even the most perfect production does not reach the same high level as the creative genius himself.

It must emphatically be recognized that failure is the fate that awaits all embodiments of the creative fire, in consequence of the fact that it is in the objective world that it is given effective realization. Which stands at the higher level, St Francis of Assisi himself, the actual appearance of his religious genius which is unique in the history of Christianity, or the Franciscan Order which he founded and in which his spirit has been extinguished and the dull commonplace routine has triumphed? Which reaches the higher level, Luther and the flaming religious drama which was his experience, or the Lutheran Church which he founded, with its pastors and theologians of the eighteenth and nineteenth centuries among whom rationalism and moralism flourished victoriously? Which is the higher, the new emotional experience revealed in J. J. Rousseau, or the doings of his followers, the Jacobins? Once again, which is the higher, Nietzsche himself with that human tragedy experienced by his burning genius, or the men and the movements which so shamefully exploit him? The answers are all too clear.

But the history of the world knows of one most terrible creative failure, the failure of Christianity, of the work of Christ in the world. All too often the history of Christianity has amounted to a crucifixion of Christ. There is nothing more horrifying and more gloomy than the objectification in history of that fire which Christ brought down from heaven. Supreme failure has defeated all the great constructive efforts of history, and all designs which planned the social ordering of men. Athenian democracy did not succeed, nor did the world-wide empire of Alexander the Great. The Roman Empire did not achieve success, and the same is true of the Christian theocracies. The Reformation, the French Revolution, Communism, all alike met with failure.

This is not to say that it was all without meaning and pure loss. But it does mean that the result of every flaming creative effort and every creative design makes itself known as a true image not within this phenomenal world of objects, but in a different world, in another order of existence. Creative failure in this world is a sad and tragic thing. But there is success on the grand scale in the fact that the results of every true creative act of man enter into the Kingdom of God.

This then is the eschatology of creative energy. The failure of the creative act consists in this, that it does not achieve its purpose of bringing this world to an end, of overcoming its objectivity. Its success, on the other hand, lies in the preparation it makes for the transformation of the world, for the Kingdom of God. Sin is burnt up in the creative fire. All the great creative works of man enter into the Kingdom of God. It follows, therefore, that the creative embodiments which man produces are twofold in their nature, the conflict between two worlds is, so to speak, reflected in them. But for all that, there is nothing more terrible, more hopeless, nothing more tragic than every act of realization.

3

The theme of creative activity and its embodiments has its connections with the long-standing controversy between the classical and the romantic. Here the point at issue is not one which concerns different tendencies in art. It is a matter rather of various ways of perceiving the world, of differing types of *Weltanschauung,* and of different attitudes which are adapted to creative power in every field.

The distinction between the classicists and the romantics and the contrast between them are to a large extent relative and are often exaggerated. Of the greatest creative minds, for example, of Shakespeare and Goethe or of Dostoievsky and Tolstoy, it is certainly impossible to enquire whether they were classical or romantic. Creative geniuses have always stood outside the quarrelling schools, and above them, although the disputing tendencies dragged them into their controversies. The Bible, for instance, which contains writing of most moving artistic power, stands entirely apart from any question of classical or romantic.

Second class works of art are sometimes called 'romantic' in the narrower sense of the word, such, for instance, as the productions of many German romantics. Other works which reach a greater degree of perfection and are completely successful, are called 'classical'. But none the less, the distinction itself and the antithesis do raise a serious problem in connection with creative activity.

In the first place, in what relation does creative power stand to the 'subjective', and the 'objective', what is its bearing upon the finite and the infinite, and what does the perfection of a created product mean? Creative power is in its essential nature subjective, the creating mind is a subject and it is in the subjective sphere that the creative process takes place. To speak of 'objective' creativeness is inaccurate and refers merely to the course taken by the creating subject.

But the results of the creating act, its embodiments, fall under the sway of the world's laws of objectification. Three principles may be said to operate in creative activity, and the three principles are those of freedom, grace and law. And it may be that there are various degrees in the predominance of one or another of the principles. 'Classicism' in creative action has its truth and it has its falsehood, and so also has 'romanticism'.

The truth of classicism lies in its striving after perfection and harmony, in its effort to control matter by form. But what is false in classicism is precisely due to that. For perfection of form, and harmony, are attained within the finite. Infinity in the objective world, the world of phenomena, is formlessness, an evil infinity, and therefore the effort to reach perfection in the product of creative activity falls into the power of the finite. The subjective is aiming at a transition into the objective.

Classicism falls a prey to the illusion that perfection can be attained in the finite, in the object. Having created beauty, classicism would leave us in this world for ever. On this basis great things may be achieved, they were to be seen in the culture of Greece. Greece had its romanticism as well, of course. But classical creative activity displays a ready liability to lose the freshness of its life and to become withered and numbed. This again is the process of objectification which moves further and further away from the springs of life. And then the creative reaction of romanticism becomes inevitable.

Romanticism aims at expressing the life of the creator in what he creates. The truth of romanticism lies in its striving towards the infinite, in its dissatisfaction with all that is finite. In romanticism the truth of the 'subjective' is opposed to the falsity of the 'objective'. Romanticism does not believe that perfection is attainable in this world of objects. In this world there can only be signs, symbols of the perfection of the other world. This holds good alike in knowledge and in art.[13]

Pure classicism seeks no knowledge of the transcendent. A yearning after the transcendent is, however, in the highest degree a property of romanticism, although it is usually accompanied by a sense of impossibility of attaining it. To romanticism, creative activity is before all else the way of life of the subject

---

13 The French, who are hostile to romanticism, are inclined to reduce it to what E. Seillière, the author of numerous books on romanticism and imperialism, calls 'mystical naturalism'. See his *Le mal romantique,* an essay on 'irrational imperialism'. It all goes back to Rousseau and the recognition of the goodness of human nature. See also P. Lasserra: *Le romantisme français.* All this has little application to German romanticism and in general is not true.

himself, it is his experience of uplifting impulse and ecstasy, of an interior act of transcendence, and it may lead him out beyond the limits of romanticism.

To classicism, on the other hand, everything is concentrated upon perfection of form in the created product, upon the object. But romanticism also gives rise to illusions though they are of a different kind from the classical. There has been not a little falsity, uncleanness, and stirring up of mud in the creative work of the romantics. There is a form of falsity in romantic subjectivity; it is revealed in the inadequacy of the outlet it provides for escape from the closed circle of the self and from submersion in self. There is also a lack of capacity for real acts of transcendence. The ego has been split into two by the romantics and their expression of personality is weak. Pretentiousness and a sense of failure have readily assumed the form of romanticism and have sought in this way to justify themselves.

The sense of value is not merely a psychological experience of the subject, there is also a value in the reality upon which the subject is engaged. Romanticism may indicate a loss of the sense of reality, while classicism, on the other hand, is inclined to interpret reality exclusively in terms of objects. In point of fact both classical and romantic elements are brought concretely together in creative action. Classical and romantic tendencies are already revealed in the world of objectification. But it is in a different world that the whole truth lies.

There were some remarkable and far-reaching ideas about beauty and art in Kant's *Critique of Judgment.* That is beautiful which, without a concept, pleases *allgemein.* Beauty is adaptability to an end without bringing the end into notice. The beautiful pleases, without serving any interest. The beautiful pleases, not in its reception by the senses, not in a concept, but in an act of judgment, in appraisal. The beauty of nature is a beautiful thing. The beauty of art is a beautiful representation of a thing.

This stresses the significance of the creative subject. A judgment of taste does not depend upon reality in the sphere of things. Art, as indeed all creative expression, rises above the commonplace, that is to say above the reality which belongs to the objective world, the world of things. It is usual to say that art depicts only what is essential, significant and intense, that it is not an imitation or a reflection of nature considered as an assembly of objects. But that is to say that the creative act breaks through to a deeper reality, to the noumenal which lies behind the phenomenal.

The problem of creative power raises the question of true and false realism. The romantics from Rousseau onwards have defended the truth and rightness of 'nature' against rationalization and mechanization, which follow in the train of civilization. There was some truth in their position, but the actual concept of 'nature' was left ambiguous. Confusion arose between the objectified nature of this phenomenal world, the nature of the mechanical way of looking at things, nature in Darwin's sense, on the one hand, and the nature of the noumenal, ideal cosmos, on the other.

Beyond the dispute between the classical and the romantic (in which there is a great deal which is a matter of convention) stands genuine realism or realistic symbolism, and that is what actually characterizes the greatest creative minds. Human creative power is realist to the extent that it is theurgic, that is to say, in proportion as it is directed towards the transformation of the world, towards a new heaven and a new earth. Truly creative realism is eschatological realism. It takes the line not of reflecting the natural world and not of adjustment to it, but of changing and transforming the world.

Creative knowledge, creative art, in the same way are not a reflection and expression of the eternal world of ideas (in the Platonic sense) in this world of the senses. They are the activity of free spirit which continues to carry on the creation of the world, and prepares for its transformation. The limits of human creative activity, of human art, are imposed by this objective world. They make it symbolical, although this symbolism is realist, not idealist. But the final transformation of the world will be the passing of the symbols into reality. Human creative power will create life itself, another world, and not things, in which the breach between subject and object always remains. Then no sacrifice will be offered by life and love for the sake of creative power, such as for instance those of Goethe, Ibsen and others, but creative power and life will be made one and the same.

Creative power will then be neither classical nor romantic. Then thought, perfected after its own kind, whether in Greece or in China, will not be characterized as classical and rationalist. At that time it will not be enough to combine (as it was said that Hegel did) the values of protestant theology and those of classical antiquity. At that time there will be a unity of nature and freedom, the thing that is true and good will be the thing that is beautiful.[14] Creative power must be theurgic, the cooperation of God and man; it must be divine-human. It is the answer of man to the call of God.

The religious difficulty of this problem lies in the fact that the will of God concerning the creative vocation of man, the need of God for the creative activity of man, could not be revealed to man by God, it had to be brought to light by the daring of man himself. Otherwise there would be no freedom of creative power, there would be no answer made by man.[15] Redemption comes from God, from the fact of the Crucified and Sacrificed God, whereas creative activity derives from man. To oppose creativity and redemption, however, is to succumb to the rules of objectified and fallen consciousness.

Man finds an outlet from the closed circle of subjectivity in the creative act of spirit by two routes, that is, by the way of

---

14 Boldwin asserts this as already attained. See his *Théorie génétique de la réalité*.

15 See *The Meaning of the Creative Act*.

objectification and by the way of transcendence. By the way of objectification the creative act is adjusted to the circumstances of this world and does not reach its final state, it is cut off short. By the way of transcendence the creative act breaks through to noumenal reality and sets its bearing upon the final transformation of the world.

In reality what actually happens is that both ways are combined in human creative activity with some preponderance of one or the other. It would be a mistake to conclude that objectified creative power is devoid of importance and meaning. Without it man would be unable to endure the conditions of his existence in this world, or to improve those conditions. Man is called upon to expend his labour upon the material of this world and to subjugate it to spirit. But the limits of this way of objectification must be understood, and so must the danger of its exclusive use, for it clinches and strengthens the wrong state of the world. This is a matter of the correlation of law with freedom and grace.[16] There will come a time, a new historical aeon, when the eschatological meaning of creative power will finally and definitely be made clear. The problem of creativeness leads on to the problem of the meaning of history.

---

from

The Meaning of the Creative Act

CREATIVITY AND FREEDOM: INDIVIDUALISM AND UNIVERSALISM

CREATIVITY IS INSEPARABLE from freedom. Only he who is free creates. Out of necessity can be born only evolution; creativity is born of liberty. When we speak in our imperfect human language about creativity out of nothing, we are really

16 See *The Destiny of Man.*

speaking of creativity out of freedom. Viewed from the standpoint of determinism, freedom is "nothing", it surpasses all fixed or determined orders, it is conditioned by nothing else; and what is born of freedom does not derive from previously existing causes, from "something". Human creativity out of "nothing" does not mean the absence of resistant material but only an absolute increment or gain which is not determined by anything else. Only evolution is determined: creativity derives from nothing which precedes it. Creativity is inexplicable: creativity is the mystery of freedom. The mystery of freedom is immeasurably deep and inexplicable. Just as deep and inexplicable is the mystery of creativity. Those who would deny the possibility of creation (creativity) out of nothing must inevitably place creativity in a certain determined order and by this very fact must deny the freedom of creativity. In creative freedom there is an inexplicable and mysterious power to create out of nothing, undetermined, adding energy to the existing circulation of energy in the world. As regards the data of the world and the closed circle of the world's energy, the act of creative freedom is transcendent. The act of creative freedom breaks out of the determined chain of the world's energy. From the viewpoint of an immanent world datum this act must always represent creation out of nothing. The timid denial of creation out of nothing is submission to determinism, obedience to necessity. Creativity is something which proceeds from within, out of immeasurable and inexplicable depths, not from without, not from the world's necessity. The very desire to make the creative act understandable, to find a basis for it, is failure to comprehend it. To comprehend the creative act means to recognize that it is inexplicable and without foundation. The desire to rationalize creativity is related to the desire to rationalize freedom. Those who recognize freedom and do not desire determinism have also tried to rationalize freedom. But a rationalization of freedom is itself determinism, since this denies the boundless mystery of freedom. Freedom is the ultimate: it cannot be derived from anything; it cannot be made the equivalent of anything. Freedom is the baseless foundation of being: it is deeper than all being. We cannot penetrate to a rationally-perceived base for freedom. Freedom is a well of immeasurable depth—its bottom is the final mystery.

But freedom is not a negative and ultimate concept, merely indicating the boundaries beyond which reason cannot pass. Freedom is positive and full of meaning. Freedom is not only a denial of necessity and determinism. Freedom is not a realm of chance and wilfulness, as distinguished from the realm of law-abiding and of necessity. Those, also, fail to understand the mystery of freedom who see in it only a special form of spiritual determinism—i.e. consider that everything is free which is born of causes within the human spirit. Although freedom is neither rational nor acceptable, this is the most rational and acceptable explanation of it. In so far as the human spirit is part of the order of nature, everything in the spirit is determined, just as are all natural phenomena. The spiritual is no less determined than the material. The Indian doctrine of Karma is a form of spiritual determinism. The Karma doctrine of reincarnation does not know freedom. Man's spirit is free only in so far as it is supernatural, transcending and going beyond the order of nature. Determinism is an inevitable form of natural being, i.e. including the being of man as a natural being, even though causality in man is spiritual rather than physical. Within the determined order of nature creativity is impossible: we can have only evolution. Freedom and creativity tell us that man is not only a natural, but a supernatural being. And this means that man is not only a physical being and not only a psychic being, in the natural meaning of the word. Man is a free, supernatural spirit, a microcosm. Spiritualism, like materialism, can see in man only a natural, although a spiritual, being and then subjects him to a spiritual determinism, just as materialism subjects to the material. Freedom is only the production of spiritual phenomena out of preceding spiritual phenomena in the same being. Freedom is a positive creative force, unconditioned by anything else and based upon nothing else, flowing up from a spring of boundless depth. Freedom is the power to create out of nothing, the power of the spirit to create out of itself and not out of the world of nature. Freedom is one's positive expression and assertion is creativity. Free energy, i.e. creative energy, is substantially inherent in man. But man's substantiality is not a closed circle of energy within which everything is spiritually determined. In man's very substantiality there are bottomless well-springs. Creative energy is increasing energy, not energy which merely rearranges itself. The mystery of freedom denies everything finite and all limitations. The old spiritualism understood spiritual substance statically and by this fact revealed its own non-creative character. For the old spiritualism, freedom was merely justification of moral responsibility, rather than a justification of creativity. Traditional spiritualism is a concept of the pre-creative epoch: it exists in the law and the redemption. The powers of evil, rather than of good, have resorted to freedom for their sustentation.

The lack of base, the infinite depth and the mysteriousness of freedom do not mean arbitrariness. Freedom cannot be rationalized—it is not subject to rational categories, but in it the divine reason is alive. Freedom is positive creative power rather than negative arbitrariness. The negative consciousness of one's freedom as arbitrary free will is a falling into sin. Negative freedom, freedom as arbitrary free will, is freedom without content and void. To desire freedom for its own sake, freedom without purpose or content, is to desire emptiness, to turn away towards non-being. Freedom, conceived only formally, without purpose or content, is nothing, emptiness, non-being. Freedom in the Fall was this kind of negative, formal freedom and emptiness and non-being—it was freedom for freedom, i.e. freedom *from* rather than freedom *for*. Freedom in the Fall was not freedom for creativeness, not creative freedom. The falling away from God deprives freedom of its content and its purpose, impoverishes it, deprives it of power. Negative, formal, empty freedom is reborn in necessity: in it being is degraded. The positive, creative purpose and content of freedom could not yet be conceived at that stage of creation, the seven-day stage, since in creation there had not yet been revealed the Absolute Man, the Son of God, the revelation of the Eighth Day. In the seven-day creation there was possible only a trial of freedom. The position Adam occupied in paradise was not yet the position of man: the active-creative calling of man had not yet been revealed. The freedom of the all-man Adam had not yet been joined with the freedom of the Absolute Man, Christ, and in that earlier freedom were contained the seeds of the Fall and of sin. It might be said that Adam had the choice between absolute obedience and absolute wilfulness. Creative freedom is not revealed at this stage of creation. Adam's freedom was formal, rather than material. Material freedom is attained in another epoch of creation, the epoch of the revelation of the Absolute Man. This freedom is born of the union of the human nature of Jesus with the divine nature of Christ. The cosmic mystery of the redemption overcomes formal and empty freedom and the necessity which is born of it. Human nature, become son of God, rises to the consciousness of material freedom full of creative purpose. Freedom is penetrated by universal love. Freedom is henceforth inseparable from its universal content. Freedom *from* is in sin: freedom *for* is in creativeness. Adam's freedom in the seven-day creation is different from his freedom in the creation of the eighth day. The freedom of the new Adam, joined with the Absolute Man, is creative freedom, freedom which continues the work of God's creativity, freedom which does not revolt against God in negative arbitrary wilfulness.

There are two freedoms: divine and diabolic. The freedom of the first Adam could not be diabolic freedom, because divine freedom in its positive content could not be revealed in the seven-day creation. Adam's freedom was the first stamp of man's likeness to the Creator. And even in paralysing sin there was still a sign of man's power. The fall of the first man, Adam, had positive meaning and justification, as a moment in the revelation of creativity, preparing for the appearance of the Absolute Man. Theodicy, the justification of God, is also a justification of the meaning of evil. Evil, as absolute meaninglessness and loss, denies the absolute meaning of being and leads to dualism. The traditional Christian consciousness in the doctrine of evil approaches dualistic duotheism. This doctrine of evil, denying all immanent meaning in the experience of evil, was a pedagogic for the immature. There was no room for the truth of evil's antinomic nature. An exclusively transcendent view of evil gives rise to slavish fear. This slavish fear prevented man from comprehending his fall away from God as a tragic moment in the revelation and development of man's freedom from the old to the new form. But any antinomic solution to the problem of evil is impossible. It is equally true that a dark source of evil exists in the world and that in the final sense of the word there is no evil. The freedom of Adam the first man had to be destroyed in his experience of good and evil; it had to be swallowed up by necessity so that the true and higher freedom might be revealed through the Absolute Man, Christ. The fall of the first Adam was a necessary cosmic moment in the revelation of the new Adam. This was the way to a higher completeness by means of a falling-apart. In Christianity the experience of sin is peripheral, exoteric. The deep experience of resisting God, of being deceived by God as an inward way of falling apart and division in divine life is esoteric. All the mystics have known this. Diabolic freedom was born after the appearance of the new Adam. Final evil is possible only after Christ. Diabolic freedom is a final and ultimate resistance against Christ: the destruction of man, the choice of the way of non-being. Diabolic freedom is revealed only in the eighth day of creation as a false likeness of creative freedom. The devil's creativity creates only non-being: it steals from God in order to create a caricature of being, a false image of being. Diabolic freedom is final necessity, final enslavement. Necessity is only a form of freedom. In Adam's fall freedom was reborn into necessity which was subject to the fallen angel. But this was still no final loss of freedom. Final loss of freedom and final enslavement are possible only in that epoch of creation where there is already the revelation of the Absolute Man, Christ, and when the Antichrist, a false image and caricature of the Absolute Man, tempts man by the blessed condition of non-being. Here we approach an eschatological problem. For the moment it has been important to state that two forms of freedom exist, corresponding to the two epochs of creation and revelation. The fall of Adam did not mean deciding the fate of the world. This was merely tempting a youth. The first Adam was not yet a part of the Divine mystery of the Trinity through the Absolute Man and hence did not yet know his creative freedom: he is only the first stage of creation. The final truth about evil is included in the genial works of J. Boehme. From the *Ungrund,* the abyss, light is born, God: the theogonic process takes place and out of it flows darkness, evil, a shadow over the light of divinity. Evil takes its source not in the God that is born but in the foundations of God, in the abyss, from which proceed both light and darkness. We can give reasoned meaning to evil only if we accept the principle of development in divine life.

§

Necessity is a creation of the freedom of the first Adam, a result of wrongly directed freedom, the freedom of the Fall. Freedom is not consciously accepted necessity, as the German idealists taught. Necessity is an evil, sub-conscious freedom, a freedom not illumined by the Logos. Obligatory necessity is only the reverse side of the world's fall away from, and estrangement from God. Those substances or beings of the world-hierarchy, which are estranged from each other and continue in strife and dissension, which are not united inwardly and freely, are inevitably bound and fettered outwardly. Man can be a slave only to that which is foreign and hostile. What is near and dear to man does not compel him. Those who love each other and are thus united are free: only those who are at enmity and not united are enslaved and know necessity. The materialization of the world, the compulsory and cumbersome relation of one of its parts to another—all this is born of alienation and enmity, i.e. of the fall of Adam the all-man. Necessity is fallen freedom, a freedom of enmity and dissolution, a freedom of chaos and anarchy. Obligatory necessity is always the reverse side of the medal of inner chaos and anarchy, a movement in the hierarchic system of the universe. True freedom is an expression of the cosmic (as opposed to the chaotic) condition of the universe, its hierarchic harmony, the inward unitedness of all its parts. The cosmic is always free; in it there is no obligatory necessity, no burden or pressure, no materialization of one of its parts for another. In the cosmos everything is alive, nothing is inert or overburdened, nothing compels by its material consistence. Every time that man's living spirit encounters the resistance of heavy and for him lifeless material bodies, he feels the fall of the all-man and the strife and alienation which were born of it. The lower ranks of being were deadened, made burdensome, materialized by the fall of the all-man and by the strife and enmity engendered by that fall. The obligatory "materiality" of being is born of man himself. It is the result of man's loss of his hierarchic position in the universe, his inward estrangement from the lower orders of the cosmic hierarchy, the result of dualizing being. And the degree of obligatory "materiality" is in direct proportion to the degree of inward estrangement. The rocks are most obligatory for us and we feel them to be the least living of all things because we are the most estranged and separated from them. People who are near to us in spirit are the least obligatory for us, and we feel them to be the most alive of all things because they are nearest to us, dear to us, joined with us. Love burns up all necessity and gives freedom. *Love is the content of freedom—love is the freedom of the new Adam, the freedom of the eighth day of creation.* The world is bewitched by evil and can be released from the spell only by love. The world's necessity is enchantment; the world's material "obligatoriness" is letting evil take the lead; it is an illusory being, born of dissension. The inert, heavy and oppressive material of the world can be released from bewitchment, can be unfettered, made alive, only by the power of the unifying love which the Absolute Man, the new Adam, brings with him into the world. Love is creativeness.

Man is responsible for the materialization of the world, for the necessity and compulsion which reign in it; for man is called to be king of the universe—and the world lives or dies by him. The world is deadened by man's fall and it is revived by man's uprising. But the all-vivifying and spiritualizing rise of fallen man is possible only through the advent of the Absolute Man, bringing man's nature into communion with divine nature. The Redeemer and Saviour of the world exorcizes the spell and casts off the fetters of necessity. He is the Liberator. *Without Christ the Liberator, the world would have remained for all time shattered in necessity and determinism would be for ever true.* Determinism is finally overcome only in Christ the Liberator. Any philosophy which does not accept Christ the Liberator, which is not illumined by Christ the Logos, inevitably contains within itself to a greater or less degree an undissolved remnant of determinism. Without Christ the Liberator, freedom itself must appear to be the result of necessity. Freedom without Christ the Liberator is the freedom of the old Adam, freedom without love, freedom of the seven-day creation. Freedom with Christ is the freedom of the new Adam, freedom which by love removes the spell from the world—freedom of the eighth day of creation. After Christ, man is a new creature, knowing new freedom. For determinism only the old creature exists, under the spell of necessity. The naturalistic view of man and the world is the old view, born of the old consciousness, consonant with the epoch of unfinished seven-day creation. Determinism and naturalism will always persist until man's human nature is joined with divine nature through the Absolute Man. Individualism carries on a tragic but powerless struggle against the power of determinism and naturalism. Individualism is only an evidence of the crisis of naturalism and determinism—not a victory over them.

§

Individualism, which became so acute at the close of the nineteenth century, rose against the power of natural and social order over man's individuality. *Individualism is a convulsion of the freedom of the old Adam, of the old freedom.* Hence, in individualism, freedom is not creating the cosmos but rather resisting it. Freedom in individualism is a disunited freedom, estranged from the world. And all separation or estrangement from the world leads to slavery to the world, since everything foreign and distant from us is for us compelling necessity. For the individualist, the world is always violating him. Extreme individualism tries to identify man's individuality with the world and to cast off the whole world outside this inflated human individuality. But this identification of man with the world is realized only as an illusion. This is demonic self-deception. In reality individualism denies that man is a microcosm and that he is in a cosmic situation. Individualism demeans man—does not wish to know his world-wide universal content. The individualist tries convulsively to free himself from the world, from the cosmos—and attains only slavery; for to separate oneself inwardly from the universe is inevitably to enslave oneself to it outwardly. Individualism is a devastation of individuality, its impoverishment, a diminution of its universal content, i.e. a tendency towards non-being. If individuality should attain absolute separation and alienation from the universe, from the hierarchy of living beings, it would turn into non-being—it would destroy itself completely. Individuality and individualism are opposites. Individualism is the enemy of individuality. Man is an organic member of the universal cosmic hierarchy, and the richness of his content is in direct proportion to his union with the cosmos. Man's individuality finds complete expression only in universal, cosmic life. In individualism, the individuality is empty, without content. In individualism, freedom is only an unhealthy convulsion. Did Ibsen's Peer Gynt affirm his individuality? Did he possess freedom? Convulsively asserting his individuality, he was deprived of it; he was not himself, a personality, but rather a slave of necessity. *Peer Gynt* is a work of genius presenting the tragedy of individualism. Individualism is the tragedy of empty freedom. Individualism does not say "I want this" (content): it says "I want what I want" (emptiness). But a free act of will must have content, an object, a purpose—it cannot be empty, purposeless, without an object. The free act of will desires something, and not just "what it desires". In this insistence upon the right to "want what I want" there is a slavish psychology, a psychology which has lost its freedom, a psychology of the age of childhood. The truly free affirm their will with definite content, not merely formally. They know what they want. Formal and empty freedom is the freedom of the old Adam, the freedom of the Fall, the freedom of the world's childhood. This formal and vacant freedom arises in individualism.

Individualism may be a symptom of world crisis, but it still remains in the pre-creative epoch of the world; it gives expression to its immature will, its lack of freedom. In individualism freedom takes a wrong direction and gets lost. Individualism and its freedom are confirmed only in universalism. A mature and free will directs its act of desire, its action on cosmic and divine life, towards a rich content for life, rather than towards vacuity. Mature and free will is creative will going out from itself into cosmic life. By its nature, individualism is not creative; it is negative and empty, since it deprives men of that universal content, towards which, alone, creativity may be directed. The whole concept of individualism is still confused and insufficiently explained. Sometimes individualism is understood as meaning the liberation of individuality from external pressure, natural or social, the pressure of an established moral or social order. If we understand individualism in this fashion, then we must recognize positive value in it. We cannot, for instance, deny the healthful elements in the individualism of the Renaissance. The human spirit is of greater value than the state, or customs and *mores,* or any external value—the human spirit is worth more than the whole external world. But in a strict sense, which is appearing only now in our time, individualism is opposed to universalism; it is the disunion of the human individuality from the universe; it is self-idolization. Such an individualism leads to the destruction of man, to his fall into non-being. Man is infinitely poor and empty if there is nothing higher than himself, if there is no God; and man is infinitely rich and meaningful if there is something higher, if God does exist. Movement is impossible for man if there is nothing higher, nothing divine—he has nowhere to move. The liberation of man's individuality from God and from the world is murder; it is a diabolic enslavement. Man's freedom is bound up with the freedom of the world and is realized only in the world's liberation. The world's necessity must be unfettered, released from the spell, in order that man should attain higher, free life. Individualism merely confirms that atomization, that estrangement among parts of the world, which is really enchantment and thralldom in compelling necessity.

§

The enslavement and bondage of the world's hierarchy of beings submit man to lower, moribund levels of being; they compel man by their material heaviness. This bondage, this heaviness of the lower hierarchy, conceal from us the creative secret of being. We see the world in an aspect of necessity, of moribund and petrified materialization. But is creativeness possible for necessity and out of necessity? We have already seen that in the realm of necessity only evolution is possible—the rearrangement of a given quantity of energy. Only freedom can create absolute increase in the world—only the free man creates. The determinism which is so compulsively forced upon us is false because freedom of personality does exist, creatively breaking the chains of necessity. We cannot understand the creative secret of being in a passive way, in an atmosphere of obedience to the world's heavy materialism. It can be understood only actively, in the atmosphere of the creative act itself. To know the creative activity of the person means being a creatively active person. Like knows like. The inner relationship between the subject of knowing and the object of knowing is a necessary condition of true knowing. Only the free man knows freedom; only the creating man knows creativity. Only the spirit knows the spiritual. Only the microcosm knows the macrocosm. To know anything in the world is to have this in oneself. Knowing is a creative act and we cannot expect to have knowledge of freedom from a slavish submission to necessity. We cannot expect to have knowledge of world freedom and of the world's creative mystery from an individualism which has separated and torn itself away from the world and set itself up against the world. The free creative power of individuality presupposes its universalism, its quality of the microcosm. Every creative act has universal, cosmic significance. The creative act of the personality enters the cosmic hierarchy, gives it deliverance from the power of lower materialized hierarchies, unfetters being. In its freedom and its creativeness the personality cannot be separated from the cosmos, cannot be divorced from universal being.

§

We find this anti-universalism which destroys individuality not only in individual schism but in the schism of sects. In the universe man is free: in a sect he is a slave. The error and untruth in all sectarianism lies in this breaking away from the cosmos, from cosmic breadth, in this refusal to accept the universal responsibility of every one for all men and all things. A sect wishes to be saved alone: it does not wish to be saved together with the world. In the sectarian psychology there is self-satisfaction, absorption with one's self, self-centredness. The sectarian psychology despises the world and is ever ready to condemn a great portion of it to destruction, as something of a lower order. In essence the sectarian psychology is not Christian: it has not got the Christian universalism or the Christian world-wide love. It does not want to recognize that Christ is not only saviour of me and my little ship, but the world's saviour as well. This schismatic psychology does not wish to bear the burden of responsibility for the fate of the lower hierarchic orders of being. Even in historic orthodoxy and Catholicism there is a tendency towards sectarianism, an insufficiency of the universal spirit. Individuality is smothered where there is no universal spiritual breath. The Christian conscience, the conscience of the universal Logos, cannot be reconciled either to individualism or to sectarianism: the apostasy and self-satisfaction of the single individual are equally repugnant to Christian conscience as are the apostasy and self-satisfaction of some small group. There may be an individualism of a small group, its schism from the cosmos, its self-satisfaction with itself. Sectarianism is worse than individualism, for it produces an illusion of universalism, it appears to offer an escape from separatism, from the individual's diversion from the whole. And the individualism of a separate small group is more difficult to overcome than the individualism of one person. A sect is a false church, a pseudo-universalism: there is in sectarianism a super-personal magic from which it is difficult to be liberated. The wine of sectarianism intoxicates, gives an illusion of ecstatic uplift of being. In a sect, a false union takes place, a union outside the cosmic, universal hierarchy. In its mystic essence the Church is universality, a cosmic organism, a universal, cosmic hierarchy with Christ in the heart of being. In a sect, on the other hand, there is developed a false organism, a fiction. Everything which is not cosmic, not universal in spirit, is already a tendency towards sectarianism, although it may bear the stamp of official ecclesiastical authority. For the Christian conscience, the hermit is more acceptable than the sectarian. Individuality is, after all, a genuine reality and value: along its life's way, individuality may experience a condition of loneliness, of crisis; it may outgrow the old forms of union. But a sect is always a phantom, an illusion; it is unreal and does not possess value in and for itself. What the Church officially calls sectarianism may be a symptom and a sign of religious thirst for a higher spiritual life. But here I am using the sectarian spirit in its inward meaning and I can discover more of it in official ecclesiasticism than in the sects. Hence the sectarian spirit is worse than that of the lonely individual.

Solitude may be combined with genuine universality *sobornost* and true churchliness. And a man of œcumenical consciousness and churchly experience may be quite alone in his creative courage and initiative. Solitude is possible for the Christian in a transition-epoch, preceding the new world-epoch of creativeness. A sect, on the other hand, is a pseudo-church and hence it can scarcely have genuine œcumenicity and churchliness. Solitude is not necessarily individualism. Solitude, a man's being alone, is not alienation from the cosmos. It may be only a symptom of the fact that a personality has outgrown certain conditions under which others live, and its universal content is not yet recognized by the others. The supreme solitude is divine. God, Himself, knows great and anguished solitude. He has the experience of being deserted by the world and by men. Christ was solitary and not understood during His life. Men accepted and understood Christ only after His death on the Cross. Solitude is quite compatible with universality: there may be more of the universal spirit in solitude than in a herded society. Every act of courage, every creative initiative, gives a sense of solitude, of being unrecognized—transcends every given community. And there is always the temptation to overcome this solitude by some sectarian community rather than by the universal community. Solitude lies outside the contradistinction between individualism and universalism, hence there may be both universalism and individualism in solitude. The one may be more universal and œcumenical than a whole collective. In the single, lone Nietzsche there was more of the universal spirit than in many a sect, many a social collective. We must never forget that the religious way moves from the personality to society, from the inward to the outer, toward the cosmos by way of individuality.

§

God expects from man the highest freedom, the freedom of the eighth day of creation. This, God's expectation, lays on man a great responsibility. *The final, ultimate freedom, the daring of freedom and the burden of freedom, is the virtue of religious maturity.* To arrive at religious maturity means to know final freedom. The immaturity of Christian consciousness has hitherto made impossible a knowledge of man's ultimate freedom. Christianity has always been a training, a guardianship of the immature. And hence Christianity has not yet revealed itself in fullness, as an experience of freedom. The religion of freedom is a religion of apocalyptic times. Only the final time will know the final freedom. Christianity, as a religion of training and guardianship of the immature, as a religion of the fear of temptation for the immature, is being deformed and is becoming torpid. But only a religion of freedom, a religion of daring and not of fear, can answer to man's present age, to the times and seasons of to-day. We can no longer refuse the time of freedom: Christian men are now too old, not only ripe but over-ripe for that. At the end of the Christian path there dawns the consciousness that God expects from man such a revelation of freedom as will contain even what God Himself has not foreseen. God justifies the mystery of freedom, having by His might and power set a limit to His own foreseeing. Those not free are not needed by God, they do not belong in the divine cosmos. Hence freedom is not a right: it is an obligation. Freedom is a religious virtue. He who is not free, the slave, cannot enter the kingdom of God: he is not a son of God; he is subject to lower spheres. There is a freedom which corresponds to the world's creative epoch. Before that there was only a freedom of the law and the redemption. What are the ways of freedom? Is asceticism which leads to sainthood the only way of liberation or is there another?

Other books by Berdyaev:

The Destiny of Man, 1931.
The Divine and the Human, 1949.
Freedom and the Spirit, 1935.
Slavery and Freedom, 1940.
Spirit and Reality, 1937.

Other books on the same problem:

Barth, Karl. *The Holy Ghost and the Christian Life,* 1938.
Dillistone, F. W. *The Holy Spirit in the Life of Today,* 1947.
Harper, Ralph. *The Sleeping Beauty,* 1955.
Printer, Regin. *Spiritus Creator,* 1953.
Sayers, Dorothy L. *The Mind of the Maker,* 1941.
Van Dusen, H. P. *Spirit, Son and Father,* 1958.
Williams, Charles. *The Descent of the Dove,* 1950.

III. THE INCARNATION

7. Time and the Eternal: Oscar Cullmann
   from *Christ and Time*

8. Christ and the Kingdom of Caesar: H. Richard Niebuhr
   from *Christ and Culture*

9. Faith and the Forms of Culture: Richard Kroner
   from *Culture and Faith*

> *"Render, therefore, unto Caesar the things that are Caesar's and unto God the things that are God's."*
>
> *Matthew 22: 21.*

With the advent of Christianity there emerged in human consciousness an attitude toward history and toward the cultural life of man that was decisive for the subsequent history of western thought. This attitude recognized the fact that man's life is neither totally swallowed up by the all consuming power of time's passage, nor wholly circumscribed by those cultural forms whose stability guaranteed the community a permanence amidst change, an endurance beyond the brevity and fortuitousness of the individual life. This new dimension of consciousness embodied in the Incarnation—Crucifixion—Resurrection sequence and in the metaphorical distinction between the Kingdom of God and the Kingdom of Caesar, established a position from which man could stand beyond finite time, history and culture while yet subject to them. Henceforth the tension between time and eternity, finitude and infinity, faith and culture, history and meta-history have been major concerns of theology.

In the 20th century the collapse of confidence in ideas of progress and in the inevitable upward march of culture toward its own historical fulfillment gave rise to renewed questioning of the self-sufficiency of culture and the meaning of history. The selections in Part III of our anthology are the products of such questioning of culture, faith and history in the light of the Biblical revelation.

OSCAR CULLMANN

OSCAR CULLMANN, like Bultmann, is primarily a New Testament scholar and, like Bultmann, attempts through rigorous criticism of texts to uncover the original "kernel" or essence of Christianity by freeing it from the falsifications or accretions that have gathered around it as a result of interpretations that spring from extra-Biblical presuppositions, that is, from previously established philosophical or psychological presuppositions. In many respects, however, his methods and conclusions differ from those of Bultmann with whom he takes issue on many points.

Christ and Time, from which the following chapters are taken, is an attempt to define the specifically Christian element of the New Testament revelation, that is, to determine that which it does not have in common with philosophical or other religious systems. For Cullmann this "kernel" or central point of Christianity, in which all Christian theology must be rooted and in the light of which, alone, all else must be interpreted, is the New Testament conception of time and history.

For him the Christian conception of time is first of all linear and not cyclic. Secondly, this time line has a mid-point from which the rest of time derives its meaning—the Incarnation of Christ. This event, itself located in time as an historical event, is the central event to which all other events, past and future are related and from which they are to be understood and judged. God's self-revelation in the birth, crucifixion and resurrection of Christ is itself a history—the "Christ-process"—which unfolded in history and which reveals the Biblical message of redemption to be essentially *historical.* And, conversely, it reveals the meaning of history to be the temporal arena within which God's work of redemption of the world takes place.

Thirdly, for Cullmann, eternity in the New Testament is not the opposite of time, a timelessness that provides an escape from time. Eternity is rather endless time, unlimited time, measurable in time, though endless and therefore known only to God. Hence, salvation is not salvation *from* time, but salvation in time. As such, however, it is a future event to be accomplished with the Parousia or final coming of Christ at the end of history, that event which shall bring into being the final era of time—the endless time of eternity. But with the Incarnation the process of redemption which is to be consummated with the Parousia was already begun and continues in history toward its fulfillment.

Christ and Time is a study of the relationship of tension between secular and Biblical history and hence between the actions of men and the action of God. It is an interpretation of history which precludes ascetic withdrawal from the world on the one hand and avoids the meaninglessness of historical relativism on the other. An ethics of responsible human decision and action in the concrete historical situation is possible, argues Cullmann, only if grounded in the Biblical revelation of redemptive history, that is, in a faith in the redemptive work of Christ in history.

Cullmann's conclusions do not go unchallenged in theological circles. Nevertheless, his study will remain a major contribution to the understanding of both the problem of time and the problem of history.

OSCAR CULLMANN

from

CHRIST AND TIME*

1

THE SIGNIFICANCE OF THE NEW TESTAMENT TERMINOLOGY FOR TIME

PRIMITIVE CHRISTIAN FAITH and thinking do not start from the spatial contrast between the Here and the Beyond, but from the time distinction between Formerly and Now and Then. In saying this we do not mean that the mainly spatial contrast between visible and invisible does not here exist. There is in the New Testament an invisible heaven and a visible earth; invisible powers and authorities are at work, while man observes only the visible deeds executed by the earthly agents of those powers.[1] But this invisible course of events is itself completely subjected to the progress of time. The essential thing is not the spatial contrast, but the distinction which faith makes between the times. Thus the author of The Epistle to the Hebrews, in his famous definition of faith (ch. 11:1), names first of all the "assurance of things *hoped for,*" that is, things which are future. Thereby he also gives to the further definition, the "conviction of things not seen," a reference to the time process.

The emphatically temporal character of all expressions of faith is connected in the New Testament with the Jewish

1 Thus the executive power of the State is the administrative organ for the "rulers of this age" (I Cor. 2:8). In the light of this fact we should also understand that the "authorities" of Rom. 13:1, in keeping with the meaning which this plural always has for Paul, are the powers that stand behind the actual executive power of the State. On this subject, see Part III, Chapter 3.

valuation of time,[2] and this in turn shows close contacts with Parsiism.[3] Nevertheless, it will be shown in this and the following chapters that the New Testament writings for the first time give to all revelation an essential anchorage in time; here for the first time the time line is consistently carried through in its central significance for salvation and faith. Thus it is not as if we had to do with a Jewish survival; rather, that which is intimated in Judaism is here completely carried out.

In this respect the terminology of the New Testament is characteristic. Here, in decisive passages, all the expressions for time that were available in the Greek language occur with special frequency; prominent are the words for "day" (*hêmera*), "hour" (*hôra*), "season" (*kairos*), "time" (*chronos*), "age" (*aiôn*), and "ages" (*aiônes*). It is no accident that we constantly encounter these and similar expressions,[4] among which the emphatic "now" (*nun*) and the emphatic "today" (*sêmeron*) must also be mentioned; indeed, we find all the terms so used as to throw this very time aspect into a notably theological light.

For all statistical and lexicographical material which relates to these words we may refer to the older and the more recent New Testament lexicons, especially that of G. Kittle, which seeks to bring out the theological significance of the words in question. To be sure, theological understanding necessarily

2 Gerhard Delling, in *Das Zeitverständnis des Neuen Testaments,* 1940, wrongly seeks to show that in the problem of time there is a gulf between Judaism and Christianity. In any case, the difference does not lie where he seeks it. See footnote 25 of this chapter.

3 This is to be fully conceded in spite of the scientific nonsense which has been put forth concerning Parsiism in New Testament publications of the past decade, in order to give to Christianity the appearance of an "Aryan" home.

4 Such vague time formulas of transition as "after these things," "straightway," etc., which in the Synoptic Gospels connect the various fragments of tradition, do not come into consideration here, since they were introduced by the authors only to create a literary framework. See Karl Ludwig Schmidt, *Der Rahmen der Geschichte Jesu,* 1919.

encounters limits in the separate treatment of a single word. Therefore we here desire to show in a connected survey how even this terminology expresses the distinctive quality of the Primitive Christian thinking concerning time.

The two ideas that most clearly elucidate the New Testament conception of time are those usually expressed by *kairos* ("a point of time"), and *aiôn* ("age"). It is not easy to find an adequate translation for the various expressions that refer to time. The translation at times must be determined by the theological content which results from the context. That these terms can also be used in the New Testament without special theological reference becomes clear as one uses the lexicons.

The characteristic thing about *kairos* is that it has to do with a definite *point of time* which has a fixed content, while *aiôn* designates a duration of time, a defined or undefined *extent of time*. In the New Testament both terms serve, in a manner that corresponds remarkably well to the matter in hand, to characterize that time in which the redemptive history occurs.

Kairos in secular usage is the moment in time which is especially favorable for an undertaking; it is the point of time of which one has long before spoken without knowing its actual date; it is the fixed day, which in modern jargon, for example, is called D day. It is human considerations that cause a point of time to appear especially adapted for the execution of this or that plan, and thus make it a *kairos*. In this secular sense Felix says to Paul: "When I have a convenient season, I will call for thee" (Acts 24:25).

The New Testament usage with reference to redemptive history is the same. Here, however, it is not human deliberations but a divine decision that makes this or that date a *kairos*, a point of time that has a special place in the execution of God's plan of salvation. Because the realization of the divine plan of salvation is bound to such time points or *kairoi* chosen by God, therefore it is a redemptive *history.* Not all fragments of ongoing time constitute redemptive history in the narrower sense, but rather these specific points, these *kairoi,* singled out from time as a whole.

What we said in the Introduction concerning the relation of the redemptive history to general history finds its confirmation in this central New Testament time concept of the *kairos.* Regarded from the historical standpoint as man sees it, the choice of the *kairoi* that constitute the redemptive history is arbitrary. The New Testament, therefore, gives as the principle of this divine "selection" of the *kairoi* only the "sovereign divine power": "the *kairoi* which the Father in his sovereign power has fixed" (Acts 1:7). To men, even to the disciples, it is not granted to know the date of the still future *kairoi.* The apostle Paul reminds the Thessalonians of the sudden inbreaking of these *kairoi* (I Thess. 5:1 f.).

The Apocalypse of John (chs. 1:3; 11:18) also designates the decisive moment of the eschatological drama as a *kairos* and says of it that it is "near," in the same sense in which the nearness of the Kingdom of God is announced in the Synoptic Gospels. *Kairos* appears likewise in the Synoptic Gospels with this eschatological application (Luke 19:44; 21:8), and the same usage occurs in I Peter 1:5. As in the passage just named, so also in the Pastoral Epistles the *kairoi* refer to the still future stages of the redemptive history.[5] In these Epistles, especially by the addition of the adjective (*idios*), "appropriate,"[6] it is emphasized that the sovereign power of God fixes these *kairoi* in the context of his entire plan of salvation: "the appearance of our Lord Jesus Christ, which the blessed

---

5 See also II Thess. 2:6, where we hear that even for the revelation of the Antichrist the *Kairos* is fixed.

6 The word *idios* is also understood by W. Bauer, in his *Griechisch-Deutsches Wörterbuch zu den Schriften des N.T.,* 1928, as an expression that lays particular emphasis upon the "appropriate time."

and only Sovereign will show at the appropriate *kairoi*" (I Tim. 6:14, 15).

In the same Epistle to Timothy we are shown the relation of these still future *kairoi* to an already past *kairos* of this same divine line of salvation: "Jesus Christ has given himself as a ransom for all, as a witness to appropriate *kairoi*" still to come (I Tim. 2:6).

Quite in agreement with this, however, the Epistle to Titus designates the time of the "revelation" of the proclamation of Christ, a time that already lies in the *past,* by precisely the same term "appropriate *kairoi*" (Titus 1:3). So also The First Epistle of Peter describes as a *kairos* the time of the Christ-event, which from the standpoint of the author had already been completed. The Old Testament "prophets searched to learn what or what manner of *kairos* was meant by the Spirit dwelling in them, when it testified to the sufferings destined for Christ and to the subsequent glory" (I Peter 1:11).

It is not merely in the faith of the Church after the death of Christ that this role of a central *kairos* in the divine plan of salvation is ascribed to the work that the incarnate Christ performed. Rather, Jesus himself, according to the Synoptic witness, characterizes his Passion as his *kairos;* by this Greek word the Evangelist, no doubt accurately translates the Aramaic word which Jesus used. At the time of the preparation for the Last Supper Jesus sends forth his disciples with the message: "The Master sends word: My *kairos* is near" (Matt. 26:18). We are reminded of the first preaching of Jesus: "The kingdom of God has come near." To the *kairos* to which Jesus points as the completion of his own work is thus ascribed a quite decisive significance in the course of events which lead to the Kingdom of God. We know this from other sayings of Jesus, altogether apart from the occurrence of the word *kairos.* We hear that even in the very fact of Jesus' appearance, above all in his healings, the Kingdom of God has broken in. That the decisive *kairos* of Christ's death and resurrection, and of the victory thereby achieved over the world of demons, is already announced in preceding *kairoi* of his earthly career, becomes clear to us in another passage of the Gospel of Matthew when the demon-possessed speak thus: "Hast thou come hither to torment us *before* the *kairos?*" (Matt. 8:29).

Nowhere does that which the New Testament understands by *kairos* come to clearer expression than in John 7:3 ff., a passage which in this regard is truly classic. In it Jesus says to his unbelieving brothers: "*My kairos* [to go up to Jerusalem] has not yet come; *your kairos* is always ready" (v. 6). This means: For you there is no *kairos* in the meaning found in the New Testament redemptive history, no times that God in his sovereign power has fixed and that therefore have a special significance in relation to his plan of salvation.[7] For the others there applies only the secular use of the word *kairos,* where everything depends solely on the human decision as to whether a *kairos* is favorable or not. They can go up to Jerusalem at any time; Christ cannot, for he stands in the midst of the divine plan of salvation, whose *kairoi* are definitely fixed by God.[8]

Upon the basis of the deed of Christ, however, there also exists in the present period of the Primitive Christian Church a divine *kairos* for the believer: "The *kairos* has come for the judgment to begin at the house of God" (I Peter 4:17). Hence the demand in Colossians and Ephesians (Col. 4:5;

---

7 Without the use of the word *Kairos,* precisely the same idea is present in the Cana story in John 2:4, which as a whole forms an exact parallel to the section John 7:1-13; cf. O. Cullmann, *Urchristentum und Gottesdienst* (*Abhandlungen zur Theologie des Alten und Neuen Testaments,* No. 3), 1944, pp. 42 ff. When Jesus here says to his mother: "Madam, why do you interfere in my affairs; my hour has not yet come," his words have the same meaning as does the answer given in John 7:6. The words *ti emoi kai soi* correspond to *ho de kairos ho humeteros pantote estin etoimos.*

8 R. Bultmann, in *Das Evangelium des Johannes,* 1941, p. 220, is here again interested only in the question of decision, not in that of the genuine time quality of the *kairos* concept in its relation to the entire redemptive line.

Eph. 5:16) to "redeem" the *kairos;* and if the "Western" reading in Rom. 12:11 is correct, Paul there summons his readers to place themselves at the service of the *kairos.* In these passages is meant the present *kairos,* whose significance in the entire plan of salvation is known to the believer upon the basis of the past *kairos,* that is, the death and resurrection of Christ.

Thus we see that in the past, the present, and the future there are special divine *kairoi,* by the joining of which the redemptive line arises.[9] The necessity of connecting the *kairoi* with one another has become clear to us especially in I Tim. 2:6, in connection with the two other passages cited from the Pastoral Epistles.[10]

This conception of special points of time at which the self-revealing God, in the execution of his plan, effects salvation is by no means bound to the one expression *kairos.* On the contrary, the specifically New Testament usage of other words for time serves to express the same idea, and does so once again in reference to the past, the present, and the future. As first in importance we must here mention the expressions "day" and "hour."

To designate the beginning of the eschatological drama which still lies in the future, Primitive Christianity took over from Judaism the concept of the "day of the Lord" (*yôm Yahweh*).[11] In Mark 13:32 Jesus speaks of "that day and hour," concerning time of which no one knows.

Here again those decisive events connected with the work of Jesus, who appeared in the flesh, are called in a special sense

9 That the entire "secular" process is determined by divine *kairoi* we hear in the Areopagus speech (Acts 17:26). God has "determined in advance the *kairoi* of all peoples on the face of the earth." Here emerges the problem of the relation between the redemptive history and general history; to this we shall devote a separate section (Part III).

10 See pp. 310 f.

11 See Acts 2:20 (from Joel 2:31); II Tim. 1:12; 1:18; 4:8; Acts 17:31.

"day" or, as the Gospel of John prefers to say, "hour." The above-mentioned utterance of Jesus in the Gospel of John, in which he explains that he himself is bound to fixed *kairoi,* is inevitably brought to mind when Jesus says in the Gospel of Luke (ch. 13:32): "I cast out demons and perform healings today and tomorrow, and on the third day I am perfected."

Above all, however, we must here recall the numerous Johannine passages in which Jesus speaks of his "hour" and where in every case the hour of his death is meant.[12] It is the central point, the central hour in the Christ-event. But from it a light falls on the other instances in the Johannine narrative concerning the life of Jesus where the hour is fixed. Indeed, it is in itself noteworthy that precisely the Gospel of John, which otherwise shows much less interest than the Synoptics for the chronological and geographical framework of the history of Jesus, presents an amazingly precise chronological placing of certain narratives: "it was about such and such an hour." This probably can be explained only by concluding that the Fourth Evangelist thereby intends to show that this life is really a redemptive event and so is bound to the time fixed for it by God. The time of Christ is not "always ready" as it is for the unbelieving brothers (John 7:6).

In this connection we must likewise place the emphatic "now" (*nun*), which we often find used in the New Testament to stress the fact that the present period of the Apostolic Age belongs in an outstanding way to the redemptive history and is thus distinguished from all other times. For example, it is said in Col. 1:26 that "the mystery which has been hidden for ages and generations has *now* been revealed to the saints, to whom God has willed to make it known."[13] It is in a similar sense that the author of The Epistle to the Hebrews speaks of his own time as "today" (*sêmeron,* ch. 3:7, 13, 15).

---

12 O. Cullmann, *Urchristentum und Gottesdienst* (*Abhandlungen zur Theologie des Alten und Neuen Testaments,* No. 3), 1944, pp. 41 ff.

13 Cf. Eph. 3:5; Rom. 16:25 f.

Thus here also we reach the result that all these expressions refer to moments or at least to sharply defined periods of time in the past as well as in the present and future. God chooses these moments or periods of time for the realization of his plan of salvation, and does so in such a way that the joining of them in the light of this plan forms a meaningful time line.

The terms treated thus far cluster around the central concept of *kairos* and characterize the decisive stages of time individually in their separate significance. The other word, *aiôn* ("period of time," "age"), that is so frequent in the New Testament, is to be so defined that it focuses upon the extension of time and expresses duration.

This word, like the Hebrew *ôlâm,* takes on at times a spatial meaning and so comes to mean "world"; it thus becomes a synonym of "world," "universe" (*kosmos*).[14] In the overwhelming majority of passages, however, we find the original use of the word, that is, as an expression of time.

The quite varied use of *aiôn* in the New Testament writings is extremely instructive for the understanding of the Primitive Christian conception of time. It can be shown that this one word serves here to designate both an exactly defined period of time and an undefined and incalculable duration, which we then translate by the word "eternity." Thus it comes about that the same expression that refers to the present "evil" age (Gal. 1:4) can be a characteristic of God, the "King of the ages" (I Tim. 1:17).[15] This ambiguous usage of the same

---

14 See, for example, Heb. 1:2. Further material excellent for orientation is given in the article on *aiôn* by H. Sasse in the *Theologisches Wörterbuch zum Neuen Testament,* Vol. 1, pp. 203 f.

15 We probably should agree with H. Sasse, *op. cit.,* p. 201, when he, in connection with the late Jewish usage in which these same words are linked, understands the genitive here in the sense of the Hebrew construct state, and accepts as the *original* meaning only that of "eternal king." To be sure, he leaves open the possibility that the meaning "Lord over the Ages" is also subsequently introduced into the expression. This is what

word, which has its counterpart in the usage of the Hebrew *ôlâm* and the Persian *zrvan,* will help us, in a separate later chapter, to determine correctly the relation between time and eternity in the New Testament.

Even here, however, the conclusion should be laid down that eternity, as meant in this linguistic usage, is not to be interpreted in the Platonic and modern philosophical sense, where it stands in contrast to time; it must rather be taken as endless time.[16] This is clear, indeed, from the fact that the use of the plural "ages" is particularly preferred when eternity is mentioned. Although the rhetorical tendency to liturgical pathos is certainly a contributing factor here, yet the fact that one can speak of eternity in the plural proves that it does not signify cessation of time or timelessness. It means rather endless time and therefore an ongoing of time which is incomprehensible to men; or, as it may be still better expressed, it means the linking of an unlimited series of limited world periods, whose succession only God is able to survey.

Thus in the New Testament field it is not time and eternity that stand opposed, but limited time and unlimited, endless time. Moreover, the thoroughly temporal manner of thinking is not surrendered even when the New Testament speaks of this limitless time. This latter time is not different from the former. The difference consists only in the fact that it is not

---

E. Stauffer, in his *Theologie des Neuen Testaments,* 1941, p. 59, assumes has happened in our passage.

16 This has been quite correctly recognized by H. Sasse, *op. cit.,* pp. 201 f. Even the Jewish conception of eternity (with the exception of Slavonic Enoch 65) is not that of timelessness, but that of endless time, and for the New Testament also it holds true that "statements concerning the eternal existence and action of God are made in the form of *prae* (before) and *post* (after)." Unfortunately Sasse, in his further discussion in the same article, obscures this insight when he writes on p. 202 that the eternity of God and the time of the world "stand in deepest contrast to one another," and when on p. 205, in the section concerning the present and the future age, he speaks of the dualistic teaching of the Bible concerning time and eternity.

limited. When the Christian writers, in their statements concerning calculable time, look backward, they write *ek tou aionos* ("out of the age"), *ap aiônes* ("from the age"), or even *apo tôn aiônôn* ("from the ages");[17] when they look forward, they write *eis aiôna* ("into the age") or *eis tous aiônas* ("into the ages"). Both usages agree completely with those of the Old Testament. Eternity, accordingly, is designated by the term *aiôn,* which carries a time meaning.[18]

By remembering this fact we can understand the familiar New Testament usage, which likewise roots in Judaism, in which the age "age" is used to express the divine division of time into this present age (*aiôn hoûtos enestôs*) and the coming age (*aiôn mellôn*).[19] Here too it is not the case that by this distinction time and eternity are set in contrast as opposites; nor is it true that "this age" means time while "the coming age" means timelessness. Rather, the coming age's future character, expressed in the added participle,[20] is to be taken seriously. The coming age is not, for example, already present as eternity. To be sure, there exists a radical contrast between the two ages, of which the one is characterized as "evil" (Gal. 1:4); but this is not meant in the sense that the one is temporal while the other is timeless—in both cases, indeed, the thing meant is called "age." The contrast and the

17 The expression "before the ages" (I Cor. 2:7) does not prove that eternity would be timeless because lying "before time." Either "ages" is used here in the sense of limited time (between the Creation and the end) or, as is also possible, we have here the spatial use of "ages" (see above). In this latter case "before the ages" would be exactly parallel to "before the foundation of the world" (Eph. 1:4; John 17:24; I Peter 1:20).

18 Concerning the Old Testament terminology for time, see C. v. Orelli, *Die hebräischen Synonyma der Zeit und Ewigkeit,* 1871.

19 The numerous supporting passages are cited by H. Sasse, *op. cit.,* pp. 205 f.

20 This future idea is expressed not only by *mellôn,* but also by *erchomenos* or *eperchomenos.*

evil character of the one age are not connected with the time quality as such, but with the event that stands with determinative role at the beginning of this period of time. That event is the Fall. The fall into sin did not create the time category itself, but it involved in the power of evil the course of events that fills this age, while the course of events that fills the coming age is marked by the conquest of the evil powers.

There also exists, to be sure, a distinction in time between the two ages, the present and the future. But here too the question involved is only that of the limits. The present age is limited in *both* directions: in the backward direction by creation, in the forward direction by the eschatological drama. The coming age is limited on *one* side but unlimited on the other; its beginning is limited, inasmuch as it begins with the events that are pictorially described in the apocalypses, but no limit is set for its end. In other words, it is without end but not without beginning, and only in this sense is it "eternal." Precisely from the fact that the coming age of the Bible has a beginning in time we perceive that its eternity is not that, for example, of the Platonic view.

If we wish to understand the Primitive Christian use of *aiôn* ("age"), we thus must free ourselves completely from all philosophical concepts of time and eternity. In summary, it may be said that in the temporal sense of the word in the singular and in the plural has in view a longer duration of time, and specifically:

1. Time in its entire unending extension, which is unlimited in both the backward and the forward direction, and thus is "eternity." [21]

21 To this use of *aiôn* corresponds the adjective *aiônios*, "agelong," "eternal." Since eternity in this sense comes into consideration only as an attribute of God, the adjective *aiônios* has the tendency to lose its time sense and is used in the qualitative sense of divine-immortal.

2. Limited time, which lies between Creation and the eschatological drama, and thus is identified with the "present" age, "this" age.[22]

3. Periods of time that are limited in one direction but unlimited in the other, and specifically:

a. The period to which the phrase *ek tou aiônos,* "out of the age," points back,[23] i.e., the time that lies before the Creation. On the side of Creation it has an end and so a limit; but in the backward direction it is unlimited, unending, and only in this sense is it eternal.

b. The time that extends beyond the end of the present age (*aiôn mellôn,* the "coming age"). It thus has in the so-called eschatological drama its beginning and so a limit; but in the forward direction it is unlimited, unending, and only in this sense is it eternal.

This schematic survey shows that only this simple rectilinear conception of unending time can be considered as the framework for the New Testament history of redemption. Along this consistently rectilinear line of the ages lie the *kairoi* determined by God. Thus just as God fixed the individual providential points or seasons of the redemptive history, so also he determined the just named divisions of the ages in which this history occurs.

None of the New Testament expressions for time has as its object time as an abstraction. This is not even the meaning of *chronos,* "time." This word is not used as it is in Greek philosophy, where it serves to designate time as such, in its problematic character. In the New Testament we find this word for "time" used in concrete reference to the redemptive history;

---

22 In this sense of limited "ages," I Cor. 10:11 speaks of "the ends of the ages." With Christ the final phase of the limited world period has dawned.

23 See p. 317.

it may have the meaning of "season" or of "age," or it may signify simply some space of time that is to elapse. Thus even the well-known passage in Rev. 10:6, where it is said that there will be no more *chronos,* is not to be understood as if the era of timelessness were meant; rather, on the analogy of Hab. 2:3 and Heb. 10:37, we must translate: "There will be no more *delay.*" [24]

The terminology of the New Testament teaches us that, according to the Primitive Christian conception, time in its unending extension as well as in its individual periods and moments is given by God and ruled by him. Therefore *all* his acting is so inevitably bound up with time that time is not felt to be a problem.[25] It is rather the natural presupposition of all that God causes to occur. This explains the fact that in a great majority of cases the terminology of the Primitive Christian writings has a time reference. Each individual item of the redemptive history has its fixed place in time. Of the law it is said quite concretely, in a section which is thoroughly theological and doctrinal, that it came 430 years after the

---

24 So also, in agreement with almost all expositors, E. Lohmeyer, *Die Offenbarung des Johannes,* in the *Handbuch zum Neuen Testament,* edited by H. Lietzmann, 1926, *ad. loc.,* although he also cites Bede's interpretation, which leans toward a philosophical understanding: *"mutabilis saecularium temporum varietas cessabit,"* "the changeful variety of this world's periods of time shall cease."

25 G. Delling, in *Das Zeitverständnis des Neuen Testaments,* 1940, thinks that in Judaism time was not felt to be a problem, but that for Hellenism, on the contrary, it was a difficult problem never solved. Christianity, he thinks, is distinguished from both in so far as it overcame time by the knowledge of the inbreaking of eternity. This would presuppose that for Primitive Christianity time as such was after all a problem to be overcome. This, however, is not the case. Rather, Primitive Christianity stands in this point much closer to Judaism than Delling supposes. Time is not something hostile to God that must be overcome. Certainly not by eternity, as though this meant a contrast to time. That which Delling calls the inbreaking of eternity is in reality something quite different; it has to do with the new time division effected by the work of Christ. See Part I, Chapters 4 and 5.

promise (Gal. 3:17); on the other hand, it is said that in the redemptive process this law "entered in along the way" (Rom. 5:20); moreover, the preceding survey in Rom. 5:12-14 is in its theological import completely anchored in chronology.

Christ, however, who is the divine revelatory Word himself, the mediator of all divine action, is so fully and closely connected with endless divine time that the author of The Epistle to the Hebrews can actually set forth his nature in time terminology: *"Jesus Christ, the same yesterday and today and into the ages"* (Heb. 13:8).

Similarly, The Revelation of John ascribes to him participation in God's eternity, when it designates him as the one who is "the first and the last, the beginning and the end" (chs. 1:17; 2:8; 22:13).

2

THE LINEAR CONCEPTION OF TIME IN THE REVELATORY HISTORY OF THE BIBLE AS CONTRASTED WITH THE CYCLICAL CONCEPTION OF HELLENISM

OUR STUDY of terminology has shown that in the Primitive Christian conception time is not a thing opposed to God, but is rather the means of which God makes use in order to reveal his gracious working. On the one side, time does not stand in contrast to God's eternity; on the other side, it is thought of as a straight line, not as a circle. Mention is made of a "beginning" (*archê*) and an "end" (*telos*). As soon as "beginning" and "end" are distinguished, the straight line is the suitable illustration to use.

All philosophical speculation concerning the nature of time, such as is carried on throughout the whole course of Greek philosophy without ever coming to a solution of the question,[1]

1 G. Delling offers a summary in *Das Zeitverständnis des Neuen Testaments,* 1940, Chapter 1, pp. 5 ff.

is quite foreign to Primitive Christianity. Indeed, we can clearly define the conception of the course of time which the New Testament presupposes by stating it in opposition to the typically Greek idea, and we must start from this fundamental perception, that the symbol of time for Primitive Christianity as well as for Biblical Judaism[2] and the Iranian religion is the *upward sloping line,* while in Hellenism it is the *circle.*[3]

Because in Greek thought time is not conceived as an upward sloping line with beginning and end, but rather as a circle, the fact that man is bound to time must here be experienced as an enslavement, as a curse. Time moves about in the eternal circular course in which everything keeps recurring. That is why the philosophical thinking of the Greek world labors with the problem of time. But that is also why all Greek striving for redemption seeks as its goal to be freed from this eternal circular course and thus to be freed from time itself.

---

2 The situation is different in Philo of Alexandria, who also in this respect is strongly influenced by Platonism.

3 G. Hölscher, *Die Ursprünge der jüdischen Eschatologie,* 1925, p. 6, has pointed out this radical contrast which exists between the eschatological thinking of Judaism and the cyclical conception of Hellenism. For the New Testament, Gottlob Schrenk, in "Die Geschichtsanschauung des Paulus" (*Jahrbuch der theologischen Schule Bethel,* 1932, pp. 59 ff.), a work which is noteworthy for our problem in still another respect, has distinguished the Pauline conception of time from the cyclical conception of Hellenism (Posidonius). In addition, M. Doerne, in "Annus Domini" (*Luthertum,* 1936, pp. 17 ff.), has strongly emphasized, in opposition to Th. Knoelle and W. Stählin, the conception of time as a straight line. So has G. Delling in *Das Zeitverständnis des Neuen Testaments,* 1940, p. 148, where he refers to Aristotle's statement in the *Physics,* 4:14: "For indeed time itself seems to be a sort of circle." See also J. Guitton, *Le temps et l'éternité chez Plotin et Saint-Augustin,* 1933. Note further my article, "La pensée eschatologique d'après un livre récent," in *Revue d'Histoire et de Philosophie religieuses,* 1938, pp. 347 ff. On the other hand, it is confusing when J. Jeremias, *Jesus als Weltvollender,* 1930, pp. 8 ff., accepts for the New Testament the conception that world history proceeds in circular movements.

For the Greeks, the idea that redemption is to take place through divine action in the course of events in time is impossible. Redemption in Hellenism can consist only in the fact that we are transferred from existence in this world, an existence bound to the circular course of time, into that Beyond which is removed from time and is already and always available. The Greek conception of blessedness is thus spatial; it is determined by the contrast between this world and the timeless Beyond; it is not a time conception determined by the opposition between Now and Then.[4] On the basis of the cyclical conception of time, it cannot be determined by the time factor.

In the Primitive Christian preaching, on the contrary, salvation, in keeping with the Bible's linear understanding of time, is conceived strictly in terms of a time process. The expectation of the coming Kingdom of God is not to be so dissolved that it means "always standing in the situation of decision." [5] Were that done, the event of the coming of God's reign would not be "an event in the course of time." The coming consummation is a real future, just as the past redemptive deed of Jesus Christ, in spite of the fact that it is the interpreting mid-point of all times, is from the standpoint of the Church a real past, and just as the present of the Church, stamped as it is with a thoroughly time-conditioned character,

---

4 See on this point, E. v. Dobschütz, "Zeit und Raum im Denken des Urchristentums" (*Journal of Biblical Literature,* 1922, pp. 212 ff.).

5 So R. Bultmann, *Jesus,* 1926; see especially pp. 49-54 (Eng. tr., *Jesus and the Word,* 1934, pp. 51-56.) When nevertheless Bultmann holds fast to the view that the divine Lordship is "pure future," this is after all only a concession to the Biblical *terminology.* For a future that is stripped of its time character is no future. The "expectation of an end of the world which is to come in time" belongs, according to Bultmann, to "mythology" (*ibid.,* p. 53; Eng. tr., p. 56). It is really strange that there has been so much excitement over the appearance of Bultmann's work *Offenbarung und Heilsgeschehen,* 1941; this conception of "myth" is already essentially present in his 1926 book on *Jesus.*

is bound back to this past and forward to that future.[6] The New Testament knows only the linear time concept of Today, Yesterday, and Tomorrow; all philosophical reinterpretation and dissolution into timeless metaphysics is foreign to it. It is precisely upon the basis of this rectilinear conception of time that time in Primitive Christianity can yield the framework for the divine process of revelation and redemption, for those *kairoi* which God in his omnipotence fixes, for those ages into which he divides the whole process. Because time is thought of as an upward sloping line, it is possible here for something to be "fulfilled"; a divine plan can move forward to complete execution; the goal which beckons at the upper end of the line can give to the entire process which is taking place all along the line the impulse to strive thither; finally, the decisive mid-point, the Christ-deed, can be the firm hold that serves as guidepost for all the process that lies behind and for all that lies ahead.

In Biblical thinking there exists, we may say, congenial harmony between the redemptive process thus understood and time thus understood. Indeed, we have seen that in the New Testament time is never spoken of in an abstract manner, but is always mentioned in connection with the redemptive process. The New Testament's favorite expression of "fulfillment," of the "completion" of time (*plêrôma, plêroûsthai*), also points to this connection and faithfully represents the rectilinear conception of time and history.

Because time in Hellenism is not conceived in a rectilinear manner, the scene of the working of providence (*pronoia*) can never be history as such but only the fate of the individual. History is not under the control of a *telos* or end goal. From this standpoint, in so far as the need of man for revelation and

6 Moreover, the emphasis on our being "contemporaneous" with that event of the past, a position so dear to the heart of Kierkegaard, must not lead us to use this position to abolish the time character of the redemptive process. See pp. 146, 168 f.

redemption is to be satisfied, it can take place only in the direction of timeless mysticism, which thinks in spatial concepts.

If today, in the prevailing attitude, the radical contrast between Hellenistic metaphysics and Christian revelation is often completely lost, this is due to the fact that very early the Greek conception of time supplanted the Biblical one, so that down through the history of doctrine to the present day there can be traced a great misunderstanding, upon the basis of which that is claimed as "Christian" which in reality is Greek. The root of the heresy, if we are to designate as heresy what is really apostasy from Primitive Christianity, is the dissolving into metaphysics of the Primitive Christian conception that redemptive history is bound to the upward sloping time line.

If Platonic Greek influence on The Epistle to the Hebrews were actually so profound and decisive as it is often asserted to be, it should show itself precisely in this central point. But, as a matter of fact, here also the invisible is thought of primarily in terms, not of space, but of time. The Epistle speaks not only of the Beyond but also of the *future* Jerusalem, of the future city (Heb. 11:10, 16; 13:14). Therefore it is said that we "wait" for it. To be sure, even now in the present an invisible process is going on, but it is a process that takes place in time; it therefore stands in connection with that unique process of the past and the future.

The first apostasy from the Primitive Christian understanding of time is not found in The Epistle to the Hebrews, nor in the Johannine writings. In this central question, as we have already seen in the discussion of the *kairos* concept and shall see again later, these writings are not controlled by a Hellenistic slant. The first apostasy comes rather in *Gnosticism.*

The marks of ancient Christian Gnosticism are manifold, and can be classified in various ways. In the last analysis, they may all be traced back to the Greek, and so to an un-Biblical, concept of time. From that point of view the redemptive history can only be rejected as barbarism, or else it must be given a radically new meaning.

Thus it happens that in all Gnostic systems the following features go hand in hand:

1. Rejection of the Old Testament, both in its explanation of history as the creative action of God and in its claim that the history of Israel constitutes a redemptive history.

2. Docetism, which is not exhaustively presented in the theory that has given the name to this heresy, the theory according to which Jesus possessed only the semblance of a body but had no actual human body; its chief distinguishing mark is rather to be seen in its rejection of the judgment that redemptive history passes on the quite ordinary particular historical event that occurred in the incarnate Christ, and that includes the offensively ordinary fact of the death on the cross. Thus here also we have to do with the denial of the redemptive significance of an event that occurred in time.[7]

3. Rejection of the Primitive Christian eschatological expectation, whose characteristic distinction in terms of time between the present and the future age is replaced by the Greek

---

7 We shall show (Part II, Chapter 1) that ancient Christian Docetism assumes two different forms. It is common to both that the redemptive worth of Christ's death is rejected, and in connection therewith the fact itself is denied. Especially favored is the theory according to which, in the instant at which the suffering of Jesus began, a substitution took place; Simon of Cyrene was crucified while Christ ascended to heaven (Irenaeus, *Against Heresies,* I, 24, 4; see also I, 27, 1). According to the Gnostic view, so complete an entrance into history as the suffering on the cross under Pontius Pilate presents is not compatible with the redemptive activity of Christ. We return to the question of Docetism in Part II. It is a real problem today; for it can be shown that Docetism is also present in all the modern Christological discussions in which a choice is made as to what is and is not central for salvation on the basis of this or that idealistic position, rather than on the basis of what the Gospels themselves present in the history that they transmit.

metaphysical distinction between this world and the timeless Beyond.

Whoever takes his start from Greek thought must put aside the entire revelatory and redemptive history. Hence it is not accidental that in the older Gnosticism, as in modern philosophical reinterpretations of the New Testament witness, all of the three Biblical positions named above are given up in one complete surrender.

It is also no accident, however, that among the theologians of the second century none fought Gnosticism with such acuteness as did Irenaeus, who with unyielding consistency carried through the time line of redemptive history from the Creation to the eschatological new creation. Down to the theologians of the "redemptive history" school in the nineteenth century, Joh. Tobias Beck, Joh. Chr. K. von Hofmann, Carl Aug. Auberlen, and Martin Kähler,[8] there has scarcely been another theologian who has recognized so clearly as did Irenaeus that the Christian proclamation stands or falls with the redemptive history, that the historical work of Jesus Christ as Redeemer forms the mid-point of a line which leads from the Old Testament to the return of Christ. Therefore also no theologian of antiquity grasped so clearly as did Irenaeus the radical opposition which emerges between Greek and Biblical thinking as to this point, namely, the question of the conception of time. Irenaeus is the theologian of antiquity who understood the Greek world in its innermost nature, and yet undertook no such violent reductions and reinterpretations of the New Tes-

---

8 In a certain sense the federal theology of Joh. Cocceius can already be regarded as the forerunner of theology presented as redemptive history (see Gottlob Schrenk, *Gottesreich und Bund im älteren Protestantismus, vornehmlich bei Johannes Cocceius,* 1923). Concerning the nineteenth century representatives of the theology which centers in redemptive history, see Gustav Weth, *Die Heilsgeschichte, Ihr universeller und ihr individueller Sinn in der offenbarungsgeschichtlichen Theologie des 19. Jahrhunderts,* 1931, and Folke Holmström, *Das eschatologische Denken der Gegenwart,* 1936.

tament message as were practiced, not only by the Gnostics, but also by the Alexandrian scholars Clement and Origen.[9]

It is by this contrast between the Greek and the Biblical conceptions of time that the unusually severe clash between Hellenism and Biblical Christianity is explained; in the same way is also explained the initial process of the Hellenizing transformation of Christianity.[10] These two things, the hostile clash and the Hellenizing of Christianity, constituted together the chief theme of doctrinal debate in antiquity, and fundamentally they have remained so to this day, in so far as modern philosophical thinking roots in Hellenism.

There can be no real reconciliation when the fundamental positions are so radically different. Peaceful companionship is possible only when either Hellenism is Christianized on the

---

9 In Irenaeus, to be sure, we may say that this rectilinear character of the redemptive history actually overreaches itself and collapses. Hence it comes about that Irenaeus does not understand the sinful fall of Adam as the positive act of revolt and disobedience, but rather ascribes it to the natural immaturity of Adam, as somewhat counted on from the outset; thereby, of course, its significance is minimized. For Irenaeus the line runs on in so straight a course that the break which resulted from the fall into sin is not sufficiently taken into account. Everything is merely fulfillment. With this is connected the fact that for Irenaeus the redemptive line strains so intently to its goal that on its course the intermediate period between the resurrection and return of Christ is not sufficiently taken into account. This becomes clear when Irenaeus, in interpreting the ancient Christian confession, transfers into the future the subjection of the "lordships and powers" which according to Phil. 2:6ff. and the other earliest confessions has already taken place from the time of Christ's death. See my work, *Die ersten christlichen Glaubensbekenntnisse*, 1943, p. 56 (Eng. tr., *The Earliest Christian Confessions*, 1949, pp. 61f.) Having taken this position, Irenaeus must then reject also the reference of the "authorities" of Rom. 13:1 to the invisible lordships who stand behind the State (*Against Heresies*, V, 24, 1), since no time is left to them for a temporary activity connected with Christ.

10 The contrast between Hellenism and Christianity is well presented by L. Laberthonnière, *Le réalisme chrétien et l'idéalisme, grec*, 1904; and also in the already mentioned work by Jean Guitton, *Le temps et l'éternité chez Plotin et Saint-Augustin*, 1933.

basis of the fundamental Biblical position or Christianity is Hellenized on the basis of the fundamental Greek position. The first-named possibility, the Christianizing of Hellenism, has never really been achieved. Tendencies in this direction, however, are found in the New Testament itself, especially in the Johannine literature, which has its orientation in the redemptive history and whose time concept, as we have already said, is thoroughly Christian and Biblical, but which, on the other hand, takes up and Christianizes such Hellenistic concepts as that of the Logos.

Wherever in the course of doctrinal development there has occurred a debate between Hellenism and Christianity, it has almost always had its fundamental outcome in the realization of the second-named possibility, the Hellenizing of Christianity. This has meant that the New Testament's time-shaped pattern of salvation has been subjected to the spatial metaphysical scheme of Hellenism.

This is shown most tangibly—but not only there—in the collapse of the Primitive Christian eschatological expectation. In the confirmation of this fact we must agree completely with M. Werner, who intensively studies this problem in his explanation of the origin of the Christian doctrine.[11] But against Werner's *explanation* of this fact it must be strongly emphasized that this question as to how, under Hellenistic influence, the collapse of the Primitive Christian eschatological expectation occurred must not be considered in an isolated way; it must rather be given its place in the larger problem as to how the entire Biblical scheme of redemptive history, in which eschatology is only one member, came to be Hellenized. In this process of Hellenization we have to do with the question not only of the future but of *time in general*. For this reason alone it is misleading when Werner makes the nonoccurrence of the Parousia responsible for the process of Hellenization. This

11 Martin Werner, *Die Entstehung des christlichen Dogmas,* 1941.

process affected not only Christianity but all ancient religions, even those in which there was no eschatology in the Biblical sense, and so no expectation of the Parousia. If, however, the debate with Christianity ran its course in a much more sharpened form than did the debate with any other religion, this is due precisely to the radically un-Greek conception of time which the Christian redemptive history presupposes.

Although Christianity shares this conception of time with Judaism and to a certain degree with Parsiism, our investigation will show that in Primitive Christianity the line of redemptive history is carried through as a connected and upward sloping line in a much more consistent way than was possible in the Old Testament. This is connected with the fact that in the New Testament the present also can be drawn into the redemptive process in a special way, as the "time between Resurrection and Parousia." An event of the past, the death and resurrection of Christ, is regarded as the decisive mid-point of the entire line of revelation, and in this way the connection of the future with what has previously happened is no longer left vague and undefined; rather now for the first time, on the basis of the fixed orientation to *that mid-point in time,* the line can be clearly drawn from the beginning on, in its unbroken continuity. The point of view that redemptive history presents is indeed found in the Old Testament, but nevertheless only in a preparatory way; it can be constructed into a straight and complete line only in the light of the fulfillment which has already taken place in time, in the death and resurrection of Christ. To this there is no analogy in any other religion, not even in Parsiism. That is the reason why the debate with Hellenism presents from the beginning the great problem of Christian theology.[12]

---

12 In saying this I have also given an implicit answer to the objection which M. Werner, in the *Schweizerische theologische Umschau* for September, 1942, made in reply to my criticism of his thesis. In the *Kirchenblatt für die Reformierte Schweiz,* June, 1942, I had sought to refute

If we did not desire as a matter of principle to avoid all theological slogans, we would be tempted to oppose to the slogan of the "consistently eschatological" way of looking at the New Testament that of the viewpoint marked by the "consistently historical method of revelation." He who speaks only of eschatology sees the entire question in a cramped perspective.[13]

3

TIME AND ETERNITY

THE CONTRAST which we have shown to exist between the Greek and the Biblical conception of time appears in a particularly clear way in the determination, so important for our problem, of the relationship between time and eternity. We must here refer back to Chapter 1, concerning the New Testa-

---

Werner's assertion that the Hellenization of Christianity is explained only by the delay in the Parousia. My argument was that the process of Hellenization was a universal phenomenon in the religious history of antiquity; this process laid hold not only of Christianity but also of other ancient religions in which the delay of the Parousia plays no role. To this M. Werner, in the above-named article, objected that in no other religion did the conflict with Hellenism have such far-reaching consequences as in the Christian religion, and that this fact is explained only by the delay in the Parousia. The observation that the collision is here seen in a particularly accentuated form is correct, but it is explained, as we have seen, by Hellenism's radically different understanding of time, which excludes any and all revelation in history.

13 In Karl Barth's discussions of the situation before time, above time, and after time (*Kirchliche Dogmatik,* II, Part 1, 1940, pp. 698 ff.), we believe that we find (see pp. 62 f., 66) the last traces of a philosophical and non-Biblical statement of the relation between time and eternity. Yet it seems to us that in this section he has well shown the necessity of treating the problem of time *as a whole;* hence we are not to give a one-sided emphasis which treats the situation before time along the lines of the Reformers' theology, the state above time along the lines of the theology of the eighteenth and nineteenth centuries, and the situation after time ceases along the lines of "consistent eschatology."

ment terminology dealing with time, and we must now go on to define more closely the conclusions there reached. We do this in order to show how these conclusions differ from the Greek conception, present above all in Platonism, of the way in which time and eternity are related.[1]

For Greek thinking in its Platonic formulation there exists between time and eternity a qualitative difference, which is not completely expressed by speaking of a distinction between limited and unlimited duration of time. For Plato, eternity is not endlessly extended time, but something quite different; it is timelessness. Time in Plato's view is only the *copy* of eternity thus understood. How much the thinking of our days roots in Hellenism, and how little in Biblical Christianity, becomes clear to us when we confirm the fact that far and wide the Christian Church and Christian theology distinguish time and eternity in the Platonic-Greek manner. This then has important consequences, and when the New Testament perspective of redemptive history is thereby affected, it leads to a radical transformation of the Primitive Christian preaching.[2]

To Primitive Christianity, as to Judaism, the Greek manner of distinguishing between time and eternity is quite foreign. The reason is that here the relation between time and eternity is never the object of a speculation; if the relation comes to discussion at all, this results from faith in a divine revelation which is anchored in time. We have seen that Primitive Christianity knows nothing of timelessness, and that even the passage Rev. 10:6 is not to be understood in this sense.[3] From all that has been said in the two preceding chapters it

1 From another point of view, namely, that of a debate with the "dialectic theology," the problem is treated in a more philosophical manner by Hans Wilhelm Schmidt, *Zeit und Ewigkeit, die letzten Voraussetzungen der dialektischen Theologie,* 1927.

2 As in Martin Dibelius, *Geschichtliche und übergeschichtliche Religion im Christentum,* 1925.

3 See p. 320.

results rather that eternity, which is possible only as an attribute of God, is time, or, to put it better, what we call "time" is nothing but a part, defined and delimited by God, of this same unending duration of God's time. Nowhere does this come so clearly to expression as in the already established fact that the word used to express eternity, *aiôn* ("age"), is *the same word* that is also applied to a limited division of time; otherwise expressed, between what we call eternity and what we call time, that is, between everlastingly continuing time and limited time, the New Testament makes absolutely no difference in terminology. Eternity is the endless succession of the ages (*aiônes*). In order, therefore, to do justice to the Primitive Christian conception, we should possess a terminology that would take account of this fact.[4] Since such does not exist, we in what follows will preserve the usual terminology, but constantly remind ourselves that above the distinction between "time" and "eternity" stands the one time concept of the age (*aiôn*), which includes both.

Karl Barth also, in contrast to his earlier publications, lays very strong emphasis in his *Dogmatik* (Vol. II, Part 1, 1940, pp. 685 ff.) on the temporal quality of eternity. But the philosophical influence which controls the conception of time in his earlier writings, especially in the Commentary of Romans,[5] is still operative in the *Dogmatik* of 1940; here still, in spite of everything, he takes as his starting point a fundamental distinction between time and eternity, and refuses to regard eternity as "time stretching endlessly forward and backward" (p. 686). The time-marked character of eternity, which Karl Barth strives so urgently to bring out in this section of his book,

4 The demand for the introduction of a special terminology is also raised by H. W. Schmidt, *Zeit und Ewigkeit,* 1927.

5 For the presentation and criticism of his earlier conception of time see Folke Holmström, *Das eschatologische Denken der Gegenwart,* 1936, pp. 212 ff., 325 ff., and especially Karl Barth's self-correction in *Kirchliche Dogmatik,* Vol. II, Part 1, 1940, pp. 714 ff.

is understood in the Biblical sense only when the symbol of the straight line is applied to both, to time and to eternity, so that this very time during which the creation exists appears as a limited portion of the same line, and not as something essentially different. Of this fact Karl Barth's figurative manner of expression fails to take account when he says that eternity "surrounds" time on all sides (p. 698), or "accompanies" it (p. 702). Here emerges the danger that, after all, eternity may again be conceived as qualitatively different from time, and so as a result there may again intrude that Platonic conception of timeless eternity which Karl Barth in the *Dogmatik* is nevertheless plainly striving to discard.

Thus time and eternity share this time quality. Primitive Christianity knows nothing of a timeless God. The "eternal" God is he who was in the beginning, is now, and will be in all the future, "who is, who was, and who will be" (Rev. 1:4). Accordingly, his eternity can and must be expressed in this "naïve" way, in terms of endless time.[6] This time quality is not in its essence something human, which first emerged in the fallen creation.[7] It is, moreover, not bound to the creation.

When it is said in Heb. 1:2 that God has "created the ages," the meaning here is not that "time" has been created; we

---

6 This holds true also against Folke Holmström, *Das eschatologische Denken der Gegenwart,* 1936, pp. 204 ff., who demands on p. 209 that the "naïve" concept of time ("chronologically limited duration") be accepted in Christian theology, but that the "naïve" concept of eternity ("endless duration of time") be as decisively rejected.

7 So Karl Heim, *Glauben und Denken,* 1934, pp. 376 ff. Also Walter Künneth, *Theologie der Auferstehung,* 1933, in which time is understood as a "creation" and as the "world form of the fall," and therefore as "identical in form and content with the existence of man" (p. 170). In this linking of time and sin the Greek time concept most clearly continues to work; this is true, indeed, of by far the most of the theologians who have dealt with the problem, including still Karl Barth in his *Dogmatik* of 1940. In the next chapter it will be shown how sin in fact does have something—indeed, a great deal—to do with the division of time, but not with time itself.

have rather the spatial use of the word *aiôn,* a usage which is also attested elsewhere (see H. Sasse, in Kittel's *Theologisches Wörterbuch zum Neuen Testament,* article on *aiôn,* p. 204). The word is here identical in meaning with "world" (*kosmos*).

If we wish to grasp the Primitive Christian idea of eternity, we must strive above all to think in as unphilosophical a manner as possible. To be sure, there appears on the margin in the New Testament a primitive beginning; the prologue to the Gospel of John, in the opening verses, speaks not in the historical tense of the aorist, but in the imperfect tense: "in the beginning *was* [*ên*] . . . ," that is, before the Creation (John 1:1). But the imperfect indicates only that at that time no revelatory event in the real sense had as yet taken place. Nevertheless, this series of events is already being prepared, in the foreordination of God (John 17:24; I Cor. 2:7; Col. 1:26; Eph. 3:11). Similarly, on the outermost limit of that which is reported in the New Testament, we hear concerning a "Sabbath rest of God" (Heb. 4:9), where God will be "all in all" (I Cor. 15:28). But by this too it is meant only that the Biblical process of revelation then comes to its conclusion. Only on the very margin of the New Testament is there mention of that original condition in which this process has not yet occurred and of this final condition, following the eschatological drama, where this process is no longer going on. The time of "rest" is never the really independent object of attention in the New Testament, not even—especially not—in the Apocalypse of John. For it regularly belongs to the essential nature of the Bible that it speaks only of God's revelatory action.[8] Accordingly, where the Biblical statements go beyond

8 To the question as to the rest of God before the Creation, Calvin, as is well known, gave the answer which had already been given before him: "God was not idle, but was creating hell for curious questioners." Luther too rejected all questioning as to God's activity before the Creation with the answer: "He went into the woods and cut rods with which to punish good-for-nothing questioners!"

the beginning and the end of this action, this always happens only in order to show how God's revelatory action connects with that existence of his which lies before the Creation and after the end of the world. Hence, in the last analysis, that condition of rest which appears on the margin is after all fitted into the series of revelatory events, in that during the rest this process is first prepared and then becomes operative in its effects. The Primitive Christian preaching views that condition of rest only in the light of that process. The very consideration that all Biblical statements deal with God's revelation, with God's action, should keep us from proceeding to an understanding of the Biblical thought about time—the Old Testament thought as well as that of the New Testament—by taking as starting point a speculative concept of eternity; we must not start from an eternity concept which is separated from this revelatory happening; we must not start, for example, from a speculation concerning the "rest" of God. For this reason eternity can be conceived in Primitive Christianity only as endlessly extended time.

It should be added that the erroneous importation into Primitive Christian thinking of the Platonic contrast between time and timeless eternity has no connection with the few "marginal passages" that mention the existence of God before the Creation and after the end of the world. It connects rather with the Biblical distinction between the two ages, the "present" and the "future" ages. It is a favorite practice to identify the "present" age with "time" and the "future" one with "eternity." To this, however, it must at once be replied that the future age in the New Testament is an actual future, that is, a future *in time*. All talk about the coming age that does not take this time quality in full earnest is philosophical reinterpretation.

When Karl Barth, in his *Kirchliche Dogmatik* (Vol. II, Part 1, 1940, pp. 709 f.; cf. also Vol. I, Part 1, 1932, pp. 486 f.), makes eschatology into the "state subsequent to time," where "there will be time no longer," when he gives future character to this "state subsequent to time" only with the qualification that this holds good merely "from our point of view," and when he goes on to declare that the final state (*to eschaton*) is "still future" only from our point of view, there evidently lies at the basis of these statements a philosophical standpoint which is foreign to the New Testament. The Bible knows no other point of view about time than that of the revelation that has come to us; it regards a particular event as the mid-point of time, and so for this point of view future simply means future, and not a timeless eternity that is future only "for us." We believe that we are fair to the ultimate *intention* of Karl Barth when we stress the fact that upon the ground of the Biblical revelation everything divine, including God's eternity, can be seen only "from our point of view," that is, from the revelation that came to us in Jesus Christ in the years 1–30. Whatever ideas one may form concerning God's eternity "in itself," they must not destroy the characteristic perspective in which Primitive Christianity sees all revelation. This perspective is that of a point of time.

The time character of the future becomes especially clear from the fact that the eschatological drama, as it is pictured in the Apocalypses, including the New Testament ones, takes place in a thoroughly chronological progression; this is true in the more detailed Johannine and Synoptic apocalypses as well as in the Pauline eschatological passages. In this connection we must bear in mind not only the millennial Kingdom of the book of Revelation and the numerical data which point to the limited duration of certain events, but also the entire structure, which characterizes this process not as timeless but rather as occurring in time.[9] In these writings we hear of

9 This should be emphasized also in opposition to the "timeless" exposition of the Apocalypse of John by E. Lohmeyer, *Die Offenbarung des Johannes*, 1926 (*Handbuch zum Neuen Testament*, edited by H. Lietzmann).

"afterward" and "then," and this occurs not merely in the book of Revelation, but particularly in Paul. Read, for example, the short passage I Cor. 15:23-28, and note the heaping up of expressions for time: "thereafter" (*epeite*), "then," "next" (*eita*), "whenever" (*hotan*), "then" (*tote*). Moreover, we dare not weaken the time character of the coming age by pointing out that after all, at the end of this whole process which takes place within that phase, God is "all in all" (I Cor. 15:28). The new age does not begin only then; rather, all that the preceding passage has announced concerning the eschatological drama already falls in the coming age. *Within* the new age the Lordship of Christ, which has been established ever since the ascension, *continues on in time,* until the Son himself at a definite time is "subjected to the Father who subjected all things to him." But independently of that fact, this conclusion that God is "all in all" signifies, as already said, only the end of the Biblical revelatory process.

Another reason why the future age cannot be taken as timeless eternity and contrasted with the present age is that the coming age is *not a mere return to the primitive beginning.*[10] In this fact also is shown its time character. In reality the New Testament, as we have seen, recognizes not only two but at least three ages:

1. The age before the Creation, in which the revelatory process is already being prepared in the divine predestination and in the Logos, who is already with God.

2. The "present" age, which lies between the Creation and the end.

3. The "coming" age, in which the eschatological drama falls. The first and third by no means coincide. In the first, the Creation is not yet present; it is only being prepared. In the

---

10 The difference between the time of the beginning and the end must not be obscured by the foggy concept of "primal history."

third, the first Creation is replaced by the new creation. All this can take place only in a time framework that continuously moves straight forward; it cannot occur in the framework of a dualism between time and timeless eternity.

In the next chapter we shall show how the two-part division is superimposed upon the three-part scheme. A decisive event is regarded as the mid-point of the entire time line. From this point, then, the entire section that lies before this center appears as preparation for this one point where time is fulfilled. The decisive red line in a thermometer of endless extension is there reached, but the thermometer itself extends still farther above the red line. The red line introduces a two-part division. This does not do away with the previously mentioned three-part scheme: before the Creation, Creation, new creation; but it is superimposed upon that scheme.

This, however, means that the worth of an epoch of time does not consist in its reference to a timeless eternity; each epoch has its own full meaning precisely as a portion of time. This meaning is recognized, however, only from the mid-point which itself is time. We shall show this for the entire line of salvation in Part II. Thus the reason that the present phase of time, which began with the resurrection of Christ and still continues, is of interest for redemptive history is not that it stands in relation to a timeless eternity which surrounds it; rather, it has its own worth precisely in its time character and in its connection with the fact of Christ's resurrection at a specific point of time.

The so frequently cited[11] and famous word of L. v. Ranke, that "every age is immediately related to God," is emphatically not meant in this New Testament sense. Instead, it carries the idea of relation to a timeless God, as becomes clear from the

---

11 Here we should mention, among others, E. Hirsch, Karl Barth, Paul Althaus, Emil Brunner, and Heinrich Barth.

subsequent part of that sentence.[12] According to the Primitive Christian conception, on the contrary, the inherent worth of every epoch is determined by its relation to a central event in time.

Other books by Cullmann:

Baptism in the New Testament, 1950.
Early Christian Worship, 1953.
The Early Church: Studies in Early Christian History and Theology, 1956.
Peter: Disciple, Apostle, Martyr, 1953.
The State in the New Testament, 1950.

Other books on the same problem:

Brabant, F. H. *Time and Eternity in Christian Thought,* 1937.
Brandon, S. G. F. *Time and Mankind,* 1951.
Farrer, Austin. *Finite and Infinite,* 1943.
Gunn, J. Alexander. *The Problem of Time,* 1929.
Heidegger, Martin. *Sein und Zeit,* 1927.
Marsh, John. *The Fulness of Time,* 1952.
Poulet, George. *Studies in Human Time,* 1956.

12 L. v. Ranke, *Ueber die Epoche der neuern Geschichte,* 1917, p. 217. On this point see F. Holmström, *Das eschatologische Denken der Gegenwart,* 1936, p. 203.

H. RICHARD NIEBUHR

H. Richard Niebuhr, brother of the more widely known Reinhold Niebuhr, has written largely in the field of Christian Ethics where the implications of the revelation for human behavior is the central problem. If the New Testament is the revelation of the redemptive action of God for man, what then is the status and meaning of human action? What relationship does man's action in and through the life of culture bear to God's accomplished through the religious life of faith? The tension between the "Kingdom of God" and the "Kingdom of Caesar" emerges again today as a crucial problem because of 18th and 19th century tendencies to identify the two to the point where the first term of the pair has disappeared and the second faces the possibility of self-extinction.

Niebuhr's *Christ and Culture* is an attempt to clarify for contemporary man the multiple ambiguous dimensions of the Biblical metaphor by developing a typology of the numerous and conflicting interpretations given to the metaphor in the history of western thought. As the study develops the reader becomes increasingly aware of the validity and necessity of these two "Kingdoms", their mutual dependency upon each other and the impossibility of absorbing either into the other. The realm of faith and the realm of culture become more clearly defined and one is forced both to examine one's own position with respect to their relationship and to assume a position with respect to the five types of traditional solution so clearly presented. The following selection contains Niebuhr's elaboration of one of the five types.

H. RICHARD NIEBUHR

from

CHRIST AND CULTURE

CHAPTER 1. THE ENDURING PROBLEM

IV. THE TYPICAL ANSWERS

GIVEN THESE TWO complex realities—Christ and culture—an infinite dialogue must develop in the Christian conscience and the Christian community. In his single-minded direction toward God, Christ leads men away from the temporality and pluralism of culture. In its concern for the conservation of the many values of the past, culture rejects the Christ who bids men rely on grace. Yet the Son of God is himself child of a religious culture, and sends his disciples to tend his lambs and sheep, who cannot be guarded without cultural work. The dialogue proceeds with denials and affirmations, reconstructions, compromises, and new denials. Neither individual nor church can come to a stopping-place in the endless search for an answer which will not provoke a new rejoinder.

Yet it is possible to discern some order in this multiplicity, to stop the dialogue, as it were, at certain points; and to define typical partial answers that recur so often in different eras and societies that they seem to be less the product of historical conditioning than of the nature of the problem itself and the meanings of its terms. In this way the course of the great conversation about Christ and culture may be more intelligently followed, and some of the fruits of the discussion may be garnered. In the following chapters such typical answers are to be set forth and illustrated by reference to such Christians as John and Paul, Tertullian and Augustine, Thomas Aquinas and Luther, Ritschl and Tolstoy. At this point brief and summary descriptions of these typical answers is offered as a guide to what follows.

Five sorts of answers are distinguished, of which three are closely related to each other as belonging to that median type in which both Christ and culture are distinguished and affirmed; yet strange family resemblances may be found along the whole scale.

Answers of the first type emphasize the *opposition* between Christ and culture. Whatever may be the customs of the society in which the Christian lives, and whatever the human achievements it conserves, Christ is seen as opposed to them, so that he confronts men with the challenge of an "either-or" decision. In the early period of church history Jewish rejection of Jesus, defended by Klausner, found its counterpart in Christian antagonism to Jewish culture, while Roman outlawry of the new faith was accompanied by Christian flight from or attack upon Graeco-Roman civilization. In medieval times monastic orders and sectarian movements called on believers living in what purported to be a Christian culture to abandon the "world" and to "come out from among them and be separate." In the modern period answers of this kind are being given by missionaries who require their converts to abandon wholly the customs and institutions of so-called "heathen" societies, by little groups of withdrawing Christians in Western or "Christianized" civilization, and in partial manner, by those who emphasize the antagonism of Christian faith to capitalism and communism, to industrialism and nationalism, to Catholicism and Protestantism.

Recognition of a fundamental *agreement* between Christ and culture is typical of the answers offered by a second group. In them Jesus often appears as a great hero of human culture history; his life and teachings are regarded as the greatest human achievement; in him, it is believed, the aspirations of men toward their values are brought to a point of culmination; he confirms what is best in the past, and guides the process of civilization to its proper goal. Moreover, he is a part of culture in the sense that he himself is part of the social heritage that must be transmitted and conserved. In our time answers of this kind are given by Christians who note the close relation between Christianity and Western civilization, between Jesus' teachings or the teachings about him and democratic institutions; yet there are occasional interpretations that emphasize the agreement between Christ and Eastern culture as well as some that tend to identify him with the spirit of Marxian society. In earlier times solutions of the problem along these lines were being offered simultaneously with the solutions of the first or "Christ-against-culture" type.

Three other typical answers agree with each other in seeking to maintain the great differences between the two principles and in undertaking to hold them together in some unity. They are distinguished from each other by the manner in which each attempts to combine the two authorities. One of them, our third type, understands Christ's relation to culture somewhat as the men of the second group do: he is the fulfillment of cultural aspirations and the restorer of the institutions of true society. Yet there is in him something that neither arises out of culture nor contributes directly to it. He is discontinuous as well as continuous with social life and its culture. The latter, indeed, leads men to Christ, yet only in so preliminary a fashion that a great leap is necessary if men are to reach him or, better, true culture is not possible unless beyond all human achievement, all human search for values, all human society, Christ enters into life from above with gifts which human aspiration has not envisioned and which human effort cannot attain unless he relates men to a supernatural society and a new value-center. Christ is, indeed, a Christ of culture, but he is also a *Christ above culture* This *synthetic* type is best represented by Thomas Aquinas and his followers, but it has many other representatives in both early and modern times.

Another group of median answers constitutes our fourth type. In these the duality and inescapable authority of both Christ and culture are recognized, but the opposition between them is also accepted. To those who answer the question in this way it appears that Christians throughout life are subject to the tension that accompanies obedience to two authorities who do not agree yet must both be obeyed. They refuse to accommodate the claims of Christ to those of secular society, as, in their estimation, men in the second and third groups do. So they are like the "Christ-against-culture" believers, yet differ from them in the conviction that obedience to God requires obedience to the institutions of society and loyalty to its members as well as obedience to a Christ who sits in judgment on that society. Hence man is seen as subject to two moralities, and as a citizen of two worlds that are not only discontinuous with each other but largely opposed. In the *polarity* and *tension* of Christ and culture life must be lived precariously and sinfully in the hope of a justification which lies beyond history. Luther may be regarded as the greatest representative of this type, yet many a Christian who is not otherwise a Lutheran finds himself compelled to solve the problem in this way.

Finally, as the fifth type in the general series and as the third of the mediating answers, there is the *conversionist* solution. Those who offer it understand with the members of the first and the fourth groups that human nature is fallen or perverted, and that this perversion not only appears in culture but is transmitted by it. Hence the opposition between Christ and all human institutions and customs is to be recognized. Yet the antithesis does not lead either to Christian separation from the world as with the first group, or to mere endurance in the expectation of a transhistorical salvation, as with the fourth. Christ is seen as the converter of man in his culture and society, not apart from these, for there is no nature without culture and no turning of men from self and idols to God save in society. It is in Augustine that the great outlines of this answer seem to be offered; John Calvin makes it explicit; many others are associated with these two.

When the answers to the enduring problem are stated in this manner it is apparent that a construction has been set up that is partly artificial. A type is always something of a construct, even when it has not been constructed prior to long study of many historic individuals and movements. When one returns from the hypothetical scheme to the rich complexity of individual events, it is evident at once that no person or group ever conforms completely to a type.[1] Each historical figure will show characteristics that are more reminiscent of some other family than the one by whose name he has been called, or traits will appear that seem wholly unique and individual. The method of typology, however, though historically inadequate, has the advantage of calling to attention the continuity and significance of the great *motifs* that appear and reappear in the long wrestling of Christians with their enduring problem. Hence also it may help us to gain orientation as we in our own time seek to answer the question of Christ and culture.

* * *

Chapter 5. Christ and Culture in Paradox

I. The Theology of the Dualists

Efforts to synthesize Christ and culture have been subject to sharp attacks throughout Christian history. Radicals have protested that these attempts are disguised versions of cultural accommodation of the rigorous gospel, and that they broaden the narrow way of life into an easy highway. Cultural Christians have objected that synthesists retain as evangelical vestigial remnants of old, immature ways of thought. The strongest opposition, however, has been voiced by neither left- nor right-

---

1 C. J. Jung's *Psychological Types,* 1924, is suggestive and illuminating as an example of typological method. On the applicability to individuals of type descriptions see especially pp. 10 f., 412 ff.

wing parties but by another central group, that is to say, by one which also seeks to answer the Christ and culture question with a "both-and." This is the group which, for want of a better name, we have called *dualist,* though it is by no means dualistic in the sense that it divides the world in Manichaean fashion into realms of light and darkness, of kingdoms of God and Satan. Though the members of this group dissent from the synthesists' definitions and combinations of Christ and culture they also seek to do justice to the need for holding together as well as for distinguishing between loyalty to Christ and responsibility for culture.

If we would understand the dualists, we must note the place where they stand and take up our position with them as they deal with our problem. For them the fundamental issue in life is not the one which radical Christians face as they draw the line between Christian community and pagan world. Neither is it the issue which cultural Christianity discerns as it sees man everywhere in conflict with nature and locates Christ on the side of the spiritual forces of culture. Yet, like both of these and unlike the synthesist in his more irenic and developing world, the dualist lives in conflict, and in the presence of one great issue. That conflict is between God and man, or better—since the dualist is an existential thinker—between God and us; the issue lies between the righteousness of God and the righteousness of self. On the one side are we with all of our activities, our states and our churches, our pagan and our Christian works; on the other side is God in Christ and Christ in God. The question about Christ and culture in this situation is not one which man puts to himself, but one that God asks him; it is not a question about Christians and pagans, but a question about God and man.

No matter what the dualist's psychological history may have been, his logical starting point in dealing with the cultural problem is the great act of reconciliation and forgiveness that has occurred in the divine-human battle—the act we call Jesus

Christ. From this beginning the fact that there was and is a conflict, the facts of God's grace and human sin are understood. No dualist has found it easy to arrive at this starting point. Each is quick to point out that he was on the wrong road until he was stopped and turned round in his tracks by another will than his own. The knowledge of the grace of God was not given him, and he does not believe it is given to any, as a self-evident truth of reason—as certain cultural Christians, the Deists for instance, believe. What these regard as the sin to be forgiven and as the grace that forgives are far removed from the depths and heights of wickedness and goodness revealed in the cross of Christ. The faith in grace and the correlate knowledge of sin that come through the cross are of another order from that easy acceptance of kindliness in the deity and of moral error in mankind of which those speak who have never faced up to the horror of a world in which men blaspheme and try to destroy the very image of Truth and Goodness, God himself. The miracle with which the dualist begins is the miracle of God's grace, which forgives these men without any merit on their part, receives them as children of the Father, gives them repentance, hope, and assurance of salvation from the dark powers that rule in their lives, especially death, and makes them companions of the one they willed to kill. Though His demands on them are so high that they daily deny them and Him, still He remains their savior, lifting them up after every fall and setting them on the road to life.

The fact that the new beginning has been made with the revelation of God's grace does not change the fundamental situation as far as grace and sin are concerned. Grace is in God, and sin is in man. The grace of God is not a substance, a *mana*-like power, which is mediated to men through human acts. Grace is always in God's action; it is God's attribute. It is the action of reconciliation that reaches out across the no-man's land of the historic war of men against God. If something of the graciousness of Christ is reflected in the thankful responses of a

Paul or a Luther to the gracious action of Christ, they themselves cannot be aware of it; and those who behold it cannot but see that it is only reflection. As soon as man tries to locate it in himself it disappears, as gratitude disappears in the moment when I turn from my benefactor to the contemplation of this beneficial virtue in me. The faith also with which man acknowledges and turns in trust to the gracious Lord is nothing that he can bring forth out of his native capacities. It is the reflection of the faithfulness of God. We trust because he is faithful. Therefore in the divine-human encounter, in the situation in which man is after as well as before he hears the word of reconciliation, grace is all on God's side. And Jesus Christ is the grace of God and the God of grace.

But sin is in man and man is in sin. In the presence of the crucified Lord of glory, men see that all their works and their work are not only pitifully inadequate, measured by that standard of goodness, but sordid and depraved. The dualist Christians differ considerably from the synthesists in their understanding of both the extent and the thoroughness of human depravity. As to extent: Clement, Thomas, and their associates note that man's reason may be darkened, but is not in its nature misdirected; for them the cure of bad reasoning lies in better reasoning; and in the aid of the divine teacher. Moreover, they regard man's religious culture in its Christian form—the institutions and doctrines of the holy church—as beyond the range of sinful corruption, however many minor evils calling for reform may now and again appear in the sacred precincts. But the dualist of Luther's type discerns corruption and degradation in all man's work. *Before the holiness of God* as disclosed in the grace of Jesus Christ there is no distinction between the wisdom of the philosopher and the folly of the simpleton, between the crime of the murderer and his chastisement by the magistrate, between the profaning of sanctuaries by blasphemers and their hallowing by priests, between the carnal sins and the spiritual aspirations of men. The dualist does not say that there are no differences between these things, but that before the holiness of God there are no significant differences; as one might say that comparisons between the highest skyscrapers and the meanest hovels are meaningless in the presence of Betelgeuse. Human culture is corrupt; and it includes all human work, not simply the achievements of men outside the church but also those in it, not only philosophy so far as it is human achievement but theology also, not only Jewish defence of Jewish law but also Christian defence of Christian precept. If we would understand the dualist here we must keep two things in mind. He is not passing judgment on other men—save as in the sinfulness to which he is subject he abandons his position before God—but testifies rather to the judgment that is being passed on him and on the whole of mankind, with which he is inseparably united not only by nature but in culture. When he speaks of the sinfulness of the law-abiding man he does so as a Paul who has been zealous in observance of the law, and as a Luther who has rigorously sought to keep the letter and the spirit of the monastic vows. When he speaks about the corruption of reason, he does so as a reasoner who has tried ardently to ascend to the knowledge of truth. What is said about the depravity of man is said therefore from the standpoint and in the situation of cultured, sinful man confronting the holiness of divine grace. The other thing that must be kept in mind is that for these believers the attitude of man before God is not an attitude man takes in addition to other positions, after he has confronted nature, or his fellow men, or the concepts of reason. It is fundamental and every-present situation; though man is forever trying to ignore the fact that he is up against God, or that what he is up against when he is "up against it" is God.

The dualist differs from the synthesist also in his conception of the nature of corruption in culture. Perhaps the two schools share that religious sense of sin that can never be translated into moral or intellectual terms, and the dualist only feels more profoundly the sordidness of everything that is creaturely, human, and earthly when it is in the presence of the holy.[1] Having contended like Job for his own goodness, he also joins in the confession: "I had heard of thee by the hearing of the ear; but now mine eye seeth thee: wherefore I abhor myself and repent in dust and ashes." Yet the holiness of God as presented in the grace of Jesus Christ has too precise a character to permit definition of its negative counterpart, human sin, in the vague terms of primitive feeling. The sense of sordidness, of shame, dirtiness, and pollution is the affective accompaniment of an objective moral judgment on the nature of the self and its society. Here is man before God, deriving his life from God, being sustained and forgiven by God, being loved and being lived; and this man is engaged in an attack on the One who is his life and his being. He is denying what he must assert in the very act of denial; he is rebelling against the One without whose loyalty he could not even rebel. All human action, all culture, is infected with godlessness, which is the essence of sin. Godlessness appears as the will to live without God, to ignore Him, to be one's own source and beginning, to live without being indebted and forgiven, to be independent and secure in one's self, to be godlike in oneself. It has a thousand forms and expresses itself in the most devious ways. It appears in the complacency of self-righteously moral and of self-authenticatedly rational men, but also in the despair of those for whom all is vanity. It manifests itself in irreligion, in atheism and antitheism; but also in the piety of those who consciously carry God around with them wherever they go. It issues in desperate acts of passion, by which men assert themselves against the social law with its claims to divine sanction; but also in the zealous obedience of the law-abiding, who desperately need the assurance that they are superior to the lesser breeds without

---

1 Cf. Otto, Rudolf, *The Idea of the Holy,* 1924, pp. 9 ff.; also Taylor, A. E., *The Faith of a Moralist,* 1930, Vol. I, pp. 163 ff.

the law. Thwarted in its efforts to found divine, enduring empires, the desire to be independent of God's grace expresses itself in attempts to establish godlike churches that have stored up all necessary truth and grace in doctrines and sacraments. Unable to impose its will on others through the morality of masters, the will to be god tries the methods of slave morality. When man cannot any longer assure himself that he is the master of his physical fate, he turns to the things he believes are really under his control, such things as sincerity and integrity, and tries to shelter himself under his honesty; in this domain, at least, he thinks he can get along without grace, an independent good man, needing nothing he cannot himself supply. The dualist likes to point out that the will to live as gods, hence without God, appears in man's noblest endeavors, that is, those that are noblest according to human standards. Men whose business it is to reason exalt reason to the position of judge and ruler of all things; they call it the divine element in man. Those who have the vocation of maintaining order in society deify law—and partly themselves. The independent, democratic citizen has a little god inside himself in an authoritative conscience that is not under authority. As Christians we want to be the forgivers of sins, the lovers of men, new incarnations of Christ, saviors rather than saved; secure in our own possession of the true religion, rather than dependent on a Lord who possesses us, chooses us, forgives us. If we do not try to have God under our control, then at least we try to give ourselves the assurance that we are on His side facing the rest of the world; not with that world facing Him in infinite dependence, with no security save in Him.

Thus in the dualist's view the whole edifice of culture is cracked and madly askew; the work of self-contradicting builders, erecting towers that aspire to heaven on a fault in the earth's crust. Where the synthesist rejoices in the rational content of law and social institutions, the dualist, with the skepticism of the Sophist and positivist, calls attention to the lust for power and the will of the strong which rationalizes itself in all these social arrangements. In monarchies, aristocracies, and democracies, in middle-class and proletarian rules, in episcopal, presbyterian, and congregational polities, the hand of power is never wholly disguised by its soft glove of reason. In the work of science itself reason is confounded; as on the one hand it humbly surrenders itself to the given in disinterested questioning, and on the other hand seeks knowledge for power. In all the synthesists' defences of rational elements in culture the dualist sees this fatal flaw, that reason in human affairs is never separable from its egoistic, godless, perversion. The institution of property, he points out, not only guards against theft but also sanctions the great seizures of alien possessions, as when it protects the settler in his rights over lands taken by force or deceit from Indians. The reasonable institution rests on a great irrationality. Institutions of celibacy and marriage prevent and also cover a multitude of sins. Hence the dualist joins the radical Christian in pronouncing the whole world of human culture to be godless and sick unto death. But there is this difference between them: the dualist knows that he belongs to that culture and cannot get out of it, that God indeed sustains him in it and by it; for if God in His grace did not sustain the world in its sin it would not exist for a moment.

In this situation the dualist cannot speak otherwise than in what sound like paradoxes; for he is standing on the side of man in the encounter with God, yet seeks to interpret the Word of God which he has heard coming from the other side. In this tension he must speak of revelation and reason, of law and grace, of the Creator and Redeemer. Not only his speech is paradoxical under these circumstances, but his conduct also. He is under law, and yet not under law but grace; he is sinner, and yet righteous; he believes, as a doubter; he has assurance of salvation, yet walks along the knife-edge of insecurity. In Christ all things have become new, and yet everything remains as it was from the beginning. God has revealed Himself in Christ, but hidden Himself in His revelation; the believer knows the One in whom he has believed, yet walks by faith, not sight.

Among these paradoxes two are of particular importance in the dualists' answer to the Christ-culture problem: those of law and grace, and of divine wrath and mercy. The dualist joins the radical Christian in maintaining the authority of the law of Christ over all men, and in stating it in its plain literal sense, objecting to the attenuations of the gospel precepts by cultural or synthetic Christians. The law of Christ is not, in his understanding, an addition to the law of man's nature but its true statement, a code for the average, normal man, and not a special rule for spiritual supermen. Yet he also insists that no human self-culture, in obedience to that law or any other, can avail to extricate man out of his sinful dilemma. Nor are institutions that claim this law as their basis—monastic orders or pacifist customs or communistic communities—less subject to the sin of godlessness and self-love than are the cruder forms of custom and society. The law of God in the hands of men is an instrument of sin. Yet as coming from God and heard from His lips it is a means of grace. But, again, it is a kind of negative means, driving man to despair of himself and so preparing him to turn away from himself to God. When, however, the sinner throws himself on the divine mercy and lives by that mercy alone, the law is reinstated in a new form, as something written on the heart—a law of nature, not an external commandment. Still, it is the law of God which the forgiven receives as the will of the Other rather than as his own. Thus the dialogue about law proceeds. It sounds paradoxical, because the effort is being made to state in a monologue a meaning that is clear only in the dramatic encounters and re-encounters of God and the souls of men. In his shorthand synopsis of the great action, the dualist seems to be saying that the law of life is not law but grace; that grace is not grace but law, an infinite demand made on man; that love is an impossible possibility and hope of salvation an improbable assurance. These are the abstractions; the reality is the continuing dialogue and struggle of man with God, with its questions and answers, its divine victories that look like defeats, its human defeats that turn into victories.

The situation the dualist is attempting to describe in his paradoxical language is further complicated by the fact that man encountering God does not meet a simple unity. The dualist is always a Trinitarian, or at least a binitarian, for whom the relations of the Son and the Father are dynamic. But besides this he notes in God as revealed in nature and Christ and the Scriptures the duality of mercy and wrath. In nature man meets not only reason, order, and life-giving goodness, but also force, conflict, and destruction; in the Scriptures he hears the word of the prophet, "Shall evil befall a city and the Lord hath not done it?" On the cross he sees a Son of God who is not only the victim of human wickedness but is also one delivered to death by the power that presides over all things. Yet from this cross there comes the knowledge of a Mercy which freely gives itself and its best-beloved for the redemption of men. What seemed to be wrath is now seen to have been love, which chastised for the sake of correction. But this love is also a demand, and appears as wrath against the despisers and violators of love. Wrath and mercy remain to the end intermingled. The temptation of the dualist is to separate the two principles; and to posit two gods, or a division in the Godhead. The true dualist resists the temptation, but continues to live in the tension between mercy and wrath. When he deals with the problems of culture, he cannot forget that the dark sides of human social life, such things as vices, crimes, wars, and punishments, are weapons in the hands of a wrathful God of mercy, as well as assertions of human wrath and man's godlessness.

II. THE DUALISTIC MOTIF IN PAUL AND MARCION

In the case of dualism even more than in that of the previous answers to the Christ and culture question we ought to speak of a *motif* in Christian thinking rather than of a school of thought. It is more difficult to find relatively clear-cut, consistent examples of this approach than of the others; and the *motif* often appears in some isolation, confined to special areas of the cultural problem. It may be used in dealing with reason and revelation by a thinker who does not employ it when he considers political questions. It may appear in discussions about Christian participation in government and war, by believers whose solution of the reason-revelation problem sounds more like that of the synthesists. Important in the thought of many Christians, it is so strongly emphasized a *motif* in the writings of some, such as Luther, that it may be permissible to speak also of a group or a school, relatively distinct from the others.

Whether or not Paul may be counted a member of such a group, it is evident that its later representatives are his spiritual descendants, and that the *motif* is more pronouncedly present in his thought than are synthetic or radical, not to speak of cultural, tendencies. The issue of life, as Paul sees it, lies between the righteousness of God and the righteousness of man, or between the goodness with which God is good and desires to make men good on the one hand, and on the other the kind of independent goodness man seeks to have in himself. Christ defines the issue, and solves the problem of life by his continuous action of revelation, reconciliation, and inspiration. There is no question about the centrality of Jesus Christ in the life and thought of the man for whom Christ was "the power of God and the wisdom of God," the mediator of divine judgment, the offering for sin, the reconciler of men to God, the giver of peace and eternal life, the spirit, the interceder for men, the head of the church and progenitor of a new humanity, the image of the invisible God, the "one Lord, through whom are all things and through whom we exist." On his cross Paul had died to the world and the world had died to him; henceforth to live meant to be with Christ and for Christ and under Christ, knowing nothing and desiring nothing save him. This

Christ of the apostle was Jesus. The time is past when the identity of Paul's Lord with the Rabbi of Nazareth could be questioned. The one he had seen, who dwelt in his mind and possessed him body and soul, was most evidently that friend of sinners and judge of the self-sufficiently righteous, that prophet and lawgiver of the Sermon on the Mount, and that healer of diseases who had been condemned by Paul's fellow Jews, crucified by his fellow Romans, and seen in resurrected as in mortal existence by his fellow apostles.[2]

In a double sense the encounter with God in Christ had relativized for Paul all cultural institutions and distinctions, all the works of man. They were all included under sin; in all of them men were open to the divine ingression of the grace of the Lord. Whether men were by culture Jews or pagans, barbarians or Greeks, they stood on the same level of a sinful humanity before the wrath of God, "revealed from heaven against all ungodliness and unrighteousness." Whether law was known by reason or made known through past revelation it condemned men equally, was equally ineffective in saving them from lawlessness and self-seeking, and was equally instrument of divine wrath and mercy. God by the revelation of His glory and grace in Jesus Christ had convicted all religion of faithlessness, whether it was the worship of images resembling men, birds, beasts, and reptiles, or trust in the Torah, whether it stressed ritual observances or the keeping of ethical laws. Both the knowledge that found its basis in reason, and the one that looked to revelation for its foundation, were equally remote from the knowledge of the glory of God in the face of Jesus Christ. Christ destroyed the wisdom of the wise and the righteousness of the good, which had rejected him in different ways but to the same degree. But he did not sanction the folly of the unwise or the iniquity of transgressors; these also were included under sin, the evident subjects of its rule. If human

2 Cf. especially Porter, F. C., *The Mind of Christ in Paul,* 1930.

spiritual attainments fell short of the glorious achievement of Christ and appeared corrupted when illuminated by his cross, the total inadequacy and depravity of physical values was also evident. Had Paul spoken in this connection more explicitly than he did of the institutions of culture—family, school, state, and religious community—he would, it seems clear, have had to deal with them in the same fashion. Christ had brought to light the unrighteousness of every human work.

Yet in every position in culture and in every culture, in all the activities and stations of men in civilized life, they were also equally subject to his redemptive work. Through his cross and resurrection he redeemed them from their prison of self-centeredness, the fear of death, hopelessness and godlessness. The word of the cross came to married and unmarried, to moral and immoral, to slaves and freemen, to the obedient and disobedient, the wise and the righteous, the fools and the unrighteous. By the redemption they were born anew, given a new beginning which was not in themselves but in God, a new spirit which proceeded from Christ, a love to God and neighbors which constrained them to do without constraint what law had never been able to accomplish. In freedom from sin and freedom from law they were empowered by love to rejoice in the right, to bear all things, to be patient and kind. Out of the inner fountains of the spirit of Christ there would flow forth love, joy, peace, patience, kindness, goodness, faithfulness, gentleness, self-control. Not as lawgiver of a new Christian culture but as the mediator of a new principle of life—a life of peace with God—Christ did and does this mighty work in the creation of a new kind of humanity.

It would be false to interpret all this in eschatological terms, as if Paul looked upon human culture from the point of view of a time when it would be judged at a final assize, and a new era of life would be inaugurated. In the cross of Christ man's work was not judged; by his resurrection the new life had now been introduced into history. Whoever had had his eyes opened to the goodness with which God is good and to His wrath upon all godlessness saw clearly that human culture had been judged and condemned; if long-suffering patience kept such men and their works alive a little longer, if the final assize was delayed, that was not an invalidation but a further demonstration of the Pauline gospel. The new life, moreover, was not simply a promise and a hope but a present reality, evident in the ability of men to call upon God as their Father and to bring forth fruits of the spirit of Christ within them and their community. The great revolution in human existence was not past; neither was it still to come: it was now going on.

With this understanding of the work of Christ and the works of man, Paul could not take the way of the radical Christian with his new Christian law by attempting to remove himself and other disciples out of the cultural world into an isolated community of the saved. He warns, as a matter of course, against participation in actions and customs that are flagrant exhibitions of human faithlessness, lovelessness, hopelessness, and godlessness. "The works of the flesh are plain: immorality, impurity, licentiousness, idolatry, sorcery, enmity, strife, jealousy, anger, selfishness, dissension, party spirit, envy, drunkenness, carousing and the like. . . . Those who do such things shall not inherit the kingdom of God."[3] But he is far from suggesting that those who refrain from such conduct will therefore inherit the kingdom, or that training in good moral habits is a step in preparation for the gift of the spirit. His experience with Galatian and Corinthian, with Judaizing and spiritualizing Christians had taught him—if after his years of wrestling with Christ and the gospel he needed to be taught—that the anti-Christian spirit could not be evaded by any measures of isolation from pagan culture, by any substitution of new laws for old ones, or by supplanting the pride of Hellenistic philosophy with the pride of a Christian *gnosis*. The pervasive

---

3 Gal. 5:19-21.

reign of sin could manifest itself in the actions and customs of Christians, in their lovelessness at love feasts, their speaking in tongues, their pride in spiritual attainments, their almsgivings, and their martyrdoms. Since the battle was not with flesh and blood but against spiritual principles in the minds and hearts of men, there was no hiding place from their attacks in a new, Christian culture. The Christians' citizenship was in heaven, their hiding place was with the risen Christ. As far as this world was concerned it was their task to work out their salvation, and their gift to live in the spirit of Christ in whatever community or station in life they had been apprehended by the Lord. It was not possible to come closer to the reign of Christ by changing cultural customs, as in matters of food and drink or the keeping of holy days, by abandoning family life in favor of celibacy, by seeking release from chattel slavery, or by escaping from the rule of political authorities.

And yet Paul added to his proclamation of the gospel of a new life in Christ a cultural Christian ethics; for the new life in faith, hope, and love remained weak, and subject to struggle with Satan, sin, and death. It had to be lived, moreover, in the midst of societies evidently subject to the dark powers. This ethics was in part an ethics of Christian culture, in part an ethics for intercultural relations. For Christian culture it provided injunctions against sexual immorality, theft, idleness, drunkenness, and other common vices. It regulated marriage and divorce, the relations of husbands and wives, of parents and children; it dealt with the adjustment of quarrels among Christians, sought to prevent factions and heresies, gave directions for the conduct of religious meetings, and provided for the financial support of needy Christian communities. In so far as this ethics concerned itself with the relations of Christians and their churches to non-Christian social institutions, its provisions were various. Political authorities were recognized as divinely instituted, and obedience to their laws was required as a Christian duty; yet believers were not to make use of the law courts in pressing claims against each other. Economic institutions, including slavery, were regarded with a certain indifference or taken for granted. Only the religious institutions and customs of non-Christian society were completely rejected. This ethics of Christian culture and of Christian life in culture had various sources. Little effort was made to derive it directly from the teachings of Jesus, though in a number of instances his words were of basic importance. For the rest it was based on common notions of what was right and fitting, on the Ten Commandments, on Christian tradition, and on Paul's own common sense. Direct inspiration, apart from such use of tradition and reason, is not referred to as source of the laws and the counsels.

Thus Paul seems to move in the direction of a synthetic answer to the Christ-and-culture problem; and yet the manner in which he relates the ethics of Christian culture to the ethics of the spirit of Christ is markedly different from the way in which a Clement and a Thomas proceed from the one to the other. For one thing, the order is different; since the synthesists move from culture to Christ, or from Christ the instructor to Christ the redeemer, whereas Paul moves from Christ the judge of culture and the redeemer to Christian culture. The variation in order is connected with something more significant. The synthesist regards the cultural life as having a certain positive value of its own, with its own possibilities for the achievement of an imperfect but real happiness. It is directed toward the attainment of positive values. But for Paul it has a kind of negative function. The institutions of Christian society and the laws for that society, as well as the institutions of pagan culture in so far as they are to be recognized, seem more designed, in his view, to prevent sin from becoming as destructive as it might otherwise be, rather than to further the attainment of positive good. "Because of the temptation to immorality, each man should have his own wife and each woman her own husband." The governing authorities are servants of God "to execute his wrath on the wrong-doer."[4] The function of law is to restrain and expose sin rather than to guide men to divine righteousness. Instead of two ethics for two stages on life's way or for two kinds of Christians, the immature and the mature, Paul's two ethics refer to contradictory tendencies in life. The one is the ethics of regeneration and eternal life, the other is the ethics for the prevention of degeneration. In its Christian form it is not exactly an ethics of death, but it is an ethics for the dying. Hence there is no recognition here of two sorts of virtues, the moral and the theological. There is no virtue save the love that is in Christ, inextricably combined with faith and hope. From this all other excellence flows. The ethics of Christian culture, and of the culture in which Christians live, is as such without virtue; at its best it is the ethics of non-viciousness—though there are no neutral points in a life always subject to sin and to grace.

In this sense Paul is a dualist. His two ethics are not contradictory, but neither do they form parts of one closely knit system. They cannot do so, because they refer to contradictory ends, life and death, and represent strategies on two different fronts—the front of the divine-human encounter, and the front of the struggle with sin and the powers of darkness. The one is the ethics of Christians as they yield to the overwhelming mercy of God; the other has in view His inclusive wrath against all unrighteousness. Paul's dualism is connected not only with this view of Christian life as being lived in the time of the final struggle and of the new birth, but also with his belief that the whole cultural life together with its natural foundations is so subject to sin and to wrath that the triumph of Christ must involve the temporal end of the whole temporal creation as well as of temporal culture. "Flesh" in his thought represents not only an ethical principle, the corrupt element in human spiritual life, but also something physical from which man must be redeemed. Life in grace is not only life coming from God, but

4 I Cor. 7:2; Rom. 13:4.

life outside the human body. "While we are still in this tent, we sigh with anxiety; . . . while we are at home in the body we are away from the Lord." [5] Dying to self and rising with Christ are spiritual events, yet remain incomplete without the death of the terrestrial body and its renewal in celestial form. As long as man remains in the body he has need then, it seems, of a culture and of the institutions of culture not because they advance him toward life with Christ but because they restrain wickedness in a sinful and temporal world. The two elements in Paul are by no means of equal importance. His heart and mind are all devoted to the ethics of the kingdom and eternal life. Only the necessities of the moment, while the new life remains hidden and disorder reappears in the churches themselves, wring from him the laws, admonitions, and counsels of a Christian cultural ethics.

In the second century the dualistic answer to the Christ-and-culture question was confusedly and erratically offered by Paul's strange follower Marcion. He is often counted with the Gnostics, for he was almost violent in his efforts to wrest Christian faith free from its associations with Jewish culture, particularly in his attempt to exclude the Old Testament and all elements derived from it from the Christian Scriptures. At the same time he used Gnostic ideas in his theology. On the other hand we must associate him with the radical Christians, for he founded a sect separated from the church and marked by rigorous asceticism. He is often thought to have gone beyond this and to have become a kind of Manichaean, who distinguished two principles in reality and divided the world between God and the power of evil. But as Harnack and others have made clear, Marcion was first of all a Paulinist, for whom the gospel of divine grace and mercy was the wonder of wonders, arousing astonishment and ecstasy, something which could not be compared with any-

---

5 II Cor. 5:4, 6.

thing else.[6] He did not begin with the law of Christ, but with the revelation of divine goodness and mercy. But there were two things he could not rhyme with that gospel. One of these was the Old Testament presentation of God as the wrathful guardian of justice, and the other was the actual life of man in this physical world with the demands, the indignities and the horrors to be faced in it. Had only the Old Testament bothered him he might have dismissed it, and developed a theology of a kind Father Creator and an ethics of love bound to be successful in a world fashioned for grace. But the actual world as Marcion saw it was "stupid and bad, crawling with vermin, a miserable hole, an object of scorn." How was it possible to think that the God of all grace, the Father of mercies, had made it, and was responsible among other things for "the disgusting paraphernalia of reproduction and for all the nauseating defilements of the human flesh from birth to final putrescence"?[7] In such a world, family, state, economic institutions, and harsh justice doubtless had their place; but the whole arrangement was evidently a botched piece of work, the product of poor workmanship and vile material. The life in Christ and his spirit, the blessedness of mercy responding to mercy, belonged to a wholly different sphere.

With this understanding of Christ, and of a culture founded on nature, Marcion sought for his solution. He found his answer in the belief that men were dealing with two gods: the just but bungling and limited deity who had created the world out of evil matter; and the good God, the Father, who through Christ rescued men from their desperate plight in the mixed world of justice and matter. He recognized two moralities, the ethics of justice and the ethics of love; but the former was inextricably bound up with corruption, and Christ lived,

---

6 Harnack, A. v., *Marcion, Das Evangelium vom Fremden Gott,* chaps. iii and vi; cf. Lietzmann, H., *The Beginnings of the Christian Church,* pp. 333 ff.

7 So Harnack describes Marcion's view; *op. cit.,* pp. 144, 145; cf. pp. 94, 97.

preached, and communicated only the latter.[8] Hence Marcion sought to draw Christians out of the physical as well as the cultural world as much as possible, and formed communities in which the sex life was sternly suppressed—even marriage being prohibited to believers—in which fasting was more than religious rite, but in which also relations of mercy and love between men were to be realized in accordance with the gospel.[9] Even so, while men remained physically alive they could only live in hope of and in preparation for their salvation by the good God.

Marcion's answer, then, in effect was not truly dualistic but more like that of an exclusive Christian. The true dualist lives in tension between two magnetic poles; Marcion broke the poles apart. Justice and love, wrath and mercy, creation and redemption, culture and Christ, were sundered; and the Marcionite Christian endeavored to live not only outside the world of sin but as far as possible, outside the world of nature, with which sin and justice were inextricably united. Under these circumstances the gospel of mercy became for him a new law, and the community of the redeemed a new cultural society.

The dualistic motif is strong in Augustine; but since the conversionist note seems more characteristic of his thought we defer consideration of his views in a later connection. In medieval Christianity the dualistic solution appears in special areas, as when Scotists and Occamists abandon the synthetic way of dealing with revelation and reason yet seek to maintain the validity of each. It is offered also in connection with the problem of church and state, as in Wycliffe's reply to that question.

III. DUALISM IN LUTHER AND MODERN TIMES

Martin Luther is most representative of the type, though he like Paul is too complex to permit neat identification of an historic individual with a stylized pattern. The strongly dualistic

8 Harnack, *op. cit.*, p. 150.

9 *Ibid.*, pp. 186 ff.

note in his answer to the Christ-culture problem is apparent when we place alongside each other his two most widely known (though by no means best) works, the *Treatise on Christian Liberty* and the call to resistance *Against the Robbing and Murdering Hordes of Peasants.* They differ from each other somewhat as Paul's hymn on the love which is not irritable or resentful differs from his attack on the Judaizers, with its wish that those who unsettle the new Christians with their talk about circumcision would mutilate themselves.[10] But the distance between these writings of Luther is far greater than anything of the sort to be found in Paul. Doubtless personal temperament plays its role here; but another factor must also be considered. Luther had a responsibility for a total national society in a time of turmoil which Paul could have shared only if he had been Cicero or Marcus Aurelius and Paul in one person. Yet, be that as it may, it is a far cry from Luther's celebration of the faith that works by love, suffering all things in serving the neighbor, to his injunction to the rulers to "stab, smite, slay, whoever can." In *Christian Liberty* he writes, "From faith flow forth love and joy in the Lord, and from love a joyful, willing and free mind that serves one's neighbor willingly and takes no account of gratitude or ingratitude, of praise or blame, of gain or loss. . . . For as his Father does, distributing all things to all men richly and freely, causing His sun to shine upon the good and upon the evil, so also the son does all things and suffers all things with that freely bestowing joy which is his delight when through Christ he sees it in God, the dispenser of such great benefits." [11] But in the pamphlet against the peasants we read that "a prince or lord must remember in this case that he is God's minister and the servant of his wrath to whom the sword is committed for use upon such fellows. . . . Here there is no time for sleeping; no place for patience or mercy. It is the

---

10 Gal. 5:12.

11 *Works of Martin Luther,* Philadelphia, 1915-1932, Vol. II, p. 338.

time of the sword, not the day of grace."[12] The duality which is so evident in the juxtaposition of these statements appears at many other points in Luther, though it is not usually quite so sharp. He seems to have a double attitude toward reason and philosophy, toward business and trade, toward religious organizations and rites, as well as toward state and politics. These antinomies and paradoxes have often led to the suggestion that Luther divided life into compartments, or taught that the Christian right hand should not know what a man's worldly left hand was doing. His utterances sometimes seem to support this view. He makes sharp distinctions between the temporal and spiritual life, or between what is external and internal, between body and soul, between the reign of Christ and the world of human works or culture. It is very important for him that there should be no confusion of these distinctions. Accordingly in defending his pamphlet against the peasants he writes, "There are two kingdoms, one the kingdom of God, the other the kingdom of the world. . . . God's kingdom is a kingdom of grace and mercy . . . but the kingdom of the world is a kingdom of wrath and severity. . . . Now he who would confuse these two kingdoms —as our false fanatics do—would put wrath into God's kingdom and mercy into the world's kingdom; and that is the same as putting the devil in heaven and God in hell."[13]

Luther does not, however, divide what he distinguishes. The life in Christ and the life in culture, in the kingdom of God and the kingdom of the world, are closely related. The Christian must affirm both in a single act of obedience to the one God of mercy and wrath, not as a divided soul with a double allegiance and duty. Luther rejected the synthesist solution of the Christian problem, but was at least equally firm in maintaining the unity of God and the unity of the Christian life in culture. He rejected it for a number of reasons: it tended to make the radical commandments of Christ relevant only to the few more perfect

12 *Ibid.*, Vol. IV, pp. 251 f.

13 *Works*, Vol. IV, pp. 265, 266.

Christians, or to a future life, rather than to accept them as they stood—unconditional demands on all souls in every present moment; it tended both to disquiet and to comfort the consciences of men in ways hard to reconcile with the gospel; it passed over too easily the sin of godlessness which infects both the efforts to live an ordinary, virtuous life and the striving after saintliness; it did not adequately present the singular majesty of Christ both as lawgiver and as savior, associating him too much with other masters and redeemers. The basis for Luther's thought and for his career as a reformer of Christian morals was laid when he came under the conviction that what was demanded of man in the gospel was absolutely required by an absolute Lord.[14]

If this realization seemed to direct him to take the exclusive Christian position and to reject life in culture as incompatible with the gospel, he was prevented from making that choice by the realization that the law of Christ was more demanding than radical Christianity believed; that it required complete, spontaneous, wholly self-forgetful love of God and neighbor, without side glances toward one's temporal or eternal profit. The second step in Luther's moral and religious development came, then, when he thoroughly understood that the gospel as law and as promise was not directly concerned with the overt actions of men but with the springs of conduct; that it was the measure by which God recreated the souls of men so that they might really perform good works. As lawgiver Christ

14 An excellent description of Luther's development as Christian ethical thinker and reformer is given in Prof. Karl Holl's article "Der Neubau der Sittlichkeit" in his *Gesammelte Aufsaetze zur Kirchengeschichte,* Vol. I, 6th ed., pp. 155 ff. Holl's treatment unfortunately is marked by an anti-Catholic bias, corresponding to the anti-Lutheran animus of such writers as Grisar, and by a desire to show how original Luther was even in comparison with Augustine. The article, however, is superior to the widely used treatment of Luther's ethics by Ernst Troeltsch in his *Social Teachings of the Christian Churches,* Vol. II. Holl's interpretation of Luther's attitude toward culture makes him more of a conversionist than the present writer finds tenable.

puts all men under the conviction of their sinfulness, their lovelessness and faithlessness. He shows them that an evil tree cannot bring forth good fruit, and that they are evil trees; that they cannot become righteous by acting righteously, but can act righteously only if first of all they are righteous; and that they are unrighteous.[15] But as savior he creates in those in whom he destroyed self-confidence that trust in God out of which can flow love of neighbor. As long as man mistrusts his Creator he will in his anxiety for himself and his goods be unable to do anything in all his service of others but serve himself. He is involved in the vicious circle of self-love, which leads him to look for credit for every apparently altruistic action, and which makes even his service of God a work for which he expects the reward of approval. Christ by his law and by his deed of redemption breaks this circle of self-love, and creates trust in God and reliance on Him as the only one who can and does make men righteous—not within themselves but in the response to Him of their humbled and grateful hearts. Luther understood that the self could not conquer self-love, but that it was conquered when the self found its security in God, was delivered from anxiety and thus set free to serve the neighbor self-forgetfully.

This is the basis of Luther's dualism. Christ deals with the fundamental problems of the moral life; he cleanses the springs of action; he creates and recreates the ultimate community in which all action takes place. But by the same token he does not directly govern the external actions or construct the immediate community in which man carries on his work. On the contrary, he sets men free from the inner necessity of finding special vocations and founding special communities in which to attempt to acquire self-respect, and human and divine approval. He releases them from monasteries and the conventicles of the pious for

---

15 Cf. "Treatise on Good Works," *Works,* Vol. I, "Treatise on Christian Liberty," *Works,* Vol. II; cf. Holl, *op. cit.,* 217 ff., 290 f.

service of their actual neighbors in the world through all the ordinary vocations of men.

More than any great Christian leader before him, Luther affirmed the life in culture as the sphere in which Christ could and sought to be followed; and more than any other he discerned that the rules to be followed in the cultural life were independent of Christian or church law. Though philosophy offered no road to faith, yet the faithful man could take the philosophic road to such goals as were attainable by that way. In a person "regenerate and enlightened by the Holy Spirit through the Word" the natural wisdom of man "is a fair and glorious instrument and work of God."[16] The education of youth in languages, arts, and history as well as in piety offered great opportunities to the free Christian man; but cultural education was also a duty to be undertaken.[17] "Music," said Luther, "is a noble gift of God, next to theology. I would not change my little knowledge of music for a great deal."[18] Commerce was also open to the Christian for "buying and selling are necessary. They cannot be dispensed with and can be practiced in a Christian manner."[19] Political activities, and even the career of the soldier, were even more necessary to the common life, and were therefore spheres in which the neighbor could be served and God be obeyed.[20] A few vocations were ruled out, of course, since they were evidently irreconcilable with faith in God and love of neighbor. Among these Luther eventually included the monastic life. In all these vocations, in all this cultural work in the service of others, the technical rules of that

---

16 Kerr, H. T., *A Compend of Luther's Theology,* pp. 4-5; cf. Holl's remarks on the effect of the Reformation on philosophy, *op. cit.,* 529 ff.

17 Cf. "To the Councilmen of All Cities in Germany That They Establish and Maintain Christian Schools," *Works,* Vol. IV, pp. 103 ff.

18 Kerr, *op. cit.,* p. 147.

19 "On Trading and Usury," *Works,* Vol. IV, p. 13.

20 "Secular Authority: To What Extent It Should Be Obeyed," *Works,* Vol. III, pp. 230 ff.; "Whether Soldiers, Too, Can Be Saved," *Works,* Vol. V, pp. 34 ff.

particular work needed to be followed. A Christian was not only free to work in culture but free to choose those methods which were called for, in order that the objective good with which he was concerned in his work might be achieved. As he cannot derive the laws of medical procedure from the gospel when he deals with a case of typhus, so he cannot deduce from the commandment of love the specific laws to be enacted in a commonwealth containing criminals. Luther had great admiration for the geniuses among men, who in their various spheres hit upon novel procedures rather than followed the traditional processes.

We may say, then, that the dualism in Luther's solution of the Christ-and-culture problem was the dualism of the "How" and the "What" of conduct. From Christ we receive the knowledge and the freedom to do faithfully and lovingly what culture teaches or requires us to do. The psychological premise of Luther's ethics is the conviction that man is a dynamic being, forever active. "The being and nature of man cannot for an instant be without doing or not doing something, enduring or running away from something, for life never rests." [21] The drive to action, it seems, comes from our God-given nature; its direction and spirit is a function of faith; its content comes from reason and culture. Hunger drives us to eat; our faith or lack of it determine whether we eat as good neighbors, with concern for others and to the glory of God, or anxiously, immoderately, and selfishly; our knowledge of dietetics and the dietary customs of our society—not Hebraic legislation about clean and unclean or church laws about fasting—determine what and when to eat. Or, our curiosity makes us seek knowledge; our religious attitude determines how we seek it, whether with anxiety for reputation or for the sake of service, whether for the sake of power or for God's glory; reason and culture show us by what methods and in what areas knowledge may be gained. As there is no way of deriving knowledge from the gospel about

21 "Treatise on Good Works," *Works,* Vol. I, pp. 198 f.

what to do as physician, builder, carpenter, or statesman, so there is no way of gaining the right spirit of service, or confidence and hopefulness, of humility and readiness to accept correction, from any amount of technical or cultural knowledge. No increase of scientific and technical knowledge can renew the spirit within us; but the right spirit will impel us to seek knowledge and skill in our special vocations in the world in order that we may render service. It is important for Luther that these things be kept distinct despite their interrelations, for to confuse them leads to the corruption of both. If we look to the revelation of God for knowledge of geology, we miss the revelation; but if we look to geology for faith in God, we miss both Him and the rocks. If we make a rule for civil government out of the structure of the early Christian community, we substitute for the spirit of that community, with its dependence on Christ and his giving of all good gifts, a self-righteous independence of our own; if we regard our political structures as kingdoms of God, and expect through papacies and kingdoms to come closer to Him, we cannot hear His word or see His Christ; neither can we conduct our political affairs in the right spirit.

Great tensions remain, for technique and spirit interpenetrate, and are not easily distinguished and recombined in a single act of obedience to God. Technique is directed toward temporal things; but spirit is a function of the Christian's relations to the eternal. The spirit is something highly personal; it is the deepest thing in man; technique is a habit, a skill, a function of the office or vocation he has in society. The Christian spirit of faith is oriented toward the divine mercy; the techniques of men are often designed to prevent the evils that arise from the flouting of divine justice. The Christian is dealing every moment, as a citizen of the eternal kingdom and over-arching empire of God, with the immediate transitory values of physical men, his own but above all his neighbors'. The sort of conflict a statesman must feel when he causes crops of cereal to be plowed under for the sake of the long-range prosperity of a nation is here immensely increased. Temporally we employ our best knowledge to gain our daily bread; as citizens of eternity we are (or ought to be) without anxiety. This tension is made the more acute by the fact that it is combined with the polarity of person and society. For himself, as an individual infinitely dependent on God and trusting in Him, a person feels the demand and perhaps the possibility of doing his work without hope of earthly reward; but he is also father and breadwinner, an instrument by which God supplies daily food to children. As such he cannot in obedience to God forgo his claims to his wages. The tension becomes still more acute when what is required of man in his service of others is the use of instruments of wrath for the sake of protecting them against the wrathful. Luther is quite clear on this point. So far as a person is responsible only for himself and his goods, faith makes possible what the law of Christ demands, that he do not defend himself against thieves or borrowers, against tyrants or foes. But where he has been entrusted with the care of others, as father or governor, there in obedience to God he must use force to defend his neighbors against force. The greater sin here is to want to be holy or to exercise mercy where mercy is destructive.[22] As God does a "strange" work—that is, a work not apparently merciful but wrathful—in natural and historical calamities, so He requires the obedient Christian to do "strange" work that hides the mercy of which it is the instrument.

Living between time and eternity, between wrath and mercy, between culture and Christ, the true Lutheran finds life both tragic and joyful. There is no solution of the dilemma this side of death. Christians along with other men have received the common gift of hope that the present evil state of affairs in the world will come to an end and a good time will come. And yet there is no two-fold happiness for them, since as long as life

22 Cf. especially "Secular Authority," *Works,* Vol. III, pp. 236 ff. Cf. Kerr, *op. cit.,* pp. 213 ff., for other relevant passages.

lasts there is sin. The hope of a better culture "is not their chief concern, but rather this, that their own particular blessing should increase, which is the truth as it is in Christ. . . . But besides this they have . . . the two greatest future blessings in their death. The first, in that through death the whole tragedy of this world's ills is brought to a close. . . . The other blessing of death is this, that it not only concludes the pains and evils of this life, but (which is more excellent) makes an end of sins and vices. . . . For this our life is so full of perils—sin, like a serpent, besetting us on every side—and it is impossible for us to live without sinning; but fairest death delivers us from these perils, and cuts our sin clean away from us." [23]

Luther's answer to the Christ-and-culture question was that of a dynamic, dialectical thinker. Its reproductions by many who called themselves his followers were static and undialectical. They substituted two parallel moralities for his closely related ethics. As faith became a matter of belief rather than the fundamental, trustful orientation of the person in every moment toward God, so the freedom of the Christian man became autonomy in all the special spheres of culture. It is a great error to confuse the parallelistic dualism of separated spiritual and temporal life with the interactionism of Luther's gospel of faith in Christ working by love in the world of culture.

The dualistic *motif* has appeared in post-Lutheran Christianity in nonparallelistic forms also. But most of its expressions when compared with Luther's seem thin and abstract. In paradoxical sayings and ambivalent writings Søren Kierkegaard sets forth the dual character of the Christian life. He is himself an essayist, an aesthetic writer, who wants to be understood as a man of his culture, yet not as aesthetic writer and man of culture but as a religious author.[24] He seeks to argue philosophically the impossibility of stating philosophically the truth that is "truth for me." The Christian life has for him the double

---

23 "The Fourteen of Consolation," *Works,* Vol. I, pp. 148 f.

24 Cf. *The Point of View for My Work as an Author,* Part I.

aspect of an intense inward relation to the eternal, and a wholly nonspectacular external relation to other men and to things. In these respects he appears to represent rather than to argue for the dual ethics of Luther; he is a man in his office, using the instruments of his office in the spirit of faith. In consciousness of sin, in utter humility, and in reliance on grace, Kierkegaard, a cultured man in his culture, goes about his work as *litterateur* and aspirant to the ministry (another duality in him). But this is not his essential problem, that as a Christian he should do the dubious work of an aesthetic writer and the possibly more dubious work of writing edifying discourses. The dualism with which he wrestles is that of the finite and the infinite; and because this characterizes all his writings he skirts but never comes to grips with the problem of Christ and culture. The debate in which he is engaged is a lonely debate with himself. Sometimes it seems that he doesn't want so much to become a Christian as a kind of Christ; one in whom the infinite and the finite are united, and one who suffers for the sins of the world rather than one for whom first of all the eternal victim has suffered. In his isolation as "the individual" he beautifully analyzes the character of true Christian love, but is more concerned with the virtue than with the beings to be loved. So far as he deals with the Christ and culture problem, it is much more in the spirit of exclusive Christianity than as synthesist or dualist; even so, it is the exclusive Christianity of the hermit rather than of the cenobite. "The spiritual man," he writes, "differs from us men in being able to endure isolation, his rank as a spiritual man is proportionate to his strength for enduring isolation, whereas we men are constantly in need of 'the others,' the herd. . . . But the Christianity of the New Testament is precisely reckoned upon and related to this isolation of the spiritual man. Christianity in the New Testament consists in loving God, in hatred to man, in hatred of oneself, and thereby of other men, hating father, mother, one's own child, wife, etc., the strongest expression for the most agonizing isolation." [25] So extreme an expression, which deals so abstractly with the New Testament, can of course be balanced by other Kierkegaardian dicta. But the theme of isolated individuality is dominant; there is no genuine sense of the fact that persons exist only in "I-Thou" relations, and the feeling for the "We" is almost completely absent. Hence cultural societies do not concern Kierkegaard. In state, family, and church he sees only the defections from Christ. He assumes that he alone in Denmark is struggling hard to become a Christian; he seems to think that social religion, the state church, should be able to express more easily than his literary productions do what it means to be contemporaneous with Christ.[26]

Kierkegaard in effect is protesting as a Christian in nineteenth century culture against the cultural Christianity or Christianized culture of his day, which in Central Europe had used Luther's dualism as a way of domesticating the gospel and easing all tensions. More truly dualistic answers were offered by others, who could not in obedience to Christ avoid the claims of culture yet also understood how much Christ was entangled with culture. Ernst Troeltsch experienced the problem as a double dilemma. On the one hand he wrestled with the question of the absoluteness of a Christianity that was the cultural religion of the West; on the other hand he was concerned with the conflict between the morality of conscience and the social morality directed toward the attainment and conservation of the values represented by state and nation, science and art, economics and technology. Was not Christianity itself a cultural tradition, with no greater claims than any of the other parts of a historical and transitory civilization? Troeltsch could not give this question the answer of the cultural Christian; Christianity

25 *Attack upon "Christendom,"* p. 163.

26 The best introductions to Kierkegaard are Bretall, Robert (ed.), *A Kierkegaard Anthology;* Dru A. (ed.), *The Journals of Soren Kierkegaard;* Swenson, David, *Something about Kierkegaard.*

indeed was relative, but through it there came to men an absolute claim; even if that claim came only to Western men, it was still an absolute one in the midst of relativity.[27] The claim of Jesus was identified by Troeltsch with the ethics of conscience. However historical the growth of conscience may be, still it confronts historical men with the demand to attain and defend free personalities, independent from mere fate, internally unified and clarified; and at the same time to honor free personality in all men and to unite them in the moral bonds of humanity. The morality of conscience will no doubt always be engaged in a struggle with nature. "The kingdom of God, just because it transcends history, cannot limit and shape history. Earthly history remains the foundation and the presupposition of the final personal decision and sanctification; but in itself it goes on its way as a mixture of reason and natural instinct, and it can never be bound in any bonds except in a relative degree and for a temporary space." [28] This struggle with nature, however, is not the only one man must endure. There is in his ethical consciousness another morality besides that of conscience. He is directed toward the attainment of the cultural values, the objective and obligatory goods which his institutions represent—justice, peace, truth, welfare, etc. Though conscience and the morality of cultural values are closely related, the "two spheres meet only to diverge." Conscience is transhistorical; it scorns death, for "no evil can befall a good man in life or in death"; but the morality of cultural values is historical, and concerned with the maintenance of perishable things. No synthesis is possible save in individual acts of achievement. At the end we are justified only by faith.[29] Troeltsch himself experienced these tensions in acute fashion as he undertook to carry on political tasks in the Weimar Republic. It is clear that his

---

27 *Glaubenslehre,* pp. 100 ff.; also *Christian Thought,* 1923, pp. 22 ff.

28 *Ibid.,* Section II, Pt. I, "The Morality of the Person and of Conscience," pp. 39 ff.

29 *Ibid.,* Pt. II, "The Ethics of Cultural Values," pp. 71 ff.

version of the claims of Christ was more akin to the cultural Christian interpretation of the New Testament prevalent in his day than to a more literal and radical reading of the gospels. Even so, a tension between Christ and culture remained, and could not be solved save in a life of continuous struggle.

In our time many versions of the dualistic solution are current.[30] It is often maintained, for instance, that faith and science can be neither in conflict with each other nor in positive relation, since they represent incommensurable truths. Man is a great amphibian who lives in two realms, and must avoid using in one the ideas and methods appropriate to the other.[31] Dualism appears in practical measures and theoretic justifications for the separation of Church and state. Roger Williams has become the symbol and example of such dualism in America. He rejected the synthetic and conversionists attempts of Anglicanism and Puritanism to unite politics and the gospel, both because the union corrupted the gospel by associating spiritual force with physical coercion, and because it corrupted politics by introducing into it elements foreign to its nature. He dismissed also the Quaker effort to found a commonwealth on the foundations of Christian spirituality, because it was politically as inadequate as it was Christianly perverse.[32] The problem of combining loyalty to Christ with the acceptance of social religion was even more difficult for him than that of Christ and Caesar. The attitude of Seeker which he took after leaving Anglican, Puritan, and Baptist churches represented a *modus*

---

30 Among these dualisms that eschew parallelism or the compartmentalization of the moral life may be mentioned Reinhold Niebuhr's *Moral Man and Immoral Society*, 1932, and A. D. Lindsay's *The Two Moralities*: *Our Duty to God and to Society*, 1940.

31 For a typical statement of this position see J. Needham, *The Great Amphibium*, 1931.

32 Cf. *The Bloudy Tenent of Persecution, George Fox Digg'd Out of His Burrowes, Experiments in Spiritual Life and Health*, and *Letters*. All these, except the *Experiments*, are most readily available in the *Publications of the Narragansett Club*.

vivendi rather than a solution of the problem. In both instances, the political and the ecclesiastical, Williams remains representative of a common dualism in Protestantism.

The dualistic answer has also been accepted in theory and practice by exponents of culture. Political defenders of the separation of church and state, economists who contend for the autonomy of the economic life, philosophers who reject the combinations of reason and faith proposed by synthesists and cultural Christians, are often far removed from an anti-Christian attitude. A Nikolai Hartmann, for instance, having set up the antitheses between Christian faith and cultural ethics, allows the antimonies to stand without suggesting that they must be resolved in favor of culture. Even positivists who cannot find a basis for faith in the life of reason may be unwilling to dismiss it; it belongs to a different order of human existence.[33]

Often such solutions, whether offered by churchmen or others, lack moral seriousness as well as rational depth. Dualism may be the refuge of worldly-minded persons who wish to make a slight obeisance in the direction of Christ, or of pious spiritualists who feel that they owe some reverence to culture. Politicians who wish to keep the influence of the gospel out of the realm of "Real-Politik," and economic men who desire profit above all things without being reminded that the poor shall inherit the kingdom, may profess dualism as a convenient rationalization. But such abuses are no more characteristic of the position itself than are the abuses associated with each of the other attitudes. Radical Christianity has produced its wild monks, its immoral cloisters, and its moral exhibitionists. Cultural Christianity and synthesis have allowed men to justify the lust for power and the retention of old idolatries. Moral integrity and sincerity does not follow the adoption of one or the other of these positions; though each of them, including dual-

---

33 See Ayer, A. J., *Language, Truth and Logic,* 1936. Religion and ethics are here described as meaningless in the strict sense; they express emotion only.

ism especially, has been taken by men in consequence of sincere and earnest striving for integrity under Christ.

IV. THE VIRTUES AND VICES OF DUALISM

There is vitality and strength in the dualistic *motif* as this is set forth by its great exponents. It mirrors the actual struggles of the Christian who lives "between the times," and who in the midst of his conflict in the time of grace cannot presume to live by the ethics of that time of glory for which he ardently hopes. It is a report of experience rather than a plan of campaign. If on the one hand it reports the power of Christ and his spirit, on the other it does not balk at the recognition of the strength and prevalence of sin in all human existence. There is an impressive honesty in Paul's description of the inner conflict and in Luther's "Pecca fortiter" that is too often lacking in the stories of the saints. Their recognition of the sin that is not only in believers but also in their community is more in accord with what the Christian knows about himself and about his churches than are the descriptions of holy commonwealths and perfect societies set forth by radicals and synthesists. Whether or not the dualistic accounts are intelligible from the viewpoint of their inner consistency, they are intelligible and persuasive as corresponding to experience.

The dualists, however, are not only reporters of Christian experience. Far more than any of the preceding groups with which we have dealt they take into account the dynamic character of God, man, grace, and sin. There is something static about the radical Christians' idea of faith; it is for him a new law and a new teaching. To a great extent this is true of the synthesists also, except as in the higher reaches of the Christian life a dynamic element is recognized. The dualist, however, is setting forth the ethics of action, of God's action, man's and the wicked powers'. Such an ethics cannot consist of laws and virtues nicely arranged in opposition to vices, but must be suggested and adumbrated; for living action can only be suggested and indicated. It is an ethics of freedom not in the sense of liberty from law, but in the sense of creative action in response to action upon man. With their understanding of the dynamic nature of existence, the dualists have made great and unique contributions both to Christian knowledge and to Christian action. They have directed attention to the profundity and the power of the work of Christ, how it penetrates to the depths of the human heart and mind, cleansing the fountains of life. They have put aside all the superficial analyses of human viciousness, and have tried to bring into view the deep roots of man's depravity. Accompanying these insights and partly in consequence of them, they have been reinvigorators of both Christianity and culture. To Christianity they have mediated new apprehensions of the greatness of God's grace in Christ, new resolution for militant living, and emancipation from the customs and organizations that have been substituted for the living Lord. To culture they have brought the spirit of a disinterestedness that does not ask what cultural or gospel law requires directly, or what profit for the self may be gained; but rather what the service of the neighbor in the given conditions demands, and what these given conditions really are.

It is evident, of course, that dualism has been beset by the vices that accompany its virtues; and to these other groups in Christianity continue to call attention. We may leave out of account those abuses of the position to which reference has been made, and deal only with the two most frequently voiced charges: that dualism tends to lead Christians into antinomianism and into cultural conservatism. Something is to be said for both of these indictments. The relativization of all the laws of society, of reason and all other works of men—through the doctrine that all are comprehended under sin no matter how high or low they stand when measured by human standards—has doubtless given occasion to the light-minded or the despairing to cast aside the rules of civilized living. They have claimed Luther or Paul as authority for the contention that it makes no difference whether men are sinfully obedient or sinfully disobedient to law, whether they are obedient or disobedient to sinful law, whether they sinfully seek truth or live as sinful skeptics, whether they are self-righteously moral or self-indulgently amoral. It is evidently far from the dualists' intention to encourage sublegal and subcultural behavior, because he knows of a superlegal life and discerns the sin in culture. Yet he must accept responsibility for putting, if not temptation, at least forms of rationalization for refusing to resist temptation, in the way of the wayward and the weak. The fact that this is so by no means invalidates what he has to say about the prevalence of sin and the difference between grace and all human work. It does indicate that he cannot say everytihng that needs to be said; and that cultural and synthetic Christians need to stand at his side with their injunctions to obedience to cultural law—though they in turn cannot say what dualism must preach about the sinfulness that attaches to obedience. The church chose more wisely than Marcion did when it associated with the epistles of Paul, the Gospel of Matthew and the Letter of James.

Both Paul and Luther have been characterized as cultural conservatives. Much can be said for the ultimate effect of their work in promoting cultural reform; yet it seems to be true that they were deeply concerned to bring change into only one of the great cultural institutions and sets of habits of their times—the religious. For the rest they seemed to be content to let state and economic life—with slavery in the one case and social stratification in the other—continue relatively unchanged. They desired and required improvement in the conduct of princes, citizens, consumers, tradesmen, slaves, masters, etc.; but these were to be improvements within an essentially unchanged context of social habit. Even the family, in their view, retained its dominantly patriarchal character, despite their counsels to husbands, wives, parents, and children to love each other in Christ.

Such conservatism seems indeed to be directly connected with the dualist position. If it has nevertheless contributed to social change, this has resulted largely without its intention, and not without the assistance of other groups. Conservatism is a logical consequence of the tendency to think of law, state, and other institutions as restraining forces, dykes against sin, preventers of anarchy, rather than as positive agencies through which men in social union render positive service to neighbors advancing toward true life. Moreover, for the dualists such institutions belong wholly to the temporal and dying world. A question arises in connection with this point. There seems to be a tendency in dualism, as represented by both Paul and Luther, to relate temporality or finiteness to sin in such a degree as to move creation and fall into very close proximity, and in that connection to do less than justice to the creative work of God. The idea which in Marcion and Kierkegaard is set forth in heretical fashion is at least suggested by their great predecessors. In Paul the idea of creation is used significantly only for the sake of reinforcing his first principle of the condemnation of all men because of sin; while his ambiguous use of the term "flesh" indicates a fundamental uncertainty about the goodness of the created body. For Luther the wrath of God is manifested not only against sin, but against the whole temporal world. Hence there is in these men not only a yearning for the new life in Christ through the death of the self to itself, but also a desire for the death of the body and for the passing of the temporal order. Denying to self and rising with Christ to life in God are doubtless more important; but self-centeredness and finiteness belong so closely together that spiritual transformation cannot be expected this side of death. These thoughts lead to the idea that in all temporal work in culture men are dealing only with the transitory and the dying. Hence, however important cultural duties are for Christians their life is not in them; it is hidden with Christ in God. It is at this point that the conversionist *motif,* otherwise very similar to the dualist, emerges in distinction from it.

Other books by Niebuhr:

The Kingdom of God in America, 1937.
The Meaning of Revelation, 1941.
The Social Sources of Denominationalism, 1929.

Other books on the same problem:

Butterfield, Herbert. *Christianity and History,* 1950.
Löwith, Karl. *Meaning in History,* 1949.
Niebuhr, Reinhold: *Faith and History,* 1949.
Piper, Otto A. *God in History,* 1939.
Rust, Eric Charles. *The Christian Understanding of History,* 1948.
Shinn, Roger L. *Christianity and the Problem of History,* 1953.
Tillich, Paul. *The Interpretation of History,* 1926 (Engl. trans. 1936).

RICHARD KRONER

RICHARD KRONER is more a philosopher than a theologian. His background training and major pursuits have been primarily philosophical. His impact upon contemporary theology has been strongest in those works in which he seeks to bring about a reconciliation between philosophical speculation and religious reflection, between the realms of culture and faith. Philosophy and theology cannot be two different and independent sciences; there cannot be two kinds of truth. Their separation ultimately disrupts the consciousness and even the life of man. This conviction is the driving force of Kroner's thought.

As the thinking of the theologian Tillich became progressively more philosophical, so that of Kroner became progressively inclined toward theological concerns. This parallel reverse movement of two great minds in different sciences is both symptomatic and prophetic in contemporary thought. It not only brings to focus the tension between the valid claims of culture and faith but also indicates one direction in which contemporary thought is moving—that of synthesis rather than diastasis.

The crisis of modern culture may be seen in its atomization, that is, in the isolated development of the various spheres of culture in terms of highly specialized and independent methods and modes of thought and in their pulling apart from each other to the point where there is no longer communication between them. At the same time each discipline has come to a kind of dead end or impasse where its conclusions seem self-contradictory or where the questions raised in each cannot be answered from within its own conceptual framework. The self-sufficiency of each is questioned as well as the self-sufficiency of secular culture itself as an adequate basis for man's fulfillment in history.

Both Kroner and Tillich seek to achieve a rapprochement between the spheres of culture and faith. Both recognize the demonic destructive possibilities for each in their continued separation. Both seek a new synthesis, though their methods differ.

In *The Primacy of Faith* Kroner sets out to show that faith has been and must be the necessary presupposition of all speculative philosophy. In *The Religious Function of Imagination* this "faculty" (imagination) which had been relegated to the spheres of "mere subjectivity" and artistic creation is placed again at the apex of reason as its crown and fulfillment.

In *Culture and Faith* Kroner develops a systematic philosophy, or better, theology of culture. Part I presents an analysis of the structure of experience in terms of the fundamental antinomies of ego and world, individuality and universality, oneness and manifoldness, freedom and necessity, time and eternity—fundamental antinomies which give rise to the inner discordant, contradictory and antagonistic motivations of human experience, and which tend to disrupt the unity of the Self. Part II, from which the following selection is taken, contains an analysis of the principal modes of cultural activity through which man performs his work of self-realization. In this part Kroner analyses the character, intent and limitations of the major spheres of cultural life. Part III begins with an analysis of the structure of faith and of the religious experience and proceeds to demonstrate that faith is both the consummation as well as the limitation of man's efforts and achievements. "It (Part III) tries to construct a bridge from secular philosophy to Christian theology, from an understanding of culture to an understanding of faith, and from the self-comprehension of man to the comprehension of the Word of God."

As with all systems of thought, the merit of this work, as Kroner himself implies, lies not in a claim for final validity but rather in the degree to which it illuminates and clarifies the problems it approaches and thereby provides a basis for further reflection, self-understanding and creative action.

RICHARD KRONER

from

Culture and Faith*

Chapter 4. Science—Art—State

science: (a) the intelligible universe or nature

Heinrich Rickert, my teacher at the University of Freiburg in Baden, used to say that nature is a product of culture. This bon mot hits an important truth. Nature, as we conceive it today in the light of the natural sciences, is a product of the intellect, which makes the world intelligible by comprehending it in accordance with its own rules and principles. These rules and principles are not merely conventional or capricious; rather, they constitute the order of the world which we experience and in which we live or, more correctly, the order of that province which exists as the natural subhuman background of human life and history. Of course, this order is intellectual and therefore intelligible because it answers the question of the intellect or because it is produced by the subordination of sense data to the unity of the understanding, which investigates and reasons about the natural phenomena. In this definite sense nature is intelligible: it is ordered in the way man's intellect finds it ordered. In another sense nature is much more than this intelligible world. It reveals a deeper order to the intuition of the artist and of everyone who views it with the eyes and the heart of the artist, and it is perfectly true to say that, at bottom, nature is a work of art, beautifully shaped, the harmonious cosmos of the ancients.

As there is a mathematical order in music, though only as its skeleton; as there is a kind of arithmetic in verse meter; as there is geometry in the plastic arts and especially in architecture, so nature, too, is fundamentally mathematical. Plato proclaimed this truth in his old age; the Pythagoreans had seen it earlier;

but not until the dawn of modern times was it methodically applied and carried through in the various fields of natural knowledge. The new mathematics of nature marks the beginning of the modern era in the contemplative sphere of civilization. Man confronts the world with a new kind of courage and curiosity. He feels sure that his intellect is able to read the writing of nature, if he builds his theories on the ground of careful and specific observation and analysis with the help of mathematics; he discovers that the language in which nature speaks is not the language of speculation or philosophic thought, as Aristotle believed, but rather the language of geometry and arithmetic. The former attempt to unseal the book of nature by means of general concepts which were supposed to rule physical change and growth was abandoned, and the place of those concepts or "substantial forms" was taken by equations expressing quantitative relations between the main factors involved in the facts under investigation.

This method turned out to be not only much more reliable but also better adapted to the ultimate goal of science: the subordination of the facts to the intellect. The reduction of natural science to a mathematics of nature was not merely a gain, however, it was also an abandonment and eventually evoked the temptation to replace the old Platonic and Aristotelian metaphysics by a new one based upon mathematics and physics. To the eternal glory of Galileo, it must be said that he recognized at once all these aspects of the Nuova Scientia. He protested again and again that the method which he devised and applied would not lead to a knowledge of the "nature of things," as had been the aim of the ancient systems; that the exactitude of experimental results was bought at a high price—the price of restricting the scope of opposites to be united. Greek speculation had tried to depict a panorama of the world comprising its uttermost extremes, the poles of its absolute unity and absolute manifoldness, its universality and its individuality, its material and its spiritual structure. Modern physics gave up this gigantic task; it abandoned metaphysics.

Whereas Galileo had warned that the mathematical method cannot penetrate into the ultimate constitution and the ultimate fulness of things, his philosophical successors—Descartes, Spinoza, Leibniz, and others—disregarded this warning and aimed at a new metaphysics, either directly based upon the mathematical method or imitating this method and transforming it into a "geometry of God." Only Hume and Kant renewed the warning of Galileo, making his restriction the principle of their own philosophies (with the difference that Hume doubted even the empirical truth of physics, whereas Kant confirmed this truth in the spirit of Galileo). Kant showed that the intellect is able to spell the language of nature, if it confines itself to the phenomenal realm, i.e., if it does not pretend to give a world-picture—to solve the absolute task of contemplation.[1] He showed that the natural sciences do reach an empirical truth by subordinating the phenomena to a general unity—the unity of a general understanding—and to general concepts and principles of knowledge, thereby uniting all the empirical data under general rules or laws. But he also showed that they can never reach a speculative truth which could rival the intuitive and imaginative work of art in uniting the extreme poles of experience, thereby presenting the "things-in-themselves."

Science does achieve its task by reconciling oneness and manifoldness in a limited way. The mathematical method can discharge this task better than any other logical procedure, e.g., classification, can because it permits more thoroughly and more effectively the subordination of the particular to the general. If the complexity and impermeability of individual occasions and events are left behind and if, in their stead, quantitative relations

---

1 The term "phenomenal" as used by Kant is frequently misinterpreted as meaning what appears psychologically in the human consciousness, whereas Kant means what is finite and fragmentary, corresponding to the ever finite and fragmentary status of the intellect.

are investigated, then it is possible to dominate the facts by means of symbols which can be replaced by definite numbers, in order to describe their "individual" reality. This individuality is then no longer, on the one hand, sensuous and, on the other, meaningful in a human sense; rather, it is made intelligible, transparent to the intellect. Numbers are themselves products of intellectual operation. They represent, unlike the species in a classificatory system, concepts which cannot be derived from higher, more abstract and generic concepts because they have specific attributes *(differentiae specificae)*; numbers are, rather, as much generic as they are specific because they are produced in accordance with general rules which underlie the whole system of numbers. In this way the facts are completely subordinated to the intellect; nothing incomprehensible, nothing irreducible, no irrational, individual residuum remains. This is the "magic wand" of modern physics.[2]

But it is evident that this ingenious method does not really solve the problem of individuality. It neglects and suppresses the fulness of the individual features of the world, paying attention only to the generality of its quantatitive relations. Now these relations do exist; they are an intelligible and rational element within the individual world of experience. Science has been successful because mathematics is inherent—as it were, in nature. To deny the metaphysical ambition of science does not mean to deny its empirical truth, which, on the contrary, can be understood and appreciated only if its empirical restriction, as stated by Galileo and interpreted by Kant, be acknowledged.

The picture of the world as science sees it is correct as far as it goes, but it is fragmentary and abstract. The "higher" truth of art is not reached; yet it is not precluded. Science's interpretation of the world on the lower level of subordination is most brilliantly carried through by the mathematical method. This

---

2 Cf. the brilliant discussion of this point by Ernst Cassirer in *Substanzbegriff und Functionsbegriff: Untersuchungen über die Grundfragen der Erkenntnis Kritik* (Berlin: B. Cassirer, 1910).

method has still another advantage. By eliminating the full individuality and the absolute universality of the world of experience, science also eliminates the individuality of the ego more successfully and more thoroughly than speculative physics and metaphysics have ever done and can ever do. Mathematics has a kind of universal validity which can never be attained by speculation. No one would deny the conclusiveness of Euclidean geometry (though modern geometry has made it the special form of a more general geometry). There was never a Euclidean "school" concerning geometry as there were philosophic schools. Euclid's individuality is completely absorbed and, as it were, annihilated by his own system. And today mechanics is no longer tinged by the personality of the founders. If the modern physics of Einstein is correct, his individuality is of no significance (though, of course, it will be remembered and will be of great interest to the biographer). It is effaced to the degree to which his theory is true, i.e., generally valid.

In this way the antinomy between oneness and manifoldness, between individuality and universality, is solved by modern science; this is its contribution to the task of culture. This contribution is restricted, of course, and so is the truth of science. The antinomies are not absolutely solved. What has been said about the polarity of oneness and manifoldness, of universality and individuality, is also valid with respect to the polarity of freedom and necessity, as well as of time and eternity. It is even more obvious here because these antinomies are concerned with oppositions within the self and not with oppositions within the world. In so far as science eliminates the ego from its world-contemplation, science cannot solve the antinomies of the self; it does not even recognize and acknowledge them. In the view of science, freedom and eternity, in their proper sense, simply do not exist.

However, in a certain sense they do exist. Although science intends to find out the necessity in the processes of nature and although it succeeds, inasmuch as it subordinates what seems to be accidental to laws and rules, the very existence of laws points to a court higher than the necessity of those natural processes. The laws themselves cannot be so necessary as the facts subordinated to them. The facts, as it were, "obey" the laws, and this "obedience" is the source of their necessity. The facts are necessary just because they occur in agreement with the content of the laws. But the laws themselves cannot be necessary in the same way. They do not "obey" higher laws; they "command" the facts; they (or Nature through them) determine the course of events. Nature as the lawgiver of the natural processes is not coerced by the laws but is free. Science here encounters the problem of freedom on its own ground or, more correctly, at the fringe of its territory, for science as such is not interested in solving this problem; its task is circumscribed by the investigation of the facts and their necessity.

The antinomy between time and eternity is touched upon in a similarly indirect way. The facts exist in time; the events occur according to the temporal succession of cause and effect. But the laws do not exist in the same fashion. They do not "exist" at all, if existence is understood in a scientific sense, just because they do not exist in time. They are not "facts" or "events" in the way that natural phenomena and processes are. They belong to the Platonic realm of eternal Ideas; indeed, they partly fulfil the mission which the ideas in the system of Plato were supposed to fulfil. But, again, the scientist is not interested in raising the question of how and where the laws exist. The scientist is interested only in the investigation of temporal processes, although he claims timeless validity for the truth he finds. The antinomy of time and eternity enters the realm of science not directly but only indirectly, at the fringe of its realm.

SCIENCE: (b) THE SCIENTIST

The scientist does not figure within science and its world. He is the tacit, hidden actor behind the scene. The world he investigates and presents is the world of facts and events; in this world he himself has no place, for he is neither a fact nor an event but the author of the play and the stage manager of its performance. Science may succeed in explaining everything that happens in the world; it will never succeed in explaining the scientist and his work in terms of science. The problem of science is not a scientific problem, nor is the problem of the scientist such a problem. Neither science nor scientist belongs to nature (in the sense of the natural sciences); they are presupposed by the sciences, just as the ego is presupposed by experience. The world of science consists of objects and objective events, but the scientist is a subject, namely, that subject for whom objects exist and who investigates and explains them. This subject must necessarily exist outside the scientific world, as its bearer and constructor. The scientist belongs to the cultural world in which he actively participates, which he helps to build up, and in which science is one of the realms.

It is not science but the philosophy of culture which alone can solve the problem of the scientist. I have already mentioned that the individuality of the scientist must not encroach upon his work; it does not enter the truth he seeks. This truth is as "objective" as is the object about which it is the truth. In both cases objectivity means subordination of the particular to the general. Objects are objects of science only in so far as they can be subordinated to general laws or rules, and the truth of science is objective only if it is discovered by that general intellect to which the particular scientist submits his individual subjectivity. The general intellect must therefore control the scientific experience of the individual scientist. And the scientist, in turn, has to train and discipline himself in order to reach "objectivity."

This means that the scientist has to eliminate all the sources of knowledge which are not controlled by the intellect, because they may become sources of error. His senses may deceive him, since they are always exposed to all kinds of illusion; he has to submit their message to the examination of the intellect. For this purpose the intellect devises special methods, capable of eliminating all "subjective" aberrations. The main device concerns the means of observation. The experiment supplants individual judgment with instruments which register the data of observation in an impersonal and objective way. Another device is the continuous collaboration of a manifold of scientists, who mutually check their findings and thereby exclude merely individual influences. This collaboration is not confined to observation, of course, but extends also to theories and hypotheses. Whereas the artist is the only critic of his work as long as he is creating it, the scientist is permanently criticized and controlled by the community of scientists, so that the manifoldness of their worlds is permanently reduced to the oneness of that world which is recognized to be accurate by all of them. The idea of a "national" or "political" difference of scientific theories is therefore a challenge to the very principle of science as such.

"Hypotheses non fingo" is the often quoted catchword of Newton. The same is expressed by Laplace when he dismisses every theory which is not the "résultat de l'observation ou du calcul." [3] The scientist must therefore regard an unbridled imagination as his greatest enemy, to be defeated at all costs. This does not imply that imagination has absolutely no part in scientific discovery or the creation of theories. A certain scientific imagination is even indispensable, in order to anticipate insights and to set forth hypotheses which later experimental experience might or might not verify. But this imagination should not be mistaken for her sister in the realm of poetry, and even less for mere fancy or caprice; neither should it be confused with what the rationalists of the seventeenth century called "imagination," by which they meant sense-perception as over against rational explanation. Scientific imagination is as much an intellectual operation as is the analysis of facts; it is an imagination that serves this analysis and prepares theories; it is an

---

3 In *Exposition du système de monde* (1796).

operation that undergoes the same kind of control and discipline which dominates all scientific work; it is in no sense individual. On the contrary, to the degree that it is individual, it is on a false track and can never lead to scientific results. The genius in the field of the natural sciences is not inspired by an imagination which binds together the two extremes of experience and the world, but is a genius of the intellect. Kant denied categorically that the scientist could ever be a genius, reserving this word for the poet and the artist alone. I think he is right, if we take the word in its accurate meaning.

The scientist, as contrasted with the artist, does not create an imaginative work and an imaginative world, but he observes the world methodically and compels nature to give answers to intelligent questions, under circumstances freely chosen and arranged by the observer and experimentalist. In this respect one might say that the scientist is nearer to "reality" than is the poet or the composer, the architect or the painter; "reality" in this sense means, of course, not the ultimate but the phenomenal reality of scientific objects. The scientist is a "realist" in the sense that he has to disenchant the half-poetical, half-mythical visions of nature which have their place in almost all speculative systems. Thus he might seem to be the opponent of an artistic and of a mythical world-view; but he is this opponent only if he oversteps the limits of science and encroaches upon the prerogative of the arts and of religion.

The scientist can discharge his task only if he is inclined to discipline and control his imagination and his will for the sake of his intellectual purpose; he has to subordinate the nonintellectual forces of the individual to the intellect. It is paradoxical that this very subordination cannot be carried out by the intellect alone but also requires the moral will. Without the activity of the moral self, the scientist cannot be a scientist. This relation points to the power of morality even within the contemplative sphere. The scientist can achieve his own purpose only if he exercises those virtues which point to the conquest of time by eternity: endurance, perseverance, patience, loyalty, and so on. The "pure" intellect needs these virtues in the scientist, although the result of scientific labor and toil does not preserve the individual effort and virtue; it is impersonal, objective, abstract, and rational. But it is culturally important to realize that scientific work has an educational influence upon the person in the direction of virtues indispensable not only in the field of science but in all cultural efforts as well. Thus science transcends science within the scientist.

The same can be said with respect to the collaboration of the scientists, which is demanded by scientific work. Here, too, science fosters an effort which transcends the proper aims and ends of the sciences. The scientists are legitimately conscious of this social contribution which they produce. Precisely because of the objectivity and generality of the intellect, as well as the truth which underlies scientific work, this work can unite all individuals on the earth. The *république des savants* as conceived in the seventeenth century thus paves the way to the peaceful collaboration of all races and all nations, even to a world-state. The solidarity of all scientists refuses to acknowledge any frontiers and political barriers. It is the spirit of the active spheres of cultural life which animates the community of the scientists the world over. In spite of the "world-solution" which science offers, the primacy of the "ego-solution" makes science instrumental to the end of active culture.

This same primacy is also obvious in another way. It is, after all, the ego which operates in the scientist; he can subordinate the world to the intellect and, within the world, the material and changing surface to eternal and intellectual rules only because his intellect is the same intellect as that which, according to Kant, "prescribes to nature its laws." Indeed, if the intellect of the scientist and the intellect which is the true lawgiver of the natural processes were not one and the same intellect, the work of the scientist could never succeed. Only because there is a universal primacy of the ego over the world can scientific labor achieve what it does achieve. This points to the great mystery which hides behind the polarity of ego and world, of contemplation and action, of the phenomenal and the ultimate, and which pushes cultural life forward to ever new solutions of the antinomies, and finally to faith and religion.

THE LIMIT OF SCIENCE

In the course of my discussion I have frequently touched upon the limit of science. Although science is one of the activities of civilization, it is by no means the only one or the most prominent or the sum total of them all. Science leaves room for other activities which supplant and limit it. The world as propounded by science is by no means the "world-in-itself" or the whole of experience; it is a limited, definite, fragmentary view of the world, correct within its scope and exact in its knowledge. Science is, therefore, not even the only branch of contemplative culture, as I have shown above. It is rivaled by art, which also offers a "world-solution" of the supreme problem, but on a higher level.

Science is limited in a twofold way; first, because it is contemplative only, aiming at a "world-solution," and, second, because it subordinates one pole to the other, while art co-ordinates the poles in their extreme opposition. Between absolute unity and absolute plurality science interpolates the intermediate stratum of generic laws, a kind of scientific realm of Platonic Ideas. They have in common with the absolute oneness the power to unite a manifold of phenomenal facts under one head, and they have in common with the multiplicity of phenomena a concrete and definite content which facilitates the subordination of the facts to the laws. The facts themselves are adapted to the laws by their subordination; they are not merely perceived but are comprehended as particular specimens of the generic laws. This intermediate stratum abstracts one aspect from the world of experience, but it does not offer a picture of the world in its all-embracing unity and its full, vast multiplicity.

The stratum of the laws also reconciles the universality and individuality of the world of experience, as indicated, in a limited and relative fashion. The consequence of this limitation is that the world is broken up by science into several classes of phenomena corresponding to the classes of laws which prevail over them. The individual multiplicity of phenomenal facts is so ordered that all of them can be subordinated to definite classes of general laws represented by definite natural sciences, like mechanics, optics, and the other branches of physics; chemistry in its various divisions; astronomy; geology; geography; biology; and so on. There is no single science of nature; neither is there one nature comprehended by science. Instead, there are several provinces of nature, but none of the sciences tells what the whole is. There is no true and absolute universality in any of the sciences, although mechanics claimed, and claims sometimes even now, to represent the basic essence of nature to which all the other phenomena should be reduced. This claim is in conformity with the mathematical priority of mechanics, but it disregards the difference between generality and universality. It ignores the truth inherent in individuality itself. This world of ours is not a mechanism, precisely because it is individual in all its manifestations. Indeed, the world itself is a kind of individual which cannot be dissolved into particulars dominated by general laws.

Some writers have suggested that the most modern phase of scientific development has opened the door to the understanding of freedom. Physics, they argue, no longer holds to the principle of strict causal necessity but provides for the reality of the accidental, which, in turn, is at the root of freedom. Even scholars of considerable training in the intricacies of epistemology and the methodology of science have supported this suggestion. Does the modern method of statistical probability really permit the introduction of freedom into the conception of the world?

This seems highly improbable from the outset, since freedom in its genuine and proper meaning belongs to the will and action of man as a self and since man's selfhood is methodically excluded from the scientific world. It is true that, by acknowledging the limitation of causal necessity within the natural processes, science approaches the limit of its own world and thereby the "supernatural" world-hemisphere of man and the self. As far as I understand it, the step made by the modern development of physics was brought about by the attempt to subordinate the individuality of the world more closely to general laws than had ever been done before. This attempt met the barrier between the particular, which can be subordinated, and the individual, which cannot. The nearer the scientist comes to that barrier, the more obstacles he must encounter to his undertaking. The more closely he approaches the full reality of observed facts, the clearer it becomes that his method cannot penetrate into the individual kernel of reality. This kernel cannot be subjugated to a strict necessity; it can be grasped only by statistical methods, which replace necessity by probability.

But we should not forget that probability is not a principle of freedom or of self-determination but is itself a principle of necessity, though of a restricted kind. Statistical laws in the realm of human acts do not support the insight into the operation of the free will; on the contrary, they show that this operation is subject to necessity of a certain sort. If we learn that under definite circumstances a definite number of persons commit suicide, this does not say anything about the individual motives and the individual views of those who are the unhappy ones. Instead, it disregards all these individual factors on behalf of a general rule which limits the freedom of the will. The contrast and contradiction between natural necessity and moral freedom is not mitigated by statistical laws; it is rather enhanced and brought into the open. The atom particles, electrons, or whatever, for all the indeterminateness that quantum mechanics ascribes to their motions, have no freedom at all; and this indeterminateness can in no way reconcile freedom and necessity—it is simply a limited necessity. Indirectly, of course, this limited necessity does point to the limits of science and its world and in that way to the existence of something that transcends those limits.

Man can certainly be subjected to the principles and methods of science, as biology, physiology, psychology, and sociology show; man is definitely a part of nature, exposed to all the necessities of natural existence. Even historical life in all its cultural manifestations and ramifications is not exempt from this general rule. Natural necessity plays a part—and sometimes a very decisive part—in the historical trend of events; but how far the whole course of cultural development is determined by general laws we do not know. Whether Spengler is right in asserting that a certain rhythm recurs over and over again in that development (when we abstract from his thesis that this rhythm is bound up with the rise and fall of new cultures) it is hard to determine. It is certainly true that man, even as creator of cultural values of the highest kind, is yet a being controlled by psychological laws which he cannot evade. How deeply this necessity permeates the creativity of the mind, whether the flourishing and the decay of cultural life is partly caused by a natural rhythm that encroaches upon intellectual and spiritual impulse and vitality, I would not dare to judge. But it is certain that circumstances and conditions of a unique and individual character are involved in all historical change and that they offer the occasion on which man's free will comes to the fore.

Rhythm, i.e., the reiteration of a sequence of equal stages in a development, is a phenomenon that occurs frequently in nature and also in the arts. Organic life provides many illustrations of rhythm. Many processes in the organic body—for instance, breathing—take place in a rhythmical sequence. Birth and death, although not regulated by definite periods, are nevertheless also a kind of rhythmical reiteration. We find rhythm, however, not only in the realm of organic life but also in inorganic nature, as the change of the seasons, brought about by the rhythmical movement of the earth, shows. As the lack of determination can be regarded as the negative substitute for freedom in the world of science, thus rhythm is a kind of negative substitute for eternity.

Rhythm is the phenomenal image of the timeless validity of natural laws. It manifests this validity in a visible form. The reiteration of the same stages or phases in a movement demonstrates to sense-experience the eternal order of nature in special cases and seems to superimpose eternity upon time and the temporal processes. It is, as it were, the temporalization of eternity. Plato calls time "the moving image of eternity," referring thereby to what appeared to him to be the visible, circular movement of the sun around the earth, which determines the change of day and night and which serves as the measure of time.

Science is limited to this image of eternity. The idea of cycles is the scientific substitute for eternity. Nietzsche, whose thoughts were influences by scientific patterns (in so far as they had any logical coherence at all), dreamed of the eternal return of all things as the highest fulfilment of his longing, since he "loved" eternity, as he says in one of his most beautiful poems. But Nietzsche was not a scientist after all, though he was (at least in some of his utterances) a representative of scientism.

SCIENTISM

Scientism transgresses the limits of science. Rarely has the scientist himself fallen victim to the temptation of this transgression, at least during the last two hundred years. In the sixteenth and seventeenth centuries, during that period of great metaphysical systems based upon the natural sciences when scientism was in its heyday, even outstanding scientists like Descartes and Leibniz indulged in the adventure of expanding scientific thought-forms to cover the universe. Today scientism is the vice of those who do not practice science itself but are intoxicated by the triumph of scientific, and even more of technological, discoveries and devices, i.e., the vice of the masses in almost all countries on the earth. Scientism has become the most dangerous pseudo-religion, pseudo-metaphysics, and pseudo-theology that has ever been devised.

The roots of scientism lie deeper than its proponents know. They extend to the very springs of culture and life. Culture tries to overcome the antinomies of experience. Science partly solves them; but a partial solution is no solution—it only generates new unsolved and scientifically insoluble problems. It thus postulates other ways of culture. But the very existence of a plurality of solutions contradicts the goal of culture; it tears anew the human consciousness which culture aims to reconcile; it generates a competition among the branches of culture, instead of bringing peace and unity. We are accustomed to the manifold of cultural activities and realms and no longer take offense at this plurality, until some tragic clash between the realms or the persons representing them reveals that there is no peace in their mere coexistence, if they are not united inwardly. But no single branch of culture seems to be entitled to unite them all or to represent their inner unity and totality. Scientism pretends that science is called upon and is enabled to carry through this high task.

The limitation of each of the cultural realms is not a mere fact, it is something that upsets the thinking mind as much as the persons who suffer from it. If the antinomies are not solved by any of the cultural activities, what good is in them? Why does mankind labor and toil for the goal of culture when the very manifoldness and diversity of activities only enhance the original split within the experiencing subject? Does not the whole undertaking of civilization thus frustrate itself? Is its meaning not endangered, if not outright destroyed, by its eventual failure to reach its goal?

These questions lie behind all attempts of any special branch of civilization to extend over the whole range of culture in order to solve definitely the common antinomies. Scientism, as we will see, is only one of the many attempts aiming at the same goal, undertaken by each of the manifold realms of culture. As science oversteps its limit and falls into the trap of scientism, so art falls into that aestheticism, politics into that of totalitarianism (or statism), morality into moralism, philosophy into absolutism, history into historicism, and so on. Each branch has the ambition of finishing the job and giving mankind what mankind strives for in all its single efforts and works. At bottom it is a religious longing which inspires and presses man toward the final solution, the perfect unity, the absolute peace, in all these disparate aberrations.

People begin to adore science after science has deprived them of their proper object of adoration, because they need such an object and are fond of adoration. The adoration of science leads to the fallacy of scientism. Since science has achieved almost miraculous results, it has taken over the function of the miracle-worker, and, because most people need miracles in order to believe in the existence of a power greater than man, they begin to believe that the scientist is a kind of superman.

It is a strange paradox, however, that science—this intellectual undertaking, this methodical and exact way of finding truth, this most unromantic, most disenchanting procedure—should play the role of a universal savior of mankind, a quasi-divine source of wisdom, of the Logos (in the sense of the preamble to the Fourth Gospel). And yet one cannot doubt that to many—perhaps to the majority of people today—science has become the spiritual support and the inner strength to which they appeal in all the troubles and dangers of our time. Even the Christian faith has bowed down before this new deity in founding the denomination of a "Christian Science."

The most grotesque scientism was proclaimed by Auguste Comte, the initiator of so-called "positivism," which is a philosophical or pseudo-philosophical fashion of scientism. He was not satisfied to assert that the natural sciences are the only solid basis and the entire content of philosophy, but he went on to proclaim that this philosophy should be regarded as the only valid religion, and he even proposed the establishment of a "church" derived from his principles. This is the most explicit prototype of all the following attempts at a cultural system dominated by science.

The nineteenth century and the beginning of the twentieth were more or less convinced that science alone could bring salvation to mankind; that in the long run it could and would cure all human evils, not only those which originated from ill health or natural deficiencies within man or from natural enemies without, but also all social, political, and moral shortcomings and frailties; that psychology, sociology, and political science, if conducted in the exact spirit of scientific observation and analysis, would build up a better civilization, free from the superstition and anxiety of former, less happy ages. Scientism was firmly intrenched in the heart and mind of man.

The devastating effect of this new form of superstition can be seen everywhere. The scientific spirit invaded all the other branches of culture and organized them according to its own methods and ideals. This led to a general paralysis of man's spiritual imagination, which blighted the arts, enervated faith, and produced illusionary political and social ideas. The decay of poetry, painting, sculpture, and music and the rise of utopianism and ideology were the immediate consequences. Sensitive artists took refuge in an abstract symbolism or in an often artificial and sophisticated style and manner.

The most insidious and invidious influence of scientism is felt in the noncontemplative spheres of culture, which are most remote from the spirit of science. Action rests upon strong conviction, not upon experimental observation and calculation. It rests upon insight in individual and practical necessities and in the discovery of the right ways of dealing with them. Science can put means and tools into the hands of the statesman, but it certainly cannot determine the end and the goal of action. The word "ideology" arose in minds which believed that science was able to guide and to direct action. The best-known example is so-called "historical materialism," a misleading term, since the theory (or ideology) which it is supposed to designate is neither truly historical nor truly materialistic; it claims, however, to be true in a scientific sense.

Historical materialism is a pseudo-philosophy of history based upon the dogma that the physical needs of man and the economic institutions which serve the satisfaction of those needs are the backbone and primary cause of all social and political realities—and even of all the higher realms of culture. These higher realms are called a "superstructure" by the adherents of this pseudo-philosophy, which today has assumed the dimensions of a new fanaticism pretending to the authority of dogmatic truth. Economic conditions and institutions undoubtedly have a great influence upon the whole of cultural life; but, even so, they themselves are, in turn, always influenced by religious, political, and social traditions or revolutions.[4] But more important than this historical question is the hierarchical order of the cultural branches, because it is this order which should determine the action and the evaluation of good and bad in the social and political spheres. Only a philosophy of culture which distinguishes lower and higher spheres can decide this question. Scientism is unable to do so because, in principle, it confuses scientific and philosophic points of view, and this confusion generates ever new confusions.

If historical materialism were right, it should conclude that it is itself the product of economic facts; but then it would become false at the moment when economic conditions alter; since economic conditions have greatly altered in countries in which historical materialism was made the slogan of revolution, the theory or philosophy should have altered too. In other words, if historical materialism is right, it is an outcome of a capitalistic situation and should cease to be true when this situation disappears. This conclusion obviously contradicts its own logic. It demonstrates that it is altogether nonsense to make truth

4 Cf. Max Weber, *Gesammelte Aufsätze zur Religionssoziologie* (Tübingen: J. C. B. Mohr, 1923-34).

dependent upon economic conditions of whatever kind. Historical materialism is only an example of the confusion originating from the superstitious belief in the omnipotence of science and especially from the belief that any scientific theory can become a possible guide to political action. This is a fundamental error, based upon the imperialistic tendency to exalt science to the pinnacle of the supreme and absolute solution of the world-ego antinomy.

Another example of scientific imperialism's disregard for the legitimate limits of science is the attempt on the part of psychopathology and psychotherapy to claim a philosophical and religious authority and to replace philosophy and religion by scientific methods and ideas. I do not speak about the medical value of psychoanalysis; I leave the decision about this to the experts. But in the name of a philosophy of culture I must protest against the arrogant attempts to extend psychoanalysis beyond the reach of its relative merits and to presume that from its vantage point alone one is permitted to evaluate religion and to speak as the judge in any and all matters of culture, as Freud has done. Atheism based upon scientific reasons all too often forgets that it infringes the limits of a special branch of culture; it ignores the simple fact that science is incompetent to speak about matters not belonging to its territory. A philosophy of culture has to be on guard against all violations of the frontier of cultural realms and to push back invaders.

Psychoanalysis is in danger of disregarding this limitation, if the physician assumes the function of the moral educator (or of the priest). He who wishes to cure emotional perturbations is easily tempted to assume that role. Since, however, the method of psychoanalysis is devoid of ethical standards—as, indeed, all purely scientific methods necessarily are—the danger is imminent that the physician may take his healing art as a substitute for moral advice. Psychoanalysis tries to liberate the patient from inhibitions which (according to the theory) produced mental disturbances; the physician may then forget that moral life to a great extent rests upon wholesome self-control, which, seen from a psychological point of view, closely resembles inhibition.[5]

ART: (a) THE IMAGE-WORLD

Art is another of man's efforts to solve the basic contradiction of experience which endangers his inner integrity and selfhood. Art, like science, offers its contribution in the fashion of a "world-solution." Although art does not eliminate the human ego, it takes it as only a part of the world, as determined by surroundings and involved in the universal nexus of temporal events. Art continues the work of science on a higher plane; it offers a higher truth, more comprehensive and more radical than the one presented by science.

Such a statement probably upsets and challenges most modern men. They are accustomed to think of scientific intelligence as the supreme judge in questions of truth and reality. They are proud of having defeated earlier views of the world created by an imagination allied, to a great extent, with fancy and caprice. Is it not the glory of modern science to have dismissed groundless speculations of ancient and medieval world-constructions, as Bacon demanded that it should do? Do we not know by now that only the disciplined mind of science is able to find out truth in a realistic sense, while imagination may conquer the heart and generate lofty and noble ideals but cannot tell us anything about the real nature of things? Much has been said already in rejection of this whole argument.

Art does not challenge science on the ground of science. It transcends the whole scientific level. It works where science can-

5 Cf. William E. Hocking, *Science and the Idea of God* (Chapel Hill: University of North Carolina Press, 1944): "It is not the business of psychiatry to say what life is about nor what for any individual makes life worth living" (p. 41). C. G. Jung, *Modern Man in Search of a Soul*: "The patient does not feel himself accepted, unless the very worst of him is accepted too" (p. 270, quoted by Hocking, *op. cit., p.* 44). See, however, the chapter on "Moralism" in David E. Roberts, *Psychotherapy and a Christian View of Man* (New York: Charles Scribner's Sons, 1950).

not work, though both have the approach of contemplation in common. What science never accomplishes—the depiction of the world in one image—is the particular and singular intention of art. The whole of the world is not subject to the principles and methods of science; it can be grasped and comprehended only by imaginative means. The world as a whole is not intelligible. It is, however, imaginable; and to this degree speculation was right, although it erroneously conferred the method of imagination upon the field of rational thought. Imagination is more powerful than the intellect, if the task be to reach the uttermost polarities of experience and to reconcile them. No intellect whatever can perform this task. It is therefore not man's finitude or the limitations of his intellect which prevents the solution achieved by art from being translated into the language of science. Rather, it is the limitation of the intellect per se which frustrates any such attempt. Even an infinite intellect, as long as it is an intellect, not endowed by and enlarged through imagination, cannot encompass the scope of the world as a whole.

Only imagination can accomplish this. Only through an image can the universe be known. The world as a whole does not exist in the way in which all the details of the world do. It belongs to another kind of reality, and it is this reality which can be grasped only by imagination. The senses are confined to single impressions and perceptions; the intellect embraces genera by means of concepts and laws; but imagination is able to adumbrate the universe. This is a wondrous capacity indeed, and the intellect will always suspect its results. The intellect is perfectly right in doing so, since the result reached by imagination completely overshadows intellectual truth and can never be made acceptable to the intellect by intellectual means. One has to have imagination, one has to know it from within, in order to measure its performance and to assess its truth.

Imagination alone can reconcile the extremes of experience—the absolutely individual and the absolutely universal, the sensuous and the spiritual. No abstract concept, no mere idea, no generic law, can ever hope to grasp the individual and concrete universe; only artistic creativity can produce the world in a mirror, a little world, a kind of microcosm in which the macrocosm is reflected. It is not the method of subordination but only the method of co-ordination which brings about this wondrous solution. The little world of art is as sensuous as it is spiritual; the opposite poles of experience are most intimately united, without any chasm. The individual features of whatever phenomena are so depicted as to obtain at the same time a universal significance. The multiplicity of detail is not subjected to an outer abstract unity but is inwardly united. The microcosmic world of the work of art does not embrace, like the macrocosm, all the details of the world but only a tiny fragment, some peculiar events, some particular persons, some individual feelings. Even so, it images the world in and through its form.

It is this form which reconciles the extremes with each other. Whereas in science the realm of laws is an intermediate stratum interpolated between the extremes of unity and plurality, of universality and individuality, the artistic form is one with the content of the artistic work, although it is possible to distinguish them *in abstracto*. The laws order real processes not contained in them; the aesthetic form orders its own content and has no relation to anything outside itself. The image-world of a work of art and the image-form of that world are actually one and the same whole. The form penetrates and permeates the content in all its detail. This wholeness generates the impression of world-totality. The image-world is absolutely independent of anything outside itself; it is, as it were, closed up, perfectly self-sufficient, balanced within itself, based upon itself, like the One of Parmenides (who was probably influenced by the experience of art, as most Greek philosophers were, especially those who think of the cosmos as the Absolute).

This form of the image-world makes the content a whole in which every part derives its existence, function, and meaning from the whole, which is the underlying, creative idea of the parts: its immanent end or *telos*. As Kant points out, the aesthetic form resembles the organic form in nature. Of course, this analogy is limited, since the image-world is a product of the human mind, while the organism is a product of nature. The organism as a living entity is related to the outside world and depends upon it; it is not absolutely ordered by the idea of the whole (the idea of organic self-preservation and self-propagation) but permits contingent elements caused by inorganic factors. Still there is an analogy between the organic and the artistic form. Recently the thesis has been defended that the development of artistic styles from a primitive to a more and more complicated and integrated form resembles the development of the organic forms in the evolution of the species. I do not dare to take sides in this discussion.

The analogy between organism and image-world has caused those systems of philosophy which assert that the world is both an organism and a work of art (as did Plato and, after him, innumerable other thinkers, outstanding among them Augustine, Giordano Bruno, Shaftesbury, and Schelling). In this way they tried to unite nature and mind by the same idea of a whole organizing itself and producing itself as the artist produces his work.

The more perfect a work of art is, the more are the whole and the parts actually one and the same unit, the whole growing out from the parts, the parts developing into the whole and determined by the whole, as the idea of the universe demands it. The contradictions within the world seem to be dissolved. Harmony is the aesthetic category expressing this solution. Indeed, as long as we live in the contemplation of the image-world, we are at rest. We feel that the tensions of the antagonistic poles are subdued, preserved but overcome. In that way the truth presented by art is not merely physical, as is the truth of science, but metaphysical. It concerns not only the existence of the phenomena of the world and their necessary connection but, at the same time, the meaning of the world, its purpose as expressed and exemplified by the phenomena. And thus not only the contradictions within the world but even the contradiction between world and ego are mastered—of course, in the manner and within the limits of the "world-solution."

"To the great poets I ascribe the power to gaze fixedly at the whole of life and bring into harmony that which is within and that which is without them." [6] Not only oneness and manifoldness, universality and individuality, but also freedom and necessity and even eternity and time are somehow reconciled to one another. This is achieved because the image-world of art depicts not only the visible universe but also the soul of man. In fact, man is even in the center of the artistic image; he is the real focus of artistic imagination. The world appears only as the reflex of man. The primacy of the ego is thus maintained in spite of the primacy of the world and in spite of the "world-solution" offered by art. Of course, man is merely a depicted man in the artistic image; it is an image-man we see in that picture, not the actual man we meet in life. This depicted man, however, is the pivot upon which the universe hinges. Therefore, drama and lyric and epic poetry, more than architecture, are the prototypes of the image-world. Music presents the inner soul, painting and sculpture present the outer appearance of man, though indirectly his soul also.

Art is more adequate than any psychology to mediate the truth about man. Who can doubt that there are infinitely more profound and more comprehensive insights into the nature, character, heart, and soul of man in the works of great poets than can be found in scientific psychology, which often denies even the existence of the soul and certainly does not undertake the study of its inner life? Homer, the Greek tragedians and lyrical poets, Dante and Shakespeare and Goethe, know more about this inner life than all the volumes of technical psychology

---

6 Thornton Wilder, *The Ides of March* (New York: Harper & Bros., 1948), p. 33.

contain. And this is not at all the fault of the psychologists; it is the necessary consequence of the limit of science as compared with the scope, the task, and the method of the arts.

The will and action of man as depicted by the poets are not deprived of their prerogative to manifest freedom. On the contrary, they appear within the image-world in the same or, more accurately, in a manner similar to their appearance in actual life, i.e., endowed with the capacity of deliberation and decision and encumbered by the judgment of conscience, which presupposes responsibility and freedom. But—and this is the wonder of art—at the same time the conflict between freedom and necessity seems to be straightened out. Although in art the person is not deprived of the freedom which we know from experience belongs to him, the utterances of his freedom appear, nevertheless, as necessitated by his character and by the causal nexus of events and decisions. Thus universal causality is brought into harmony with personal freedom: the great riddle of metaphysics is solved. Even so Christian a theologian as Augustine has made much of the aesthetic wholeness of the world, in order to demonstrate that individual freedom and universal causality (in the form of the will of God) are compatible. In that way the most tragic afflictions and sufferings can be assuaged: "The sinners," Augustine says, "enhance the beauty of the Whole." [7]

Finally, time and eternity are also conciliated and conjoined, as far as this is possible, by contemplative creativity. Schiller says: "Was sich nie und nirgends hat begeben, das allein veraltet nie" ("What has never and nowhere occurred, that alone never becomes obsolete"). Art exalts all events and all actions to the level of eternity. Time, as depicted by the poet, the composer, the dramatist, is not the time which the scientist

---

7 Not only in his early work, *De ordine,* but as late as *De civitate Dei* (xii. 4 ff.). Cf. Nicolas Berdyaev, *The Divine and the Human* (London: Geoffrey Bles, 1949), p. 86, where he speaks about the form of theodicy adopted by Augustine and adds: "It means the prevalence of the aesthetic point of view over the ethical" (chap. vi, "Evil").

knows in his equations as one of the determining factors of natural processes. Neither is it that time within which biological development proceeds (organic time), nor is it that time which we measure in actual life (actual time). Rather, it is a time scheme peculiar to the work of art, an especially aesthetic or artistic time. And this peculiar time is in a profound unison with eternity; it is no longer endless, but complete.

Whereas science is compelled to separate the timeless validity of laws from the temporal processes, such a separation does not take place in the image-world of art because the opposite poles are united by co-ordination. The timeless validity of the work of art is not dissociated from the temporal content which unfolds in it, since form and content are only two aspects of one and the same whole. To be sure, the ten years during which the siege of Troy by the Greeks lasts do not actually pass in the epic of Homer; they have a merely aesthetic existence. Nevertheless, they have the function of actual time in the image-world depicted by the poet; they are depicted years, as the persons are depicted persons, their acts are depicted acts, and so on. Depicted time is time, though it passes only in the image-world and has an imaginative character.

This imaginative time is reconciled to eternity. Indeed, it is itself "the image of eternity" in a sense more true than is the circular movement of the sun around the earth, which Plato had in mind, precisely because this time scheme is not circular or cyclical. It extends like actual time and yet differs from it in that it has an absolute beginning and an absolute end and is thereby self-sufficient, as eternity is. Actual time stretches indefinitely, endlessly. Its contents are not inwardly connected with one another in a meaningful coherence but are interrupted by divergent, disconnected events and circumstances which chance or fate allows to follow one another in our life. There are empty periods without meaning, lost moments and intermissions; and no meaningful whole generates the succession of its various contents, although we are always seeking and longing for such a continuous flow of meaningful moments and periods in our life, in the life of other persons, and, finally, in the history of mankind. This state marks the finite and endless time of history.

Imaginative time is both finite and infinite, just as the whole image-world is both a fragmentary segment of life and yet the whole of life. Time thus takes on the nature of the whole. In spite of its finitude, it does not point to any "before" or "after," any past or future which would extend outside the frame of the work. Although the plot of a novel does not always begin on the first page but sometimes many years before the first described scene opens, nevertheless the time span filled by the novel has its beginning and its end within the covers of the book; it is complete and fulfilled together with the unfolding plot. It is the time scheme of a little world which neither needs nor can tolerate any supplement, if the work is truly perfect. The image-time exists by itself; it hovers above the ocean of nothingness and possesses all its strength within itself. The beautiful "is blessed by itself" (Moericke). The image-time is a temporal eternity, an eternal temporality.

Like the cyclical return of the stages in a natural process, the image-time of the image world also may return at any actual time, i.e., at any moment, when we turn to it, read the epic or novel again, see the performance of a tragedy again, and so forth. But nevertheless this time scheme is not cyclical, because it happens only within its own world and in no way in our actual life. It belongs to a blessed island or oasis, and therefore it does not return but is unique. It is complete not only in that it has its beginning and its end within its own little world but also because in a masterpiece it is so rounded that the end returns to the beginning, being its necessary consequence and definitive fulfilment. This is particularly evident in music.

The image-world of art exists in its own eternity, just as its time exists within that eternity and is one with it. This is the unique glory of that reconciliation and self-realization which is achieved by artistic creation. Hegel in his *Encyclopedia* tried to imitate this self-contained, closed, and blessed character of the image-world, in order to generate the impression of a comprehension of all existence, a comprehension which would successfully rival the work of art and even surpass it because it would not be imaginative, but scientific and speculative. He did not realize that the peculiar glory and perfection of the masterpiece of art is based precisely upon the imaginative character of its performance.

The contribution of art to the activity of culture thus consummates contemplation. Art reaches the highest summit in the whole sphere of "world-solution." The antinomies of experience seem to be overcome, the human consciousness seems to be completely satisfied, totally united within self. No wonder the poet often claims a quasi-religious significance for his work. Goethe calls true poetry a "secular gospel," [8] and Graf Platen sings:

> Um Gottes eigene Glorie zu schweben
> Vermag die Kunst allein und darf es wagen,
> Und wessen Herz Vollendetem geschlagen,
> Dem hat der Himmel weiter nichts zu geben.[9]

ART: (b) THE ARTIST

Art reveals the primacy of the ego in still another way. The image-world is, even more than has yet been shown, centered around the ego. Not only is it centered in man, as poetry, music, and also, to a lesser degree, painting and sculpture illustrate, but the image-world, being the product of human imagination, is also rooted in the self of the artist; it is an image of the world, and it is also indirectly an image of the soul of its creator.

---

8 *Dichtung und Wahrheit,* Book III.

9 *Venetianische Sonette.* "Art alone is able to attain to God's own glory and is entitled to attain to it; and he whose heart is struck by the master's work cannot expect anything which heaven could give him beyond this."

Every work of art is unmistakably stamped by the individual way in which the artist sees, feels, and interprets the world. The image-world is not like the intelligible world of the sciences, an abstract, schematic, and conceptual world, the reflex of highly theoretical doctrines. Instead, it is a concrete and individual world which reflects the concrete and individual personality of its author. The artist lends, as it were, his own soul to the world which he creates, so that this individual soul assumes the function of the soul of the image-world. The animating principle in the artistic work is not the general intellect but the personality of the artist.

The image-world is therefore much more in line with the world of experience, which also centers around the experiencing self. Indeed, artistic imagination and creation spring directly from total experience; they are much nearer to experience than are the theories and laws of the sciences. The world which we experience is like the world which we confront in the work of art, and not like the world devised by physics and chemistry and the other branches of science (although biology and psychology are, of course, nearer to immediate experience than are the mathematical disciplines). For this reason it is easier to read a novel than it is to study Einstein's theory of relativity, although it is less easy to penetrate great masterpieces and to understand them fully than it might be to understand physics, if one were trained for this purpose. In principle, every man should be able to understand physics as well as mathematics because both rest upon the general intellect, while the appreciation of a work of art demands a kind of kindred soul.

Although the artistic creation is nearer to experience than is science, this very affinity between art and experience makes it more difficult to understand how art can achieve a reconciliation of the polarities and how it can solve the antinomies which arise out of experience. Is not the generality of the intellect precisely the reconciling principle in the sciences? Does not the elimination of the individual features of the self enable the scientist to arrive at a "world-solution" no longer encumbered by the contrast between the universality and the individuality of the ego? When the artist, on the contrary, does not eliminate his individuality but even makes it the very soul of the world he creates, how can such a product reconcile the opposition mentioned? And yet the fact cannot be denied that the work of the artist does perform this miracle and (what is even more startling) performs it the better, the more original the individuality of the artist is, that is to say, the more individual it is!

However, we already have the key to this riddle in our hands. If it is true that the world of experience is always the world of an individual self and not of an abstract intellect only, then it is evident that only the reconciliation of the individuality and the universality of the ego can bring about a full and true image of the world, one which concerns not only fragmentary aspects but the totality of all aspects. Therefore, we can well comprehend that a universal personality can achieve what science cannot: the reproduction of the world in an image that echoes his own soul and, at the same time, appeals to all souls which feel the harmony between the individuality and the universality of the genius reflected in his work.

The artist has to be "inspired" in order to achieve his work. He does not produce out of rational and intellectual reflections and calculations, although reflections and calculations do participate in the transposition of the inspired conception into the actuality of the work. The artist cannot generate his work by sheer will power. As a merely individual person, he cannot create. Inspiration means the fusion of the universal and the individual ego within the operation of the artist. When this fusion occurs, the precondition of creation is achieved. But it cannot be "achieved" at all, when this word implies that the effort and the aspiration of the artist alone decide. They do not decide; the artist depends not only upon himself but also upon the favor of the Muses whom he invokes.

No phrase can better describe his inner state of mind. It is not accidental that a mythological metaphor creeps in when one tries to express the peculiar method of the artist. Mythology is the poetical solution of the religious "problem." And it is the religious problem which enters when we analyze the miraculous process of imaginative creation. The artist depends upon "grace" in a pagan sense. As the fragmentary and individual character of the imaginative content of the artistic work does not hamper the universal significance of the image-world, so also the individuality of the artist does not obstruct his universal greatness. On the contrary, in both cases the fusion itself is the moving power of the reconciliation achieved.

Although the religious sphere is somehow anticipated and foreshadowed in the act of artistic creation, still the artist is not a prophet. Poet and prophet are brothers. But the poet belongs to the contemplative sphere, the prophet to that of action. The poet acts, but for the sake of, and commissioned by, contemplation; the prophet contemplates, but for the sake of, and commissioned by, action. The artist is a messenger not of the Living God but of the Muses, whose virtue and spirit are entirely contemplative. The poet, Schelling says, is born a pagan. No wonder that the great poets have some inclination toward the pagan gods, to which they frequently appeal. Even Dante chooses Vergil as his leader through hell, and his audacious idea of making the beloved woman the mediator between himself and the Blessed in heaven is certainly not Christian.

Both prophet and genius act under a kind of compulsion which does not exclude, but rather presupposes, individual freedom. The wonder of inspiration in both rests upon the fusion of freedom and necessity in their creative state of mind. Here again we see that the antinomies of experience are surmounted by and in the artist. He is certainly not coerced, as are the beasts by their instincts; and yet he is driven toward his intuition, and only when he is driven is his intuition genuinely artistic. The split between necessity and freedom as it opens in experience is closed in the blessed situation of genuine creativity.

The artist "redeems" the world in a secular sense. Depicting even man's cruelest deeds, his most tragic destinies, his most depressing frustrations, his most destructive forces, the artist exalts them to the level of eternal beauty, endows them with nobility, and spiritualizes them. His deity is Beauty. He adores her in creating his work, and thereby he produces a kind of theodicy which is more effective than any thought out by a philosopher or theologian. After all, Augustine only imitates the artist when he insists that everything truly and really existing is included in the universal order of beauty.

The instrument by which the genius accomplishes so great an effect is his imagination, which combines the opposite poles of the personality, thereby integrating man as a self. Wordsworth calls the imagination of the artist "the mind's internal heaven." Initiating the dream world of fairy tales and fables, fiction and fancy, romance and myth, and all the arts, this creative force is itself akin to its products, equally fabulous and miraculous, super-rational, and to be understood only in an imaginative fashion. If it is true that man is created in the image of God, then the artist, in spite of his pagan affinity, most resembles the Creator (although the Creator in the biblical sense is more than an artist). The identity of the word "creator" in both cases is not accidental. The artist does create, as God does, "out of nothing." He is not bound by the laws of nature but is free in depicting the world as he sees fit, for the purpose of interpretation. He possesses the power to arrest the fleeting wave of time and events and to impress eternity upon the transitory moment. His hero will live as long as his work:

> So long as man can breathe, or eyes can see,
> So long lives this, and this gives life to thee

Shakespeare proudly exults. Indeed, as the image-world is a little world of its own, so the artist is a little god of his own.

THE LIMIT OF ART

In art the contemplative solution of the antinomies of experience culminates, but this solution itself is limited for the very reason that it is contemplative. Contemplation can never absolutely reconcile world and ego because it offers a "world-solution," which either completely disregards the existence of the human self, as science does, or treats this existence only as a part of the image-world of art. To be sure, the self of the artist impinges upon this world, but it does not figure within it. The artist as such is not known by artistic means; he, as the creator, does not appear in his work except in autobiography (which is not purely a work of art but in most cases is either historical or at least half-historical, as in Goethe's *Dichtung und Wahrheit*). A self-portrait is an artistic mirror of the artist, but this mirror makes the artist an image of his own world; it must "objectify" his self, precisely in order to be a work of art. The self as such, the living subject, can never be transformed into an image; this is the limit of art. It is the final limit of contemplation and of the contemplative solution of the antinomies.

The artist is not only the image he creates in his work, if he portrays himself, but also a living being. In fact, he is such a being in the first place and is only secondarily a creative being and the author of his works. The contradictions of experience are felt by him in an actual way, and they could be absolutely transcended only in an actual way, i.e., by means of an actual community in which the contrast of ego and ego, of world and world, is finally settled. Contemplation cannot perform this task because it does not take the other self as an acting, existing person but transforms him into an imaginative person who lives in the imaginary world of the artistic work. In other words, the limit of art springs from the fact that everything and everyone undergo a metamorphosis in the mirror of art and that this metamorphosis deprives the actual person of his actuality. This explains why the actual self-contradiction of the experiencing ego cannot be absolutely conquered by any contemplative solution, be it scientific or artistic.

This basic limitation of the whole sphere of art again generates a new tension, a new inner division of the self, and so aggravates the evil it would conquer; it generates a split between the actual and the imaginative worlds. This split is felt, and the more the artist succeeds in portraying himself in his works, the more he becomes merged in the world of his creation, and the more his actual life is regarded as merely a means for his artistic intentions. The actual world can never be completely absorbed and, as it were, replaced by its imaginative counterpart. Since this counterpart is infinitely more harmonious and reflects the inner reconciliation of the art sphere, the insufficiency and the contradictions of actual life are only the more deeply and the more painfully notable; the contrast between the two spheres underlines the imperfection and the unredeemed character of the actual one. The artist and the sensitive lover of art suffer more from the deficiencies, tensions, and tragic conflicts of human existence than do insensitive and unaffected men immersed in the pursuit of active purposes and ends.

This fundamental limit of art could not be removed, even if it were possible to contemplate the great world in the fashion of the little world of art, or if it were possible to comprehend the all as the macrocosm, as Greek thinkers and even their Christian successors, like Augustine, thought they could. In *Faust* Goethe shows how the hero is completely dissatisfied with knowledge, even that knowledge which enables him to look at the world as a harmonious whole, because he feels that it does not still the infinite thirst of his mind for actual life, for a satisfaction that no contemplation of whatever kind can possibly grant. Observing the sign of the Macrocosm, he explains:

> Like heavenly forces rising and descending,
> Their golden urns reciprocally lending,
> With wings that winnow blessing
> From Heaven through Earth I see them pressing,

Filling the All with harmony unceasing!
How grand a show! but ah! a show alone.
Thee boundless Nature, how make thee my own?

It is this infinite desire which prompts Faust to leave his study, where he has investigated nature and enjoyed the arts, to immerse himself in the floods of life and the tumult of action. Led by this desire, he is driven first from pleasure to pleasure;[10] but finally he acquires the insight that only social work can absolutely satisfy his thirst for life and that a community in which all are free to collaborate with one another for the sake of all could alone redeem his heart and bring peace to the storm of his passion. Goethe in this way expresses his conviction that it is not contemplation but action alone which can calm a man's unrest, because this unrest originates from an inner conflict which no contemplation of the world, even of a perfectly harmonious cosmos, can pacify. Whether Goethe's solution is eventually satisfying is, of course, a question not to be discussed here.

Art is limited because the ego ceases to be the ego when it figures within the world as a quasi-object. The chasm between the self as an object belonging to the world and as a subject not belonging to the world cannot be filled by any "world-solution" of the basic antinomy of experience. The impossibility becomes further evident, when we consider the relation between individuality and universality in the ego of the artist. Although this contrast is reconciled in the creative genius, it is never fully so, since the universality of the genius is somewhat restricted by the fact that there are many artists and many arts and that even one and the same artist creates many works, so that art offers many "worlds," each of which claims universality. The only universal world is imaged in many forms, since there are many individual artists and even the same artist produces his

---

10 It is remarkable that among those pleasures which Faust enjoys, but only for a short time, even artistic creation and contemplation, symbolized by his marriage with beautiful Helen, figure.

works in many individual situations. This is the price which has to be paid for the prerogative of artistic creation in reaching the goal of art in many works.

To be sure, it is possible to establish a scale of the artists and to distinguish the greatest among them as the one who alone deserves the predicate "universal" in the fullest sense. One might call Homer the greatest of the epic poets, Shakespeare the greatest of the dramatists, Goethe the greatest of the lyric poets, and so on. But all such judgments might evoke some protest; besides, it might be difficult to distinguish any single one of the creations of each as the epitome of greatness (e.g., the *Iliad* or the *Odyssey*). Whatever we might design to reduce the manifold of masterpieces to one only, we will always meet difficulties. In fact, such an undertaking is impossible.

In spite of the universality of the genius, artistic imagination is still the imagination of the individual man, even if he is inspired by the Muses, i.e., by universal powers imaged in a poetical fashion. The genius is the creator of his work, not the Muses. In other words, the individual man is universal inasmuch as he is a genius; but, even so, he is human and finite and hence exposed to failures and defects, not only as a moral being, but also as an artist, as any attempt to arrange his works with respect to their greatness illuminates. It is not that the universal ego is individualized in him but that his individual peculiarity takes on the dimensions of universality in his work. The artist is not a messenger of the Loving God, or even of the gods. To put it another way, art is limited because it is not religion, though it may have a religious significance.

This limitation seems to encroach upon the principle of coordination as compared with that of subordination. The scientist can unite scientists the world over because they are, as it were, incarnations of the Logos, that reason which "prescribes to nature its laws," while the artists have not such an inner solidarity and the art-lovers are divided by their different tastes and assessments. In this respect the scientist and science seem to be free from the restriction of art. This is true, but only in a qualified way. Scientific universality is less restricted indeed, simply because it achieves not universality, strictly speaking, but generality only, an abstract universality which sacrifices individuality and thereby wins a wider scope of acknowledgment and applicability. To conclude: both science and art are restricted, though in different ways and on different levels. If it were possible to combine the absolute generality of science with the relative universality of art, so that an absolute universality would result, this hypothetical synthesis might achieve what none of the branches of contemplation can achieve by itself. But alas, such a synthesis does not exist in the field of contemplation, precisely because it is this field.

The image-world of art is limited, also, because it images but a fragmentary detail of the world and exalts it to the height of universality. Homer might seem to embrace the whole cosmos of human feelings, situations, relations, and so on. Even so, all these contents are only a segment of the all of human possibilities, which is, in fact, inexhaustible. But each of the possibilities selected by the artist somewhat circumscribes the image of the world and thus the world itself as imaged in this peculiar way. Thus we arrive at many "worlds" again. As in the case of the artist, so in that of the world, individual items or instances are exalted as representative of the whole universe; it is not the universe itself which appears before us in an individual image, as it does when we read that God created it in six days.

Art can integrate the soul of the spectator because the work is the result of a self-integration on the part of the creator. But, as the process of creation is restricted, so is the process of its effect upon the lover of art. In both cases the redemption—if I may use this religious term—lasts only as long as the work is conceived and perceived, although the value of the work may be eternal. The reconciling power of the work cannot penetrate the whole of life (as faith can); it depends upon the presence of the work and the state of the spectator, reader, or listener, who must be engrossed in the contemplation of it in order to feel its redemptive efficacy. There is an analogy with respect to the sacrament, the sermon, and so on in the religious realm, but I will postpone discussion of this point.

AESTHETICISM

Aestheticism refuses to respect the boundaries of art and tends to expand art over the whole range of culture, making it the consummation, the absolute. Such a transgression necessarily violates all the other realms of culture, invades their legitimate territory, and distorts the meaning of their contributions. It creates the semblance of an absolute reconciliation achieved by art, whereas, in reality, this reconciliation itself is distorted by enlarging it beyond its prerogative. Aestheticism would like to make art a religion and religion an aesthetic contemplation.

In a way, all mythological religions are a result of aestheticism, inasmuch as they discharge the task of religion by artistic imagination, expressing their religious feelings by artistic production in painting and sculpture, song and poetry, music and drama, as the Greeks above all nations did in the most marvelous and convincing form. However, in ancient Greece art was not yet detached from the totality of cultural activity; it was itself religious in its origin and in its function, so that one should speak of a reciprocal influence of art upon religion and of religion upon art. The cultural realms were still inwardly united, none was autonomous. *L'art pour l'art* is the least Hellenic slogan conceivable. Even so, aesthetic contemplation was the highest goal and the guiding principle in all Greek civilization, as the German classics were right in interpreting the Greek spirit. "In God all things are beautiful, good and just," Heraclitos says, mentioning first the beautiful.[11] And even Aristotle calls the good the beautiful *(kalon)* throughout his *Ethics*.

---

11 Diels, *Die Fragmente der Vorsokratiker* (Berlin: Wertmannsche Buchhandlung, 1922), Frag. 102.

The "ancient quarrel between philosophy and poetry" which Plato discusses in his *Republic*[12] is fundamentally a quarrel between religion and poetry, to be sure—between a religion propagated by the philosophers, who revolted against the mythological gods and their artistic representation, as Heraclitos was the first to do. "The Greeks," he says, "pray to these statues, as if a man would converse with buildings; for they do not know the true nature of gods." This invective mirrors the indignation roused by the aesthetic influence upon religious expression. It parallels the biblical prohibition of portraying God by "graven images."

Plato himself took the most active part in this quarrel by branding all the views of Homer on the gods. "The first thing," he says, "to be established in the state will be a censorship of the writers of fiction. They are telling a lie about the gods, and what is more, a bad lie. We shall be silent about all the innumerable quarrels of gods and heroes: wrangling is unholy. All the battles of the gods in Homer: these tales must not be admitted into our state." [13] Plato rejects the claim of poets to know the truth about things divine; they are too fanciful and irresponsible to be trusted. It is not poetical imagination but political philosophy alone which can be called upon to teach this truth and to establish the right religion in the state. For religion is not a matter of artistic creation, it is rather a matter of political wisdom and philosophic insight. Plato thus restricts the sphere of art, which he otherwise admires and loves.

The most dangerous and finally disastrous consequence of aestheticism is, as Plato saw, the falsification of religious truth and the enervation of moral life. If one regards art as the ultimate and absolute interpreter of the meaning of life, the peculiar conditions of the entire active sphere of culture will be distorted in a manner analogous to the distortion generated by scientism.

---

12 *The Dialogues of Plato,* trans. B. Jowett (New York: Random House, 1920, 1937), I, 865.

13 *Ibid.*, pp. 640 ff.

Aestheticism and scientism have this in common: neither can do justice to actual life because they transplant it to the plane of contemplated life, on which it loses its own right and essence by appearing either as a scientifically observed, or as an artistically created, object. It undergoes a metamorphosis which deprives it of its peculiarity and destroys its actuality. Objectification kills the significance and reality of the living subject; it suppresses the responsibility and personality of the willing and acting person; it paralyzes and annihilates the very pulse of life. Contemplation is the opposite of action, and this opposition is not neutralized or placated by aestheticism but is, rather, ignored, so that life appears to be imaginative only, instead of being actual and real in the moral and religious sense.

Although, as we have seen, aesthetic imagination and contemplation can preserve the specifically human features of human life and the human personality better than scientific observation and explanation can, nevertheless they still deprive life and personality of their original and immediate presence. They deal with man not in an active, but in a contemplative, way which makes him an object and a mere part of the world without that moral freedom which characterizes man as man. The great achievement of art—its ability to reconcile freedom and necessity in the unity of the image-world which superimposes its own totality upon every event or decision that occurs within its scope—becomes perverted into the denial of freedom, because actual life lacks the totality of the image-world and does not reflect the soul of a creative artist. Art is not ultimate.

The greatest artists are inclined to extend their own artistic modes of viewing the world to actual life and thus to fall victim to aestheticism. It is well known that Goethe tried to lead his life as if it were a work of art[14] and thereby met difficulties and underwent temptations which he could overcome only because a great amount of moral wisdom and strength counteracted

---

14 Cf. the profound book on *Goethe* by Georg Simmel (Leipzig: Klinckhardt, 1913).

and balanced the trend of aestheticism. But his example was dangerous to those of his innumerable admirers who did not possess the same resources and yet ventured to imitate his aesthetic standards (or lack of moral standards) in their own insignificant lives. This might well be one of the many reasons why the German nation declined so surprisingly and fatefully in her moral standards and conduct during the nineteenth and twentieth centuries. Some of the Romanticists had already drawn conclusions from aestheticism with respect to moral actuality which were destructive for social morality and which weakened their own resistance when they confronted the temptation of being converted to the Roman Catholic church.[15]

In a definite way this church itself resulted partly from the blending of Christian and ancient religious tendencies and from attempting to preserve the aesthetic values and artistic inclinations of paganism[16] without giving up the moral and spiritual basis of biblical faith. This attempt certainly saved the treasures of antiquity, but it harmed the gravity and depth of the gospel and led eventually to Renaissance and Reformation.

Sometimes scientism and aestheticism covenant with each other and thereby increase the dangers involved in both tendencies. Here again Goethe is an example. The consequence of this union was that his scientific views were tinged by his aesthetic contemplation, causing him to establish a doctrine of the nature of colors which was in agreement with the sense-experience of the visible world but impaired mathematical optics and induced Goethe to assail Newton's theory. On the other hand, his scientific passion encroached upon his poetry, obscuring some passages in the second part of *Faust*.

Kierkegaard describes and analyzes profoundly, in his first great book, *Either-Or,* the sickness of aestheticism, which prob-

---

15 E.g., Friedrich Schlegel, whose early novel *Lucinde* indulged in libertinistic ideas, while in his old age he was converted.

16 The famous impressionist painter, Renoir, stresses this point in his letters.

ably threatened his own moral and spiritual health for some time, if not throughout his life. He shows that one of the conspicuous symptoms of aestheticism is its imitation of the artistic reconciliation between time and eternity in actual life. The aesthete abandons the imperative of fidelity in his love relations because he enjoys the beauty and perfection of every new erotic impulse. He lives through the moments of his life as if each were a little world in itself like that within the work of art, closed and self-sufficient and not pointing to anything beyond itself. The happy "moment" of such a life, however, contradicts the fact that life is not a series of imaginative world-moments or momentary worlds, each possessing its own eternity, but, rather, a continuous challenge to fight merely momentary desires for the sake of moral eternity, i.e., the inner consequence and wholeness of character revealing itself in loyalty and endurance and acts of resignation.

The difference between belief in Fate and Fortune and belief in Providence and Destiny rests upon the difference between aesthetic and ethical standards and views. Fate reflects the unity and universality of aesthetic world-contemplation, while Providence reflects the unity and universality of a moral and spiritual faith in God, the creator and ruler of the world. Aestheticism sacrifices the unity and universality of the holy will of God to the same features as those realized in the work of art. It sacrifices the ideal of a perfect human community to the enjoyment of looking at the world as if it were created by a world-artist or an "Artist-God," as Nietzsche worshiped him, according to his own confession.[17]

In the twentieth century the seed sown by Nietzsche flowered. German youth succumbed to the alluring charm of his style and the fascination of his refined and learned aestheticism. In the so-called "Stefan George-Kreis," this aesthetic mode of feeling and thinking reached its zenith and enervated the hearts of the

---

17 Preface to *The Birth of Tragedy* under the title "Attempt at a Self-critique" (1886).

most gifted lovers of art, so that they were unable to resist when Hitler called them back into the arena of action. National socialism was itself a half-romantic, half-scientific movement in which scientism (pseudo-biological theories) and aestheticism (mythology) joined each other on the political scene, on which the barbaric fanaticism and the sadistic insanity of a new Nero used them for his own "will to power."

Other books by Kroner:

How Do We Know God? 1943.
Kant's "Weltanschauung", 1956.
The Primacy of Faith (Gifford Lectures, 1939-40), 1943.
The Religious Function of Imagination, 1941.
Speculation in Pre-Christian Philosophy, 1956.

Other books on the same problem:

Bailie, W. John. *What Is Christian Civilization?* 1945.
Brunner, Emil. *Christianity and Civilization*, 1949.
Meland, Bernard E. *Faith and Culture*, 1953.
Religion and Culture: Essays in Honor of Paul Tillich, edited by Walter Leibrecht, 1959.
Temple, William. *Nature, Man and God* (Gifford Lectures, 1932-33), 1934.
Tillich, Paul. *Theology of Culture*, 1959.

IV. THE ETHICAL-RELIGIOUS

10. Christian Morality and Social Guilt: Reinhold Niebuhr
    from *Moral Man and Immoral Society*

11. Christian Fortitude and Existential Despair: Paul Tillich
    from *The Courage to Be*

12. The Creative Work of Love: Paul Tillich
    from *Love, Power and Justice*

"Work out your own salvation with fear and trembling."

Philippians 2: 12.

Whereas the selections in Part III of this anthology come to grips with the general problem of the relationship between faith and culture, those in Part IV are focused on the more specific problems of what it means to be a Christian in the modern world, and deal with such categories of experience as anxiety, guilt, courage, responsibility, justice and love.

The brutality of two world wars and the threat of a third global war of unprecedented destructive power, the ruthless tyranny of modern totalitarian dictators, the ambiguity of human motivation and the destructive character of guilt brought to light in the development of depth psychology, the cultural relativism of social mores and the new consciousness of man's social nature revealed in the work of the social sciences, and, finally, that haunting sense of the futility and meaninglessness of human effort rendered articulate in existential literature, art and philosophy—all have contributed to an undermining of the prestige of a humanized Christian ethic ("morality tinged with emotion") and demanded of theologians a reinterpretation of the moral situation of man in the light of the Biblical proclamation.

Foremost in this reinterpretation is the reaffirmation of the objective reality of evil and the unavoidability of guilt that form the cornerstone of Reinhold Niebuhr's thought. Second, the concealed pride and self-sufficiency underlying doctrines of moral perfectibility are exposed along with the concupiscence masked in romantic love and in the cult of success. Third, the tensions between the claims of power and those of justice, between the appeal of the good and the demands of the right, between loyalty to self and loyalty to neighbor, are revealed, in the analyses of Paul Tillich, as intransigent tensions which threaten the unity of the self and the stability of social structures. Fourth, the problem of meaninglessness emerges critically as the characteristic manifestation of finitude in contemporary life with which everyone must come to terms. Finally, since sin is reaffirmed as the state in which man exists and from which he cannot escape, the Biblical promise of salvation becomes again a powerful reality. Not freedom from sin and guilt but salvation in spite *of sin is the guarantee of faith. Or, in the language of Tillich, faith manifests itself as the "courage to be", the courage to affirm existence in spite of anxiety over guilt and meaninglessness.*

REINHOLD NIEBUHR

REINHOLD NIEBUHR's major contributions to Protestant thought have been in the area of applied Christianity where he examines the implications of Christian faith for the practical life of individual and social decision and action. With David Swenson he first introduced Kierkegaard to America and, while he disclaims his rôle as theologian, he is recognized as being one of the most vigorous leaders in America in the development of what is called neo-orthodoxy or neo-Protestantism. He has continued the Kierkegaardian "attack" against both Protestant fundamentalism for the narrowness of its uncritical literal Biblicism, and Protestant liberalism for the naïvité of its social gospel and its failure to comprehend the depth of man's moral life. His attacks have not been confined to the church alone but were directed against most of the confidently held dogmas of the early 20th century in America—political, social, economic, philosophical and historical.

The positive side of his thought springs from his reaffirmation of the Biblical account of the nature of man and his historical destiny elaborated by Niebuhr in his major work, *The Nature and Destiny of Man.* Subjecting classical and modern conceptions of the nature of man to brilliant and relentless criticism, he demonstrates their failure fully to "account for the facts" of human experience and their inadequacy to serve as bases either for dealing with the concrete problems of contemporary social, political and economic life or for a full understanding of the Self in its historical situation. Against the background of this critique he re-examines the Biblical interpretation and in this, as well as in all of his numerous other books and articles, shows its relevance for the practical problems of our individual and social life.

In his analysis of the individual he shares with Kierkegaard penetrating insights into multiple forms of self-deception whereby reason conceals from itself its egoistic motives and whereby the claims of virtue conceal hidden power drives. With Barth he reaffirms the universality of sin as the condition of human existence. In every essay we encounter new forms of individual and social pride along with their destructive consequences.

In the analysis of the social and historical scene his key term is *ambiguity* by which he emphasizes the fact that in the concrete social and historical situation the intricate network of conflicting claims never presents a course of action that is clearly and unambiguously right or wrong or in the pursuit of which one may claim to be virtuous.

Finally, Niebuhr reaffirms the importance of history as the arena in which the work of redemption takes place and in which the responsibility of the individual Christian is not a matter of arbitrary choice but of divine imperative in spite of the inevitable involvement in guilt.

In *Moral Man and Immoral Society,* from which the following chapter is taken, Niebuhr attacks the moralist's assumption that education, social techniques and the continued spread of a religiously inspired "good will" will progressively bring about social harmony between all human societies and collectives. There is a sharp distinction, he maintains, between the moral and social behavior of individuals and that of social groups. In a face to face encounter of man with man, a high degree of morality—unselfish subordination of egoism—is possible. In the encounter of group with group, of one collective will with another, however, this is not the case. Conflict of power with power is inevitable. There is an impersonal and brutal character about man's collective behavior which belongs to the order of natural necessity and can never be brought completely under the dominion of reason or conscience. Hence the paradox: moral man—immoral society.

REINHOLD NIEBUHR

from

Moral Man and Immoral Society*

Chapter 10. The Conflict Between Individual and Social Morality

A REALISTIC ANALYSIS of the problems of human society reveals a constant and seemingly irreconcilable conflict between the needs of society and the imperatives of a sensitive conscience. This conflict, which could be most briefly defined as the conflict between ethics and politics, is made inevitable by the double focus of the moral life. One focus is in the inner life of the individual, and the other in the necessities of man's social life. From the perspective of society the highest moral ideal is justice. From the perspective of the individual the highest ideal is unselfishness. Society must strive for justice even if it is forced to use means, such as self-assertion, resistance, coercion and perhaps resentment, which cannot gain the moral sanction of the most sensitive moral spirit. The individual must strive to realise his life by losing and finding himself in something greater than himself.

These two moral perspectives are not mutually exclusive and the contradiction between them is not absolute. But neither are they easily harmonised. Efforts to harmonise them were analysed in the previous chapter. It was revealed that the highest moral insights and achievements of the individual conscience are both relevant and necessary to the life of society. The most perfect justice cannot be established if the moral imagination of the individual does not seek to comprehend the needs and interests of his fellows. Nor can any non-rational instrument of justice be used without great peril to society, if it is not brought under the control of moral goodwill. Any justice which is only justice soon degenerates into something less than justice.

It must be saved by something which is more than justice. The realistic wisdom of the statesman is reduced to foolishness if it is not under the influence of the foolishness of the moral seer. The latter's idealism results in political futility and sometimes in moral confusion, if it is not brought into commerce and communication with the realities of man's collective life. This necessity and possibility of fusing moral and political insights does not, however, completely eliminate certain irreconcilable elements in the two types of morality, internal and external, individual and social. These elements make for constant confusion but they also add to the richness of human life. We may best bring our study of ethics and politics to a close by giving them some further consideration.

From the internal perspective the most moral act is one which is actuated by disinterested motives. The external observer may find good in selfishness. He may value it as natural to the constitution of human nature and as necessary to society. But from the viewpoint of the author of an action, unselfishness must remain the criterion of the highest morality. For only the agent of an action knows to what degree self-seeking corrupts his socially approved actions. Society, on the other hand, makes justice rather than unselfishness its highest moral ideal. Its aim must be to seek equality of opportunity for all life. If this equality and justice cannot be achieved without the assertion of interest against interest, and without restraint upon the self-assertion of those who infringe upon the rights of their neighbors, then society is compelled to sanction self-assertion and restraint. It may even, as we have seen, be forced to sanction social conflict and violence.

Historically the internal perspective has usually been cultivated by religion. For religion proceeds from profound introspection and naturally makes good motives the criteria of good conduct. It may define good motives either in terms of love or of duty, but the emphasis is upon the inner springs of action. Rationalised forms of religion usually choose duty rather than love as the expression of highest virtue (as in Kantian and Stoic morality), because it seems more virtuous to them to bring all impulse under the dominion of reason than to give any impulses, even altruistic ones, moral pre-eminence. The social viewpoint stands in sharpest contrast to religious morality when it views the behavior of collective rather than individual man, and when it deals with the necessities of political life. Political morality, in other words, is in the most uncompromising antithesis to religious morality.

Rational morality usually holds an intermediary position between the two. Sometimes it tries to do justice to the inner moral necessities of the human spirit rather than to the needs of society. If it emphasises the former it may develop an ethic of duty rather than the religious ethic of disinterestedness. But usually rationalism in morals tends to some kind of utilitarianism. It views human conduct from the social perspective and finds its ultimate standards in some general good and total social harmony. From that viewpoint it gives moral sanction to egoistic as well as to altruistic impulses, justifying them because they are natural to human nature and necessary to society. It asks only that egoism be reasonably expressed. Upon that subject Aristotle said the final as well as the first authoritative word. Reason, according to his theory, establishes control over all the impulses, egoistic and altruistic, and justifies them both if excesses are avoided and the golden mean is observed.

The social justification for self-assertion is given a typical expression by the Earl of Shaftesbury, who believed that the highest morality represented a harmony between "self-affections" and "natural affections." "If," said Shaftesbury, "a creature be self-neglectful and insensible to danger, or if he want such a degree of passion of any kind, as is useful to preserve, sustain and defend himself, this must certainly be esteemed vicious in regard of the end and design of nature." [1]

---

1 Third Earl of Shaftesbury, *An Inquiry Concerning Virtue or Merit,* Bk. II, Part I, sec. III.

It is interesting that a rational morality which gives egoism equality of moral standing with altruism, provided both are reasonably expressed and observe the "law of measure," should again and again find difficulty in coming to terms with the natural moral preference which all unreflective moral thought gives to altruism. Thus Bishop Butler begins his moral theorising by making conscience the balancing force between "self-love" and "benevolence." But gradually conscience gives such a preference to benevolence that it becomes practically identified with it. Butler is therefore forced to draw in reason (originally identified with conscience) as a force higher than conscience to establish harmony between self-love and conscience.[2]

The utilitarian attempt to harmonise the inner and outer perspectives of morality is inevitable and, within limits, possible. It avoids the excesses, absurdities and perils into which both religious and political morality may fall. By placing a larger measure of moral approval upon egoistic impulses than does religious morality and by disapproving coercion, conflict and violence more unqualifiedly than politically oriented morality, it manages to resolve the conflict between them. But it is not as realistic as either. It easily assumes a premature identity between self-interest and social interest and establishes a spurious harmony between egoism and altruism. With Bishop Butler most utilitarian rationalists in morals believe "that though benevolence and self-love are different . . . yet they are so perfectly coincident that the greatest satisfaction to ourselves depends upon having benevolence in due degree, and that self-love is one chief security of our right behavior to society." [3] Rationalism in morals therefore insists on less inner restraint upon self-assertion than does religion, and believes less social restraint to be necessary than political realism demands.

The dangers of religion's inner restraint upon self-assertion, and of its effort to achieve complete disinterestedness, are that

2 Cf. Joseph Butler, *Fifteen Sermons on Human Nature.*

3 Butler, *op. cit.,* Sermon I.

such a policy easily becomes morbid, and that it may make for injustice by encouraging and permitting undue self-assertion in others. Its value lies in its check upon egoistic impulses, always more powerful than altruistic ones. If the moral enterprise is begun with the complacent assumption that selfish and social impulses are nicely balanced and equally justified, even a minimum equilibrium between them becomes impossible.

The more the moral problem is shifted from the relations of individuals to the relations of groups and collectives, the more the preponderance of the egoistic impulses over the social ones is established. It is therefore revealed that no inner checks are powerful enough to bring them under complete control. Social control must consequently be attempted; and it cannot be established without social conflict. The moral perils attending such a political strategy have been previously considered. They are diametrically opposite to the perils of religious morality. The latter tend to perpetuate injustice by discouraging self-assertion against the inordinate claims of others. The former justify not only self-assertion but the use of non-rational power in reinforcing claims. They may therefore substitute new forms of injustice for old ones and enthrone a new tyranny on the throne of the old. A rational compromise between these two types of restraint easily leads to a premature complacency toward self-assertion. It is therefore better for society to suffer the uneasy harmony between the two types of restraint than to run the danger of inadequate checks upon egoistic impulses. Tolstoi and Lenin both present perils to the life of society; but they are probably no more dangerous than the compromises with human selfishness effected by modern disciples of Aristotle.

If we contemplate the conflict between religious and political morality it may be well to recall that the religious ideal in its purest form has nothing to do with the problem of social justice. It makes disinterestedness an absolute ideal without reference to social consequences. It justifies the ideal in terms of the integrity and beauty of the human spirit. While religion may involve itself in absurdities in the effort to achieve the ideal by purely internal discipline, and while it may run the peril of deleterious social consequences, it does do justice to inner needs of the human spirit. The veneration in which a Tolstoi, a St. Francis, a crucified Christ, and the saints of all the ages have been held, proves that, in the inner sanctuary of their souls, selfish men know that they ought not be selfish, and venerate what they feel they ought to be and cannot be.

Pure religious idealism does not concern itself with the social problem. It does not give itself to the illusion that material and mundane advantages can be gained by the refusal to assert your claims to them. It may believe, as Jesus did, that self-realisation is the inevitable consequence of self-abnegation. But this self-realisation is not attained on the level of physical life or mundane advantages. It is achieved in spiritual terms, such as the martyr's immortality and the Saviour's exaltation in the hearts of his disciples. Jesus did not counsel his disciples to forgive seventy times seven in order that they might convert their enemies or make them more favorably disposed. He counselled it as an effort to approximate complete moral perfection, the perfection of God. He did not ask his followers to go the second mile in the hope that those who had impressed them into service would relent and give them freedom. He did not say that the enemy ought to be loved so that he would cease to be an enemy. He did not dwell upon the social consequences of these moral actions, because he viewed them from an inner and a transcendent perspective.

Nothing is clearer than that a pure religious idealism must issue in a policy of non-resistance which makes no claims to be socially efficacious. It submits to any demands, however unjust, and yields to any claims, however inordinate, rather than assert self-interest against another. "You will meekly bear," declared Epictetus, "for you say on every occasion 'It seemed so to him.'" This type of moral idealism leads either to asceticism, as in the case of Francis and other Catholic saints, or at least to the complete disavowal of any political responsibility, as in the case of Protestant sects practicing consistent non-resistance, as, for instance, the Anabaptists, Mennonites, Dunkers and Doukhobors. The Quakers assumed political responsibilities, but they were never consistent non-resisters. They disavowed violence but not resistance.

While social consequences are not considered in such a moral strategy, it would be shortsighted to deny that it may result in redemptive social consequences, at least within the area of individual and personal relationships. Forgiveness may not always prompt the wrongdoer to repentance, but yet it may. Loving the enemy may not soften the enemy's heart; but there are possibilities that it will. Refusal to assert your own interests against another may not shame him into unselfishness; but on occasion it has done so. Love and benevolence may not lead to complete mutuality; but it does have that tendency, particularly within the area of intimate relationships. Human life would, in fact, be intolerable if justice could be established in all relationships only by self-assertion and counter-assertion, or only by a shrewd calculation of claims and counter-claims. The fact is that love, disinterestedness and benevolence do have a strong social and utilitarian value, and the place they hold in the hierarchy of virtues is really established by that value, though religion may view them finally from an inner or transcendent perspective. "The social virtues," declares David Hume, "are never regarded without their beneficial tendencies nor viewed as barren and unfruitful. The happiness of mankind, the order of society, the harmony of families, the mutual support of friends, are always considered as a result of their gentle dominion over the breasts of men." [4] The utilitarian and social emphasis is a little too absolute in the words of Hume, but it is true within limits. Even the teachings of Jesus reveal a prudential strain in which the wholesome social consequences

---

4 David Hume, *An Enquiry Concerning the Principles of Morals,* Part 2, sec. II.

of generous attitudes are emphasised. "With what measure you mete, it shall be measured to you again." The paradox of the moral life consists in this: that the highest mutuality is achieved where mutual advantages are not consciously sought as the fruit of love. For love is purest where it desires no returns for itself; and it is most potent where it is purest. Complete mutuality, with its advantages to each party to the relationship, is therefore more perfectly realised where it is not intended, but love is poured out without seeking returns. That is how the madness of religious morality, with its trans-social ideal, becomes the wisdom which achieves wholesome social consequences. For the same reason a purely prudential morality must be satisfied with something less than the best.

Where human relations are intimate (and love is fully effective only in intimate and personal relations), the way of love may be the only way to justice. Where rights and interests are closely interwoven, it is impossible to engage in a shrewd and prudent calculation of comparative rights. Where lives are closely intertwined, happiness is destroyed if it is not shared. Justice by assertion and counter-assertion therefore becomes impossible. The friction involved in the process destroys mutual happiness. Justice by a careful calculation of competing rights is equally difficult, if not impossible. Interests and rights are too mutual to allow for their precise definition in individual terms. The very effort to do so is a proof of the destruction of the spirit of mutuality by which alone intimate relations may be adjusted. The spirit of mutuality can be maintained only by a passion which does not estimate the personal advantages which are derived from mutuality too carefully. Love must strive for something purer than justice if it would attain justice. Egoistic impulses are so much more powerful than altruistic ones that if the latter are not given stronger than ordinary support, the justice which even good men design is partial to those who design it.

This social validity of a moral ideal which transcends social considerations in its purest heights, is progressively weakened as it is applied to more and more intricate, indirect and collective human relations. It is not only unthinkable that a group should be able to attain a sufficiently consistent unselfish attitude toward other groups to give it a very potent redemptive power, but it is improbable that any competing group would have the imagination to appreciate the moral calibre of the achievement. Furthermore a high type of unselfishness, even if it brings ultimate rewards, demands immediate sacrifices. An individual may sacrifice his own interests, either without hope of reward or in the hope of an ultimate compensation. But how is an individual, who is responsible for the interests of his group, to justify the sacrifice of interests other than his own? "It follows," declares Hugh Cecil, "that all that department of morality which requires an individual to sacrifice his interests to others, everything which falls under the heading of unselfishness, is inappropriate to the action of a state. No one has a right to be unselfish with other people's interests." [5]

This judgment is not sufficiently qualified. A wise statesman is hardly justified in insisting on the interests of his group when they are obviously in unjust relation to the total interests of the community of mankind. Nor is he wrong in sacrificing immediate advantages for the sake of higher mutual advantages. His unwillingness to do this is precisely what makes nations so imprudent in holding to immediate advantages and losing ultimate values of mutuality. Nevertheless it is obvious that fewer risks can be taken with community interests than with individual interests. The inability to take risks naturally results in a benevolence in which selfish advantages must be quite apparent, and in which therefore the moral and redemptive quality is lost.

---

5 Hugh Cecil, *Conservatism*, p. 182.

Every effort to transfer a pure morality of disinterestedness to group relations has resulted in failure. The Negroes of America have practiced it quite consistently since the Civil War. They did not rise against their masters during the war and remained remarkably loyal to them. Their social attitudes since that time, until a very recent date, have been compounded of genuine religious virtues of forgiveness and forbearance, and a certain social inertia which was derived not from religious virtue but from racial weakness. Yet they did not soften the hearts of their oppressors by their social policy.

During the early triumphs of fascism in Italy the socialist leaders suddenly adopted pacifist principles. One of the socialist papers counselled the workers to meet the terror of fascism with the following strategy: "(1) Create a void around fascism. (2) Do not provoke; suffer any provocation with serenity. (3) To win, be better than your adversary. (4) Do not use the weapons of your enemy. Do not follow in his footsteps. (5) Remember that the blood of guerilla warfare falls upon those who shed it. (6) Remember that in a struggle between brothers those are victors who conquer themselves. (7) Be convinced that it is better to suffer wrong than to commit it. (8) Don't be impatient. Impatience is extremely egoistical; it is instinct; it is yielding to one's ego urge. (9) Do not forget that socialism wins the more when it suffers, because it was born in pain and lives on its hopes. (10) Listen to the mind and to the heart which advises you that the working people should be nearer to sacrifice than to vengeance." [6] A nobler decalogue of virtues could hardly have been prescribed. But the Italian socialists were annihilated by the fascists, their organisations destroyed, and the rights of the workers subordinated to a state which is governed by their enemies. The workers may live "on their hopes," but there is no prospect of realising their hopes under the present regime by practicing the pure moral principles which the socialistic journal advocated. Some of them

---

6 Quoted by Max Nomad, *Rebels and Renegades,* p. 294.

are not incompatible with the use of coercion against their foes. But inasfar as they exclude coercive means they are ineffectual before the brutal will-to-power of fascism.

The effort to apply the doctrines of Tolstoi to the political situation of Russia had a very similar effect. Tolstoi and his disciples felt that the Russian peasants would have the best opportunity for victory over their oppressors if they did not become stained with the guilt of the same violence which the czarist regime used against them. The peasants were to return good for evil, and win their battles by non-resistance. Unlike the policies of Gandhi, the political programme of Tolstoi remained altogether unrealistic. No effort was made to relate the religious ideal of love to the political necessity of coercion. Its total effect was therefore socially and politically deleterious. It helped to destroy a rising protest against political and economic oppression and to confirm the Russian in his pessimistic passivity. The excesses of the terrorists seemed to give point to the Tolstoian opposition to violence and resistance. But the terrorists and the pacifists finally ended in the same futility. And their common futility seemed to justify the pessimism which saw no escape from the traditional injustices of the Russian political and economic system. The real fact was that both sprang from a romantic middle-class or aristocratic idealism, too individualistic in each instance to achieve political effectiveness. The terrorists were diseased idealists, so morbidly oppressed by the guilt of violence resting upon their class, that they imagined it possible to atone for that guilt by deliberately incurring guilt in championing the oppressed. Their ideas were ethical and, to a degree, religious, though they regarded themselves as irreligious. The political effectiveness of their violence was a secondary consideration. The Tolstoian pacifists attempted the solution of the social problem by diametrically opposite policies. But, in common with the terrorists, their attitudes sprang from the conscience of disquieted individuals. Neither of them understood the realities of political life because neither had an appreciation for the significant characteristics of collective behavior. The romantic terrorists failed to relate their isolated acts of terror to any consistent political plan. The pacifists, on the other hand, erroneously attributed political potency to pure non-resistance.

Whenever religious idealism brings forth its purest fruits and places the strongest check upon selfish desire it results in policies which, from the political perspective, are quite impossible. There is, in other words, no possibility of harmonising the two strategists designed to bring the strongest inner and the most effective social restraint upon egoistic impulse. It would therefore seem better to accept a frank dualism in morals than to attempt a harmony between the two methods which threatens the effectiveness of both. Such a dualism would have two aspects. It would make a distinction between the moral judgments applied to the self and to others; and it would distinguish between what we expect of individuals and of groups. The first distinction is obvious and is explicitly or implicitly accepted whenever the moral problem is taken seriously. To disapprove your own selfishness more severely than the egoism of others is a necessary discipline if the natural complacency toward the self and severity in the judgment of others is to be corrected. Such a course is, furthermore, demanded by the logic of the whole moral situation. One can view the actions of others only from an external perspective; and from that perspective the social justification of self-assertion becomes inevitable. Only the actions of the self can be viewed from the internal perspective; and from that viewpoint all egoism must be morally disapproved. If such disapproval should occasionally destroy self-assertion to such a degree as to invite the aggression of others, the instances will be insignificant in comparison with the number of cases in which the moral disapproval of egoism merely tends to reduce the inordinate self-assertion of the average man. Even in those few cases in which egoism is reduced by religious discipline to such proportions that it invites injustice

in an immediate situation, it will have social usefulness in glorifying the moral principles and setting an example for future generations.

The distinction between individual and group morality is a sharper and more perplexing one. The moral obtuseness of human collectives makes a morality of pure disinterestedness impossible. There is not enough imagination in any social group to render it amenable to the influence of pure love. Nor is there a possibility of persuading any social group to make a venture in pure love, except, as in the case of the Russian peasants, the recently liberated Negroes and other similar groups, a morally dubious social inertia should be compounded with the ideal. The selfishness of human communities must be regarded as an inevitability. Where it is inordinate it can be checked only by competing assertions of interest; and these can be effective only if coercive methods are added to moral and rational persuasion. Moral factors may qualify, but they will not eliminate, the resulting social contest and conflict. Moral goodwill may seek to relate the peculiar interests of the group to the ideal of a total and final harmony of all life. It may thereby qualify the self-assertion of the privileged, and support the interests of the disinherited, but it will never be so impartial as to persuade any group to subject its interests completely to an inclusive social ideal. The spirit of love may preserve a certain degree of appreciation for the common weaknesses and common aspirations which bind men together above the areas of social conflict. But again it cannot prevent the conflict. It may avail itself of instruments of restraint and coercion, through which a measure of trust in the moral capacities of an opponent may be expressed and the expansion rather than contraction of those capacities is encouraged. But it cannot hide the moral distrust expressed by the very use of the instruments of coercion. To some degree the conflict between the purest individual morality and an adequate political policy must therefore remain.

The needs of an adequate political strategy do not obviate the necessity of cultivating the strictest individual moral discipline and the most uncompromising idealism. Individuals, even when involved in their communities, will always have the opportunity of loyalty to the highest canons of personal morality. Sometimes, when their group is obviously bent upon evil, they may have to express their individual ideals by disassociating themselves from their group. Such a policy may easily lead to political irresponsibility, as in the case of the more extreme sects of non-resisters. But it may also be socially useful. Religiously inspired pacifists who protest against the violence of their state in the name of a sensitive individual conscience may never lame the will-to-power of a state as much as a class-conscious labor group. But if their numbers grew to large proportions, they might affect the policy of the government. It is possible, too, that their example may encourage similar non-conformity among individuals in the enemy nation and thus mitigate the impact of the conflict without weakening the comparative strength of their own community.

The ideals of a high individual morality are just as necessary when loyalty to the group is maintained and its general course in relation to other groups is approved. There are possibilities for individual unselfishness, even when the group is asserting its interests and rights against other communities. The interests of the individual are related to those of the group, and he may therefore seek advantages for himself when he seeks them for his group. But this indirect egoism is comparatively insignificant beside the possibilities of expressing or disciplining his egoism in relation to his group. If he is a leader in the group, it is necessary to restrain his ambitions. A leadership, free of self-seeking, improves the morale of the whole group. The leaders of disinherited groups, even when they are avowed economic determinists and scorn the language of personal idealism, are frequently actuated by high moral ideals. If they sought their own personal advantage they could gain it more easily by using their abilities to rise from their group to a more privileged one.

The temptation to do this among the abler members of disinherited groups is precisely what has retarded the progress of their class or race.

The progress of the Negro race, for instance, is retarded by the inclination of many able and educated Negroes to strive for identification and assimilation with the more privileged white race and to minimise their relation to a subject race as much as possible. The American Labor Movement has failed to develop its full power for the same reason. Under the influence of American individualism, able labor men have been more ambitious to rise into the class of owners and their agents than to solidify the laboring class in its struggle for freedom. There is, furthermore, always the possibility that an intelligent member of a social group will begin his career in unselfish devotion to the interests of his community, only to be tempted by the personal prizes to be gained, either within the group or by shifting his loyalty to a more privileged group. The interests of individuals are, in other words, never exactly identical with those of their communities. The possibility and necessity of individual moral discipline is therefore never absent, no matter what importance the social struggle between various human communities achieves. Nor can any community achieve unity and harmony within its life, if the sentiments of goodwill and attitudes of mutuality are not cultivated. No political realism which emphasises the inevitability and necessity of a social struggle, can absolve individuals of the obligation to check their own egoism, to comprehend the interests of others and thus to enlarge the areas of co-operation.

Whether the co-operative and moral aspects of human life, or the necessities of the social struggle, gain the largest significance, depends upon time and circumstance. There are periods of social stability, when the general equilibrium of social forces is taken for granted, and men give themselves to the task of making life more beautiful and tender within the limits of the established social system. The Middle Ages were such a period. While they took injustices for granted, such as would affront the conscience of our day, it cannot be denied that they elaborated amenities, urbanities and delicate refinements of life and art which must make our age seem, in comparison, like the recrudescence of barbarism.

Our age is, for good or ill, immersed in the social problem. A technological civilisation makes stability impossible. It changes the circumstances of life too rapidly to incline any one to a reverent acceptance of an ancestral order. Its rapid developments and its almost daily changes in the physical circumstances of life destroy the physical symbols of stability and therefore make for restlessness, even if these movements were not in a direction which imperil the whole human enterprise. But the tendencies of an industrial era are in a definite direction. They tend to aggravate the injustices from which men have perennially suffered; and they tend to unite the whole of humanity in a system of economic interdependence. They make us more conscious of the relations of human communities to each other, than of the relations of individuals within their communities. They obsess us therefore with the brutal aspects of man's collective behavior. They, furthermore, cumulate the evil consequences of these brutalities so rapidly that we feel under a tremendous urgency to solve our social problem before it is too late. As a generation we are therefore bound to feel harassed as well as disillusioned.

In such a situation all the highest ideals and tenderest emotions which men have felt all through the ages, when they became fully conscious of their heritage and possible destiny as human beings, will seem from our perspective to be something of a luxury. They will be under a moral disadvantage, because they appear as a luxury which only those are able to indulge who are comfortable enough to be comparatively oblivious to the desperate character of our contemporary social situation. We live in an age in which personal moral idealism is easily accused of hypocrisy and frequently deserves it. It is an age in which honesty is possible only when it skirts the edges of cynicism. All this is rather tragic. For what the individual conscience feels when it lifts itself above the world of nature and the system of collective relationships in which the human spirit remains under the power of nature, is not a luxury but a necessity of the soul. Yet there is beauty in our tragedy. We are, at least, rid of some of our illusions. We can no longer buy the highest satisfactions of the individual life at the expense of social injustice. We cannot build our individual ladders to heaven and leave the total human enterprise unredeemed of its excesses and corruptions.

In the task of that redemption the most effective agents will be men who have substituted some new illusions for the abandoned ones. The most important of these illusions is that the collective life of mankind can achieve perfect justice. It is a very valuable illusion for the moment, for justice cannot be approximated if the hope of its perfect realization does not generate a sublime madness in the soul. Nothing but such madness will do battle with malignant power and "spiritual wickedness in high places." The illusion is dangerous because it encourages terrible fanaticisms. It must therefore be brought under the control of reason. One can only hope that reason will not destroy it before its work is done.

Other books by Niebuhr:

Discerning the Signs of the Times, 1946.
Faith and History, 1949.
An Interpretation of Christian Ethics, 1935.
The Irony of American History, 1952.
Leaves From the Notebook of a Tamed Cynic, 1929.
The Nature and Destiny of Man, 1941-43.
Reflections at the End of an Era, 1934.
The Self and the Dramas of History, 1955.

Other books on the same problem:

Bonhoeffer, Dietrich. *Ethics,* 1949 (Engl. trans. 1955).
Bennet, John C. *Christian Ethics and Social Policy,* 1946.
Bennet, John C. *Christian Faith and Social Action,* 1953.
Bennet, John C. *Christians and the State,* 1958.
Brunner, Emil. *Justice and the Social Order,* 1945.
Butterfield, Herbert. *History and Human Relations,* 1931.
Tillich, Paul. *Love, Power and Justice,* 1954.
Von Hildebrand, Dietrich. *True Morality and Its Counterfeits,* 1955.

PAUL TILLICH

PAUL TILLICH is considered by many to be *the* theologian of modern Protestantism. Not only because of the systematic character of his thought but even more because of the all-embracing synthesis which he undertakes, he has been called a Protestant Thomas Aquinas. Like the latter he encompasses the entire history of Christian thought and especially the multiple conflicting currents of Protestant thought. And like Thomas he seeks to reconcile not only conflicting claims within the theological traditions but also those in the wider sphere of general culture and, above all, the modern conflicts between the claims of faith and those of culture. This latter goal, the synthesis of culture and faith, is perhaps the central consuming passion of Tillich's intellectual life and that which accounts for the great tension, excitement and widespread appeal of his thought. In his famous formula, "Religion is the substance of culture; culture is the form (expression) of religion", the inseparability and essential unity of these two spheres is expressed. The forms and styles of a given culture reveal the character and depth of its religious life. Or, conversely, the substance of an individual's or group's faith is embodied in their cultural products.

The absorbing desire to achieve for our age a synthesis of culture and faith has driven Tillich to a careful and sympathetic examination of almost every realm of modern culture—psychology and medicine, sociology and anthropology, literature and art, history, philosophy and philology. The seriousness with which he considers the findings of modern intellectual life and his refusal to compromise their validity for the sake of religious presuppositions results in an intellectual integrity and honesty that has not always characterized theologians.

Tillich is a philosophical rather than Biblical, dogmatic or historical theologian. This implies that his thinking is ontologically rooted in the rational structure of being itself. For him the forms and content of experience as well as the act of experiencing are never *merely* psychological, sociological or historical phenomena but are always grounded in structures of being which give them status, validity, and their fundamental reality. The aim of ontology is to articulate the rational order of being (the ontic-structure) in which experience is grounded. Therefore, for Tillich, anxiety, courage, alienation, love and similar forms of experience with which he deals in the following selections are not subjective states, emotions or "values" to be explained by psychological categories or theories of value. They are metaphysical categories to be fully understood only in their relationship to the structure of being in which they are grounded and which they themselves reveal. Part of his work is, therefore, to reveal the underlying structure within which the various complexities of experience operate and in the light of which they can be more fully comprehended. This is the work of existential and ontological analysis of existence.

Tillich's theology is phenomenological in that he maintains that divine revelation is always revelation *to* an individual or group. The form in which it is received and expressed or formulated is subject to the mode of consciousness of those who receive it. The original symbols, images, stories, etc., in which the revelatory experience is communicated are already interpretations of the experience and, like all interpretations, subject to the limitations of history and of the "intentionality" of consciousness underlying all communication. No interpretation, therefore, has ultimate authority. The original forms in which the Christian revelation was received and articulated are not a body of transcendental knowledge, not statements about the divine life, but symbols which have the power to point to, open a way to, become the occasion for further encounters between man and God. But every age must re-interpret these symbols for itself in the light of its own experience. This is the work of theological "correlation".

This last term is that used by Tillich to describe his method, the method followed in the two selections included here. The first stage is that of existential analysis, that is, the philosophical examination and reformulation of the urgent questions about our existence by our generation in all areas of our cultural life. Such analysis clarifies the "structure" of the situation and indicates the direction of the question. (In his existential analysis of contemporary life and the predicament of modern man Tillich has rendered invaluable aid to our self-understanding through the clarity of his definitions and the lucidity of the framework within which the problems are articulated.)

The second stage consists in formulating the answers implied in the Biblical revelation in the light of the questions raised in stage one. That is, the existential analysis of stage one provides the frame of reference, the conditions, the means whereby the substance of the revelation can be interpreted and "speak" meaningfully in response to the questioner.

In the first of the following excerpts the question raised out of our present existential situation is the general question of anxiety and the specifically contemporary question of meaninglessness and despair. How can one overcome the self-destructive power of despair over the meaninglessness of existence? This situation is subjected to ontological analysis whereby the essential structures of anxiety and meaning are revealed so as to point the direction of the question and the mode of the answer. The Protestant answer to the question—by faith and faith alone—is here answered neither dogmatically nor Biblically but in terms provided by the question itself and in the mode of questioning: Courage to accept acceptance in spite of the anxiety of meaninglessness and doubt. The acceptance of meaninglessness is in itself a meaningful act which places one in a position to become "aware of a hidden meaning within the destruction of meaning".

In the second excerpt the question emerges from the confusion we encounter individually and in groups (ethnic, economic or political) when we are faced by conflicting claims of love, power and justice. In this study Tillich again subjects each of these terms to a lucid structural analysis in the light of which the reuniting, healing power of love as *agapê* is the Christian answer to the existential dilemma.

Since the essence of the Christian revelation is that God is love, and grace the healing, reuniting power of love, it is fitting that this anthology conclude with an attempt to rescue this word from its degraded and almost useless condition and to return to it its ontological status where it can operate effectively as the powerful symbol it is.

PAUL TILLICH

from

The Courage to Be

Chapter 2. Being, Nonbeing, and Anxiety

An Ontology of Anxiety

THE MEANING OF NONBEING

COURAGE IS SELF-AFFIRMATION "in-spite-of," that is in spite of that which tends to prevent the self from affirming itself. Differing from the Stoic–Neo-Stoic doctrines of courage, the "philosophies of life" have seriously and affirmatively dealt with that against which courage stands. For if being is interpreted in terms of life or process or becoming, nonbeing is ontologically as basic as being. The acknowledgment of this fact does not imply a decision about the priority of being over nonbeing, but it requires a consideration of nonbeing in the very foundation of ontology. Speaking of courage as a key to the interpretation of being-itself, one could say that this key, when it opens the door to being, finds, at the same time, being and the negation of being and their unity.

Nonbeing is one of the most difficult and most discussed concepts. Parmenides tried to remove it as a concept. But in order to do so he had to sacrifice life. Democritus re-established it and identified it with empty space, in order to make movement thinkable. Plato used the concept of nonbeing because without it the contrast of existence with the pure essences is beyond understanding. It is implied in Aristotle's distinction between matter and form. It gave Plotinus the means of describing the loss of self of the human soul, and it gave Augustine the means for an ontological interpretation of human sin. For Pseudo-Dionysius the Areopagite nonbeing became the principle of his mystical doctrine of God. Jacob Boehme, the Protestant mystic and philosopher of life, made the classical statement that all things are rooted in a Yes and a No. In Leibnitz' doctrine of finitude and evil as well as in Kant's analysis of the finitude of categorical forms nonbeing is implied. Hegel's dialectic makes negation the dynamic power in nature and history; and the philosophers of life, since Schelling and Schopenhauer, use "will" as the basic ontological category because it has the power of negating itself without losing itself. The concepts of process and becoming in philosophers like Bergson and Whitehead imply nonbeing as well as being. Recent Existentialists, especially Heidegger and Sartre, have put nonbeing *(Das Nichts, le néant)* in the center of their ontological thought; and Berdyaev, a follower of both Dionysius and Boehme, has developed an ontology of nonbeing which accounts for the "me-ontic" freedom in God and man. These philosophical ways of using the concept of nonbeing can be viewed against the background of the religious experience of the transitoriness of everything created and the power of the "demonic" in the human soul and history. In biblical religion these negativities have a decisive place in spite of the doctrine of creation. And the demonic, anti-divine principle, which nevertheless participates in the power of the divine, appears in the dramatic centers of the biblical story.

In view of this situation it is of little significance that some logicians deny that nonbeing has conceptual character and try to remove it from the philosophical scene except in the form of negative judgments. For the question is: What does the fact of negative judgments tell about the character of being? What is the ontological condition of negative judgments? How is the realm constituted in which negative judgments are possible? Certainly nonbeing is not a concept like others. It is the negation of every concept; but as such it is an inescapable content of thought and, as the history of thought has shown, the most important one after being-itself.

If one is asked how nonbeing is related to being-itself, one can only answer metaphorically: being "embraces" itself and nonbeing. Being has nonbeing "within" itself as that which is eternally present and eternally overcome in the process of the divine life. The ground of everything that is is not a dead identity without movement and becoming; it is living creativity. Creatively it affirms itself, eternally conquering its own nonbeing. As such it is the pattern of the self-affirmation of every finite being and the source of the courage to be.

Courage is usually described as the power of the mind to overcome fear. The meaning of fear seemed too obvious to deserve inquiry. But in the last decades depth psychology in cooperation with Existentialist philosophy has led to a sharp distinction between fear and anxiety and to more precise definitions of each of these concepts. Sociological analyses of the present period have pointed to the importance of anxiety as a group phenomenon. Literature and art have made anxiety a main theme of their creations, in content as well as in style. The effect of this has been the awakening of at least the educated groups to an awareness of their own anxiety, and a permeation of the public consciousness by ideas and symbols of anxiety. Today it has become almost a truism to call our time an "age of anxiety." This holds equally for America and Europe.

Nevertheless it is necessary for an ontology of courage to include an ontology of anxiety, for they are interdependent. And it is conceivable that in the light of an ontology of courage some fundamental aspects of anxiety may become visible. The first assertion about the nature of anxiety is this: anxiety is the state in which a being is aware of its possible nonbeing. The same statement, in a shorter form, would read: anxiety is the existential awareness of nonbeing. "Existential" in this sentence means that it is not the abstract knowledge of nonbeing which produces anxiety but the awareness that nonbeing is a part of one's own being. It is not the realization of universal transitoriness, not even the experience of the death of others, but the impression of these events on the always latent awareness of our own having to die that produces anxiety. Anxiety is finitude, experienced as one's own finitude. This is the natural anxiety of man as man, and in some way of all living beings. It is the anxiety of nonbeing, the awareness of one's finitude as finitude.

THE INTERDEPENDENCE OF FEAR AND ANXIETY

Anxiety and fear have the same ontological root but they are not the same in actuality. This is common knowledge, but it has been emphasized and overemphasized to such a degree that a reaction against it may occur and wipe out not only the exaggerations but also the truth of the distinction. Fear, as opposed to anxiety has a definite object (as most authors agree), which can be faced, analyzed, attacked, endured. One can act upon it, and in acting upon it participate in it—even if in the form of struggle. In this way one can take it into one's self-affirmation. Courage can meet every object of fear, because it is an object and makes participation possible. Courage can take the fear produced by a definite object into itself, because this object, however frightful it may be, has a side with which it participates in us and we in it. One could say that as long as there is an *object* of fear love in the sense of participation can conquer fear.

But this is not so with anxiety, because anxiety has no object, or rather, in a paradoxical phrase, its object is the negation of every object. Therefore participation, struggle, and love with respect to it are impossible. He who is in anxiety is, insofar as it is mere anxiety, delivered to it without help. Helplessness in the state of anxiety can be observed in animals and humans alike. It expresses itself in loss of direction, inadequate reactions, lack of "intentionality" (the being related to meaningful contents of knowledge or will). The reason for this sometimes striking behavior is the lack of an object on which the subject (in the state of anxiety) can concentrate. The only object is the threat itself, but not the source of the threat, because the source of the threat is "nothingness."

One might ask whether this threatening "nothing" is not the unknown, the indefinite possibility of an actual threat? Does not anxiety cease in the moment in which a known object of fear appears? Anxiety then would be fear of the unknown. But this is an insufficient explanation of anxiety. For there are innumerable realms of the unknown, different for each subject, and faced without any anxiety. It is the unknown of a special type which is met with anxiety. It is the unknown which by its very nature cannot be known, because it is nonbeing.

Fear and anxiety are distinguished but not separated. They are immanent within each other. The sting of fear is anxiety, and anxiety strives toward fear. Fear is being afraid of something, a pain, the rejection by a person or a group, the loss of something or somebody, the moment of dying. But in the anticipation of the threat originating in these things, it is not the negativity itself which they will bring upon the subject that is frightening but the anxiety about the possible implications of this negativity. The outstanding example—and more than an example—is the fear of dying. Insofar as it is *fear* its object is the anticipated event of being killed by sickness or an accident and thereby suffering agony and the loss of everything. Insofar as it is *anxiety* its object is the absolutely unknown "after death," the nonbeing which remains nonbeing even if it is filled with images of our present experience. The dreams in Hamlet's soliloquy, "to be or not to be," which we may have after death and which make cowards of us all are frightful not because of their manifest content but because of their power to symbolize the threat of nothingness, in religious terms of "eternal death." The symbols of hell created by Dante produce anxiety not because of their objective imagery but because they express the "nothingness" whose power is experienced in the anxiety of guilt. Each of the situations described in the *Inferno* could be met by courage on the basis of participation and love. But of course the meaning is that this is impossible; in other words they are not real situations but symbols of the objectless, of nonbeing.

The fear of death determines the element of anxiety in every fear. Anxiety, if not modified by the fear of an object, anxiety in its nakedness, is always the anxiety of ultimate nonbeing. Immediately seen, anxiety is the painful feeling of not being able to deal with the threat of a special situation. But a more exact analysis shows that in the anxiety about any special situation anxiety about the human situation as such is implied. It is the anxiety of not being able to preserve one's own being which underlies every fear and is the frightening element in it. In the moment, therefore, in which "naked anxiety" lays hold of the mind, the previous objects of fear cease to be definite objects. They appear as what they always were in part, symptoms of man's basic anxiety. As such they are beyond the reach of even the most courageous attack upon them.

This situation drives the anxious subject to establish objects of fear. Anxiety strives to become fear, because fear can be met by courage. It is impossible for a finite being to stand naked anxiety for more than a flash of time. People who have experienced these moments, as for instance some mystics in their visions of the "night of the soul," or Luther under the despair of the demonic assaults, or Nietzsche-Zarathustra in the experience of the "great disgust," have told of the unimaginable horror of it. This horror is ordinarily avoided by the transformation of the anxiety into fear of something, no matter what. The human mind is not only, as Calvin has said, a permanent factory of idols, it is also a permanent factory of fears—the first in order to escape God, the second in order to escape anxiety; and there is a relation between the two. For facing the God who is really God means facing also the absolute threat of nonbeing. The "naked absolute" (to use a phrase of Luther's) produces "naked anxiety"; for it is the extinction of every finite self-affirmation, and not a possible object of fear and courage. But ultimately the attempts to transform anxiety into fear are vain. The basic anxiety, the anxiety of a finite being about the threat of nonbeing, cannot be eliminated. It belongs to existence itself.

Types of Anxiety

THE THREE TYPES OF ANXIETY AND THE NATURE OF MAN

Nonbeing is dependent on the being it negates. "Dependent" means two things. It points first of all to the ontological priority of being over nonbeing. The term nonbeing itself indicates this, and it is logically necessary. There could be no negation if there were no preceding affirmation to be negated. Certainly one can describe being in terms of non-nonbeing; and one can justify such a description by pointing to the astonishing prerational fact that there is something and not nothing. One could say that "being is the negation of the primordial night of nothingness." But in doing so one must realize that such an aboriginal nothing would be neither nothing nor something, that it becomes nothing only in contrast to something; in other words, that the ontological status of nonbeing as nonbeing is dependent on being. Secondly, nonbeing is dependent on the special qualities of being. In itself nonbeing has no quality and no difference of qualities. But it gets them in relation to being. The character of the negation of being is determined by that in being which is negated. This makes it possible to speak of qualities of nonbeing and, consequently, of types of anxiety.

Up to now we have used the term nonbeing without differentiation, while in the discussion of courage several forms of self-affirmation were mentioned. They correspond to different forms of anxiety and are understandable only in correlation with them. I suggest that we distinguish three types of anxiety according to the three directions in which nonbeing threatens being. Nonbeing threatens man's ontic self-affirmation, relatively in terms of fate, absolutely in terms of death. It threatens man's spiritual self-affirmation, relatively in terms of emptiness, absolutely in terms of meaninglessness. It threatens man's moral self-affirmation, relatively in terms of guilt, absolutely in terms of condemnation. The awareness of this threefold threat is anxiety appearing in three forms, that of fate and death (briefly, the anxiety of death), that of emptiness and loss of meaning (briefly, the anxiety of meaninglessness), that of guilt and condemnation (briefly, the anxiety of condemnation). In all three forms anxiety is existential in the sense that it belongs to existence as such and not to an abnormal state of mind as in neurotic (and psychotic) anxiety. The nature of neurotic anxiety and its relation to existential anxiety will be discussed in another chapter. We shall deal now with the three forms of existential anxiety, first with their reality in the life of the individual, then with their social manifestations in special periods of Western history. However, it must be stated that the difference of types does not mean mutual exclusion. In the first chapter we have seen for instance that the courage to be as it appears in the ancient Stoics conquers not only the fear of death but also the threat of meaninglessness. In Nietzsche we find that in spite of the predominance of the threat of meaninglessness, the anxiety of death and condemnation is passionately challenged. In all representatives of classical Christianity death and sin are seen as the allied adversaries against which the courage of faith has to fight. The three forms of anxiety (and of courage) are immanent in each other but normally under the dominance of one of them.

THE ANXIETY OF FATE AND DEATH

Fate and death are the way in which our ontic self-affirmation is threatened by nonbeing. "Ontic," from the Greek *on,* "being," means here the basic self-affirmation of a being in its simple existence. (Onto-logical designates the philosophical analysis of the nature of being.) The anxiety of fate and death is most basic, most universal, and inescapable. All attempts to argue it away are futile. Even if the so-called arguments for the "immortality of the soul" had argumentative power (which they do not have) they would not convince existentially. For existentially everybody is aware of the complete loss of self which biological extinction implies. The unsophisticated mind knows instinctively what sophisticated ontology formulates: that reality has the basic structure of self-world correlation and that with the disappearance of the one side the world, the other side, the self, also disappears, and what remains is their common ground but not their structural correlation. It has been observed that the anxiety of death increases with the increase of individualization and that people in collectivistic cultures are less open to this type of anxiety. The observation is correct yet the explanation that there is no basic anxiety about death in collectivist cultures is wrong. The reason for the difference from more individualized civilizations is that the special type of courage which characterizes collectivism, as long as it is unshaken, allays the anxiety of death. But the very fact that courage has to be created through many internal and external (psychological and ritual) activities and symbols shows that basic anxiety has to be overcome even in collectivism. Without its at least potential presence neither war nor the criminal law in these societies would be understandable. If there were no fear of death, the threat of the law or of a superior enemy would be without effect—which it obviously is not. Man as man in every civilization is anxiously aware of the threat of nonbeing and needs the courage to affirm himself in spite of it.

The anxiety of death is the permanent horizon within which the anxiety of fate is at work. For the threat against man's ontic self-affirmation is not only the absolute threat of death but also the relative threat of fate. Certainly the anxiety of death overshadows all concrete anxieties and gives them their ultimate seriousness. They have, however, a certain independence and, ordinarily, a more immediate impact than the anxiety of death. The term "fate" for this whole group of anxieties stresses one element which is common to all of them: their contingent character, their unpredictability, the impossibility of showing their meaning and purpose. One can describe this in terms of the categorical structure of our experience. One can show the contingency of our temporal being, the fact that we exist in this and no other period of time, beginning in a contingent moment, ending in a contingent moment, filled with experiences which are contingent themselves with respect to quality and quantity. One can show the contingency of our spatial being (our finding ourselves in this and no other place, and the strangeness of this place in spite of its familiarity); the contingent character of ourselves and the place from which we look at our world; and the contingent character of the reality at which we look, that is, our world. Both could be different: this is their contingency and this produces the anxiety about our spatial existence. One can show the contingency of the causal interdependence of which one is a part, both with respect to the past and to the present, the vicissitudes coming from our world and the hidden forces in the depths of our own self. Contingent does not mean causally undetermined but it means that the determining causes of our existence have no ultimate necessity. They are given, and they cannot be logically derived. Contingently we are put into the whole web of causal relations. Contingently we are determined by them in every moment and thrown out by them in the last moment.

Fate is the rule of contingency, and the anxiety about fate is based on the finite being's awareness of being contingent in every respect, of having no ultimate necessity. Fate is usually identified with necessity in the sense of an inescapable causal determination. Yet it is not causal necessity that makes fate a matter of anxiety but the lack of ultimate necessity, the irrationality, the impenetrable darkness of fate.

The threat of nonbeing to man's ontic self-affirmation is absolute in the threat of death, relative in the threat of fate. But the relative threat is a threat only because in its background stands the absolute threat. Fate would not produce inescapable anxiety without death behind it. And death stands behind fate and its contingencies not only in the last moment when one is thrown out of existence but in every moment within existence. Nonbeing is omnipresent and produces anxiety even where an immediate threat of death is absent. It stands behind the experience that we are driven, together with everything else, from the past toward the future without a moment of time which does not vanish immediately. It stands behind the insecurity and homelessness of our social and individual existence. It stands behind the attacks on our power of being in body and soul by weakness, disease, and accidents. In all these forms fate actualizes itself, and through them the anxiety of nonbeing takes hold of us. We try to transform the anxiety into fear and to meet courageously the objects in which the threat is embodied. We succeed partly, but somehow we are aware of the fact that it is not these objects with which we struggle that produce the anxiety but the human situation as such. Out of this the question arises: Is there a courage to be, a courage to affirm oneself in spite of the threat against man's ontic self-affirmation?

THE ANXIETY OF EMPTINESS AND MEANINGLESSNESS

Nonbeing threatens man as a whole, and therefore threatens his spiritual as well as his ontic self-affirmation. Spiritual self-affirmation occurs in every moment in which man lives creatively in the various spheres of meaning. Creative, in this context, has the sense not of original creativity as performed by the genius but of living spontaneously, in action and reaction, with the contents of one's cultural life. In order to be spiritually creative one need not be what is called a creative artist or scientist or statesman, but one must be able to participate meaningfully in their original creations. Such a participation is creative insofar as it changes that in which one participates, even if in very small ways. The creative transformation of a language by the interdependence of the creative poet or writer and the many who are influenced by him directly or indirectly and react spontaneously to him is an outstanding example. Everyone who lives creatively in meanings affirms himself as a participant in these meanings. He affirms himself as receiving and transforming reality creatively. He loves himself as participating in the spiritual life and as loving its contents. He loves them because they are his own fulfillment and because they are actualized through him. The scientist loves both the truth he discovers and himself insofar as he discovers it. He is held by the content of his discovery. This is what one can call "spiritual self-affirmation." And if he has not discovered but only participates in the discovery, it is equally spiritual self-affirmation.

Such an experience presupposes that the spiritual life is taken seriously, that it is a matter of ultimate concern. And this again presupposes that in it and through it ultimate reality becomes manifest. A spiritual life in which this is not experienced is threatened by nonbeing in the two forms in which it attacks self-affirmation: emptiness and meaninglessness.

We use the term meaninglessness for the absolute threat of nonbeing to spiritual self-affirmation, and the term emptiness for the relative threat to it. They are no more identical than are the threat of death and fate. But in the background of emptiness lies meaninglessness as death lies in the background of the vicissitudes of fates.

The anxiety of meaninglessness is anxiety about the loss of an ultimate concern, of a meaning which gives meaning to all meanings. This anxiety is aroused by the loss of a spiritual center, of an answer, however symbolic and indirect, to the question of the meaning of existence.

The anxiety of emptiness is aroused by the threat of nonbeing to the special contents of the spiritual life. A belief breaks down through external events or inner processes: one is cut off from creative participation in a sphere of culture, one feels frustrated about something which one had passionately affirmed, one is driven from devotion to one object to devotion to another and again on to another, because the meaning of each of them vanishes and the creative eros is transformed into indifference or aversion. Everything is tried and nothing satisfies. The contents of the tradition, however excellent, however praised, however loved once, lose their power to give content *today*. And present culture is even less able to provide the content. Anxiously one turns away from all concrete contents and looks for an ultimate meaning, only to discover that it was precisely the loss of a spiritual center which took away the meaning from the special contents of the spiritual life. But a spiritual center cannot be produced intentionally, and the attempt to produce it only produces deeper anxiety. The anxiety of emptiness drives us to the abyss of meaninglessness.

Emptiness and loss of meaning are expressions of the threat of nonbeing to the spiritual life. This threat is implied in man's finitude and actualized by man's estrangement. It can be described in terms of doubt, its creative and its destructive function in man's spiritual life. Man is able to ask because he is separated *from,* while participating *in,* what he is asking about. In every question an element of doubt, the awareness of not having, is implied. In systematic questioning systematic doubt is effective; e.g. of the Cartesian type. This element of doubt is a condition of all spiritual life. The threat to spiritual life is not doubt as an element but the total doubt. If the awareness of not having has swallowed the awareness of having, doubt has ceased to be methodological asking and has become existential despair. On the way to this situation the spiritual life tries to maintain itself as long as possible by clinging to affirmations which are not yet undercut, be they traditions, autonomous convictions, or emotional preferences. And if it is impossible to remove the doubt, one courageously accepts it without surrendering one's convictions. One takes the risk of going astray and the anxiety of this risk upon oneself. In this way one avoids the extreme situation—till it becomes unavoidable and the despair of truth becomes complete.

Then man tries another way out: Doubt is based on man's separation from the whole of reality, on his lack of universal participation, on the isolation of his individual self. So he tries to break out of this situation, to identify himself with something transindividual, to surrender his separation and self-relatedness. He flees from his freedom of asking and answering for himself to a situation in which no further questions can be asked and the answers to previous questions are imposed on him authoritatively. In order to avoid the risk of asking and doubting he surrenders the right to ask and to doubt. He surrenders himself in order to save his spiritual life. He "escapes from his freedom" (Fromm) in order to escape the anxiety of meaninglessness. Now he is no longer lonely, not in existential doubt, not in despair. He "participates" and affirms by participation the contents of his spiritual life. Meaning is saved, but the self is sacrificed. And since the conquest of doubt was a matter of sacrifice, the sacrifice of the freedom of the self, it leaves a mark on the regained certitude: a fanatical self-assertiveness.

Fanaticism is the correlate to spiritual self-surrender: it shows the anxiety which it was supposed to conquer, by attacking with disproportionate violence those who disagree and who demonstrate by their disagreement elements in the spiritual life of the fanatic which he must suppress in himself. Because he must suppress them in himself he must suppress them in others. His anxiety forces him to persecute dissenters. The weakness of the fanatic is that those whom he fights have a secret hold upon him; and to this weakness he and his group finally succumb.

It is not always personal doubt that undermines and empties a system of ideas and values. It can be the fact that they are no longer understood in their original power of expressing the human situation and of answering existential human questions. (This is largely the case with the doctrinal symbols of Christianity.) Or they lose their meaning because the actual conditions of the present period are so different from those in which the spiritual contents were created that new creations are needed. (This was largely the case with artistic expression before the industrial revolution.) In such circumstances a slow process of waste of the spiritual contents occurs, unnoticeable in the beginning, realized with a shock as it progresses, producing the anxiety of meaninglessness at its end.

Ontic and spiritual self-affirmation must be distinguished but they cannot be separated. Man's being includes his relation to meanings. He is human only by understanding and shaping reality, both his world and himself, according to meanings and values. His being is spiritual even in the most primitive expressions of the most primitive human being. In the "first" meaningful sentence all the richness of man's spiritual life is potentially present. Therefore the threat to his spiritual being is a threat to his whole being. The most revealing expression of this fact is the desire to throw away one's ontic existence rather than stand the despair of emptiness and meaninglessness. The death instinct is not an ontic but a spiritual phenomenon. Freud identified this reaction to the meaninglessness of the never-ceasing and never-satisfied libido with man's essential nature. But it is only an expression of his existential self-estrangement and of the disintegration of his spiritual life into meaninglessness. If, on the other hand, the ontic self-affirmation is weakened by nonbeing, spiritual indifference and emptiness can be the consequence, producing a circle of ontic and spiritual negativity. Nonbeing threatens from both sides, the ontic and the spiritual; if it threatens the one side it also threatens the other.

THE ANXIETY OF GUILT AND CONDEMNATION

Nonbeing threatens from a third side; it threatens man's moral self-affirmation. Man's being, ontic as well as spiritual, is not only given to him but also demanded of him. He is responsible for it; literally, he is required to answer, if he is asked, what he has made of himself. He who asks him is his judge, namely he himself, who, at the same time, stands against him. This situation produces the anxiety which, in relative terms, is the anxiety of guilt; in absolute terms, the anxiety of self-rejection or condemnation. Man is essentially "finite freedom"; freedom not in the sense of indeterminacy but in the sense of being able to determine himself through decisions in the center of his being. Man, as finite freedom, is free within the contingencies of his finitude. But within these limits he is asked to make of himself what he is supposed to become, to fulfill his destiny. In every act of moral self-affirmation man contributes to the fulfillment of his destiny, to the actualization of what he potentially is. It is the task of ethics to describe the nature of this fulfillment, in philosophical or theological terms. But however the norm is formulated man has the power of acting against it, of contradicting his essential being, of losing his destiny. And under the conditions of man's estrangement from himself this is an actuality. Even in what he considers his best deed nonbeing is present and prevents it from being perfect. A profound ambiguity between good and evil permeates everything he does, because it permeates his personal being as such. Nonbeing is mixed with being in his moral self-affirmation as it is in his spiritual and ontic self-affirmation. The awareness of this ambiguity is the feeling of guilt. The judge who is oneself and who stands against oneself, he who "knows with" (conscience) everything we do and are, gives a negative judgment, experienced by us as guilt. The anxiety of guilt shows the same complex characteristics as the anxiety about ontic and spiritual nonbeing. It is present in every moment of moral self-awareness and can drive us toward complete self-rejection, to the feeling of being condemned—not to an external punishment but to the despair of having lost our destiny.

To avoid this extreme situation man tries to transform the anxiety of guilt into moral action regardless of its imperfection and ambiguity. Courageously he takes nonbeing into his moral self-affirmation. This can happen in two ways, according to the duality of the tragic and the personal in man's situation, the first based on the contingencies of fate, the second on the responsibility of freedom. The first way can lead to a defiance of negative judgments and the moral demands on which they are based; the second way can lead to a moral rigor and the self-satisfaction derived from it. In both of them—usually called anomism and legalism—the anxiety of guilt lies in the background and breaks again and again into the open, producing the extreme situation of moral despair.

Nonbeing in a moral respect must be distinguished but cannot be separated from ontic and spiritual nonbeing. The anxiety of the one type is immanent in the anxieties of the other types. The famous words of Paul about "sin as the sting of death" point to the immanence of the anxiety of guilt within the fear of death. And the threat of fate and death has always awakened and increased the consciousness of guilt. The threat of moral nonbeing was experienced in and through the threat of ontic nonbeing. The contingencies of fate received moral interpretation: fate executes the negative moral judgment by attacking and perhaps destroying the ontic foundation of the morally rejected personality. The two forms of anxiety provoke and augment each other. In the same way spiritual and moral nonbeing are interdependent. Obedience to the moral norm, i.e. to one's own essential being, excludes emptiness and meaninglessness in their radical forms. If the spiritual contents have lost their power the self-affirmation of the moral personality is a way in which meaning can be rediscovered. The simple call to duty can save from emptiness, while the disintegration of the moral consciousness is an almost irresistible basis for the attack of spiritual nonbeing. On the other hand, existential doubt can undermine moral self-affirmation by throwing into the abyss of skepticism not only every moral principle but the meaning of moral self-affirmation as such. In this case the doubt is felt as guilt, while at the same time guilt is undermined by doubt.

THE MEANING OF DESPAIR

The three types of anxiety are interwoven in such a way that one of them gives the predominant color but all of them participate in the coloring of the state of anxiety. All of them and their underlying unity are existential, i.e. they are implied in the existence of man as man, his finitude, and his estrangement. They are fulfilled in the situation of despair to which all of them contribute. Despair is an ultimate or "boundary-line" situation. One cannot go beyond it. Its nature is indicated in the etymology of the word despair: without hope. No way out into the future appears. Nonbeing is felt as absolutely victorious. But there is a limit to its victory; nonbeing is *felt* as victorious, and feeling presupposes being. Enough being is left to feel the irresistible power of nonbeing, and this is the despair within the despair. The pain of despair is that a being is aware of itself as unable to affirm itself because of the power of nonbeing. Consequently it wants to surrender this awareness and its presupposition, the being which is aware. It wants to get rid of itself—and it cannot. Despair appears in the form of reduplication, as the desperate attempt to escape despair. If anxiety were only the anxiety of fate and death, voluntary death would be the way out of despair. The courage demanded would be the courage *not* to be. The final form of ontic self-affirmation would be the act of ontic self-negation.

But despair is also the despair about guilt and condemnation. And there is no way of escaping it, even by ontic self-negation. Suicide can liberate one from the anxiety of fate and death—as the Stoics knew. But it cannot liberate from the anxiety of guilt and condemnation, as the Christians know. This is a highly paradoxical statement, as paradoxical as the relation of the moral sphere to ontic existence generally. But it is a true statement, verified by those who have experienced fully the despair of condemnation. It is impossible to express the inescapable character of condemnation in ontic terms, that is in terms of imaginings about the "immortality of the soul." For every ontic statement must use the categories of finitude, and "immortality of the soul" would be the endless prolongation of finitude and of the despair of condemnation (a self-contradictory concept, for "finis" means "end"). The experience, therefore, that suicide is no way of escaping guilt must be understood in terms of the qualitative character of the moral demand, and of the qualitative character of its rejection. Guilt and condemnation are qualitatively, not quantitatively, infinite. They have an infinite weight and cannot be removed by a finite act of ontic self-negation. This makes despair desperate, that is, inescapable. There is "No Exit" from it (Sartre). The anxiety of emptiness and meaninglessness participates in both the ontic and the moral element in despair. Insofar as it is an expression of finitude it can be removed by ontic self-negation: This drives radical skepticism to suicide. Insofar as it is a consequence of moral disintegration it produces the same paradox as the moral element in despair: there is no ontic exit from it. This frustrates the suicidal trends in emptiness and meaninglessness. One is aware of their futility.

In view of this character of despair it is understandable that all human life can be interpreted as a continuous attempt to avoid despair. And this attempt is mostly successful. Extreme situations are not reached frequently and perhaps they are never reached by some people. The purpose of an analysis of such a situation is not to record ordinary human experiences but to show extreme possibilities in the light of which the ordinary situations must be understood. We are not always aware of our having to die, but in the light of the experience of our having to die our whole life is experienced differently. In the same way the anxiety which is despair is not always present. But the rare occasions in which it is present determine the interpretation of existence as a whole.

Periods of Anxiety

The distinction of the three types of anxiety is supported by the history of Western civilization. We find that at the end of ancient civilization ontic anxiety is predominant, at the end of the Middle Ages moral anxiety, and at the end of the modern period spiritual anxiety. But in spite of the predominance of one type the others are also present and effective.

Enough has been said about the end of the ancient period and its anxiety of fate and death in connection with an analysis of Stoic courage. The sociological background is well known: the conflict of the imperial powers, Alexander's conquest of the East, the war between his followers, the conquest of West and East by republican Rome, the transformation of republican into imperial Rome through Caesar and Augustus, the tyranny of the post-Augustan emperors, the destruction of the independent city and nation states, the eradication of the former bearers of the aristocratic-democratic structure of society, the individual's feeling of being in the hands of powers, natural as well as political, which are completely beyond his control and calculation—all this produced a tremendous anxiety and the quest for courage to meet the threat of fate and death. At the same time the anxiety of emptiness and meaninglessness made it impossible for many people, especially of the educated classes, to find a basis for such courage. Ancient Skepticism from its very beginning in the Sophists united scholarly and existential elements. Skepticism in its late ancient form was despair about the possibility of right acting as well as right thinking. It drove people into the desert where the necessity for decisions, theoretical and practical, is reduced to a minimum. But most of those who experienced the anxiety of emptiness and the despair of meaninglessness tried to meet them with a cynical contempt of spiritual self-affirmation. Yet they could not hide the anxiety under skeptical arrogance. The anxiety of guilt and condemnation was effective in the groups who gathered in the mystery cults with their rites of expiation and purification. Sociologically these circles of the initiated were rather indefinite. In most of them even slaves were admitted. In them, however, as in the whole non-Jewish ancient world more the tragic than the personal guilt was experienced. Guilt is the pollution of the soul by the material realm or by demonic powers. Therefore the anxiety of guilt remains a secondary element, as does the anxiety of emptiness, within the dominating anxiety of fate and death.

Only the impact of the Jewish-Christian message changed this situation, and so radically that toward the end of the Middle Ages the anxiety of guilt and condemnation was decisive. If one period deserves the name of the "age of anxiety" it is the pre-Reformation and Reformation. The anxiety of condemnation symbolized as the "wrath of God" and intensified by the imagery of hell and purgatory drove people of the late Middle Ages to try various means of assuaging their anxiety: pilgrimages to holy places, if possible to Rome; ascetic exercises, sometimes of an extreme character; devotion to relics, often brought together in mass collections; acceptance of ecclesiastical punishments and the desire for indulgences; exaggerated participation in masses and penance, increase in prayers and alms. In short they asked ceaselessly: How can I appease the wrath of God, how can I attain divine mercy, the forgiveness of sin? This predominant form of anxiety embraced the other two forms. The personified figure of death appeared in painting, poetry, and preaching. But it was death and guilt together. Death and the devil were allied in the anxious imagination of the period. The anxiety of fate returned with the invasion of late antiquity. "Fortuna" became a preferred symbol in the art of the Renaissance, and even the Reformers were not free from astrological beliefs and fears. And the anxiety of fate was intensified by fear of demonic powers acting directly or through other human beings to cause illness, death, and all kinds of destruction. At the same time, fate was extended beyond death into the preultimate state of purgatory and the ultimate states of hell or heaven. The darkness of ultimate destiny could not be removed; not even the Reformers were able to remove it, as their doctrine of predestination shows. In all these expressions the anxiety of fate appears as an element within the all-embracing anxiety of guilt and in the permanent awareness of the threat of condemnation.

The late Middle Ages was not a period of doubt; and the anxiety of emptiness and loss of meaning appeared only twice, both remarkable occasions, however, and important for the future. One was the Renaissance, when theoretical skepticism was renewed and the question of meaning haunted some of the most sensitive minds. In Michelangelo's prophets and sibyls and in Shakespeare's *Hamlet* there are indications of a potential anxiety of meaninglessness. The other was in the demonic assaults that Luther experienced, which were neither temptations in the moral sense nor moments of despair about threatening condemnation, but moments when belief in his work and message disappeared and no meaning remained. Similar experiences of the "desert" or the "night" of the soul are frequent among mystics. It must be emphasized however that in all these cases the anxiety of guilt remained predominant, and that only after the victory of humanism and Enlightenment as the religious foundation of Western society could anxiety about spiritual nonbeing become dominant.

The sociological cause of the anxiety of guilt and condemnation that arose at the end of the Middle Ages is not difficult to identify. In general one can say it was the dissolution of the protective unity of the religiously guided medieval culture. More specifically there must be emphasized the rise of an educated middle class in the larger cities, people who tried to have as their own experience what had been merely an objective, hierarchically controlled system of doctrine and sacraments. In this attempt, however, they were driven to hidden or open conflict with the Church, whose authority they still acknowledged. There must be emphasized the concentration of political power in the princes and their bureaucratic-military administration, which eliminated the independence of those lower in the feudal system. There must be emphasized the state absolutism which transformed the masses in city and country into "subjects" whose only duty was to work and to obey, without any power to resist the arbitrariness of the absolute rulers. There must be emphasized the economic catastrophes connected with early capitalism, such as the importation of gold from the New World, expropriation of the peasants, and so on. In all these often-described changes it is the conflict between the appearance of independent tendencies in all groups of society, on the one hand, and the rise of an absolutist concentration of power on the other that is largely responsible for the predominance of the anxiety of guilt. The irrational, commanding, absolute God of nominalism and the Reformation is partly shaped by the social, political, and spiritual absolutism of the period; and the anxiety created in turn by his image is partly an expression of the anxiety produced by the basic social conflict of the disintegrating Middle Ages.

The breakdown of absolutism, the development of liberalism and democracy, the rise of a technical civilization with its victory over all enemies and its own beginning disintegration—these are the sociological presupposition for the third main period of anxiety. In this the anxiety of emptiness and meaninglessness is dominant. We are under the threat of spiritual nonbeing. The threats of moral and ontic nonbeing are, of course, present, but they are not independent and not controlling. This situation is so fundamental to the question raised in this book that it requires fuller analysis than the two earlier periods, and the analysis must be correlated with the constructive solution.

It is significant that the three main periods of anxiety appear at the end of an era. The anxiety which, in its different forms, is potentially present in every individual becomes general if the accustomed structures of meaning, power, belief, and order disintegrate. These structures, as long as they are in force, keep anxiety bound within a protective system of courage by participation. The individual who participates in the institutions and ways of life of such a system is not liberated from his personal anxieties but he has means of overcoming them with well-known methods. In periods of great changes these methods no longer work. Conflicts between the old, which tries to maintain itself, often with new means, and the new, which deprives the old of its intrinsic power, produce anxiety in all directions. Nonbeing, in such a situation, has a double face, resembling two types of nightmare (which are perhaps, expressions of an awareness of these two faces). The one type is the anxiety of annihilating narrowness, of the impossibility of escape and the horror of being trapped. The other is the anxiety of annihilating openness, of infinite, formless space into which one falls without a place to fall upon. Social situations like those described have the character both of a trap without exit and of an empty, dark, and unknown void. Both faces of the same reality arouse the latent anxiety of every individual who looks at them. Today most of us do look at them.

* * *

Chapter 6. Courage and Transcendence

[The Courage to Accept Acceptance]

Courage is the self-affirmation of being in spite of the fact of nonbeing. It is the act of the individual self in taking the anxiety of nonbeing upon itself by affirming itself either as part of an embracing whole or in its individual selfhood. Courage always includes a risk, it is always threatened by nonbeing, whether the risk of losing oneself and becoming a thing within the whole of things or of losing one's world in an empty self-relatedness. Courage needs the power of being, a power transcending the nonbeing which is experienced in the anxiety of fate and death, which is present in the anxiety of emptiness and meaninglessness, which is effective in the anxiety of guilt and condemnation. The courage which takes this threefold anxiety into itself must be rooted in a power of being that is greater than the power of oneself and the power of one's world. Neither self-affirmation as a part nor self-affirmation as oneself is beyond the manifold threat of nonbeing. Those who are mentioned as representatives of these forms of courage try to transcend themselves and the world in which they participate in order to find the power of being-itself and a courage to be which is beyond the threat of nonbeing. There are no exceptions to this rule; and this means that every courage to be has an open or hidden religious root. For religion is the state of being grasped by the power of being-itself. In some cases the religious root is carefully covered, in others it is passionately denied; in some it is deeply hidden and in others superficially. But it is never completely absent. For everything that is participates in being-itself, and everybody has some awareness of this participation, especially in the moments in which he experiences the threat of nonbeing. This leads us to a final consideration, the doubt question: How is the courage to be rooted in being-itself, and how must we understand being-itself in the light of the courage to be? The first question deals with the ground of being as source of the courage to be, the second with courage to be as key to the ground of being.

* * *

ABSOLUTE FAITH AND THE COURAGE TO BE

We have avoided the concept of faith in our description of the courage to be which is based on mystical union with the ground of being as well as in our description of the courage to be which is based on the personal encounter with God. This is partly because the concept of faith has lost its genuine meaning and has received the connotation of "belief in something unbelievable." But this is not the only reason for the use of terms other than faith. The decisive reason is that I do not think either mystical union or personal encounter fulfills the idea of faith. Certainly there is faith in the elevation of the soul above the finite to the infinite, leading to its union with the ground of being. But more than this is included in the concept of faith. And there is faith in the personal encounter with the personal God. But more than this is included in the concept of faith. Faith is the state of being grasped by the power of being-itself. The courage to be is an expression of faith and what "faith" means must be understood through the courage to be. We have defined courage as the self-affirmation of being in spite of nonbeing. The power of this self-affirmation is the power of being which is effective in every act of courage. Faith is the experience of this power.

But it is an experience which has a paradoxical character, the character of accepting acceptance. Being-itself transcends every finite being infinitely; God in the divine-human encounter transcends man unconditionally. Faith bridges this infinite gap by accepting the fact that in spite of it the power of being is present, that he who is separated is accepted. Faith accepts "in spite of"; and out of the "in spite of" of faith the "in spite of" of courage is born. Faith is not a theoretical affirmation of something uncertain, it is the existential acceptance of something transcending ordinary experience. Faith is not an opinion but a state. It is the state of being grasped by the power of being which transcends everything that is and in which everything that is participates. He who is grasped by this power is able to affirm himself because he knows that he is affirmed by the power of being-itself. In this point mystical experience and personal encounter are identical. In both of them faith is the basis of the courage to be.

This is decisive for a period in which, as in our own, the anxiety of doubt and meaninglessness is dominant. Certainly the anxiety of fate and death is not lacking in our time. The anxiety of fate has increased with the degree to which the schizophrenic split of our world has removed the last remnants of former security. And the anxiety of guilt and condemnation is not lacking either. It is surprising how much anxiety of guilt comes to the surface in psychoanalysis and personal counseling. The centuries of puritan and bourgeois repression of vital strivings have produced almost as many guilt feelings as the preaching of hell and purgatory in the Middle Ages.

But in spite of these restricting considerations one must say that the anxiety which determines our period is the anxiety of doubt and meaninglessness. One is afraid of having lost or of having to lose the meaning of one's existence. The expression of this situation is the Existentialism of today.

Which courage is able to take nonbeing into itself in the form of doubt and meaninglessness? This is the most important and most disturbing question in the quest for the courage to be. For the anxiety of meaninglessness undermines what is still unshaken in the anxiety of fate and death and of guilt and condemnation. In the anxiety of guilt and condemnation doubt has not yet undermined the certainty of an ultimate responsibility. We are threatened but we are not destroyed. If, however, doubt and meaninglessness prevail one experiences an abyss in which the meaning of life and the truth of ultimate responsibility disappear. Both the Stoic who conquers the anxiety of fate with the Socratic courage of wisdom and the Christian who conquers the anxiety of guilt with the Protestant courage of accepting forgiveness are in a different situation. Even in the despair of having to die and the despair of self-condemnation meaning is affirmed and certitude preserved. But in the despair of doubt and meaninglessness both are swallowed by nonbeing.

The question then is this: Is there a courage which can conquer the anxiety of meaninglessness and doubt? Or in other words, can the faith which accepts acceptance resist the power of nonbeing in its most radical form? Can faith resist meaninglessness? Is there a kind of faith which can exist together with doubt and meaninglessness? These questions lead to the last aspect of the problem discussed in these lectures and the one most relevant to our time: How is the courage to be possible if all the ways to create it are barred by the experience of their ultimate insufficiency? If life is as meaningless as death, if guilt is as questionable as perfection, if being is no more meaningful than nonbeing, on what can one base the courage to be?

There is an inclination in some Existentialists to answer these questions by a leap from doubt to dogmatic certitude, from meaninglessness to a set of symbols in which the meaning of a special ecclesiastical or political group is embodied. This leap can be interpreted in different ways. It may be the expression of a desire for safety; it may be as arbitrary as, according to Existentialist principles, every decision is; it may be the feeling that the Christian message is the answer to the questions raised by an analysis of human existence; it may be a genuine conversion, independent of the theoretical situation. In any case it is not a solution of the problem of radical doubt. It gives the courage to be to those who are converted but it does not answer the question as to how such a courage is possible in itself. The answer must accept, as its precondition, the state of meaninglessness. It is not an answer if it demands the removal of this state; for that is just what cannot be done. He who is in the grip of doubt and meaninglessness cannot liberate himself from this grip; but he asks for an answer which is valid within and not outside the situation of his despair. He asks for the ultimate foundation of what we have called the "courage of despair." There is only one possible answer, if one does not try to escape the question: namely that the acceptance of despair is in itself faith and on the boundary line of the courage to be. In this situation the meaning of life is reduced to despair about the meaning of life. But as long as this despair is an act of life it is positive in its negativity. Cynically speaking, one could say that it is true to life to be cynical about it. Religiously speaking, one would say that one accepts oneself as accepted in spite of one's despair about the meaning of this acceptance. The paradox of every radical negativity, as long as it is an active negativity, is that it must affirm itself in order to be able to negate itself. No actual negation can be without an implicit affirmation. The hidden pleasure produced by despair witnesses to the paradoxical character of self-negation. The negative lives from the positive it negates.

The faith which makes the courage of despair possible is the acceptance of the power of being, even in the grip of nonbeing. Even in the despair about meaning being affirms itself through us. The act of accepting meaninglessness is in itself a meaningful act. It is an act of faith. We have seen that he who has the courage to affirm his being in spite of fate and guilt has not removed them. He remains threatened and hit by them. But he accepts his acceptance by the power of being-itself in which he participates and which gives him the courage to take the anxieties of fate and guilt upon himself. The same is true of doubt and meaninglessness. The faith which creates the courage to take them into itself has no special content. It is simply faith, undirected, absolute. It is undefinable, since everything defined is dissolved by doubt and meaninglessness. Nevertheless, even absolute faith is not an eruption of subjective emotions or a mood without objective foundation.

An analysis of the nature of absolute faith reveals the following elements in it. The first is the experience of the power of being which is present even in face of the most radical manifestation of nonbeing. If one says that in this experience vitality resists despair one must add that vitality in man is proportional to intentionality. The vitality that can stand the abyss of meaninglessness is aware of a hidden meaning within the destruction of meaning. The second element in absolute faith is the dependence of the experience of nonbeing on the experience of being and the dependence of the experience of meaninglessness on the experience of meaning. Even in the state of despair one has enough being to make despair possible. There is a third element in absolute faith, the acceptance of being accepted. Of course, in the state of despair there is nobody and nothing that accepts. But there is the power of acceptance itself which is experienced. Meaninglessness, as long as it is experienced, includes an experience of the "power of acceptance." To accept this power of acceptance consciously is the religious answer of absolute faith, of a faith which has been deprived by doubt of any concrete content, which nevertheless is faith and the source of the most paradoxical manifestation of the courage to be.

This faith transcends both the mystical experience and the divine-human encounter. The mystical experience seems to be nearer to absolute faith but it is not. Absolute faith includes an element of skepticism which one cannot find in the mystical experience. Certainly mysticism also transcends all specific contents, but not because it doubts them or has found them meaningless; rather it deems them to be preliminary. Mysticism uses the specific contents as grades, stepping on them after having used them. The experience of meaninglessness, however, denies them (and everything that goes with them) without having used them. The experience of meaninglessness is more radical than mysticism. Therefore it transcends the mystical experience.

Absolute faith also transcends the divine-human encounter. In this encounter the subject-object scheme is valid: a definite subject (man) meets a definite object (God). One can reverse this statement and say that a definite subject (God) meets a definite object (man). But in both cases the attack of doubt undercuts the subject-object structure. The theologians who speak so strongly and with such self-certainty about the divine-human encounter should be aware of a situation in which this encounter is prevented by radical doubt and nothing is left but absolute faith. The acceptance of such a situation as religiously valid has, however, the consequence that the concrete contents of ordinary faith must be subjected to criticism and transformation. The courage to be in its radical form is a key to an idea of God which transcends both mysticism and the person-to-person encounter. . . .

PAUL TILLICH

from

Love, Power and Justice

BEING AND LOVE

The ontological question

ALL PROBLEMS OF love, power, and justice drive us to an ontological analysis. The confusions cannot be cleared up, nor can the problems be solved without an answer to the question: In what way is each of these concepts rooted in being-itself? And the question of being-itself is the ontological question. It is, therefore, appropriate that, before dealing with the ontological roots of each of our concepts, we ask: What does 'root' in this sense mean? What is the 'root-meaning' of a concept? How is the ontological question to be raised and how can it be answered?

Ontology is the elaboration of the *'logos'* of the *'on'*, in English of the 'rational word' which grasps 'being as such'. It is hard for the modern mind to understand the Latin *esse-ipsum*, being-itself, or the Greek *on ê on*, being-in-so-far-as-it-is-being. We are all nominalists by birth. And as nominalists we are all inclined to dissolve our world into things. But this inclination is an historical accident and not an essential necessity. The concern of the so-called realists of the Middle Ages was to maintain the validity of the universals as genuine expressions of being. It is however not realism to which I want you to turn from the naïve nominalism in which the modern world lives, but I want you to turn to something older than both nominalism and realism: to the philosophy which asks the question of being before the split into universal essences and particular contents. This philosophy is older than any other. It is the most powerful element in all great philosophies of the past, and it has come into its own in the important philosophical attempts of our period. It is the philosophy which asks the question: What does it mean that something *is?* What are the characteristics of everything that participates in being? And this is the question of ontology.

Ontology does not try to describe the nature of beings, either in their universal, generic qualities, or in their individual, historical manifestations. It does not ask about stars and plants, animals and men. It does not ask about events and those who act within these events. This is the task of scientific analysis and historical description. But ontology asks the simple and infinitely difficult question: What does it mean to *be?* What are the structures, common to everything that is, to everything that participates in being? One cannot avoid this question by denying that there are such common structures. One cannot deny that being is one and that the qualities and elements of being constitute a texture of connected and conflicting forces. This texture is one, in so far as it *is* and gives the power of being to each of its qualities and elements. It is one but it is neither a dead identity nor a repetitious sameness. It is one in the manifoldness of its texture. Ontology is the attempt to describe this texture, to reveal its hidden nature through the word which belongs to being and in which being comes to itself. Yet let us not make a mistake: ontology does not describe the infinite variety of beings, living and dead, subhuman and human. Ontology characterizes the texture of being itself, which is effective in everything that is, in all beings, living and dead, subhuman and human. Ontology precedes every other cognitive approach to reality. It precedes all sciences, not always historically, but always in logical dignity and basic analysis. One does not need to look back at past centuries or far-removed parts of the world to discover the primacy of the ontological question. The best method for discovering it to-day is a careful analysis of the writings of leading anti-ontological philosophers or of anti-philosophical scientists and historians. One will easily discover that on almost every page of the writings of these men a certain number of basic ontological concepts are used, but surreptitiously and therefore often wrongly. One cannot escape ontology if one wants to know! For knowing means recognizing something as being. And being is an infinitely involved texture, to be described by the never-ending task of ontology.

It is decisive for our purpose in these chapters to notice that the early philosophers, when they tried to speak in terms of the *logos* about the nature of being, could not do it without using words like love, power, and justice or synonyms for them. Our triad of terms points to a trinity of structures in being itself. Love, power, and justice are metaphysically speaking as old as being itself. They precede everything that is, and they cannot be derived from anything that is. They have ontological dignity. And before having received ontological dignity they had mythological meaning. They were gods before they became rational qualities of being. The substance of their mythological meaning is reflected in their ontological significance. *Dikê,* the goddess of justice, receives Parmenides when he is introduced into truth itself. For there is no truth without the form of truth, namely justice. And being-itself, according to the same philosopher, is kept within the bondage of eternal laws. The *logos* of being is the power which keeps the world going and the city alive, according to Heraclitus, and Mind is the divine power which swings the wheel of being, according to Xenophanes. According to Empedocles, it is hate and love, separation, and reunion which determine the movements of the elements. Love, power, and justice are ever repeated subjects of ontology. There is hardly a leading philosopher who does not put them into the very foundations of his thought. In Plato we find the doctrine of *erôs* as the power which drives to the union with the true and the good itself. In his interpretation of the ideas as the essences of everything, he sees them as the 'powers of being'. And justice for him is not a special virtue, but the uniting form of the individual and the social body. In Aristotle we find the doctrine of the universal *erôs* which drives everything towards the highest form, the pure actuality which moves the world not as a cause *(kinoumenon)* but as the object of love *(erômenon)*. And the movement he describes is a movement from the potential to the actual, from *dynamis* to *energeia,* two concepts which include the concept of power. In the line of thought which leads from Augustine to Boehme, Schelling, and Schopenhauer it is the half-symbolic use of the concept 'will' in which the element of power is preserved, while the emphasis on the *logos* of being in all of them preserves the element of justice, and the ontology of love in Augustine and all his followers shows the primacy of love in relation to power and justice. It is well known to the students of Hegel that he started in his early fragments as a philosopher of love, and it can be said without exaggeration that Hegel's dialectical scheme is an abstraction from his concrete intuition into the nature of love as separation and reunion. It should also be mentioned that in the recent psychotherapeutic literature the relation between power-drive and love is in the foreground of interest. Love has been more and more acknowledged as the answer to the question implied in anxiety and neurosis.

The historical survey shows the basic ontological significance of the triad of concepts we have to discuss. Now the question of method arises: How is ontology distinguished from what has been called metaphysics? The answer is that ontology is the foundation of metaphysics, but not metaphysics itself. Ontology asks the question of being, i.e. of something that is present to everybody at every moment. It is never 'speculative' in the (unjustified) bad sense of the word, but it is always descriptive, describing the structures which are presupposed in any encounter with reality. Ontology is descriptive, not speculative. It tries to find out which the basic structures of being are. And being is given to everybody who is and who therefore participates in being-itself. Ontology, in this sense, is analytical. It analyses the encountered reality, trying to find the structural elements which enable a being to participate in being. It separates those elements of the real which are generic or particular from those elements which are constitutive for everything that is and therefore are universal. It leaves the former to the special sciences or to metaphysical constructions, it elaborates the latter through critical analysis. Obviously this task is an infinite one, because the encounter with reality is inexhaustible and always reveals qualities of being, the ontological foundation of which must be investigated. Secondly, one must ask: Is there a way of verifying ontological judgements? There is certainly not an experimental way, but there is an experiential way. It is the way of an intelligent recognition of the basic ontological structures within the encountered reality, including the process of encountering itself. The only answer, but a sufficient answer, which can be given to the question of ontological verification is the appeal to intelligent recognition. For the following analysis this appeal is made. Finally, the question of a method cannot be answered before the method is applied successfully or unsuccessfully. Method and content cannot be separated.

An ontology of love

All problems concerning the relation of love to power and justice, individually as well as socially, become insoluble if love is basically understood as an emotion. Love would be a sentimental addition to power and justice, ultimately irrelevant, unable to change either the laws of justice or the structures of power. Most of the pitfalls in social ethics, political theory, and education are due to a misunderstanding of the ontological character of love. On the other hand, if love is understood in its ontological nature, its relation to justice and power is seen in a light which reveals the basic unity of the three concepts and the conditioned character of its conflicts.

Life is being in actuality and love is the moving power of life. In these two sentences the ontological nature of love is expressed. They say that being is not actual without the love which drives everything that is towards everything else that is. In man's experience of love the nature of life becomes manifest. Love is the drive towards the unity of the separated. Reunion presupposes separation of that which belongs essentially together. It would, however, be wrong to give to separation the same ontological ultimacy as to reunion. For separation presupposes an original unity. Unity embraces itself and separation, just as being comprises itself and non-being. It is impossible to unite that which is *essentially* separated. Without an ultimate belongingness no union of one thing with another can be conceived. The absolutely strange cannot enter into a communion. But the estranged is striving for reunion. In the loving joy about the 'other one' the joy about one's own self-fulfilment by the other is also present. That which is absolutely strange to me cannot add to my self-fulfilment; it can only destroy me if it touches the sphere of my being. Therefore love cannot be described as the union of the strange but as the reunion of the estranged. Estrangement presupposes original oneness. Love manifests its greatest power there where it overcomes the greatest separation. And the greatest separation is the separation of self from self. Every self is self-related and a complete self is completely self-related. It is an independent *centre,* indivisible and impenetrable, and therefore is rightly called an individual.

The separation of a completely individualized being from any other completely individualized being is itself complete. The centre of a completely individualized being cannot be entered by any other individualized being, and it cannot be made into a mere part of a higher unity. Even as a part it is indivisible and it is as such more than a part. Love reunites that which is self-centred and individual. The power of love is not something which is added to an otherwise finished process, but life has love in itself as one of its constitutive elements. It is the fulfilment and the triumph of love that it is able to reunite the most radically separated beings, namely individual persons. The individual person is both most separated and the bearer of the most powerful love.

We have rejected the attempt to restrict love to its emotional element. But there is no love without the emotional element, and it would be a poor analysis of love which did not take this element into consideration. The question is only how to relate it to the ontological definition of love. One can say that love as an emotion is the anticipation of the reunion which takes place in every love-relation. Love, like all emotions, is an expression of the total participation of the being which is in an emotional state. In the moment in which one is in love the fulfilment of the desire for reunion is anticipated and the happiness of this reunion is experienced in imagination. This means that the emotional element in love does not precede the others ontologically but that the ontologically founded movement to the other one expresses itself in emotional ways. Love is a passion: this assertion implies that there is a passive element in love, namely the state of being driven towards reunion. Infinite passion for God as described by Kierkegaard is, no less than the sexual passion, a consequence of the objective situation, namely of the state of separation of those who belong together and are driven towards each other in love.

The ontology of love is tested by the experience of love fulfilled. There is a profound ambiguity about this experience. Fulfilled love is, at the same time, extreme happiness and the end of happiness. The separation is overcome. But without the separation there is no love and no life. It is the superiority of the person-to-person relationship that it preserves the separation of the self-centred self, and nevertheless actualizes their reunion in love. The highest form of love and that form of it which distinguishes Eastern and Western cultures is the love which preserves the individual who is both the subject and the object of love. In the loving person-to-person relationship Christianity manifests its superiority to any other religious tradition.

The ontology of love leads to the basic assertion that love is one. This contradicts the main trend in the recent discussions of the nature of love. They were useful in so far as they directed the attention to the different qualities of love. But they were and are misleading in so far as they consider the differences of qualities as differences of types. The error was not that one distinguished the qualities of love—on the contrary, *more* distinctions should have been made in what was often comprehended under the name *erôs*. The error was that one did not start with an understanding of love as one. Such an understanding, of course, would have led to an ontological analysis. For only the relation of love to being as such can reveal its fundamental character.

If love in all its forms is the drive towards the reunion of the separated, the different qualities of the one nature of love become understandable. Traditionally *epithymia* ('desire') is considered the lowest quality of love. It is identified with the desire to sensual self-fulfilment. There is a strong interest on the part of philosophical and theological moralists in establishing a complete gap between this quality and those which are supposed to be higher and essentially different. On the other hand, there is a tendency on the naturalist side to reduce all the other qualities of love to the *epithymia* quality. A solution of this problem is only possible in the light of the ontological interpretation of love. First of all it must be said that *libido*—to use the Latin word—is misunderstood if it is defined as the desire for pleasure. This hedonistic definition is, like hedonism generally, based on a wrong psychology which itself is the consequence of a wrong ontology. Man strives to reunite himself with that to which he belongs and from which he is separated. And this is true not only of man but of all living beings. They desire food, movement, growth, participation in a group, sexual union, etc. The fulfilment of these desires is accompanied by pleasure. But it is not the pleasure as such which is desired, but the union with that which fulfils the desire. Certainly, fulfilled desire is pleasure, and unfulfilled desire is pain. But it is a distortion of the actual processes of life if one derives from these facts the pain-pleasure principle in the sense that life essentially consists of fleeing from pain and striving for pleasure. Whenever this happens life is corrupted. Only a perverted life follows the pain-pleasure principle. Unperverted life strives for that of which it is in want, it strives for union with that which is separated from it, though it belongs to it. This analysis should remove the prejudice towards libido, and it can give criteria for the partial acceptance, partial rejection of Freud's libido theory. In so far as Freud describes libido as the desire of the individual to get rid of his tensions, he has described the perverted form of libido. And he has acknowledged this implicitly (though not intentionally) by deriving the death-instinct from the infinite, never fulfilled libido. Freud describes man's libido in its perverted, self-estranged stage. But his description, in which he joins many Puritans (old and new ones who would be embarrassed by this alliance) misses the meaning of libido as the normal drive towards vital self-fulfilment. In the light of this analysis it is justified to say that *epithymia* is a quality which is not lacking in any love relation. To this extent the naturalists are right. But they are wrong if they interpret libido or *epithymia* as the striving for pleasure for the sake of pleasure.

The attempts to establish an absolute contrast between *agapê* and *erôs* usually presuppose an identification of *erôs* and *epithymia*. Certainly, there is *epithymia* in every *erôs*. But *erôs* transcends *epithymia*. It strives for a union with that which is a bearer of values because of the values it embodies. This refers to the beauty we find in nature, to the beautiful and the true in culture, and to the mystical union with that which is the source of the beautiful and the true. Love drives towards union with the forms of nature and culture and with the divine sources of both. This *erôs* is united with *epithymia* if *epithymia* is the desire for vital self-fulfilment and not for the pleasure resulting from this union. This valuation of *erôs* is attacked from two sides. Love as *erôs* is depreciated by those theologians who depreciate culture and by those who deny a mystical element in man's relation to God. But it is a rather self-defying attitude if somebody depreciates culture and does it in terms of culture, if he, e.g., uses millennia of linguistic culture in order to express his rejection of culture. Without the *erôs* towards truth, theology would not exist, and without the *erôs* towards the beautiful no ritual expressions would exist. Even more serious is the rejection of the *erôs* quality of love with respect to God. The consequence of this rejection is that love towards God becomes an impossible concept to be replaced by obedience to God. But obedience is not love. It can be the opposite of love. Without the desire of man to be reunited with his origin, the love towards God becomes a meaningless word.

The *erôs* quality of love is in a polar way related to what could be called the *philia* quality of love. While *erôs* represents the transpersonal pole, *philia* represents the personal pole. Neither of them is possible without the other. There is *erôs* quality in *philia*. And there is *philia* quality in *erôs*. They are in a polar way interdependent. This implies that without the radical separation of the self-centred self neither the creative nor the religious *erôs* is possible. Beings without a personal centre are without *erôs,* although they are not without *epithymia.* He who cannot relate himself as an 'I' to a 'thou' cannot relate himself to the true and the good and to the ground of being in which they are rooted. He who cannot love the friend cannot love the artistic expression of ultimate reality. Kierkegaard's stages of the aesthetical and the ethical and the religious are not stages but qualities which appear in structural interdependence. Conversely, *philia* is dependent on *erôs.* Concepts like participation and communion point to the *erôs* quality in every *philia* relation. It is the desire to unite with a power of being which is both most separated and most understandable and which radiates possibilities and realities of the good and the true in the manifestation of its incomparable individuality. But *erôs* and *philia* are not only united in the individual relation. They are also united in the communion of social groups. In families, and national groups, the desire for participation is directed towards the power of being which is embodied in the group, even if special relations of the *philia* type are lacking. The very fact that such groups consist of individuals with whom an I-thou relation is potentially given, distinguishes the *erôs* within a group from the *erôs* which is effective, e.g. in artistic creations. Love as *philia* presupposes some amount of familiarity with the object of love. For this reason Aristotle asserted that *philia* is possible only between equals. This is true if 'equal' is defined in a sufficiently large way and not in terms of an esoteric group.

As we have already indicated, *erôs* as well as *philia* contains an element of *epithymia.* This is most obvious in those cases in which a *philia* and *erôs* relation is united with sexual attraction or fulfilment. But it is true not only in these cases. It is always true. In this respect depth psychology has discovered a side of human existence which should not be covered again by idealistic or moralistic fears and postulates. The *appetitus* of every being to fulfil itself through union with other beings is universal and underlies the *erôs* as well as the *philia* quality of love. There is an element of libido even in the most spiritualized friendship and in the most ascetic mysticism. A saint without libido would cease to be a creature. But there is no such saint.

Up to this point the quality of love which dominates the New Testament, the *agapê* quality, has been disregarded. This has been done not because *agapê* is the last and highest form of love, but because *agapê* enters from another dimension into the whole of life and into all qualities of love. One could call *agapê* the depth of love or love in relation to the ground of life. One could say that in *agapê* ultimate reality manifests itself and transforms life and love. *Agapê* is love cutting into love, just as revelation is reason cutting into reason and the Word of God is the Word cutting into all words. This, however, is the subject of the last chapter.

At this point we must answer the questions raised in the first chapter about the concept of self-love. If love is the drive towards the reunion of the separated, it is hard to speak meaningfully of self-love. For within the union of self-consciousness there is no real separation, comparable to the separation of a self-centred being from all other beings. Certainly the completely self-centred being, man, is self-centred only because his self is split into a self which is subject and a self which is object. But there is neither separation in this structure, nor the desire for reunion. Self-love is a metaphor, and it should not be treated as a concept. The lack of conceptual clarity in the concept of self-love is manifest in the fact that the term is used in three different and partly contradictory senses. It is used in the sense of natural self-affirmation (e.g. loving one's neighbour as oneself). It is used in the sense of selfishness (e.g. the desire to draw all things into oneself). It is used in the sense of self-acceptance (e.g. the affirmation of oneself in the way in which one is affirmed by God). It would be an important step towards semantic clarification if the term 'self-love' were completely removed and replaced by self-affirmation, selfishness, and self-acceptance according to the context.

* * *

The unity of justice and love in personal encounters

Justice as proportional justice cannot fulfil the quest implied in a concrete situation, but love can. One should never say that love's work starts where the work of justice ends. For love shows what is just in the concrete situation. Nothing is more false than to say to somebody: since I love you and you love me, I don't need to get justice from you or you from me, for love eliminates the need for justice. Such language is used by people who want to avoid the obligations which are connected with justice. It is said by tyrannical rulers to their subjects and by tyrannical parents to their children. And even if they do not say it, they act accordingly. It is a clever way of trying to escape the responsibility and the self-restriction demanded by justice. Often, the love which supposedly transcends justice is nothing more than an emotional outburst of self-surrender, alternating with emotional outbursts of hostility.

Therefore it is false to say: Love gives what justice cannot give; love drives to a self-surrender which is beyond the demand of justice. There is much self-surrender which is the demand of proportional justice, e.g. death for a cause on which one's own existence depends. But there are other kinds of self-surrender which are not demanded by proportional justice. They are demanded by love. However, if they are demanded by love they are demanded by creative justice. For the creative element in justice is love.

Love, in this respect, has the same relation to justice which revelation has to reason. And this is not an accidental analogy. It is rooted in the nature of both revelation and love. Both of them transcend the rational norm without destroying it. Both of them have an 'ecstatic element'. Love in some of its expressions, e.g. in those which Paul gives in 1 Cor. xiii can be called justice in ecstasy, as revelation can be called reason in ecstasy. This also is confirmed by Paul when he derives both revelatory experiences and the working of love from the divine spirit. And as revelation does not give additional information in the realm where cognitive reason decides, so love does not drive to additional acts in the realm where practical reason decides. Both give another dimension to reason, revelation to cognitive reason, love to practical reason. Neither of them denies that to which it gives the dimensions of depth, namely to reason. As revelation does not contradict the structures of cognitive reason (otherwise revelation could not be received), so love does not contradict justice (otherwise it could not be actualized). This consideration points to something we have to deal with in the last chapter, namely the dependence of the whole realm of moral action on the presence of the Spiritual power.

The relation of justice to love in personal encounters can adequately be described through three functions of creative justice, namely, listening, giving, forgiving. In none of them does love do more than justice demands, but in each of them love recognizes what justice demands. In order to know what is just in a person-to-person encounter, love listens. It is its first task to listen. No human relation, especially no intimate one, is possible without mutual listening. Reproaches, reactions, defences may be justified in terms of proportional justice. But perhaps they would prove to be unjust if there were more mutual listening. All things and all men, so to speak, call on us with small or loud voices. They want us to listen, they want us to understand their intrinsic claims, their justice of being. They want justice from us. But we can give it to them only through the love which listens.

Love in its attempt to see what is in the other person is by no means irrational. It uses all possible means to penetrate into the dark places of his motives and inhibitions. It uses, for example, the tools provided by depth psychology which give unexpected possibilities of discovering the intrinsic claims of a human being. Through it we have learned that human expressions can mean something quite different from what they seem or are intended to mean. They seem to be aggressive, but what they express may be love, inhibited by shyness. They seem to be sweet and submissive and they are actually symptoms of hostility. Words, well meant, but uttered improperly, may produce in reaction complete injustice. Listening love is the first step to justice in person-to-person encounters. And it has also a function in encounters with living nature and nature generally. But if we tried to pursue the problem of human justice and injustice towards nature, a large new field of inquiry would be opened, too large for our present task and too much in need of references to art and poetry for an ontological analysis.

The second function of creative justice in personal encounters is giving. It belongs to the right of everyone whom we encounter to demand something from us, at least that even in the most impersonal relations the other one is acknowledged as a person. But this minimum of giving drives toward a maximum—including possible self-sacrifice if the occasion demands it. Giving is an expression of creative justice if it serves the purpose of reuniting love. It is obvious that under this criterion it may mean the demand to resist and to restrain and to deprive. Here again psychological wisdom can help to do what appears to be the opposite of giving love. Creative justice includes the possibility of sacrificing the other one in his existence, though not in his being as a person.

The third and most paradoxical form in which justice is united with love is forgiving. Their unity is indicated in the Pauline term: justification by grace. Justification literally means: making just, and it means in the context of Paul's and Luther's doctrine to accept as just him who is unjust. Nothing seems to contradict more the idea of justice than this doctrine, and everybody who has pronounced it has been accused of promoting injustice and amorality. It seems to be utterly unjust to declare him who is unjust, just. But nothing less than this is what has been called the good news in Christian preaching. And nothing less than this is the fulfilment of justice. For it is the only way of reuniting those who are estranged by guilt. Without reconciliation there is no reunion. Forgiving love is the only way of fulfilling the intrinsic claim in every being, namely its claim to be reaccepted into the unity to which it belongs. Creative justice demands that this claim be accepted and that he be accepted who is unacceptable in terms of proportional justice. In accepting him into the unity of forgiveness, love exposes both the acknowledged break with justice on his side with all its implicit consequences and the claim inherent in him to be *declared* just and to be *made* just by reunion.

Other books by Tillich:

Biblical Religion and the Search for Ultimate Reality, 1955.
Dynamics of Faith, 1957.
The Interpretation of History, 1926 (Engl. trans. 1936).
The New Being, 1955.
The Protestant Era, 1948.
The Religious Situation, 1932.
The Shaking of the Foundations, 1950.
Systematic Theology, Vol. I, 1951, Vol. II, 1957.
Theology of Culture, 1959.

Other books on the same problem:

d'Arcy, Martin C. *The Mind and Heart of Love,* 1947.
Kierkegaard, Søren. *The Works of Love,* 1847 (Engl. trans. 1946).
Nygren, Anders T. S. *Agape and Eros,* 1932.
de Rougemont, Denis. *Love in the Western World,* 1940.
Ortega y Gasset. *On Love,* 1957.
Marcuse, Herbert. *Eros and Civilization,* 1955.

SELECTED GENERAL BIBLIOGRAPHY

Brunner, Emil. *Revelation and Reason,* 1946.
Buber, Martin. *Between Man and Man,* 1947.
Buber, Martin. *Eclipse of God,* 1952.
Buber, Martin. *I and Thou,* 1922 (Engl. trans. 1937).
Cochrane, Arthur C. *The Existentialists and God,* 1958.
Dillenberger, John and Claude Welch. *Protestant Christianity,* 1955.
Fairchild, Hoxie Neale. *Religious Trends in English Poetry,* 1939——.
Flew, Anthony G. N. *New Essays in Philosophical Theology,* 1955.
Franck, Erich. *Philosophical Understanding and Religious Truth,* 1945.
Gilson, Etienne H. *Painting and Reality,* 1957.
Guardini, Romano. *The Faith and Modern Man,* 1952.
Haroutunian, Joseph. *Piety Versus Moralism,* 1932.
Herberg, Will (ed.). *Four Existentialist Theologians,* 1958.
Horton, Walter Marshall. *Can Christianity Save Civilization?* 1940.
Horton, Walter Marshall. *Realistic Theology,* 1934.
Langer, Susan. *Philosophy in a New Key,* 1942.
Lewis, Edwin. *The Christian Manifesto,* 1934.
Mackintosh, H. R. *Types of Modern Theology,* 1937.
Nash, Arnold S. *Protestant Thought in the Twentieth Century,* 1951.
Pauck, Wilhelm. *The Heritage of the Reformation,* 1951.
Pelikan, Jaroslav. *From Luther to Kierkegaard,* 1950.
Richard, George W. *Beyond Fundamentalism and Modernism,* 1934.
Roberts, David. *Existentialism and Religious Belief,* 1957.
Schweitzer, Albert. *The Quest of the Historical Jesus,* 1906.
Troeltsch, Ernst. *Christian Thought, Its History and Application,* 1923.
Troeltsch, Ernst. *Protestantism and Progress,* 1912.
Unamuno, Miguel de. *The Tragic Sense of Life,* 1912.
West, Charles C. *Communism and the Theologians,* 1958.
Wilder, Amos. *Modern Poetry and the Christian Tradition,* 1952.
Williams, Daniel D. *What Present-Day Theologians Are Thinking,* 1952.

BIOGRAPHICAL NOTES

Barth, Karl (1886——) was born in Basel, Switzerland. Educated at the universities of Bern, Berlin, Tübingen and Marburg, he began his active ministry as Vicar in Geneva in 1909. From 1911 to 1921 he served as Pastor at Safenwil. Since then he has been Professor of Systematic Theology at the University of Bonn and at the University of Basel. Reviving Evangelical theology of the Reformation he is noted as the principal advocate of "crisis" or "dialectical" theology in the 20th century. The substance of his thought is contained in the monumental *Church Dogmatics,* 1936-56.

Berdyaev, Nicholas (1874-1948) was born in Kiev into a family of the Russian aristocracy. During his student years at the University of Kiev he broke from his family social ties, allied himself with social-democratic and revolutionary groups, and, as a result of voicing liberal views, was exiled for two years. From 1904 to 1922, first in St. Petersburg and then in Moscow, he participated in the numerous literary, philosophical, religious and political societies that reflected the intellectual and spiritual ferment in Russia prior to the revolution. A leader in the Moscow Religious-Philosophical Society, he later founded his own Free Academy of Moral Science, lecturing continuously at both institutions and at the University of Moscow where he was Professor of Philosophy in 1920. In 1922 he was exiled by the Communists. For two years he carried on his activities in Berlin, establishing there the Russian Religious-Philosophical Academy and editing the publications of the Y.M.C.A. Press. In 1924 he moved to Paris where he continued active leadership of the Religious-Philosophical Academy until his death. He was awarded the Doctor of Divinity degree by Cambridge University in 1947.

Bultmann, Rudolph (1884——) was born in Wiefelstede, Oldenburg, Germany and educated at the universities of Tübingen, Berlin and Marburg. After occupying chairs of theology at the universities of Breslau and Giessen he was appointed Professor of New Testament and Early Christian History at Marburg in 1921, a position which he retained for thirty years. A pioneer in Form Criticism he remains one of the most controversial figures in contemporary New Testament scholarship.

Cullmann, Oscar (1902——) was born in Strasbourg. His education in theology and philosophy was at the universities of Strasbourg and Paris. After teaching Greek and German in

Paris he became associated with the Protestant Seminary in Strasbourg as lecturer in New Testament Greek (1927), Professor of New Testament Exegesis (1930), and Professor of Ancient Ecclesiastical History (1936). In 1938 he was appointed Professor of Ancient and Medieval Ecclesiastical History and New Testament Exegesis. Since 1949 he has also been Director of Studies of the École des Hautes-Études at the Sorbonne in Paris. He is co-editor of the *Theologische Zeitschrift* (Basel) and of the *Revue d'histoire et de philosophie religieuses* (Strasbourg).

Dostoievsky, Feodor (1821-81) was born in Moscow into the family of a well-to-do doctor. He maintained a brilliant record at the College of Military Engineers and served two years in the army. His literary career began with the success of his first novel, *Poor Folk* (1849). Arrested in 1849 for political activities he was sentenced to hard labor and deported to Siberia for five years. He was not finally pardoned until 1859. Perhaps no novelist has probed so far into the depths of the human mind and revealed more startlingly the contradictions in men's souls and personalities. And probably no single literary figure has exerted greater influence upon the minds of contemporary theologians.

Kierkegaard, Søren (1813-55) was born in Copenhagen where he remained throughout his life, devoted to prolific literary activities. His father, a prosperous woolen merchant, impressed his own severe and pietistic religious discipline upon the life of the family. Søren studied philosophy and theology at the University of Copenhagen. After finishing his studies he entered the social life of Copenhagen, playing the role of a rich man's gifted son and reflecting upon possible careers. After an unfortunate love affair and a broken engagement he fled to Berlin where for a year he attended Schelling's lectures. He then returned to Copenhagen and a life of continuous literary production. He is generally regarded as the founder of existentialist philosophy and theology.

Kroner, Richard (1884——) was educated at the universities of Breslau, Berlin, Heidelberg and Freiburg in Breisgau. Lecturer and Professor of Philosophy at the University of Freiburg from 1912, he was appointed Professor of Philosophy at the University of Dresden in 1924 and at the University of Kiel in 1929 and Research Professor in Berlin in 1934. From 1910 to 1934 he was editor of the philosophical journal *Logos* and from 1930 to 1935, President of the International Hegel League. A refugee from Nazi Germany he lectured at Oxford University in 1938 and delivered the Gifford Lectures at St. Andrews College, Edinburgh, in 1939 and 1940. From 1941 to 1952 he was Professor of the Philosophy of Religion at Union Theological Seminary in New York City. Since then he is Professor Emeritus at U. T. S. and Professor of Philosophy at Temple University in Philadelphia. Recognized as one of the great living Kant scholars he is widely known for his *Von Kant bis Hegel* (1921-24), *Kant's "Weltanschauung"* (Engl. trans. 1956) as well as for his philosophy of culture, *Die Selbstverwirklichung des Geistes* (1928) and his edition of *Hegel's Early Theological Writings* (1948).

Niebuhr, H. Richard (1894——), brother of Reinhold Niebuhr, was born in Wright City, Missouri. He was educated at Elmhurst College, Eden Theological Seminary, Washington University, Yale University and Yale Divinity School. Pastor in St. Louis from 1916 to 1918, he was appointed to a Professorship at Eden Theological Seminary where he remained until 1931, save for three years during which he was President of Elmhurst College (1924-27). In 1931 he was appointed Associate Professor of Christian Ethics at Yale Divinity School. Since 1938 he has been Professor at the same institution.

Niebuhr, Reinhold (1892——) was born in Wright City, Missouri. After his undergraduate studies at Elmhurst College, he received advanced degrees in philosophy and theology at Eden Theological Seminary and Yale Divinity School. Ordained minister in the Evangelical Synod of North America, he served as Pastor in Detroit, Michigan, from 1915 until 1928 when he was appointed Associate Professor of Philosophy of Religion at Union Theological Seminary. Subsequently he was appointed Professor of Applied Christianity and Graduate Professor of Ethics and Theology. Since 1950 he has also been Dean of the Seminary. He is widely known not only through his numerous books and articles but also through his energetic and forceful leadership in the socio-political life of the American community. He has been active in the Americans for Democratic Action and in the Liberal Party of New York.

Otto, Rudolph (1869-1937) was born at Peine near Hamburg. After completing his theological and philosophical studies at the universities of Erlangen and Göttingen he became a Lutheran Vicar at Cannes. In 1897 he was appointed lecturer and then Professor of Systematic Theology, History of Religion and History of Philosophy at Göttingen. Subsequently he became Professor of Philosophy at the University of Marburg. From 1912 to

1918 he was a member of the Prussian Parliament. He travelled extensively for religious research in Africa, India, Japan and China, Russia, Egypt, Greece and Palestine. In 1925 he was Haskell Lecturer at Oberlin College. In addition to numerous books on theology, philosophy of religion, liturgy and history of religion he translated many religious texts from Sanscrit into German, including the *Bhagavad gita* and the *Katha-Upanishad*. He is best known for his introduction into modern theological thought of the "numinous" character of God.

Tillich, Paul (1886——) was born in Starzeddel near Frankfurt on the Oder in East Prussia, the son of a Lutheran minister. His study of philosophy and theology was at the universities of Berlin, Tübingen, Breslau and Halle. He began his academic career as *Privatdozent* of Theology at the University of Berlin in 1919. In 1924 he was appointed to a theological professorship in Marburg where he began work on his *Systematic Theology.* From Marburg he was called to Dresden and then to Leipzig. In 1929 he became Professor of Philosophy at the University of Frankfurt. Dismissed from this post with the advent of Hitler, he came to America. From then until 1955 he was Professor of Philosophical Theology at Union Theological Seminary. Upon retirement from U. T. S. he was appointed University Professor of Harvard University. From the beginning of his academic career his thought has radiated from its theological center out into multiple areas of cultural life. He has conducted joint seminars and symposia with philosophers, psychoanalysts, doctors, political scientists, painters and literary artists.